Mommy's a Mole

Mommy's a Mole

Unraveling the Joan Webster Murder
& Other Secrets in a CIA Family

By Eve Carson

ISBN: 978-0-9897275-6-3

This book is printed on acid-free paper.

Printed in the United States of America

This book is for my children in hopes that someday they know what is honest. These pages are written in painful and loving memory of my sister-in-law, Joan Webster, who had the courage to be a full human being. Genuine peace and healing come with the truth. Reality matters in life to nurture the emotional connection to be complete human beings. God bless and keep you, Joan. Thank you for showing the path to the truth so my children can remember and feel my unconditional love again.

Table of Contents

Epigraph

"There is no crueler tyranny than that which is exercised under cover of law, and with the colors of justice." - *U.S. v. Jannotti*, 673 F.2d 578, 614 (3d Cir. 1982).

Prologue

Dealing with trauma requires a strong core and loving support. When crime is the source of tragedy, law enforcement and the legal system are delegated the responsibility of truth and justice, which we hope will ease our pain. A broken system compounds the problems and multiplies the number of victims left in the wake. Decent people struggle to grasp the enormity of circumstances surrounding crime and penetrate the pure evil of deranged minds that would do such things. The normal process of grief is suspended, and heartache hangs over our lives like the blade of a guillotine. My path to be heard has been an agonizing walk spiked with torment.

Society is stunned as it watches in horror the malice and reality of evil. My plight took time to settle into its proper place, but my story fits a pattern that has victimized countless innocent souls. Often victims in my position are silenced forever, unable to tell their stories. The unresolved mystery of the death of my sister-in-law, Joan Webster, in 1981, had such an ending. However, I still have a voice. Looking back, I discovered clues that could not be deciphered at the time and facts blocked from view.

Exposure to the truth can often shock those who missed seeing it earlier, and gut-wrenching stories fill the news. Scott Peterson was convicted of sinking his wife, Laci, and their unborn child into watery depths. People were stunned by his lack of emotion, and they did not buy into his feigned search for a loved one in front of the cameras. Laci's family and friends defended the man they saw as a nice person. Then a scandal exposing Scott's infidelity surfaced, and we saw Amber Frey come forward to reveal another side of Scott Peterson. Had Laci discovered his secrets? Did she lose her life confronting Scott's false image? We cannot look into a deranged mind to know what threatened Scott. Friends claimed that he was "such a nice guy" before his sentencing, but the convicted killer's secret dark side was revealed.

Lori Hacking was happily married—or at least so she thought. Then she discovered her husband, Mark, lied about his acceptance to medical school. After he discarded her body in a dumpster, Mark stood in front of the cameras and claimed he wanted to find his lost wife, the woman he loved. Her crumbled remains surfaced nearly eleven weeks later in a landfill. What was her lethal offense? She had uncovered Mark's secrets and exposed his lies. Her husband, the person she considered closest to her in the world, confessed and was convicted of her murder.

Police officer Drew Peterson took his marriage vows four times. His first wife, Carol Brown, discovered his infidelity and their marriage ended in divorce; second wife Victoria Connolly and her daughter both described the domestic abuse at his hands, and the marriage ended when Drew started dating future wife number three. During Peterson's marriage to Kathleen Savio, police were called to the home eighteen times for alleged domestic disturbances. Their conflict continued after the divorce until police were summoned to Kathleen's house. Peterson and a neighbor found her lifeless body in a waterless bathtub in the home she shared with Peterson during their marriage. Her death was initially ruled an accidental drowning by a coroner's jury, a group that included one of Drew's friends. The fellow officer defended and covered for his brother, declaring that he was "a good man who would never hurt his wife."

Long-overdue suspicions finally arose when wife number four went missing. Peterson was arrogant in front of the cameras, claiming Stacy abandoned her children and ran off with a boyfriend. He labeled all his wives crazy, and he denied any involvement in the continuing mysteries that plagued his life. Stacy confided secrets she was learning about her husband, but no one paid enough heed until tragedy forced a closer look. On September 6, 2012, a jury rendered two judgments, one spoken and one understood. Drew Peterson was found guilty of first-degree murder, and his victim, Kathleen Savio, was no longer found crazy. Stacy is still missing.

Josh Powell asserted that he took his two- and four-year-old sons camping in the middle of the night in frigid weather. The public rejected the ludicrous notion of the remote outing on the same night Josh's wife, Susan, mysteriously disappeared. Again, like Stacy Peterson, stories swirled that she had run off with a lover. More scandal erupted when allegations surfaced suggesting Susan had a sexual relationship with her father-in-law.

Susan's parents prevailed in a hearing to gain custody of their missing daughter's children. Police jailed Josh's father for possession of child pornography. Memories surfaced about the night they went camping, and the young boys remembered their mother was in the trunk of the car. The boys arrived at their father's home on February 6, 2012, for a supervised visit, but Josh locked the social worker out of the house. She pounded on the door and phoned 911 for help, smelling the gas Josh poured. Josh struck both his boys in the head with an axe, then ignited an inferno that ended all three of their lives. Secrets were coming to light against the prime suspect in his wife's disappearance. At the time of these deaths, secrets about Josh's involvement in the disappearance of Susan Powell had become known. We all shudder to think that a father could kill his defenseless children, but it happens.

The spectacle that surrounded the Casey Anthony case repulsed our senses. Her child was missing, but Casey pranced about partying. The behavior was unthinkable; a mother lied repeatedly and with-held evidence to help find her child. Police checked out Zanny the Nanny, and they learned it was a false story to explain the child's dis-appearance. What kind of mother does such things? No decent, loving parent would throw obstacles in the path to help find their child. Authorities did not uphold false stories in the Anthony case, and sus-picion logically shifted to the pretender. Scandals broke in the news and allegations swirled to divert legitimate investigation, casting dis-persion on others. The complex technicalities in court stifled common sense in the verdict. They could not place Casey at the scene, and jurors had no smoking gun evidence to conclude guilt in the obvious crime.

Dark clouds settled over State College, Pennsylvania on November 5, 2011. (After her mother remarried in 1935, Eleanor Webster, Joan's mother, moved to State College.) Icons and pillars in the community fell under scrutiny when scandal broke, and allegations of sexual child abuse became public. Pennsylvania State University defensive football coach Jerry Sandusky's conduct was the subject of rumors and investigation for years, but the man was an esteemed member of the community. Allegations include child abuse, even against a member of Sandusky's own family. The posture of colleagues swept concerns under the rug in favor of preserving image at all costs. The tragedy underscores the tendency to turn away from abhorrent images most decent people cannot process. Human nature is to reject that people we like are capable of repugnant behavior, and the attitude further victimizes those who have the courage to speak out. Years of denial have left many well-regarded citizens in the hot seat for turning their backs on the victims and struggling with conscience for not doing the right thing. The episode in State College emphasizes that the truth has a way of working its way to the surface, and the trauma ripples through a community. The routine denials and backpedaling were predictable until the façade crumbled, revealing an abhorrent reality; it is everyone's responsibility to speak out against abuse. Jerry Sandusky was convicted on forty-five out of forty-eight counts.

I was a devoted wife and mother unwittingly entangled in a family that kept secrets. There is a reasonable conclusion; Joan Webster was privy to the guarded matters of "privacy" that escaped detection to the outside observer. When I made discoveries that shattered all trust, my family of marriage banded together against the threat to their image at whatever cost.

Common sense frames a fair conclusion; criminals strive to avoid detection. Denials are the normal course. Often, gossip swirls and sensational stories deflect accountability away from the offender. Connections and insiders in an investigation tilt the balance of justice, and Boston's history unveiled a problem that existed when Joan Webster disappeared. Allegations of violent abuse surfaced in the same family guarding privacy about the unresolved murder of their daughter. However, in my case, the family blocked efforts to get necessary help with a crushing character assassination, psychological abuse, and emotional cruelty. I became another Webster to "go missing." I had glimpses of family secrets.

Essex County Massachusetts District Attorney Jonathan Blodgett posted the commitment of his office against domestic abuse. He said it is not a private family matter and we have to avoid blaming the victims. Secrecy and silence leave others vulnerable to the threat of real harm. The State of Massachusetts is obligated to Joan Webster, and authorities have a responsibility for public safety, including my children. I have the spine to confront those shielding the facts. Speaking out has left me open to the destructive efforts to discredit me, but I sincerely believe it is the legal and morally right thing to do.

CHAPTER 1

Move On

"No one will ever believe you. They'll think you're crazy."

Every time Steve said those words, my face wrinkled in complete confusion.

"Why wouldn't someone believe I was telling the truth?" I challenged.

"No one will ever believe you," he repeated. That was his strategy to preserve an image.

I pulled open my daughter's desk drawer while looking for keys. The girls were out of control, and they sabotaged every move I made to be a good mother. They had confiscated keys to open locked doors, raided tools, and riffled papers to build their case. In their minds, I was the enemy. I saw three folded pages in the back of the drawer. The blood drained from my face, and I shivered from an icy cold sweeping over my body on that warm day in June of 2001.

My stomach knotted and I rushed to the bathroom to try to throw up. The dry heaves could not expel the confused horror the letter had described, so I sat on the cold tile floor in numbed disbelief. I slipped the letter into my pocket and dialed the phone.

"Carol, I have to see you right away," I insisted.

"Can it wait until tomorrow?" Carol replied. "I can fit you in about ten."

"No, it can't wait. I need to see you as soon as possible. Tonight."

Carol Metzger was the family counselor enlisted to help my family through the turmoil that had inexplicably infected our lives. At our session, I pulled the folded letter from my pocket and she began reading my daughter's appeal to God. The allegations had to be confronted. Carol kept the letter and made copies, and we scheduled an appointment for Monday morning with Steve. When we settled on the sofa, Carol handed Steve the pages, and she and I both watched his expression as he read the words our child had written. His eyes widened and he swallowed hard.

"I'm a nice guy," Steve pleaded. Then he adamantly denied the insinuations. "This isn't true. Nothing happened."

"What do you think she meant by this, Steve?" Carol probed.

"Honest to God, I don't know," he replied as he squirmed in his seat. "I'm surprised she didn't say I hit her."

"What do you mean by that?" I wanted to know. "We are going to have to talk to the girls about this. Carol, when can you see them?"

Twenty years had passed since the mysterious unresolved murder of Steve's sister in 1981. No one knew what had really happened, but incredible stories spiced the news in the highly publicized case. By 2001, my focus was on my children, and Joan's dramatic case was rarely a topic with counselors trying to sort out baffling episodes with the girls. They did not know about George and Eleanor Webster's background, either. Steve's parents were a strong influence over my children, but counselors in the Midwest were not equipped to deal with these forces, and neither was I.

This family had secrets, secrets I did not know. They had a strong-guarded image and always assumed control. However, the Websters were dysfunctional and could not sit down to discuss any views but their own. Now horrifying allegations had surfaced in a family that still had ghosts in the closet and a daughter-in-law who relentlessly pressed to address problems that erupted with her children.

It took time to understand why I needed to look for my children and find myself. I was alone. I was half the country, and more than a quarter century, away from the devastating family mystery of Joan's murder. The death of a child is difficult to bear, but dangerous secrets surrounding this loss have utterly shattered generations of my family.

"Steve, this is no different from having Joan torn out of our lives," I reasoned. Steve and I sat in the coffee shop discussing my alienation from the children.

"I disagree with the premise. This has nothing to do with what happened to Joan," Steve dismissed. "End of subject!"

"It's no different," I continued. "I know nothing about what's going on in their lives. It's like living through Joan's nightmare all over again. How can this family do the same thing?"

"My parents would have done anything to find out what happened to Joan."

"Really? Well, I won't rest until I know what happened to my girls and find some way to help them." The bigger problem was coming into view as I faced Steve's icy glare.

"Move on, Eve," Steve callously instructed. "Get over it and move on."

The questions started first to the family, but they remained silent. I reached out to authorities in Boston, but they hung up the phone. These people should have been looking for answers, but they were not. I pulled out my daughter's desperate letter again and shook uncontrollably. I was terrified about what her words meant. The room was silent, and my thoughts drifted back to another terrifying chapter in my life. Steve's words pounded in my head: "No one will ever believe you. They'll think you're crazy."

"Was this the plan?" I said to myself. "Does my family want people to think I'm off my rocker so no one will listen to what I have to say?"

The early June sun was warm, but I trembled harder as memories drifted back to that cold autumn day in Massachusetts. On December 1, 1981, Steve had bounded into the bathroom out of breath like a child eager to tattle on his friend.

"Oh my God, Eve, are you sitting down?" he asked as he rushed up the stairs. "You're not going to believe this."

I *was* sitting. There I was on the toilet, weakened by the loss of blood following a miscarriage three days before. My hormones were fluctuating wildly, and my emotions were raw, but nothing could have prepared me for the next wave of bad news.

"Joan's missing!"

Shock and silence filled the air, and tears streamed down the confused furrows of my face. I did not know what to say. I had lost my own child, and now this. I could not help crying, but Steve became enraged at my normal human response.

"She's my sister," he said. "You have no right to cry!"

His insensitivity made me cry more. I propped my elbows on my knees and wept into my hands.

"Mom wants to know if you have Keith's phone number. Maybe Joan took a detour to go see him," Steve said. "She never made it back to the dorm, and no one has seen her."

"I just spoke with Joan a few days ago," I said. "She was excited about becoming an aunt." The sadness that had started with my miscarriage on Saturday night had blown into Massachusetts and taken Joan from us, too.

"Steve, she was so excited about her new niece or nephew," I frantically recalled. "She was so enthusiastic about how well her graduate studies were going. She just got high marks for the project she presented before the break."

When I had spoken with Joan, nothing indicated she would cut her Thanksgiving weekend short and return to Harvard on Saturday night. There was nothing unusual about her behavior, so no one called that night to see whether Joan had returned safely or not. No one even thought of calling. After a day of uncharacteristically missed classes, though, David Duncan, a concerned classmate, informed the family. Friends tried to call and tacked notes on her door in Perkins Hall. It was not like Joan to be away without informing anyone. Her absence was unusual, and everyone at school knew it. She was a dedicated student, not the type to miss class on a whim.

"We haven't seen Joan in a while, haven't heard from her," David said. "Is she still at home? She missed class."

Joan's mother took the call from David, and she told the rest of the family that Joan was missing. Evil had swept in, trampled my security and trust, and left my life and the lives of my family changed forever.

Steve said I had no right to cry. Even though it was true that Joan was not my blood sister, I was undeniably affected by this. By every legal and biological definition, she was Steve's sister and my sister-in-law. My definition of family ran much deeper than his. Even so, when the local media picked up the story of her disappearance, she became everyone's sister. Papers and broadcasts filled the news with updates on the search for Joan. It was not long before an explanation emerged that she had gone back to school early to work on an auditorium project for the next Monday. No one challenged the explanation from Joan's father. On the other hand, there were also no known witnesses to corroborate the story. Joan expended herself to finish an eleven-week project so she could enjoy time off over Thanksgiving. Her workload at the Graduate School of Design was heavy, and she had even forfeited her vacation the previous year to get her work done. The official story was that Joan waved to a friend at the luggage carousel and then simply vanished into the night.

Word reached Joan's father, George Webster. He was an executive in the telecommunications division at International Telephone and Telegraph Corporation. George was the director of budget and planning for the defense group in the conglomerate. He was exhausted from a trip to California and arrived back home late Tuesday night. The coast-to-coast trip had cut into the Thanksgiving weekend, and it was uncharacteristic for George to be so inconvenienced. Nevertheless, the car pulled up the drive late, and he slipped into the house through the mudroom door where he dropped his belongings inconspicuously in the pantry. Patrolman Thomas Guthrie stood and somberly greeted Joan's father. Then George pulled up a chair next to Eleanor at the kitchen table, and the parents filled out a missing person report with the Glen Ridge, New Jersey, police officer in the late hours of the night.

The first real clue to the lingering mystery came out of that initial police report. The report did not mention crucial information: a prearranged meeting on Sunday with classmates to work on a project. What parent would hold back anything when their child was lost? It was not until three years later that George claimed to *Boston Magazine* that he witnessed Joan placing a call on that Saturday morning to a classmate, confirming they had supplies. However, the home phone records did not support George's recollection.

The earliest indication of foul play came the next day. Anthony Belmonte was clamming on December 2, 1981, along the Lynn Marsh Road in Saugus, Massachusetts. The marshy area that sandwiched the well-traveled Route 107 on both sides was a known dumping ground. The muddy location along the road was a great spot for clamming. Bucket in hand, Belmonte strolled the area in search of a good spot to dig. What he found there between his rubber boots was a purse and wallet; they were Joan's belongings. Belmonte quickly opened the wallet. The money was gone, but it contained a checkbook, credit cards, and a card with a number to call ITT in case it was ever lost. The call from Belmonte about the missing purse came in to ITT security. Therefore, the first real lead came from George's quarters in New Jersey, and ITT directed Boston area officials where to look.

"Sgt. Dugan, this is Sgt. Meehan with the Saugus Police," the officer began. "We're doing an air search over the marsh where we found the purse and wallet. Nothing has turned up yet. I'm putting together teams of divers and searchers with scent dogs to scour the area."

Tom Dugan jotted down details of the extensive search underway. "Would it help if we can send anyone to Boston?" he offered.

"We could use the manpower if you can spare anyone from Glen Ridge," Meehan continued. "There's a tip a pickup was spotted in the area that night, and the witness thought something was buried. I'm bringing in a backhoe to dig the area up."

"Let me see what I can do to get someone up there to help," Dugan replied.

George and Eleanor Webster traveled to Boston the day after recovering the purse and settled in at the Sheraton in Cambridge. The visit was the first of countless trips to the area, and in a sense, they took up residence to stay close to the scene of the suspected crime. George set up a control center at Harvard and installed toll-free numbers to take any leads. The parents took control of the Massachusetts forces. Joan had disappeared from Logan Airport, but she resided at Perkins Hall in Cambridge, now swarmed with investigative work at a variety of levels. Joan's disappearance was a high-profile case and sucked in enormous resources for the investigation.

Another detail slipped through the cracks. The unchallenged assumption was that members of the family were in New Jersey when Joan disappeared in Boston. In other words, they had an alibi. An exhausting coast-to-coast trip cut into the executive's holiday week-end. Over the years, George threw a fit when the start of school rearranged his scheduled vacation with the family each August in Nantucket. Nor did it make any sense for Eleanor and Anne to make the half-hour drive to the airport to drop Joan off. That was not like them. They were minutes from home, and Anne had a long drive to Boston the next day. Why was Joan going back early?

On the night of her disappearance, the family stopped by the homes of two friends, the Wittpenns and the Joys, for quick cocktails before driving to Newark where Joan boarded Eastern flight 960 to Boston. The gatherings were the last time close, family friends saw her bright smile. The only thing that made sense for Eleanor and Anne to go with George to drop Joan off at the Newark Airport was if George's itinerary required it. Strangely, they were at the airport making what would be their final farewell to Joan.

Joan was a preppy. She wore a black skirt, red print blouse, navy-blue neck scarf, brown knee-high boots, and a brown Chesterfield coat when she boarded the plane. She carried her red purse, a navy-blue Lark suitcase, and a tote bag, but the contents of the tote bag were never clearly defined. Reports of shoes, books, records, and pamphlets filled the newspapers. However, she also had fragile archi-tectural drawings among the items transported in the tote bag, the carry-on that police never recovered. The fact there were crushable drawings in the tote was withheld from the media.

What was in that bag, and what police recovered, remains a mys-tery. The current custodians of Joan's files, the Essex County District Attorney's office, have denied access to verify what was in their pos-session. Rumors swirled, but it was not until 2008 that attorney Tim Burke published his theory. The facts in actual records exposed his fictitious explanations.

In the first crucial days of Joan's disappearance, Special Agent George Bertram started a file on the case. Court records in another case described him as the agent overseeing the Irish Republican Army activities for Boston's office of the Federal Bureau of Investiga-tion. Authorities in New Jersey enlisted the FBI office in Newark, too, for the operation on the parents' home turf. Over time, more and more departments touched Joan's case on both the local, state, and

Federal level, enlisting man-hours only surpassed by a case like Boston's notorious Whitey Bulger. (Bertram had a meeting with Whitey Bulger victim John McIntyre on October 17, 1984, when the informer sought to cooperate with authorities. McIntyre walked into a trap on November 30, 1984, and was tortured to his end by the FBI's protected player.)

The office of Middlesex County District Attorney John Droney handled Joan's investigation first. For several months, Assistant District Attorney Carol Ball and Massachusetts State Troopers in the Crime Prevention and Control unit were handling the Harvard graduate student's disappearance. The leads poured in.

"Joan was at a frat party Saturday night," one tipster suggested, but nothing panned out.

"There are some abandoned buildings you should check for her body." Cops took their dogs to scour the scene, but it was another dead end. There was no sign of Joan.

"There was a car parked along the Lynn Marsh Road where the purse and wallet were found," another caller revealed. Three witnesses saw the abandoned vehicle and came forward.

Authorities planned to hypnotize the alert citizens to see whether they could remember anything else. However, the exercise was a waste of time. The car was a rusted-out, ten-year-old tan Chevy. When there was finally something to compare, reported information conflicted with Tim Burke's published account. The former prosecutor's story projected a distorted illusion. Burke portrayed the junk heap as a gypsy cab that he envisioned his suspect was driving with Joan's body stuffed in the trunk. Things were not adding up.

"The story that came out," I said to myself, "was that Joan was murdered on a boat miles away from that spot. What was Burke's suspect doing parked along a road in Saugus?"

From the start, the Websters made themselves available to the press, and the story of Joan Webster sparked emotions. The baffling story got major coverage, and every heart was breaking for the poor family. Despite all these departments involved and the parents visible eagerness to have this case resolved, Joan's disappearance remained a mystery—and got more confusing by the day.

Something I could not pinpoint was upsetting about the Websters' behavior. Even from the beginning, it seemed off-putting. When I heard the news of Joan's disappearance, I wept profusely, but I never saw the Websters cry. I never got used to the Websters' stoic persona; it was such a drastic contrast to my warm and embracing, Midwest upbringing. Their detachment became especially clear only a few weeks later at Christmas. Losing a loved one makes the holidays difficult, but there was an eerie, calm resignation at this family gathering. George recited details in a matter-of-fact tone, a recitation devoid of the emotions one would expect from anguished parents searching for their daughter.

"We received the call from Mr. Belmonte, the man who found Joan's purse and wallet.

"That nice chap, David Duncan from Harvard, called the house to let us know she didn't show up for class.

"It's frustrating the police don't have any real leads.

"She's gone, and we have to move on."

George's presentation was almost robotic. The words were brief, and it was awkwardly quiet. Of all the family members present, I seemed to be the only one touched by Joan's disappearance with any display of human feelings. The only tears shed during the visit were mine. Emotions and fluctuating hormones, from my miscarriage on the same night Joan disappeared, compounded my grief and the torrential tears. In public, George gave the impression he was eager and hopeful for Joan.

"Someone out there knows what happened," George broadcast for the *Harvard Crimson*. "We have to find that person; there's a missing girl out there."

"We hold out hope, but it's hard," Eleanor added. "As long as there's no body, there's always hope."

The public words sparked every parent's worst nightmare, but at this eerie Christmas gathering they seemed perfectly resigned to the possibility that she was gone. Everything seemed odd.

What I did not know was that there was a lead. There was a composite locked away in my in-laws' files when we landed in New Jersey. Why would the Websters have suppressed this image? Eleanor had asked for Keith Krach's phone number when she called to let us know Joan was missing. Keith was a young man who had been seeing Joan; he was also my friend through my brother at Purdue. Keith was clean-shaven and an interested suitor, but the Websters had never met the Harvard MBA graduate. Why didn't they show me the sketch? In hindsight, it seemed logical that they would have wanted to know whether the composite looked like Keith, but they were mum about the clue. I did not know it existed, and they told me there were no leads. Joan and Keith had planned to get together over the Thanks- giving break, but plans inexplicably fell through.

If only I knew then that a composite had been compiled, I would have prodded them incessantly to show me the picture. In retrospect, it makes no sense why parents looking for answers would not compare Keith with the likeness of the bearded man in the police sketch, and either match or eliminate confusion in Joan's disappearance. What was the secret about the composite?

We sat down for Christmas dinner and offered thanks for our blessings, but I kept thinking that these thanks were incomplete. Under the circumstances, what were we being thankful for? Yet, in robotic unison, the family asked the blessing with George leading the way. Eleanor set one less place at the table, and there was an air of silent acceptance. I remember thinking that she should have set a place for Joan—that's what a hopeful and anguished mother would do—but she hadn't. To me, the exclusion of Joan's place at the table disconnected Joan from the family over the holidays.

A few days later, as Steve and I flew home after Christmas, we were exhausted. With all the bottled-up feelings, Christmas had been an emotionally draining gathering. Somewhere above the clouds, I passed out in the aisle of the plane to the embarrassment of my husband. While I seemed too weak, the Websters—including Steve—maintained the image of strength in the midst of crisis. Appearances were overriding at all times, even in the private moments of the family. I never saw a release of emotion from George or Eleanor. In fact, the only time I can recall Steve breaking down was under the influence of medication when his wisdom teeth were extracted. I was sad that it took sedation to get Steve to express his feelings about the loss of Joan. However, he was a Webster, after all, and the family credo in all things, including the disappearance of Joan, was to move on.

"Mom, I'm worried that Steve isn't coping with Joan's situation," I whispered to Eleanor, hoping she could help her son process the grief. I did not realize he was handling it the "Webster" way.

Although the family had moved on emotionally, the case was making some progress. The next clue to Joan's disappearance came a month later on Eleanor's birthday when authorities recovered Joan's suitcase in a Greyhound bus station in downtown Boston. Eleanor strangely waited five days before informing the local police the bag had been discovered in Boston—supposedly.

"Sgt. Dugan," Eleanor reported matter-of-factly, "the Massachusetts State Police recovered Joan's suitcase. They found it in a locker at the Boston Greyhound Bus Station."

Authorities overlooked the fact there was a three-day delay to report Joan missing. The tardy report about the bag to the local police was unsettling considering more recent revelations. Former prosecutor, Tim Burke, with privileged access to files, revealed that the police recovered the bag in New York City—not in Boston. (This information was corroborated in the *Boston Herald* on May 1, 1990, and nothing recovered supports Burke's explanation about how the bag got there.) The Port Authority on the New York side of the Lincoln Tunnel is a long way from downtown Boston, and the bag could only have been in one place. George and Eleanor probably drove past their daughter's neatly packed belongings dozens of times before a bag handler found them. It was unlikely a low-level worker in New York was aware of the baffling saga in Boston, and the station employees would be more inclined to call the number on the tag in New Jersey to return the abandoned suitcase. Nevertheless, Eleanor told Glen Ridge Police that authorities found it hundreds of miles from where Burke now says it was. So was the Lark bag in Boston or New York? It could not have been both. Somebody was not telling the truth and the discrepancy exposed another real clue. There were unusual gaps in time before the family disclosed information in the "frantic" search for their daughter.

What happened to Joan? The confusion and mystery in the case compounded as the calendar pages turned. Previously undisclosed information showed contradictory reports and evidence. Burke, for example, had access to view Joan's recovered belongings held by the Massachusetts State Police, and he claimed a pair of gray shoes was packed in the suitcase. It was not until much later that I learned there were no shoes in Joan's suitcase. However, Burke himself had reported the items were in the tote bag that the police never recovered. My heart raced with each discovery that reversed the versions I had heard at the time. The people in charge, whether innocently or not, threw obstacles in the path to find Joan.

In the Midwest, parents ingrained common sense in our thinking, and my gut was telling me there was something terribly wrong. The time to dig in and unravel what was going on with this investigation was overdue. If the people who should want answers, Joan's family and authorities, were not going to help, I was determined to find out for myself. That meant I was looking at them, too. I found out the secreted composite was not the only thing I did not know about. Unturned stones concealed what happened to Joan. Piece by piece the promoted explanation unraveled.

I became a quick study on the climate in Boston, organized crime, and the corruption prevalent at the time of Joan's disappearance. Even the infamous Zodiac murders became entwined in the investigation; one theory alleged a Harvard professor was the perpetrator of the serial killings that supposedly ended with Joan. My research uncovered deception, and there was no real evidence to support the account Tim Burke published in 2008, either. A grand jury rejected his implausible theory in 1983, years before Joan's buried remains surfaced.

Moreover, just who were the Websters, the family I trusted? Their professional background gave them skills that could cut through the tangled web of deceit, and they had the clout and connections to get answers. The way they behave toward me now, one might think I murdered Joan, despite the fact I was in the hospital hundreds of miles away when Joan landed at Logan.

Reliving the experience has left me with unsettling doubts whether those delegated the responsibility ever genuinely sought truth and justice. No one has ever been charged for the crime. The swirling maze of evidence and duplicity has troubled my life for the past thirty years, but I have dug into the dark shadows and secrets to learn what really happened to Joan.

She suffered the ultimate control, the ultimate devaluation, and the ultimate abuse. Joan Webster deserves the truth for her loss, and she should be remembered and celebrated for her courage to be a full human being.

Now, it is my life experiences and insight that may well be the missing element to uncover what happened to her. I have not moved on from remembering the value of Joan's life, and I make no apologies for it. Joan deserves better than to have her family and friends move on. Grief is suspended; it is hard to move on when the truth has not been revealed and when so many people have fought vehemently to suppress it.

"No one will ever believe you," Steve predicted. "They'll think you're crazy."

His words were a warning of what was in store.

CHAPTER 2

Form 368

The bond with my children began to deteriorate. I always told my children it was important to be open, honest, and have healthy boundaries in relationships—Joan's case was an example. When my girls were young, I would tell them about Aunt Joan, the aunt they'd never met. I recounted stories about Joan's friendly smile and her bubbly personality. I wanted them to know all about her, but there was always resistance whenever I mentioned Joan when the in-laws were around. Talking about Joan was like walking on eggshells. They did not want to talk about her, and wanted to move on.

"Eve, you're so dramatic," George said, stifling any discussion of Joan. "Talk about something else. We don't want the girls to know all the pain of what happened."

I had nothing to do with all the drama that swept over my life surrounding this case. "I want my girls to know what a wonderful person Joan was. My children can learn from lessons here and know whom to trust. God forbid anything happens to them like what happened to Joan."

"Let's just not talk about it," George dictated as he changed the subject.

The more I mentioned Joan, the more her blood-kin resisted. The family always shifted to something more fun. They were protecting the children from what was real, and substituting fun to divert their attention. The girls began making the strangest comments whenever I tried to bring up anything related to Joan, or explain the reasons why the rules were important. I wanted to keep my cherubs safe, but the elder Websters, apparently, did not see it the same way. The girls' angry arguments made no sense.

"I can't make Daddy unhappy."

"The rules mean more than if I die."

"Things happened before we were even born."

"We haven't killed anyone."

"I feel too much pressure to keep you alive."

Reason did not make a dent in their objections. As my daughters hit their teenage years, they began to rebel on a whole other scale, and it appeared as if their mutiny was encouraged by the family. The rebellion against me seemed as though they were also, in some ways, rebelling against the memory of Joan.

"When the girls start laying into me, please help correct their disrespectful behavior," I appealed to the other adults in the room.

"Eve, no one has ever talked to me that way," my mother-in-law idiotically announced.

I was dumbstruck as to how to respond to such an absurd declaration from a mother who had raised three teenagers. George, Steve and Anne all stared in my direction without saying a word. The deafening silence was finally broken when the charming Webster men shifted to the living room to play the piano.

It was difficult for my children to understand how deeply the disappearance of Joan had touched me. They were not there. They did not know Joan, and they did not know what the Websters were really like. After all, their father was a Webster, and Websters have this way of charming and persuading even the most discriminating audience. Sadly, I did not know the Websters that well either, until it was too late. They were my family, and I trusted them.

"There is just too much pressure," my youngest lamented. "It's too much trying to keep her alive. I can't do it."

The pressure was real, but her compassionate sounding words did not match with the hostile behavior. My children were spreading terrible stories. Both of them provoked arguments every waking moment, and then they twisted accounts to make it look as if I was a raving lunatic. The weight on my child's shoulders spoke to some other threat she feared, but at the time I did not comprehend what the girls meant.

"You're nothing more than a burden."

"You're an embarrassment and nobody likes you."

"We hate you and just want you to get out of our lives."

"Just tell people we died."

These were not the words of the caring children I knew. The family communicated nothing properly. The household was utter chaos and confusion. Venom poisoned every word, and I struggled in vain to hold onto the disintegrating pieces of my family and me. Family counselors were enlisted to steer us through the problems, to cope with the grief, but for me, at least, they did not help.

"Why don't you like yourself, Eve?" one of the counselors asked as I curled up in the fetal position on the sofa. Carol Metzger had recommended Sarah O'Brien to take over the challenge of my reticent and antagonistic children.

"I do, but my feedback is wrong," I replied, but without validation.

Sarah jotted down a few notes, but her scribbles echoed the confusing sentiments of my children. I lacked the feedback to know what they were saying.

"You have done something terrible," Sarah announced, "but we can't tell you what it is."

Steve nodded in satisfied agreement. "We don't want to violate her privacy, so we really can't tell you."

"How am I supposed to respond to that?" I shrugged, completely perplexed. "Did I commit some crime?"

"No, no, no," Steve assured me, "but we just can't talk about what's bothering the girls."

The professionals counseling the girls knew very little about the dramatic events that had consumed the family for years. All they understood was that Steve's sister was a murder victim, but they did not know how extraordinary the case really was, and they did not know that the case was still open. They completely ignored my instincts that there seemed to be some intentional malice undermining my efforts to help my children. Even today, my children bear an uncanny resemblance to their aunt in their demeanor and credentials. They are popular, intelligent, and well liked by others, just as Aunt Joan was. Sadly, they are also dominated by the Websters, just as Joan was.

Joan was an attractive and exceptional, twenty-five-year-old woman. She was a dean's list student and received numerous honors during and following her undergraduate years at Syracuse University. Her boyfriends were clean-cut, future professionals on the rise, and her friends were any parent's pride. Her studies consumed the bulk of her time, though her role as a dorm proctor kept her available to fellow collegians when she was not in class. Classmates and peers loved Joan, and she positively impacted her coworkers at Skidmore, Owens, and Merrill in New York before enrolling at Harvard for graduate studies.

With all of this to recommend her, I could not figure out who would want to kill Joan. Finding motives for the murder was a difficult task, though this did not stop the rumors from spreading rampantly. Despite all the scenarios and theories, no one could come up with an explanation that made sense. After a while, the conclusion that prevailed, and it prevailed for many years, was that Joan lost her life in a random act.

The facts that started to surface, however, as I continued to dig, belied that theory. This crime was not random. The irrefutable facts suggested the offense was a premeditated felony, covered up by a diverted investigation. Therefore, what made Joan a threat, and to whom? First Joan, then my children, and now me—all of us had been devalued. The time had come to unmask what secrets this family harbored.

George and Eleanor Webster met in Washington, DC, in the early years of the Central Intelligence Agency, an intelligence group established by The National Security Act in 1947. The country was still recovering from years of devastating war. The fledgling American intelligence community dismantled the remainders of the Nazis by stealthily bringing German defectors to our shores before the Soviet Union recruited them. In the postwar years, scientists, scholars, intelligence, doctors, engineers, and others were infused into the fabric of American institutions, industry, and government from the remnants of Hitler's Europe in an unsanctioned program known as Operation Paperclip. The government had no guidelines for the CIA, and pragmatism was the philosophy. The only thing that mattered was the result, no matter the consequences along the way.

George was a charming and eligible bachelor raised with the privilege of wealth. He was born in Brooklyn, studied at Yale, and attended Harvard Business School—a fertile recruiting ground for the CIA. He was an engaging, young man with sophisticated charm, allure cultivated through years of private schools, exclusive country clubs, a Greenwich, Connecticut address, and the thoroughbred owners' box at the track. These were the privileges imbued to him by his father, Reginald N. Webster, an industrialist with an Irish twinkle in his eye.

The elder Webster was President and Chief Executive Officer of the Standard Thomson Corporation headquartered in Waltham, Massachusetts. They manufactured airplane engine thermostats used during World War II to keep forces airborne. He was also a director for the ammunitions manufacturer Smith and Wesson based in Springfield, Massachusetts, and he filled a director's chair for the Heli-Coil Corporation, manufacturer of precision parts. In 1945, the board of the Otto Construction Corporation selected Reginald, known as RN, as chairman of the board. The parent organization, founded by Dr. Carlos Otto in Bochum, Germany, was in an area pulverized by the Allies in WWII. The chemical plant was the world's largest manufacturer of coke ovens before the war, and was in the center of an area vital to the Nazi effort for mining, railroads, and ammunition. After the war, the Otto Corporation fell under scrutiny, and the company was exposed and placed on the American Jewish Committee's list of firms that used slave and forced labor during Hitler's reign of terror.

Reginald was a power broker and womanizer who invested in the sport of kings—racing horses with the elite—which opened portals where his son George circulated. Entitlement, privilege, and access, simmered with a prestigious degree and his undeniable charm, made George a recruiter's ideal.

Eleanor, on the other hand, grew up in very different circumstances. She was the illegitimate daughter of Clayton Piggott during an era when such stigma branded a life with shame. To avoid the labeling, her mother, Georgia, and father, Clayton, married, but the calendar was too short to avoid the truth of Eleanor's beginning. Eleanor's parents split after a few years, estranging the young child from her father for the rest of her life. Georgia later remarried State College professor John Selsam in Pennsylvania. Eleanor embraced the decision and rejected the surname of her birth. John Selsam adopted Eleanor on August 6, 1942, and she legally denied the name that shamed her.

The alienation with Eleanor's biological father added an unusual turn to Joan's heartbreaking story. The estrangement meant Joan never met her grandfather Clayton. Though he had settled in Beverly, Massachusetts, and resided there when Joan disappeared, the printer probably did not know it was his progeny dominating the news. In a twist of fate, searchers finally found her buried nearby.

At some point, Eleanor adopted the nickname Terry, further removing her identity from her conception. After a while, wedding bells added another last name to Eleanor's profile. Thomas Hardaway was a West Point Cadet, but the couple was married barely more than a year before he was killed in action in Korea on September 8, 1950.

"Steve, where did your mom get the nickname Terry," I had once asked.

"It was a part she had in a community play," he replied as if he had heard this question before. "Dad liked it, so it just sort of stuck."

Of course, there was no reason not to accept his explanation as fact, but it was not real. The answer was probably another well-rehearsed story Steve told me. Thomas met "Terry" in 1946, three years before they married. A West Point classmate eulogized the young officer, and offered his condolences to Tom's widow, Terry.

Therefore, the nickname or alias became part of Eleanor's identity long before George Webster appeared on the scene. Why did they make up a story? What was the mystery?

Eleanor studied psychology at Mount Holyoke College. She had accumulated a long string of names that helped conceal her shame. John Selsam died during Eleanor's brief marriage; another loss. A constant feeling of rejection and disappointment pervaded Eleanor's childhood, and she became an insecure and vulnerable, young Washington woman, a model candidate for the next chapter in her life.

George and Eleanor were young idealists, drawn by the intrigue of the newly formed intelligence agency. The prerequisite for CIA employment demanded complete loyalty to the cause, and signing Form 368 guaranteed a lifelong oath of secrecy. The oath George and Eleanor were both willing to take set the stage for dire consequences that cursed the future generations. How can a person live a double life, a life of secrecy, deceit, and distrust? I am not sure I could have lived this way, but the very things that might repel many people were precisely the aspects that attracted George and Eleanor to the CIA— and the CIA to them.

"Don't tell anyone. You don't tell anyone you're in the CIA, and don't tell anyone what you do here. Just go about your lives normally and don't attract attention. As far as anyone else knows, you're just a regular person with regular interests and habits. You know nothing about the CIA."

"Don't tell." I heard those words repeated in my home.

"Don't tell your mom," Steve warned the girls.

"Don't tell," the girls cautioned their friends to punctuate their stories.

"We can't tell you, Eve," Sarah O'Brien admonished while Steve nodded approval.

"Don't tell" started with George and Eleanor. These words were implicit in the contract they'd signed. In fact, these words would probably not have even been necessary; the agency implied the dictate the moment George and Eleanor walked into the recruiting office. These were people willing to live double lives, remain stoic, and keep secrets. Both George and Eleanor honed these qualities and set the example for future generations. Theirs was a match made in an agency that assured secure and confidential pillow talk between the young couple.

George and Eleanor stood at the altar on May 17, 1952, in the St. Peter and St. Paul Episcopal Cathedral in Washington, DC. They recited vows as many people do. "To have and to hold, in sickness and in health, 'til death do us part." The couple recited their oaths without uttering the declarations they had made to the CIA. The commitment to the CIA was present at the ceremony, but present in the background, a passive observer to the religious vows, but an observer that undoubtedly took root in their minds. The agency united George and Eleanor in ways few would understand, but the world saw the image of a loving, young couple about to embark on an exciting life together.

Georgia Selsam was happy for her daughter, but also somewhat uneasy; she made a strained effort to smile at the nuptials. George exerted the Webster charm and generosity with his mother-in-law, but over the years this gradually disappeared. RN Webster was equally adept at charming the small crowd who gathered to celebrate the ceremony. Champagne flowed, introducing Eleanor to a world of the entitled few. By taking these holy pledges, financial security was guaranteed for George and Eleanor, but the secret promises to the CIA threatened to destroy the security of normal and healthy family relationships.

The larger threat, for the country at least, came from thousands of miles away in Moscow. Those years were the height of the "Red Scare." To combat this perceived menace, the CIA required unique training and skills. The countermeasures began with lessons in intelligence learned from the former foe in Germany. The CIA soon infiltrated domestic cults and organizations to study their methods of control and persuasion. The CIA studied their lessons from the very people they hoped to contain.

One such technique learned from these infiltrations was a means of supplanting false memory in an individual to suppress reality. In other words, employees of the agency substituted their version of the truth for what secreted facts would reveal. The agency addressed this by the formation of the False Memory Syndrome Foundation. Whistleblowers have described the foundation as a group dedicated to denying the existence of cult mind control and child abuse. It is a common defense; it's just their imagination, punctuated with emphatic denials that anything really happened.

CIA projects engaged in practices the public would find offensive, precisely why these exercises were kept secret for years, and enabled long periods of unrestrained experiments conducted on unwitting volunteers. George and Eleanor were involved in the CIA when the organization focused on MKULTRA, German for mind control. The project was a multifaceted, umbrella program that sought to instigate brainwashing tactics to force their view on the citizens the agency was formed to protect. Though it is hard to be specific, because of destroyed documents and sworn secrecy, it is very probable that George and Eleanor were somehow acquainted with the widespread techniques implemented in the CIA at the time.

The CIA enlisted experts with exceptional skills to train "regular people" like George and Eleanor. The CIA contracted America's most famous magician, John Mulholland, in 1953, to prepare instruction manuals for the agency. For decades, the agency believed his manuals were destroyed, but copies of *The Official CIA Manual of Trickery and Deception* were discovered in 2007 in the agency's archives, and published by H. Keith Melton and Robert Wallace. Wallace, a former CIA officer, and Melton, an intelligence historian, enlightened the public to the practices that the agency had cloaked in secrecy. It gave truly regular people a glimpse into the attitude the intelligence group cultivated. According to these documents, the CIA was not only interested in cults and vulnerable people, but also the techniques of illusionists such as Mulholland. CIA agents practiced and honed the complex, and detailed tricks and deceptions of magicians to turn it into their spy craft. The underlying premise was to conduct oneself in ordinary and acceptable ways that held attention. Meanwhile, a ruse or trick was covertly executed. The concept was simply to shield nefarious activity with normal behavior, and delude instincts into seeing only the acceptable conduct.

The agency implemented these activities for years in secrecy and denial. It took more than two decades before the CIA finally acknowledged their accountability in the death of Army Officer Frank Olson. Olson fell from a New York City hotel window on November 28, 1953, suffering from effects of the drug LSD that CIA colleagues slipped into his drink. These experiments were widespread and the results were horrific, allegedly causing Boston's infamous mobster Whitey Bulger to claim that LSD ruined his life. He volunteered for the LSD experiments during his incarceration at the Atlanta Penitentiary between 1956 and 1959. Bulger's deranged behavior and criminal life earned him a spot on the FBI's Most Wanted list until he was captured on June 22, 2011. A corrupt Boston system protected him for years as an informant before the unholy alliance was exposed.

Another project instigated in the agency under the umbrella of MKULTRA, sometimes referred to as Operation Monarch, was described in witness testimony before a President's Advisory Committee on March 15, 1995. Therapist Valerie Wolf, and victims Claudia Mullen and Chris De Nicola, detailed human experimentation ranging from rape to radiation inflicted even on the children of agency employees.

The family mindset was a lot to absorb. Understanding the foundation of Webster thinking stirred my recollections of bizarre events that played out with Steve and my children.

"We just want you to be gone," Steve coldly calculated.

"Steve, I can't go to the party tonight," I tearfully whispered. "Please take me home."

I sat in front of the television with a glass of wine trying to neutralize the venom injected by his biting words. Steve, in typical fashion, went on to the party to play. The girls heard me come home, or maybe they had been tipped that I was vulnerable to the next wave of attack.

"So what did he say to you this time, EVE?"

"You're pathetic. We hate you!"

"Why don't you just leave, and never come back?"

"It's a good time to tell you, we're going to quit swimming."

There was no question the girls needed some structured activity, but they had other ideas with their father's support. The next thing I knew, the girls bound my wrists with duct tape and summoned their conspirator home. When Steve returned, he cut the restraints and ordered the girls to retreat. My mind was fuzzy, but it was not a buzz from too much wine. I had not had that much to drink. What in hell was going on? Steve had the ammunition to paint a picture when he got Carol on the phone.

"The girls had to tie Eve up," Steve deviously implied. "They were afraid she was going to hurt them."

"I felt like I was drugged, Carol," I recounted a few days later in her office. "I don't know, but it was like someone slipped something into my drink."

"Come on, Eve," Carol discounted.

"They are twisting everything I say to make me sound like a monster," I continued. "Why am I being treated this way?"

Years passed before the CIA sat before the Senate to answer for activities the Senate declared illegal and immoral. President Clinton's apology on October 3, 1995, for the proscribed and depraved activities of the CIA during MKULTRA experiments, failed to address scarred lives adequately. Victims suffered life-altering damage by an uncontrolled agency who justified misconduct for their concept of the greater good.

"Thousands of government-sponsored experiments did take place," Clinton affirmed.

I pressed my daughter's letter to God close to my heart and wept.

"Some of them were unethical," he apologized. "They failed both the test of our national values and the test of humanity."

The thought was almost too much to bear, and I felt so alone, but others had felt similar pain.

The president declared, "When the government does wrong, we have a moral responsibility to admit it."

However, not everyone felt the conscience to own up. Richard Helms, Director of Central Intelligence, had ordered MKULTRA files be destroyed in 1973 to cover up the agency's desire to play God and control people's minds. Were George and Eleanor's names listed somewhere in the shredded CIA files? Only God knows that answer, because participants in the agency signed Form 368, but the nightmares I encountered fit the patterns. Despite the cover-up and despite his contempt for Congress, the government merely slapped Helms on the hand for his admitted perjury on November 4, 1977. He received a light, two-thousand dollar fine, and his CIA colleagues paid it, applauding his oath of secrecy. The CIA was determined to play deaf and dumb invariably, and George and Eleanor adhered to this philosophy as a part of an exclusive group disconnected from the boundaries that guide healthy, human conscience.

The CIA methods during the formative years, when the Websters were there, were completely devoid of anything resembling humanity. The Church Senate Commission hearings in 1975 examined the methods of the intelligence community. In the early days, the agency primarily employed psychological tools to promote their agenda. The media became an effective tool to disseminate disinformation and propaganda that distorted the perceptions of entire populations. While the CIA stirred and manipulated emotions through the media, they were left alone, completely unaccountable.

The agency worked closely with the Defense Department. The group controlled eighty percent of the fragmented and concealed intelligence budget, and the department was the chief consumer of the agency's product. During the early days of the Cold War, intelligence gathering was the agency's primary objective, but the organization expanded into covert operations as they broadened their reach. They used a wide variety of complex strategies that left operatives with only the information they needed to know, nothing more. The fragmentation allowed participants plausible deniability, and was a convenient method of diverting any path to the truth.

My thoughts drifted again to Joan's investigation as I studied the Senate's findings.

"Eve, we never saw any composite," Elle Gates insisted. "Who had it, and why wouldn't it have been given to our office?" Elle was ADA Carol Ball's assistant in the Middlesex DA's office that handled Joan's case when the composite was drawn from a cabbie's description in December 1981. Another department, Lt. Murphy of the Harvard Police, had constructed the image.

"No, Ms. Carson," first ADA John Dawley admitted, "we don't know anything about the extortion incident you've described." His office in Essex County, Massachusetts, was now the custodian of Joan's records, and they disingenuously maintained her nearly three-decade-old case was still under investigation. The extortion incident in October 1982, was an operation handled out of New Jersey.

"Have you reviewed the Iannuzzi murder case in your examination of what happened to Joan?" I queried.

"That case was in Suffolk County," Dawley deflected. "You'll have to speak with the DA over there."

One thing became clear; no one had all the pieces of this case except George and Eleanor Webster.

The Church report described the agency's abuses. So-called enemies of the state were routinely mistreated, but over time agency employees like George and Eleanor became disengaged and desensitized to the suffering of their victims. My personal experience trying to manage within the family is evidence of that. The CIA stripped them of their humanity, of their ability to care, reason, or trust in others. In my view, after years of struggling with the family's control, I can only conclude that decades of CIA connections had disconnected George and Eleanor from any real human emotion.

The CIA had this uncanny ability to distort everything they touched. The intelligence group even decontextualized the Bible for the agency's own nebulous gains. A carving on the wall of CIA headquarters in Langley quotes John 8:32, "And Ye shall know the truth, and the truth shall make you free." These words are the agency's motto, a Bible verse, but I cannot help believing it is quoted with a wink and nudge in a group that sought secrecy to hide the truth, not uncover it. I long for the day that the truth will set my family free, but I am certain that the CIA will not instigate the process. It is a lofty ideal to be sure, but in the agency's worldview, the truth was only what they wanted to make it. The truth was manufactured.

This artificial truth penetrated the Websters. Their association with the agency was common knowledge in close circles, but it was an unknown or unconsidered factor affecting the investigation of Joan's disappearance. The papers ignored the family background, and the parents only divulged their intelligence experience in the tight circles of those most closely involved. Every time I mentioned it, I was hushed.

"With your background in intelligence, can't you get the right people on this to find Joan?" I sensibly asked my in-laws.

"We have confidence in the people working on this," was the curt reply.

"But you were CIA, after all; trained to dig out information," I persisted.

"Don't talk about that. You really need to learn to keep quiet, Eve," Eleanor stubbornly instructed. "That's our business; don't talk about our private matters."

"They were employees of the Federal government and that's it," Steve said before changing the subject to something more fun.

It is not pleasant to air dirty laundry, but the secrets in this family reach the most dangerous level—these secrets literally veil matters of life and death. After more than three decades connected to the Websters, I have insight no one else has. The Webster family pressured me to keep quiet with methods John Mulholland instructed to hide dirty tricks.

"Were there secrets here that had put my family at risk?" I asked myself as I studied the background of my children's paternal grandparents.

After all, the family image was strong and protected at all costs. Joan's brother Steve and her father are both charming and entertaining, a seductive quality that attracted me to Steve in the first place. People always see the charm before they see the deceit, and this was certainly the case with the Websters and me. They are intelligent, interesting, and engaging, with credentials that influence outside impressions of the family. Outsiders always saw the fun side of the Websters; they laughed and played show tunes on the piano. Life with the Websters was really a lively circus filled with color and excitement. Nevertheless, as I discovered, as in any circus, what happens in the ring is really just a John Mulholland ruse to entertain the crowd and keep them distracted from the disturbing scenes backstage.

Whenever confronted with pain or difficult situations, the Websters diverted the attention by putting on a show. They were all great actors, and for a long while even I bought into the performance. All their problems were swept under the rug; their public persona entertained while they guarded the secret side with a life-binding contract. Joan grew up in this swirling world with a cryptic side of a family professionally trained to keep secrets. They had a remarkable ability to expose only the good side to the public. This evil vow unfairly compelled silence from the generations that followed George and Eleanor's choice to sign their names on Form 368.

George and Eleanor were a dominating presence during Joan's investigation. It brought the mentality of the CIA into the equation. However, what did that influence bring to the case? These were people with professional skills to control people's perceptions. They knew how to put their best image forward while more guarded things went on in the background. The fragmented search blocked paths to the truth. Joan's blood family obstructed a further probe of the facts with secrecy and declarations of privacy. These people made the truth what they wanted it to be.

CHAPTER 3

Gas Lighting

A shadowy correspondent scrawled seven words in blue ink on a full-page, diet advertisement that mysteriously appeared in my mailbox one morning.

"Eve, you should give this a try," it read.

This delivery was not the first time I received perplexing and unusual mail. I received these anonymous notes as frequently as a magazine subscription, always offering not-so-subtle hints to change this thing or that thing about my appearance. I had a slender physique, which made this particular note especially difficult to figure out. Thinking back on it now, it seems so obvious who the instigator of the notes was, but at the time I never suspected that Steve played head games to modify my appearance. The Websters obsessed about appearances, so it did not matter that I was actually quite in shape. To the Websters, my figure was irrelevant. What mattered was making sure I fit their carefully cultivated image and stayed in shape. The head games were about control.

Years later, when Steve lost his job with American Hospital Supply, he enlisted my unwitting assistance to mail an anonymous letter intentionally maligning a coworker who had embarrassed him. Mike Orscheln squeezed Steve out of a job when the human resource manager selected the Baxter counterpart to fill the one available position after the merger.

"Would you drop this in the mail for me?" my husband asked.

"But this is addressed to your office, Steve," I replied. "You're on your way there now. Why don't you just take it in and save the stamp?"

"No, just mail it for me, please," he implored, and I innocently followed his wishes not knowing what he had sealed in the envelope.

Steve's childish delight for his coworker's downfall was my first glimpse of the gas lighting tactics utilized by the Websters to maintain an image. Only in retrospect did I realize that they used the same tactics on me.

Steve certainly did not invent the devices. Eleanor obsessively clipped newspaper articles on a variety of topics, often about image. Image was all that mattered. In fact, she had even sent letters to the girls telling them not to dye their hair or shave above their knees until they were older. Imagine having to explain that sort of letter to a young girl. However, the kind of letters Mimi mailed to her granddaughters were about image.

These techniques of psychological manipulation continued for years. I enjoyed baking, and the Websters were often the grateful recipient of my culinary skills. They were especially eager to consume my grandmother's version of shortcake.

"Eve, this is delicious," Eleanor praised as she took another bite. "Can I have a copy of the recipe?"

"Mom, this is one I would rather not give out," I respectfully declined. "This is really a specialty of the house, but I'll fix it for you anytime you would like."

I remember being flattered that I had created something to her satisfaction. However, weeks later when I decided to bake the recipe again, I could not find it.

"Did you get the itinerary for our visit?" Eleanor asked. "We're looking forward to some of your good cooking. I hope you're going to fix the shortcake again?"

"No, I'm sorry," I apologetically explained. "I must have misplaced it. I couldn't find it after the last time you visited."

"Oh, well I have a copy of it in my recipes," she declared. "I'll copy it and bring it with us. Now I'll have a copy in your handwriting and you will have one in mine."

I had searched every conceivable crevice, afraid I had lost the recipe for good, only to find the recipe about a year later. The card turned up in my mother-in-law's cookbook, no doubt taken in John Mulholland fashion.

Unfortunately, a missing recipe was the least of my worries as the calendar pages turned. Years later, during the stressful times with my children, other items mysteriously disappeared and surfaced in a locked, basement closet housing the command center for the campaign my children waged against Mom. The Webster elders recruited my children just as George and Eleanor had been recruited by the CIA decades earlier, and their tactics were nearly as devious. My girls sabotaged every effort toward a harmonious, healthy, family structure and enlisted by their father with the dictate, "Don't tell Mom!"

It was not long before unfounded and unverified stories started to swirl, whispered beyond my earshot, and caused me bewildering isolation. The seeds my children planted around the community sprouted into an image of a demonic mother. One day as I was working at a local store, a parent I recognized walked in, and I could tell by the disgusted looks that something was wrong. I followed him out of the store.

"What's wrong?" I asked.

"Well, Eve, I would have never thought you were a child-beater. What a shame."

I assured him this was not the case, but I am not sure he believed me. He chose to believe false, destructive gossip spread by my daughters instead. What was going on? Little did I know that a similar scenario played out years before when Boston succumbed to the Websters' outcry for Joan's justice.

On another occasion, I found that my car key was bent, making it impossible for me to drive—impossible for me to escape the house, perhaps. My first reaction was that my daughters did it; the visible evidence did not expose any other possible culprit.

"Girls, did you have trouble unlocking the door?" I challenged. "Did you try to force the key?"

"We didn't do that!"

"I'm not really angry," I continued. "There's no one else here. I just want you to tell me the truth if it got bent when you tried to open the door."

"You don't believe us?" my oldest snapped back. "Quit accusing us of something we didn't do. Maybe the keys were dropped."

"The key didn't get bent by itself, girls, and you can't bend a steel shaft simply by dropping them on the ground," I said.

"We aren't strong enough to bend that," my youngest argued.

They were right when I thought about it, but how did the key get bent? They were visibly angry for being accused, and of course, justifiably denied any wrongdoing. A wedge was being driven between my daughters and me. Their father was the only person in the household capable of bending the steel shaft and had stealth, John Mulholland access to it. Head games were being played again, and sadly my daughters were used as pawns. The visible evidence pointed to my girls, but things were not what they appeared to be. The devious prankster framed the girls for something they could not have done. These shenanigans were not funny.

I was an unsuspecting and trusting target for the Websters' manipulative tactics in the early years, but better prepared when they covertly reignited the head games after I started asking too many questions in Joan's case. On January 22, 2009, a stealth operator tucked an anonymous letter into my mailbox. This time it was not about weight loss; this time it was a little more serious. I opened the envelope to find an article about mental disorders.

"I hope you will read this and take it seriously," the unidentified author wrote. "Acceptance and subsequent therapy are critical to knock this disorder."

I knew what they were trying to imply, but this letter signaled the truth was getting too close for someone's comfort. The suggestion was submission. "Admit you're crazy, Eve," was the implied remedy for the deepening alienation from my children. The only person who was going to benefit was Steve; he knew I had a letter that threatened his image.

However, I was not the only one to receive such a loaded and anonymous letter. A few months earlier, a covert carrier mailed an anonymous message with a South Jersey postmark to a recipient in Boston. The mail drop was suspiciously close to the new address of the Websters and raised a question who delivered the warning.

"I hope someday you will meet your justice up in heaven where you will be sent down to hell," anonymous typed. "I hope that your health will deteriorate, and you will get everything you deserve—Please God—Punish this accomplice!!!"

The addressee was Candy Weyant, the woman persecuted by authorities at the time Joan's case filled the news, and the girlfriend of the man the Websters accused of murdering Joan. The message was clear; the anonymous author supported Tim Burke's published allegations, incredulous assertions that George and Eleanor supported. Candy would have been a logical source of information to unravel the mystery surrounding Joan's case. Therefore, like me, she became a logical threat. The harassment was serious.

Indeed, I was threatening to the status quo of image cultivated by the Websters. Regardless, even though they were reluctant to receive it, I established two e-mail accounts, set up exclusively to inform George and Eleanor about things I uncovered in my research. After all, the information concerned their daughter. On May 28, 2010, I advised the Websters, through e-mail, of the parole status of the informant, Robert Bond. He was the hardened criminal whose false statement was the integral piece in the cases the state constructed to suggest Leonard Paradiso had murdered Joan. Eleanor passed away on June fifteenth, shortly after my correspondence arrived, but George read and reread the update despite his vigil.

"Robert Bond is coming up for parole. I would like to provide my children with his picture," I continued, "and information I've learned about him."

Robert Bond was a two-time murderer the state used to create their explanation for Joan's loss. The central figures in the investigation, including the parents, maintained Bond was a credible witness. Robert Bond was anything but a credible source, and I told the family that I knew it.

"I would like to discuss discrepancies in the records that have been recovered regarding Joan with the family, in a proper setting," I offered.

I also said that I had read Bond's statement and knew it was false. Investigators would have known it was false, even at the time it was taken. I wanted to talk to the family about this face-to-face, not just in e-mails. The e-mails were very clear, but it took a while to sink in for George. Paranoia set in for him soon after Eleanor met her Maker, and George forwarded the communication to Joan's sister, Anne. The dutiful daughter had to make an extra journey from Phoenix to White Horse Village in Pennsylvania and step into her mother's shoes to support her aging father.

A sneaky hand pressed the send button to deliver the latest anonymous harassment on July 12, and 16, 2010. The two e-mail addresses set up to inform the family were flooded with messages inferring that I was delusional and had a mental disorder. The deluge of malicious insinuations mirrored the anonymous letter I had received. Eleanor's tactic of copied articles sent through snail mail years before had been replaced with the instantaneous technology of the Internet. The originating Internet Protocol address of the harassing subscriptions matched the IP location of the e-mail George had forwarded with the Bond update. The trace identified the Syntellect Corporation network in Phoenix, Arizona—Anne's employer.

The cagey warning became clear; there were things I was uncovering others wished I had not. For instance, right from the beginning, the media settled on an overly simplistic account that on the day of her disappearance, Joan simply waved to a friend, then vanished. Conflicting information mentioned in the press was quickly stifled, and speculation always centered on this exceedingly basic and inaccurate account. The truth, as I discovered, is quite a bit more complex. Joan did acknowledge a friend at the crowded carousel while waiting for her luggage. She hoisted her Lark bag and moved toward the curb with her assorted belongings.

"A spokesman for the Boston Police Department said detectives are checking a report the girl was seen talking to a man at the checkout counter at the airport minutes before she was last seen by other Harvard students," the *Newark Star Ledger* reported on December 5, 1981.

"Det. Dugan, this is Jack McEwen over at ITT," the head of security began. "I'm concerned about the report I saw in the Newark paper. They've reported things the police don't know about."

"I'll check it out," the Glen Ridge officer helpfully offered.

Fellow design classmate, Beau Herr, tipped the press that classmates noticed Joan talking to someone before stepping into the chilly, November night air to assume her place in line for a taxi. A man behind the counter distracted Joan, and she stopped to talk to him. The lead was still warm when it was reported in the New Jersey paper. The report raised a red flag with Jack McEwen, head of ITT Security, the corporate connection steering the investigation for George. Jack had just returned from Boston. He participated in the extensive interviews at Logan Airport looking for clues to the missing student's whereabouts. Boston papers were not reporting it, but authorities had also spoken to a cabbie who gave a description. Therefore, authorities did know someone saw Joan. The corporate mouthpiece closest to George squelched the stories that Joan did not leave the airport unnoticed. Another important clue was suppressed from the Websters' corner.

Meanwhile in Boston, authorities pursued a whole other case, completely disconnected from the drama and information gathered in New Jersey. Tips poured in and the authorities investigated each one.

"The search on the Lynn Marsh Road didn't yield any more clues," Sgt. Neil Meehan unhappily affirmed to the press.

"Police are investigating every tip they receive no matter how farfetched," Cpl. Jack O'Rourke of the Massachusetts State Police assured the reporters from the *Harvard Crimson.*

"The purse found in Saugus may have been a diversion," Det. Richard Gordan from the Beverly Police speculated. "It looks as if the purse was thrown from a car headed south toward Logan, not headed north leaving the airport."

The Massachusetts State Police took charge of the case when local police recovered the purse and wallet on December 2, 1981. The scoured area was familiar turf to an undercover cop assigned to F Barracks at Logan Airport. Superiors assigned Trooper Andrew Palombo as the lead investigator on an unresolved 1979 murder. The culprit discarded the victim's body behind an abandoned building on the northbound side of the Lynn Marsh Road. Palombo took over the case of Marie Iannuzzi in February, 1981, but the case remained stalled, never charging either of the two named suspects. Palombo's commute from his address in Peabody passed that spot regularly as he headed south to his office. The area was a well-known dumping ground, and Palombo had a daily reminder of his cold case.

Numerous agencies stepped in to help interview cabbies, airport personnel, and countless passengers from the flights that came in around Joan's arrival. Two flights apparently arrived from Newark Airport, and passengers crowded the baggage carousel loaded with the luggage of five flights that all came in within a half hour of one another. The well-heeled, young woman did catch the attention of a cabbie waiting to help unburden Joan, overloaded with her suitcase, tote bag, and grasping to keep the purse strap on her shoulder. He was eager to help his potential fare until a bearded man diverted Joan. This observant cab driver provided authorities with enough of a description to draft a composite and help with the search.

Detective Corcoran of the Glen Ridge, New Jersey Police assembled the templates obtained from the Harvard Campus Police, and he presented the likeness to Eleanor Webster on December 21, 1981, in time for our arrival for Christmas. You would think that a mother and father eager to solve the disappearance of their daughter would be equally eager to elicit any help they could, but my in-laws never shared the picture with me. They did not mention a word about the latest lead in Joan's disappearance. The image was never broadcast to the public, nor was the likeness provided to the Middlesex County DA's office then assigned to the case.

Although the Websters covertly turned attention away from the image, they seemed eager to record any phone calls they received. Authorities tapped the Websters' home line, hoping to ensnare any callers that might know the whereabouts of their daughter. The recorder captured each voice calling in to their home, or at least this was the impression the Websters left with the police. However, according to police records, George's private line escaped scrutiny for any calls placed or taken on that number. The off-limits line sat in his restricted office upstairs, which happened to be across the hall from Joan's tiny bedroom. On December 18, 1981, only a few weeks after the disappearance, a call rang in on the home number.

"I've got Joan," the male voice said. "You'll hear her voice in a few hours."

George answered the call. "What do you want?"

"Deliver small, unmarked bills to 59th and 8th in New York. It's near the European Bank. Wear a blue hat and coat." George pretended to go along and the caller hung up.

The call was just extortion, pure and simple. Jack McEwen, with ITT's expertise, stepped in to trace the call and officials alerted the Newark FBI office. Though the dramatic call surely must have shocked George and Eleanor, the chilling event never crossed their lips at the family Christmas gathering, at least not in my presence. It's possible George and Eleanor kept some of these things secret to spare us the pain, but the web of secrecy and deceit I uncovered only obstructed the normal process of grief, reality, and truth.

An incident in New Jersey files caught my attention; a young woman got a ride from the Park Square Greyhound Station. Glen Ridge resident Ken Bramber called the police station to alert the New Jersey detectives about the episode his friend, Lynda Walsh, experienced on January 9, 1982, at the bus terminal in Boston. Det. Corcoran took down her account with the chance it might shed light locating Joan. As it turns out, their two stories did have similarities. Lynda was distraught at the Greyhound station in Boston.

"I've missed my bus," Lynda said to the woman behind the counter. "It was the bus from Park Square."

"Just a moment," the woman replied as she motioned for the large, casually dressed man to come over.

"I can give you a ride to the Trailways station if you need one," he said. He seemed friendly enough, but Lynda was not one to take rides from strange men.

"Well, I'm not sure," she said.

"Relax, honey, I'm an undercover cop," he replied, assuring her it would be safe. The man's familiarity was enough to convince Lynda, and she accepted his offer for a ride. The two moved to the unmarked car parked in the reserved area between the buses at Boston's Park Square Station.

"Everyone seemed to know him," Lynda informed Det. Corcoran. "Everyone at the Trailways station knew him, too."

This benevolent, public servant convinced his passenger he was an incognito officer helping a woman in distress. Corcoran dutifully noted these details and added pieces to the puzzle earnest searchers missed. Lynda's encounter did indeed reveal significant parallels to the enduring mystery. Trooper Palombo, the undercover cop assigned to the narcotics unit in the F Barracks at Logan, became integral in Joan's investigation. Palombo was one of only five officers that played an incognito role. Speculation that someone offered Joan a ride was the only conceivable explanation for her disappearance from the airport, and now there was evidence of a covert cop providing the service. Investigators seemingly exhausted all the other options without a clue as to her whereabouts. The incident also established the presence of undercover activity at the Boston Greyhound Station, where it was widely reported authorities recovered Joan's suitcase on January 29, 1982. It established a connection between the widely reported Boston Park Square Greyhound Station and the Massachusetts State Police—not the suspected perpetrator authorities aggressively pursued.

The search for Joan went on, but usually the leads and clues led to dead ends. An anonymous letter suggested Joan attended a fraternity party on Saturday night before most students returned to school, but Joan was not into that scene—she was not there. Enforcers searched abandoned buildings in the Boston area on a tip, but the lead produced no clues. The Harvard graduate student's disappearance was a high-profile case, and people hoped to exploit it. Police arrested three young men attempting to provide false information. The pretenders undoubtedly hoped to cash in on the $10,000 reward put up by ITT that the Websters announced on January 18, 1982. Caring citizens reported anything they thought might help, but to no avail. Joan was still missing, and authorities scrambled chasing dead ends. The lead they should have been chasing was the bearded man seen with Joan at the airport, but unfortunately, the leads they did chase only diverted the resources.

An anonymous call planted the seeds that convinced some that Joan's disappearance was connected to an alleged 1972 assault, and that Joan was the unfortunate, but random, victim of some predator still on the loose in Boston.

"Saugus Police Station," the desk sergeant answered.

"I want to report an assault," the woman declared.

"Give me the details, ma'am," the officer said. "I'll get officers dispatched right away."

"No officer," the feminine voice continued. "I was assaulted in 1972 by Leonard Paradiso. I think he had something to do with that murder you haven't solved yet, the one on the Lynn Marsh Road. I think her name was Marie something."

"Ma'am, could I have your name?" the sergeant asked. "This is 1982. Do you have any information about the Iannuzzi case in Saugus?" The woman hung up without answering.

The unidentified accuser picked up the phone again and dialed a long-distance number next. On the other end, George and Eleanor fumbled with the confounded tape recorder eavesdropping on their home phone.

"Hello, is this the Websters?" the woman inquired. "Is this the family whose daughter is missing in Boston?"

"Yes, yes," George eagerly answered. "Do you know something about Joan?"

"I was attacked within inches of my life in 1972 by a man named Leonard Paradiso," the nameless caller explained. "I think he might have had something to do with what happened to your daughter." The woman ended the call without revealing her name, or any facts that might support the dime she just dropped.

The unknown voice planted the name Leonard Paradiso. Anonymous calls to the Saugus Police and the Websters handed the state a suspect to pursue. The female caller alleged a man had assaulted her ten years before. The implication was that this supposed battering, several years before, might be connected to Joan's disappearance. Many seasons had passed without a record of the alleged assault, and there still was no known crime in Joan's case. The woman offered no details of current unresolved cases, but she coyly implicated a childhood acquaintance from the North End of Boston.

Sgt. Carmen Tammaro, an officer assigned to the narcotics unit in the F Barracks at Logan, grew up with the woman and the suspect she named. The North End was notorious for wise guys and mafia, and a neighborhood where a small-perceived slight could fester into a full-blown vendetta. The cop, the caller, and the alleged culprit were all partiers on a harbor cruise in their youth. Tempers flared and teens turned the ship into a floating brawl. Paddy wagons waited on shore when the cruise pulled up to the dock, and police arrested Carmen Tammaro for his part in the fracas. It just so happened that Sgt. Tammaro was also bearded Trooper Palombo's superior, and the two were controlling forces involved in Joan's case. Apparently, the unsubstantiated insinuations of an unknown caller were intriguing enough to George and Eleanor to set the wheels of Boston's brand of justice in motion.

The anonymous caller dangled a name for George and Eleanor just days before a bag handler discovered Joan's suitcase in either Boston or New York. The Lark bag was another clue in this confounding case. It simply did not make sense for a random perpetrator to drop off her luggage in yet another location, unless the culprit intentionally devised to avoid detection and throw off the investigation by spreading clues over a wide area. Tim Burke's recently published account, *The Paradiso Files*, claimed the Lark bag was recovered in New York. For years, seemingly credible sources constantly reported that the bag was discovered in Boston Park Square Station. Just where was Joan's suitcase?

Seeds of unsubstantiated gossip mushroomed, suggesting Burke's suspect frequented the terminal in Boston with known child molesters. Because authorities were the source of the story, they contrived a connection between the terminal and the accused, but without any real proof that there was a link. Embellishments spiced up

Burke's story, submitting Leonard Paradiso had described the contents of the suitcase to a confessor at the Charles Street Jail, but the suitcase was undisturbed when the FBI lab in Quantico examined it. The state police were now in possession of the bag, and representatives from the force provided the headlines that made the evening editions. Spin and disinformation filled the papers.

Armed with a name from an anonymous caller and a composite that looked nothing like the implicated suspect, George Webster requested a strategy meeting in February, 1982. The bureaucrat took control of the room within the austere ivied walls of Harvard. The school's motto, "Veritas," Latin for "truth," hung above their heads. The sign was sadly ironic given that the meeting did very little, in actuality, to uncover anything resembling the truth about Joan's disappearance.

The high-powered meeting underscored George's muscle to bring vast resources together. District Attorney John Droney's office was already handling the case in Middlesex County, and District Attorney Kevin Burke's Essex County office held the cold case files for the 1979 murder of Marie Iannuzzi. The Suffolk County District Attorney's office might have seemed out of place except for jurisdiction over the airport, but no crime had been established there to justify their presence.

DA Newman Flanagan mentored under his predecessor Garret Byrnes in the Suffolk County office, an office with a history of implicating the wrong offender. Suffolk County was the same public defender's office that succumbed to public outcry and pandering for votes by serving up Albert DeSalvo as the Boston Strangler. The Suffolk County DA's office based their assertions on an alleged confession DeSalvo supposedly made to an inmate, but the state lacked any real evidence to support it. Upon first impressions, it seemed Flanagan's office was there, because authorities claimed the suitcase was discovered in his jurisdiction. However, if that is not where the bag was, as Tim Burke has revealed, there had to be some other agenda for their inclusion in George's summit.

Lt. Col. John R. O'Donovan, head of the Massachusetts State Police, was used to being at odds with the Boston office of the FBI with their conflicted interests regarding the Irish mob and the Italian mafia. O'Donovan was present with his officers assigned to each DA's office. Others involved included the Harvard Campus Police, the Saugus Police, and Massachusetts State Police detectives out of F Barracks at Logan Airport. It was standing room only. This meeting was a mélange of influences and resources, people with conflicting interests and motives, all brought together by George Webster, a man with remarkable influence.

Trooper David Moran disclosed the forceful assembly convened by George Webster. The reliable source was a friend of Trooper Andrew Palombo, the central figure pursuing Leonard Paradiso. The two enforcers sometimes partnered, and Moran participated in aspects of the two cases discussed during the February 1982 meeting. The trooper was a credible source. As I reveiwed facts revealed in recovered documents, under the microscope of personal experience with George's control, it was not hard to envision what transpired in the secretive conclave.

"I've received a call," George began. "This woman has provided a name we need to get checked out. What do you know about this Leonard Paradiso?"

"The man has a record," George's disciples nodded in unison.

"He sounds like a bad actor," the missing student's father continued. "We need to get to the bottom of Joan's disappearance. The word is this fellow Paradiso had something to do with it."

"He's known as Lenny 'the Quahog,' Mr. Webster," one of the officers in the room added. "Paradiso is a suspect in a murder in Essex County that hasn't been solved."

"The case had two suspects, but we didn't have enough to charge Paradiso with the crime," An Essex County official outlined. "Trooper Palombo out of F Barracks at Logan is the lead officer on that case."

"Well, it sounds like Officer Palombo is our man to see what he can find out about Paradiso and what happened to my daughter." George persuasively guided the room to follow the anonymous tip. "I want the best minds working with Trooper Palombo on this."

"I've got a young, eager lawyer in my office working on cold homicide cases," a Suffolk County magistrate offered. "The pair will leave no stone unturned. They'll be able to dig into the Iannuzzi cold case to start."

Joan Webster was the topic on the agenda, but the direction that came out of that room had a different twist. Though the meeting ostensibly was about the missing graduate student, the strategy focused on another young woman as it adjourned. For about a year, Trooper Andrew Palombo had been the lead on the unresolved, 1979, Marie Iannuzzi murder. Soft-spoken and green, Assistant District Attorney Tim Burke, a fledgling in DA Newman Flanagan's Suffolk County office, was delegated control of the Essex County case.

"The Iannuzzi case was turned over to the Suffolk County District Attorney's office because investigators thought the young woman was murdered somewhere else and then taken to the marsh,"

Essex County DA Kevin Burke reported to the *Boston Globe*, defining the rationale for the change of jurisdiction.

According to Tim Burke's account, he wedged himself into the Marie Iannuzzi case after measuring the number of rods between the body and the county line. Technically, there was an old law on the books that allowed either county to take up a case close to the county line. It was an overly convenient coincidence, however, that the central players in Joan's investigation were also assigned to Marie's case.

The fact was that the name suggested to George Webster in an anonymous call had been considered a suspect in Marie's murder. No evidence existed to support innuendos that Leonard Paradiso was responsible for Joan's disappearance, but George's meeting set the forces in motion. The collective group at George's meeting paired ADA Tim Burke with Trooper Andrew Palombo to lead both investigations: Joan's disappearance and the Marie Iannuzzi murder. The scheme devised, by whoever was really in charge, was because of the weak circumstance that Joan's purse had been found in the same general vicinity as Marie's strangled body. They all ignored the fact that the area was a well-known dumping ground of evidence for all sorts of things. An anonymous call and a purse—that is all it took to throw off the investigation. The Harvard meeting did more damage than good, as if all the investigators lined up like horses to have saddles and blinders put on. All they could see was one direction, that Joan and Marie's cases were connected. Sadly, after that meeting, they could not see it any other way.

After leaving the meeting, Tim Burke formulated a story to justify his intrusion into the investigation of the 1979 murder. Marie Iannuzzi's sister, Kathy Leonti, would not have known the young, undistinguished attorney in a crammed, little office in another county unless his name had come to her attention. Burke had been assigned to homicide cases the previous fall, and he reviewed the case files of Basilia Melendez and her two children to try to resolve it. According to Burke's concocted story, Marie's grieving sister read an article, "AN OBSESSION TO FIND KILLER," which inspired her to finally muster the determination to call him in late February and plead for him to look at Marie's case. He had almost given up hope that anyone would call with a lead about the triple homicide when he said the phone finally rang.

"Mr. Burke, my name is Kathy Leonti," Burke chronicled in his book. "I read the article about the triple homicide case you're working on."

"Do you know about that case?" Burke asked.

"No, I'm sorry," the attorney typed Kathy's supposed response. "I thought maybe you could help me. My sister, Marie, was murdered two years ago, and I was hoping you would take a look at it."

The problem with Burke's story was that the *Boston Globe* published the article on the front page of the Metro section on Saturday, February 27, 1982. That only left Sunday, his day off, for his timeline to work for Kathy Leonti's alleged call in late February. Burke's version never mentioned the meeting with George Webster at Harvard, nor their mutual interest to go after the suspect found in the Iannuzzi case, a suspect based on an anonymous tip from an involved officer's friend.

Anyone who has experienced the wheels of the justice system knows they turn slowly. Nevertheless, by the following Tuesday, March 2, 1982, the Suffolk County DA's office issued subpoenas for a grand jury into the murder of Marie Iannuzzi. The grand jury then convened on Friday, March 5, 1982, as the *Commonwealth v. Leonard J. Paradiso.* Burke presented cause number 038655 before the court less than a week after the article appeared in the paper and Leonti's alleged call. Even though testimony implicated Marie's boyfriend, David Doyle, including testimony from Kathy Leonti, it was clear the wily attorney targeted the subject of the Websters' construction. Burke still touts this session was a John Doe grand jury, feigning an earnest interest to find Marie's true killer, but the grand jury was not given the secretive John Doe label until the next session Burke hosted on April 5, 1982.

The only logical conclusion is that the strategy of connecting the two murders was concocted at the Harvard meeting. Though the seeds of the strategy were planted at that meeting, it continued to evolve as months passed. ADA Carol Ball remained the visible presence on the case in Middlesex County and handled leads that continued to come in for the next few months. Her assistant, Elle Gates, confirmed that their office never received the crucial information that witnesses spotted Joan at the airport, nor did they ever see the composite of the bearded man.

Meanwhile, ADA Tim Burke quickly scheduled a grand jury in the *Commonwealth v. Leonard J. Paradiso* for the murder of Marie Iannuzzi. The state had not uncovered any new leads in the 1979 homicide. Burke's only justifications for the grand jury were the anonymous calls implicating Paradiso in Marie Iannuzzi's murder and Joan's disappearance. The one-sided presentation on March 5, 1982, gave the young prosecutor a preview of the challenges he faced to hang the murder on the accused. Had it begun as a John Doe as Tim Burke contends, he probably could have walked from the courtroom with an indictment against the other suspect in Marie's murder.

The strategy was tweaked when the case continued before the grand jury on April 5, 1982, and cause number 038655 was now a John Doe case, belatedly concealing the scapegoat the core group had selected.

In the week after the first grand jury session on March fifth, enforcers spread suspicions to target Leonard Paradiso for another Boston crime. Superiors dispatched Trooper Carl Sjoberg on March 11, 1982, to plant unfounded speculation with Paradiso's parole officer, Jim O'Neil.

"I'd like to speak with Jim O'Neil. This is Trooper Carl Sjoberg with the MSP," the officer announced. "I would like to talk to you about one of your parolees, Leonard Paradiso."

"This is Jim," the recently assigned parole officer acknowledged. "What can I do for you, trooper?"

"Paradiso was called before the grand jury in the Marie Iannuzzi matter. He didn't testify and said he would take the fifth." Sjoberg paused before shrewdly planting doubt with Paradiso's advisor. "He's a suspect in another case here in Boston."

"Can you give me any details?" Paradiso's assigned supervisor inquired.

"There's been a lead that your charge is involved in Joan Webster's disappearance," the designated hitter confided. The two public servants discussed the particulars of the missing student in confidence.

The seeds took root, and O'Neil spread the insinuations to his superior, Supervisor Murphy, in detail. No evidence linked Paradiso to Joan's disappearance, except accusations made by an anonymous caller and suppositions that came out of the Websters' February meeting. Both the parents and the police had the composite of a bearded man that looked nothing at all like Paradiso, but regardless, the witch-hunt was on.

These errant efforts continued. Authorities emphasized Joan's purse was crucial evidence, because some culprit tossed it in the vicinity of the 1979 victim, but they never publicly discussed the fact that this area was routinely used by criminals to discard evidence. Nor did it ever become clear where the suitcase was recovered, because no one had divulged the two different locations. An anonymous caller persuaded George and Eleanor that Paradiso was the culprit, and participants pursued the case in a direction that apparently satisfied them. The Websters, together with the police, whether intentionally or simply out of ignorance, pursued Paradiso, a suspect in Marie Iannuzzi's case, for Joan's murder.

Officials laid out Joan's recovered belongings in the Massachusetts State Police evidence room. Burke looked over the possessions that had survived that fateful night in November. Anger flushed his face thinking Paradiso had killed this beautiful, young woman. The zealous prosecutor was obsessed to find the links to connect the Websters' suspect and put him away for a very long time. He perused the items and spotted a pair of gray shoes with photographs of Joan in Nantucket tucked inside. The tanned faces smiling back from the photographs recorded happy memories from the young woman's life. Tragically, someone tore that vibrant life from people who loved her. My face smiled back at the litigator, too, from the glossy images he held in his hands, and captured the cherished moments of the last time I saw her.

George skippered the Boston Whaler up to the head of the harbor. We had the whole beach to ourselves and unloaded the picnic lunches we had packed that morning. As the tide went out, the beach widened, and we set out to explore the uncovered world in the sand dunes. An army of fiddler crabs emerged from their holes, scampering sideways to obstruct our path. All of us performed an awkward ballet, lifting ungracefully to the tips of our toes, and we ran quickly to avoid being pinched. Joan doubled over in laughter when she reached the safety of her beach towel. Her giggle was infectious, and soon we were all laughing to the point of joyful tears. I have pictured this in my mind, painfully remembering Joan, as I lay in bed trying to fall asleep.

There is no doubt in my mind that Tim Burke, the prosecutor assigned to investigate her disappearance, examined Joan's personal effects. The Massachusetts State Police were in possession of a pair of gray shoes, according to Burke's account. Lab technicians in Quantico carefully catalogued the items in Joan's suitcase on July 6, 1982. A pair of black lace leotards, a pair of gray pantyhose, and one green sock described everything that Joan could possibly wear on her feet.

"Her shoes were packed in the suitcase with some pictures of a vacation in Nantucket," Burke chronicled in his book. "I spoke to Anne. She said Joan wore gray shoes to see *The Pirates of Penzance* the night before she came back to Boston."

Where are the shoes? I thought to myself. *The photos were listed in the Lark bag, but there were no shoes at all in her suitcase, of any color.*

Burke said, "Webster was carrying a large canvas bag with shoes, books, and records." *Boston Globe* reporters took down every word when Burke took his bows for finding the touted crime scene. The September 29, 1983, article repeated the often-reported list of items that Joan carried in the tote bag, belongings authorities never recovered.

"Oh, dear God," I cried. "How did the police have an item contained in the tote bag?" My heart was pounding with the clue that had just been exposed. The Massachusetts State Police were in possession of an item, according to Burke, that connected them to Joan after she landed that night.

Current authorities, who happened to be friends and colleagues of Burke, have blocked access to the files for me or anyone else interested in verifying how "true" Burke's account really was. Joan was a member of my family.

Man-hours and tax dollars continued to be drained into the investigation of the missing Harvard graduate student. The media ate up the story sources fed them, and the headlines continued to play the baffling saga with the state's twist. The Cambridge Sheraton had their room ready when the Websters came back into town to turn over more stones. The warmth of early spring in New England was not enough to remove the chill surrounding their missing daughter. The press reported that divers braved the icy waters of Concord's Walden Pond the first week of April, 1982. Why were they there?

"Middlesex District Attorney John Droney received an anonymous letter last week stating Webster's body had been placed in a bag and dumped in the pond," Joseph Garcia reported for the *Harvard Crimson.*

"No, Eve," Elle Gates insisted. "There was no anonymous letter suggesting a search of Walden Pond. I worked on the case with ADA Carol Ball. I would have seen it. We were searching the pond because of the manifesto we received from Gareth Penn."

Disinformation implied the search came from a tip. The lead came from some Thoreau-obsessed sadist, or even worse, from someone purposely attempting to divert resources in unnecessary directions. In reality, this diversion came as a result of the bizarre theories promoted by Gareth Penn, who attempted to connect dots in his theory of the Zodiac murders.

Penn had contacted the Websters and presented a 119-page manifesto outlining his belief that Harvard Professor Michael Henry O'Hare was the Zodiac killer, responsible for the notorious crimes in California a decade before. He concluded O'Hare had also murdered Joan Webster based on cryptanalysis of the Zodiac's secret codes and complex calculations. The hypothesis assumed Penn's contention that he had cracked the baffling clues of the elusive California serial killer. George Webster sent copies to the FBI in Quantico for analysis in April, 1982, and Joan's father directed the authorities in the Middlesex office to search the areas Penn had deciphered. George handed over the overwhelming analysis to the Middlesex DA while he kept the composite locked in his files. Like sheep, Massachusetts authorities obeyed the orders from the man from New Jersey to turn every stone in the search for his daughter, despite the far-fetched claims Penn made.

"The bulk of his theory is based on speculation and a multitude of assumptions," the FBI lab concluded. "It is possible that some of Penn's assumptions are correct, but that many, if not most, appeared to be forced with the results being used selectively."

The FBI concluded that Penn's suppositions were unreliable. Despite this conclusion, the Websters continued to dally with Penn for a considerable time, and were still communicating with him a full year later when George's father passed away. This extraordinary tangent in the search emphasized three geographic points reported in Joan's case: the airport, Saugus Route 107, and the Boston Greyhound Bus Station at Park Square. Penn extended lines from the angles formed by connecting the dots, and the result pointed toward Concord. The calculations resulted in yet another futile search that sent divers into frigid waters. In any case, Tim Burke's more recent pronouncement, that the suitcase was recovered in New York, would have voided Penn's calculation in the first place if the New York location had been disclosed at the time. His geometric layout was flawed from the beginning.

Eleanor became preposterously familiar with Penn, a Mensa theorist. She became so confident with him that she even shared family matters about the dissolution of Reginald Webster's estate. Eleanor continued to fuel the man's imagination by sending him an aerial photograph, a similar item to the aerial photograph used in the case against the Suffolk County suspect. Eleanor also forwarded O'Hare's American Express authorization slip from Crimson Travel in Cambridge to Gareth Penn, and he used the confidential account information to harass the professor anonymously. How was Eleanor in possession of a slip that facilitated a diversion down a dead-end path in the investigation? Someone skilled in John Mulholland's trickery certainly explains one method to lift it. The California man made purchases delivered incognito to O'Hare's home, hoping to expose the Zodiac's identity in another one of the Websters' gaslight techniques. Eleanor inspired others to act, keeping herself removed from the strange drama of the bizarre tangent, despite the FBI analysis that rejected the theory.

Meanwhile, the police continued trying to pin Joan's murder on Paradiso. The conductor of this case summoned an FBI profiler, SA Roger DePue, from Quantico to Boston to have a meeting with representatives from the Massachusetts State Police, the Saugus Police Department, the Harvard University Police Department, the Boston Police Department, and the Beverly Police Department on April 14, 1982. This invisible authority tasked DePue with creating an image of Joan's offender. Despite being without a living or deceased victim, no evidence of a specific crime, nor even proof of the location of a crime scene, the authorities, with DePue's help, were still able to create a monster the public would be ready to lynch. Burke was a man obsessed with pinning Joan's murder on Paradiso. Authorities left the briefing armed with the profile they wanted; the hunt was underway several months before the headlines declared a "break in the case" implicating Paradiso for the crime.

A legitimate break, if anyone had known where to look, would have come from another source. George's correspondence with the FBI on April 29, 1982, ended up in the Zodiac files. Therefore, no one took note of one plausible clue suggested by a former intelligence employee. The letter also revealed George's influence to direct the efforts of the Massachusetts forces.

"I will be endeavoring to have Harvard Police continue to check airline manifests," the CIA alum outlined for the Feds. "He could have used an alias."

A stealthy assailant, or even Joan's father for that matter, who uncharacteristically traveled that same holiday weekend, could have traveled from Newark to Boston under an assumed name. The possibility that an offender covertly followed Joan to Boston was a consideration that fit with facts and more recent revelations, but the possibility had not been fully explored at the time. The condition of Joan's recovered remains in 1990, the unusual disbursement of her belongings, disinformation, and a diverted investigation all support a premeditated crime, but nothing like the absurd Zodiac or Paradiso theories. Despite all the evidence that could have helped crack the case, Joan was still lost, and her intelligence-trained parents were absorbed with incredulous explanations that sidetracked any honest investigation of the facts.

CHAPTER 4

Two Suspects

My reflex was immediate when I found the letter to God. I slipped it inconspicuously into my pocket and called the counselor who had been trying, with little success, to guide my family through these troubling times. I was already being harshly criticized, but my failings were never made clear. Pain and confusion cried from those pages, and I wrenched reading the doctrine of fresh complaint uplifted to God. My child clearly felt trapped and unable to confide in me, and she struggled with mixed images of both Steve and me. Her words clearly cast hostility and anger in my direction, but the alleged criminal behavior implicated her father. Enlisted counselors scrutinized two suspects for the obvious distress of my daughters.

"Eve," Sarah O'Brien dictated, "the girls don't want me to talk to you. They won't talk with me if I speak to you."

I did not know what to do. Counseling sessions deteriorated. The girls had their own space to confide, and I knew they desperately needed somewhere to talk. Feedback was poor, and I groped in the dark trying to figure out what was being suggested by my family in the meetings. Gossip filtered out when a parent from school restrained an obvious urge to hit me. The ruminations began to leak slowly as I heard the false perception that I had beaten my children. Abusing my children was a lie, and I was the target. At the time, I did not know how a comparable scene had played out in Boston years before when similar unsubstantiated gossip painted the image of a monster the family later accused of murdering Joan.

Steve was convincing in his denials that he had done nothing wrong, and the girls rallied around him. I was subjected to a process of devaluation and harassment that finally put me in the hospital near collapse. Depression and isolation had me on the brink of suicide, as a family, which had already lost one of their own, drove me from my children. I jumped through every hoop they set up, and conscience moved me to try whatever counselors suggested to allow healing from the unknown offenses. The forced alienation felt like exile from some secret society, or banishment from a cult afraid of exposure.

"I feel too much pressure to keep her alive," my child cried to the counselor. "I can't. It's too hard, and it's not my job."

Nevertheless, real emotions did leak into their conversations. "I need my mom," my child sobbed on the counselor's sofa. The session Sarah did share reflected my daughter's true feelings, not the intentional scheme that had brought us to this point.

My youngest daughter's words, feeling pressure to keep me alive, may have sounded sincere to the counselor, and there was noticeable distress. Nevertheless, the net nanny caught a much different side of the family's intentions; the John Mulholland lessons to keep things under the radar had been learned by the next generation. The constant harassment online was the type of bullying that fills the news, devaluing a target into despair that can end tragically. The pressure was not the concern I was a risk to myself, but the pressure was real, nonetheless. Another force influenced my children that imposed the heavy burden to keep their daddy happy.

"We're wicked ones we!"

"Yeah, I'm crying a lot."

"Let's talk about how much we hate Eve!"

"Let's go through the alphabet. Ass wipe!"

The two bantered back and forth through every letter, laughing at each other's creativity to devalue their mother. These were not the kind hearts I once knew, and these malicious rants certainly were not the actions of someone worried about my well-being.

"Z. STEVE! STEVE!"

"Oh, that was a good time—she was so humiliated!"

"As she should be, because she sounded like cattle dying!"

The girls' journals revealed more troubling assertions that bolstered my concerns about their dad's behavior, and exposed a motive.

"My mom had given Carol a journal entry my sister had written." Her sibling affirmed who wrote the troubling letter—and what it implied. "My dad wanted to talk to her about it. Everyone in the family was yelling."

Steve was unhappy because I had sought help. His well-honed image was at risk with a mom who did not follow the hushed family dictate, "Don't tell!" The girls had already expressed they couldn't make Daddy unhappy, and I was a threat to that cause.

"No one in the house had any privacy after this incident," she wrote, aping the family's concern for their secrets. "We were a team. Now we are at war."

I provided the journals to counselors, who still neglected to report the unfathomable suspicions. There was a burglary at Sarah O'Brien's secluded office the last weekend in April 2005, but the girls' advocate only reported the incident to Steve. The Webster file had been disturbed shortly after I had copied journal pages to add to O'Brien's files.

"Sarah, I want to talk to the police," I requested after Carol Metzger filled me in on the break-in. "I'm concerned about who was looking for our files. There are allegations of a felony in them."

"What felony?" Sarah idiotically asked.

"My daughter made allegations against her father," I answered, stunned that I had to explain it.

The mandate dictated by the three waging war against Mom was that Sarah not talk to me. What I did know was that my daughter had penned real terror, and I could see how diminished each of the three females in the household felt. I was shadowboxing in the dark. I knew who I was, and what I had and had not done, but I was cornered to defend myself from the unknown. I was scared. Counselors had not complied with the law, and my life was being upended. I had a meeting with the police in my community, and I reported what the professionals were obligated by law to do. I copied pages and pages to reinforce my concerns as I tried to make a coherent plea out of jumbled accusations.

Investigators knocked on the door and spoke to my girls together. Steve was not home, but the two sisters zipped their lips regardless. The response to my complaint did not expound what my children said, but rumblings of other tales emerged portraying Mom as the evil source of their pain. Ironically, I was now chastised for obeying the law that the counselors had so irresponsibly ignored.

"You hurt the girls by going to the police and reporting your concerns," Sarah scolded.

"So you do not believe a mother who is concerned about sexual abuse should call the police?" I asked, completely shocked.

"I'm not going to talk about other mothers. I'm only talking about you," Sarah replied with disdain.

"So you have a separate rule for me, as a parent, to report allegations of abuse?"

"That's right," the family counselor insanely decided.

I was a terrified mother being forced from her children and belittled for seeking appropriate help by Sarah O'Brien. No one considered that my instincts might be right, and the family banded together to discredit every word I spoke through the destructive manipulation of my children. After all, my girls were my vulnerability.

Joan's brother colluded with the girls' advocate, Sarah O'Brien, just before Steve and I discussed a divorce. Steve had manipulated the participants to devalue me further and go against the grain of established practice in the counselor's experience. Steve and Sarah told me I had done something wrong, but they could not tell me precisely what it was. He had obtained a solicited recommendation, without my knowledge, that resulted in effectively tearing me out of the lives of my children. At the same time, I was abiding by guidance from the same counselor to give my girls space for healing from this undisclosed offense.

Once again, there was a serious risk to the Webster image, and the family defended it at all costs. Steve found another counselor for my daughter, one who agreed to keep information under better wraps. Under oath in a deposition on May 13, 2008, Ari Gleckman described his observations of my child's condition.

"She has suffered with depersonalization. She has trouble differentiating between reality and illusions," he said.

He was not certain of the origin of this depersonalization, however. Gleckman had not bothered to look at what my child had written or listen to me. If he had, he would have seen how her father had consistently distorted arguments, a real event my daughter encountered, into something she had created. Steve lamented he was the victim of his child's imagination. Insight from me was blocked, and Gleckman failed to verify the outrageous allegations that formed his perception of me. He shed light on his young patient's concern about her aunt. Before Burke's book ever hit the shelves, she worried there might be publicity or legal action that would draw her into some interaction with her mom. Did all this have something to do with Joan? Perhaps this weight burdened my children, and eroded the necessary trust in healthy relationships.

"She's a whistleblower!" my mother-in-law had scorned.

Eleanor had disdainfully labeled me a whistleblower in a strange display of discontent from a mother still waiting for answers about her lost child. Newspapers and books chronicled Joan's case for years, but the dramatic events were not on the radar of local professionals dealing with my children's distress. My child's disturbing allegations compounded concerns in a family with a bizarre, unresolved murder. I knew the prosecutor's theory was implausible, and had expressed my objection to the family's support. This family was in denial.

At the time, I had not yet connected the family's background with an agency proficient in the psychological games being played. Curled in a fetal position, I pleaded for help.

"What have I done?" I sobbed as Carol listened. "What have I done to deserve this? I've loved and cared for all of them. I don't understand why I'm being treated this way."

Like Leonard Paradiso, accusations ran rampant, but I was never charged with anything. The talebearers charged nothing specific for me to defend myself, or address if I needed help. As it turned out, this tactic of manipulation was straight from the CIA handbook that documented methods of breaking down and brainwashing the enemy.

Point number three, "Feelings of Uncertainty; break down your subject by keeping them guessing, and never satisfy the target's desire to correct what is wrong." It's the same method used by police officer Popeye Doyle in the 1971 film *The French Connection*, where he barrages his witness with non-sequitur statements with the intent to confuse and disorient him until he has no choice but to comply. The CIA document OA 53-37 outlined the methods implemented against an enemy of the state, the same methods executed with precision against me. The Websters' old CIA training paid off in their objective to neutralize the leaks of the family secrets. I had knowledge that they did not want exposed, so I was consciously devalued and thrown away, but the devaluation that tore Joan from my life had not come into my awareness as a piece of the puzzle. Their son was a suspect for my children's malaise with evidence to support it, but the Websters cast me as a second suspect; a similar scenario of what had happened before.

Leonard Paradiso did not know many people at his employer's wedding, and he had only been introduced briefly to the twenty-year-old at the reception. The word-of-mouth invitation to an after-party at the Milanos' home was circulating to the guests at the Ship Restaurant when a disturbance erupted in full view. David Doyle had ripped his pants. He exploded in anger.

"Hey, David, let me sew those up for you," his girlfriend said.

"No, forget it. Just forget it. I just want to get out of here," Doyle yelled.

"Come on, David, I want to go to the Milanos' party, and I can fix that hole in your pants," she persisted. "You never want to party with me."

"Fine, go ahead," the enraged boyfriend argued, "but I'm going home!"

Doyle was embarrassed in front of his family and friends at his cousin's wedding. Rosemarie pulled her son from the argument and took him home while his girlfriend caught a ride with his cousins to carouse at the house. Lenny slipped into the passenger seat of his girlfriend's LeSabre, and Candy steered them to the parents' home in Saugus, unaware what destiny held for them.

Guests moved in and out of the house on the warm summer evening. Marie continued to drink, and flirted with Doyle's intoxicated cousin, Freddie. The groom's father tried to call David Doyle to come pick up his girlfriend, but never got an answer. He ordered a cab for the inebriated guest, who had overstayed her welcome, but Marie balked and declined the ride. Alfred Milano then appealed to a sober guest in the room if she would take Marie home. Candy Weyant, Paradiso's date, obliged her host.

"I loaded Marie into the front seat of the car," the groom's sister, Rosemary Sullivan, later told the police. "The young woman drove Marie someplace, and her boyfriend stayed behind at the house."

Marie did not want to go home to an incensed boyfriend, and insisted Candy drop her off two blocks away at the Cardinale's Nest Bar. Lenny nodded off in the living room at the Milanos' until Candy returned about eleven o'clock, and the couple lingered with the dwindling group for another hour.

Lenny picked up some papers on the front seat and showed Rosemary Sullivan when they said their goodnights about midnight. Marie had dropped some papers in Candy's car, and the couple made a detour to return them. Lenny found Marie still drinking at the bar while Candy waited outside. The belligerent, young woman had no intention to stop drinking or go home.

"No way!" she shouted as Lenny offered a ride. "I have an appointment."

Candy drove Lenny back to his place and reached for an umbrella in the back seat as they got out of the car. Lenny spotted the large key ring stuck in the seat. The couple pulled away from the curb, and Candy waited outside again as Lenny went back into the bar. The big key ring that patron Michael Kamer played with identified "Day" on the tag, and the keys rested on the counter in front of Marie. Marie had turned her limited attention to refuse Lenny's offer to drive her home. She turned to her friend, Christine DeLisi, and said she would be back in half an hour. Lenny held the door as Marie walked out about one in the morning, and he watched her walk around a corner and out of sight. Lenny sprawled out on his bed, exhausted, while Candy fixed a cup of tea before driving herself home. They were oblivious that the chance meeting with Marie and acts of kindness would eventually fuse with the fate of another young woman, and change their lives forever.

Christine did not wait, but other witnesses placed Marie back in the bar near two in the morning.

"Marie, turn the air-conditioning down," bartender Jimmy Cardinale said, while Patty Capozzi cleared glasses and turned off the lights.

It was the end of the day, but it was not the end of the story. Marie's family was worried when she did not show up as promised to celebrate her father's birthday on Sunday, but no one knew where she was. They feared the worst, and unfortunately, the worst had happened. On Sunday afternoon, passing boaters found the unemployed waitress's strangled body on the rocky bank of the Pine River behind a closed, wholesale seafood company in Saugus. Her tormenter had rolled her lifeless form down the stony hill to the water's edge.

Marie was not wearing shoes and stockings, but she was fully clothed in a red, one-piece, body suit, a matching wraparound skirt, and a black scarf double-knotted tightly around her neck. Police ruled out robbery, because no jewelry was missing, and seasoned detectives did not consider rape a motive based on how she was dressed. Autopsy photos, taken at the scene and later at the morgue, showed her clothes were intact. Marie's desperate fight was evident. Her long-manicured nails protruded like claws, but the examiner failed to scrape under the nails, and nobody bothered to ask.

Marie's mother heard the description early Monday morning as she drove home from her shift, and she frantically diverted her path to pick up Marie's sister. Mary Iannuzzi and Jean Day knocked on the Doyle's door shortly before seven o'clock Monday morning. David's mother was stunned. She covered her mouth with her hands.

"Oh, my God," she cried.

David was still foggy from his high the night before, and he sauntered into the bathroom to escape the inevitable questions about his absent girlfriend. Frantic calls gathered the family at the Iannuzzis' home, and Doyle sat silently on his hands in the corner. Inspector Arthur Cook of the Saugus Police Department affirmed some general descriptions and left for the morgue to identify the body. Marie's father was too distraught to look at the body he feared was his daughter.

"I can't look. I can't look," he said, traumatized at the thought.

Marie's brother-in-law, Tony Leonti, stood to the side as David Doyle lifted the sheet, then quickly threw it back over the tortured face. Tony saw no emotion from the man who hurriedly glared at the lifeless eyes.

"Yeah, that's her," Doyle angrily confirmed.

The lifeless victim was, indeed, the body of Marie Iannuzzi. Soon two suspects emerged in the murder case. The Saugus police began the task of reconstructing the events, and interviewed wedding guests and friends of the victim. Leonard Paradiso and David Doyle had both attended the wedding of Michael Milano with their girlfriends on August 11, 1979. Bar patrons saw Paradiso, a parolee, leaving the bar at the same time as the victim. Doyle was an unemployed drug user who lived with his girlfriend on the third floor in his parents' home. They had a known abusive relationship, and turbulence had flared again to embarrass Doyle at his cousin's wedding. Their relationship had hit the rocks, and Doyle knew Marie was seeing another man.

Word trickled out after the body was identified at 9:20 a.m. Monday morning. Lenny had already made a routine check-in call to his parole officer, Victor Anchukaitis, but never mentioned the wedding over the weekend, or lost items returned to a guest. The parolee was understandably nervous when word reached him Monday afternoon the young woman was dead, and he called Victor back later that evening.

"Cooperate with the police if they ask you any questions," Anchukaitis advised his charge.

Lenny and his girlfriend both heeded his parole officer's advice to cooperate with police, and spoke with Det. Arthur Cook and Trooper Carl Sjoberg on Tuesday. Paradiso placed another call to Victor after the officers had questioned the parolee and his girlfriend, and the counselor arranged to meet both of them later.

"Meet me at the 99 Lounge in Lynn," the aging supervisor arranged with his parolee.

Lenny and Candy had a meeting with Anchkaitis in the common setting the officer liked. When Victor made it back to his office, the supervising officer discreetly omitted the meeting place from his notes, but the typist added the entry after Victor's latest sequential entry on August 15, 1979. The retiring officer undoubtedly feared losing his pension for meeting his parolees in a bar, so his subtlety twisted account opened the window for future interpretation.

Rosemarie Doyle stayed close to her son during the wake. People whispered.

"Look at the scratches on David's hands."

"Have you seen David? He's been strung out the last two days."

The procession pulled away from the funeral home early Friday morning followed by a mass at Sacred Heart Church, but the paranoid boyfriend took flight. New Jersey law enforcement arrested him stealing suitcases from the baggage claim at Newark Airport, and Doyle gave them a false name, Edward Day. The name was familiar. Day was the name associated with the tag on Marie's returned keys, and Day was the last name of stepsiblings in her large Catholic family. Police confiscated the stolen airline ticket for a flight from LaGuardia to Boston the detainee had in his possession. At the same time Doyle sat in the clink in New Jersey, his mother answered questions and assured the police David was home on the night in question.

"I leave my second-floor bedroom door open at night. I would know if he had left," Rosemarie said before explaining the cause of the severe scratches on his hands. "There was a car accident a couple months ago on June tenth or eleventh."

Marie's siblings pointed the finger squarely on Doyle. Jean Day observed Marie's packed belongings early on Monday morning when she and her mother arrived at the Doyle's. Family members returned to pick out a dress for the wake, and they made hushed observations of another unsettling discovery—blood. There on the steps up to the couple's apartment, the group saw a drop of blood. The circumstantial evidence did not look good for David Doyle. The facts almost guaranteed Essex County a slam-dunk prosecution, but oddly, DA Kevin Burke did not indict him. Instead, the investigation stalled, despite having two suspects, and the case eventually went cold.

"Leonard is still a suspect in the Iannuzzi murder," Inspector Howard Long updated Anchukaitis. "There are two suspects, but there is nothing to arrest or even hold Paradiso for." There was not enough evidence to charge Paradiso with the crime, and some other agenda apparently usurped the common sense to arrest Doyle.

Superiors reassigned Det. Cook and removed him from the unresolved case about a year after the crime. Some higher authority also usurped Trooper Carl Sjoberg out of Essex County by February, 1981, and replaced him with an undercover detective assigned to the airport in Suffolk County. The tall and hefty cop, a former defensive lineman, worked with informants. His intimidating appearance changed as needed, but his beard and scraggly, long hair helped him mingle comfortably with unsavory elements on the street. Motorcycle gangs revved their engines on the streets of East Boston where David Doyle hustled for drugs, and Trooper Andrew Palombo's Harley helped him fit right in with the crowd.

Trooper Palombo met with Doyle twenty to thirty times. The assignment was inappropriate, and certainly unorthodox, for a lead cop in a murder case to be so closely connected to a man like Doyle. Of course, Palombo never documented or recorded the meetings he held with the murder suspect, but the relationship was clear; Doyle knew the drug world on the streets, and Palombo worked narcotics out of Logan. The pairing could hardly have been a coincidence. Doyle had an extensive rap sheet, and it seemed this close relationship between cop and criminal had distinct benefits.

In the heat of the summer in 1981, Saugus cops caught wind of a tip, and Inspector Howard Long sought out a druggie named David Dellaria. The police pulled their car to the curb and helped Dellaria carefully slip into the back seat of the squad car. Det. Charlie Gleason, Inspector James Stoddard, and Inspector Howard Long picked up the hesitant witness on July 16, 1981, and took him to an old, abandoned football stadium in East Boston.

"He killed her," Doyle's friend told the cops.

Dellaria claimed to know details of the murder, but a member of the Trampers Motorcycle Club, bikers that cruised the streets of East Boston, threatened Doyle's friend not to talk. He had reason to be frightened. Doyle battered Dellaria twice, and stuffed him in the trunk of a car until another druggie, Paul Leo, pulled Doyle away from any further assault. The cops arranged to take a complete statement a few days later, but Dellaria did not show up, too scared to say anything more. Doyle's scrapes with the law swelled his rap sheet, but offenses continued without significant deterrents.

Thanksgiving was the start of the holiday season. As winter winds blew in Boston in 1981, a chilling story about a missing graduate student from Harvard began swirling. She vanished from Logan Airport on Saturday night before most of her classmates traveled back from the break. The story filled the papers and preyed on the emotions of the public. Joan Webster's fate was a complete mystery.

While twists and turns in Joan's disappearance saturated the news in the spring of 1982, Doyle's quick temper was on public display once again. Michael DeLisi sat in the Cardinale's Nest Bar watching David Doyle's temper flare at a retreating, young woman. Michael sat down with a dejected Doyle, and the two began talking over beers. Doyle's tongue loosened as the evening wore on, and he confided, "She got what she deserved." Michael listened as Doyle spilled the details of the woman's last night alive.

"She went back to our place when the bar closed. We argued. I was on V's, you know, so she was pretty angry." DeLisi listened carefully as Doyle rambled on. "She tried to leave, but I pulled her back by her scarf. You know, I didn't mean to kill her. It just happened. I was high, so what else was I supposed to do? I remembered there was this dumpster at the airport, but I figured there might be too much security there, so I dumped her body on some rocks behind Conley and Daggets. She got what she deserved."

Marie's boyfriend had allegedly confessed to a crime of passion. He was under the influence of drugs at the time, and they had argued in front of numerous witnesses that day. He was jealous of another man Marie had been seeing, and his rage festered while Marie continued to party after the wedding.

Despite Doyle's alleged confession to a friend in the spring of 1982, the dime had already been dropped on Paradiso. Palombo's superior, Sgt. Carmen Tammaro, knew the North End woman who anonymously called implicating the Websters' suspect, Leonard Paradiso, in both crimes. The tapped ADA had already walked into the grand jury on cause number 038655, the *Commonwealth v. Leonard J. Paradiso*, for the murder of Marie Iannuzzi. The state had so much momentum to condemn Paradiso for Marie's murder that it was too late to turn back. Another agenda propelled the group to move forward. Rumors were spreading inside enforcement circles, casting suspicion on Paradiso for Joan's disappearance. No new evidence pointed to Paradiso as Marie's killer, but Joan Webster was missing.

CHAPTER 5

Not So True Bill

After being allegorically dumped and left for dead in Hamilton County, ironically, the same name of the town where Joan was recovered, my task was daunting. It was not clear what my children believed or feared, but every effort to communicate or sort things out was met with typical Webster resistance. On the twenty-fifth anniversary of Joan's disappearance, November 28, 2006, an article appeared in the *Boston Herald* announcing the book former prosecutor Tim Burke was writing. He billed his tome as "true crime," and the paper quoted George and Eleanor supporting Burke's insinuations that Paradiso murdered their daughter.

"TOME SEEKS TO CLOSE BOOK ON MURDER," was the byline for the piece in the *Boston Herald.*

"We are cooperating with the book," Eleanor trumpeted. "It keeps Joan alive."

Any rational person knew the informant's statement was false after Joan's skeleton surfaced. I, of course, was not privy to the articles that challenged the implausible theory. Numerous authorities who sincerely sought the truth told the resolute parents that Paradiso was not the likely offender.

"The girl was murdered," Chief Walter Cullen of the Hamilton Police Department grimly told the *Beverly Times.* "Personally, I think it was someone she knew."

"The modus operandi was different from the cases Paradiso was involved in." Det. Sgt. Paul Grant affirmed his superior's doubts that Paradiso was the culprit responsible for Joan's loss.

"I certainly don't believe Paradiso had anything to do with Webster, and I don't believe he had anything to do with Iannuzzi's death," private investigator Ray Morgan told *Beverly Times* reporter Kevin Wesley. "I don't like to see a guy take a screwing like that."

"I don't think Paradiso killed her [Joan]," Beverly police detective Gordon Richards told the *Bergen Record* in New Jersey.

However, Richards' observation reported to the *Beverly Times* on May 4, 1990, shed a glimmer of light into the sheer denial of facts right in front of Joan's parents.

"Paradiso had offered to take a lie detector test, but George Webster said 'no.'" The detective surmised, "In his mind, Paradiso was already guilty."

Had I seen the reports, I might have grasped the Websters' difficulty comprehending reality. Now, it was a problem my children apparently suffered, and the family was egging it on by supporting a fallacious book about the unresolved murder of the girls' aunt. Suddenly, I fully understood the significant influence the Webster family held over my children, and exactly why my girls had such difficulty discerning what was real.

For me, when the article appeared announcing Burke's book was when reality set in that had to be confronted. The grand jury rejected Tim Burke's preposterous theory in 1983, and continued efforts to badger his target failed repeatedly to gain an indictment in a climate that would have brought charges against a ham sandwich. My e-mail was firm and direct expressing concern the family would support allegations without proof.

"How is Mr. Burke going to reconcile the inconsistencies?" I challenged. "His theory has Paradiso taking Joan out on his boat. How will he explain why he didn't just dump her overboard? Why did he risk being caught bringing her back to shore, travel a long distance, and bury her?"

It defied common sense why the family believed this after they learned the informant's statement was false.

"How would Mr. Burke reconcile the stark contrast in the behavior of a family who'd lost a daughter and sister compared to the behavior I had experienced in the circumstances with the girls." I firmly focused on the hidden side of their personalities Burke had not seen.

"Perhaps my children have the fear of ending up like Aunt Joan!" I charged.

My words hit a nerve when I confronted family members with the negligent position to support such a book. My gut instincts told me my children were caught in the middle of the family's position, and my instincts got a reaction. George's e-mail bounced back, but Steve read it with anxious concern. The forwarded e-mail bounced back again from George's inbox, but the path this time was from Steve's office.

I was no longer able to ignore the questions burning in my mind. I began digging deeply into Joan's case to uncover answers while the family maintained an impossible explanation. Old wounds throbbed with pain as pieces of the puzzle fell into place. The Websters shrouded secrets and covered the reality of Joan's murder. Unfortunately, the Websters were not part of the solution; they met every question with silence. Obstruction for an independent review continued, and the family claimed privacy. They were part of the problem if they were not going to help. The Websters decided Paradiso murdered Joan, and that was apparently the determining factor. That position influenced my children to place trust in the likes of murderer Robert Bond instead of their mother. The problem was becoming clear; with my accumulated knowledge, observations, and experiences, I posed a tremendous liability to the powerful Webster family.

The grand jury had rejected Burke's premise in Joan's case, but a grand jury did believe Paradiso had raped and murdered Marie Iannuzzi enough to hand down the charges. I presumed Paradiso received a fair trial and was guilty of the 1979 crime. The players were the same as those responsible for Joan's case, so what happened? Burke tenaciously forged ahead with his suggestion that Leonard Paradiso had raped and murdered Marie Iannuzzi, despite all evidence to the contrary.

Every bit of circumstantial evidence pointed directly at Marie's boyfriend, David Doyle, but Essex County never handed down an indictment against the boyfriend. The other suspect had an unusual relationship with the lead officer that steered both cases. Shortly after the Webster meeting in February, 1982, Suffolk County scheduled a grand jury. Burke misrepresented the one-sided presentation as a John Doe inquiry to determine which of the two suspects to charge for the crime. His oratory began on March 5, 1982, in the *Commonwealth v. Leonard J. Paradiso.* Had his motives been sincere to administer justice, the hearing would have probably handed down a true bill against the boyfriend. However, the Websters' determination to target Lenny colored every syllable the handpicked prosecutor uttered and every word the public believed. As far as I can figure, the ultimate reason the Websters pursued Lenny, the root of it all, was based on some unsubstantiated anonymous phone call.

One by one, Marie's family took the stand and recounted in excruciating detail the painful events. Memories, seared with trauma and scars, were pricked open once again. Evidence continued to mount against David Doyle. Kathy Leonti, Marie's sister and the woman Burke claimed drew him into the Essex County case, was the first witness to the stand.

"Did you observe anything about Doyle?" ADA Burke asked the witness.

"He sat on the chair," Kathy somberly recollected. "He said nothing. He sat on the kitchen chair, just glazing, looking around."

"Everything was packed Sunday night?" a juror inquired. "Did he know Sunday she was dead?"

"I don't think so; Monday morning it was all packed." Kathy Leonti had just handed Burke a problem.

"Did Marie own a cat?" The prosecutor subtly gathered the facts he needed to hurdle.

"Marie told us a month before," the sister continued, "the cat ran away."

Packed belongings on Monday morning made Doyle look suspicious, but Burke could cloud the timeline with confusion. He knew he had to come up with another explanation for scratches witnesses had seen on Doyle's hands. David Doyle already told police that a cat caused the scratches on his hands and around his eye. However, there was no cat around to support the boyfriend's feeble excuse.

Next to the stand was Kathy's husband, Tony, and he described the strangely cold, callous reactions of Doyle when they viewed his girlfriend's body. Tony went with Doyle and Marie's father to the morgue to identify the body early Monday morning. The sheet was pulled back uncovering a face frozen in terror.

"It was her," Tony somberly stepped back to that moment in time. "He threw the sheet over her head in disgust. He was mad."

"Did he cry?" Burke queried.

"No!" Leonti described the emotionless boyfriend, "None whatsoever!"

That afternoon or the next morning, Tony and three other members of the family went to Doyle's house to gather belongings. All of them noticed something on the second or third step from the bottom, and stopped to discuss it.

"How did you know it was blood?" Flanagan's pupil proceeded.

"You know blood when you see it," the victim's brother-in-law confidently recalled for the counselor.

"Did you go to the wake?" Burke stepped in further. "Was David there?"

"Yes," Tony turned to the jury to describe the boyfriend's behavior. "He was on something. He was always on Valium and Angel Dust.

His mother chauffeured him around. He came in with her and left with her."

"Did you and he discuss what happened to her?" a juror posed the question.

"We talked about it at the wake. I did not see him after the wake." Tony just served up another problem for Burke's upcoming rendition of events. The witness was unaware he would later be cast as an alibi witness, but that testimony, if it were true, would have come out when he was asked about scratches Doyle suffered.

"Did you have occasion to observe David Doyle?" ADA Burke asked his next witness.

"The first day of the wake," Marie's uncle replied. "I would not shake hands; his hands were full of scratches."

"You could see them?" Incriminating evidence was piling up against the suspect Burke had not named for this hearing.

"Yes, they were terrible. It was like raw beef; wide type scratches. They were scabbed up, oozy type things; you don't put your hands on something like that." Benjamin Puzzo gave graphic testimony about the precise condition of Doyle's hands on the first day of Marie's wake.

The jurors could see from Puzzo's gestures how Doyle folded his arms on both days of the wake so nobody would see his hands. The uncle concluded Doyle was pretty well high on something, out of it at the wake, affirming what earlier witnesses said. Puzzo opined Marie's boyfriend did not know where he was. However, Burke needed to get back to the problematic scratches Puzzo recoiled from touching.

"Yes," the uncle answered Burke's question about Marie's fingernails, "always manicured, had them long."

"Would a dog or cat do that?" Burke hoped for an answer to rehabilitate Doyle.

"They were too wide. These looked like they were dug and pulled." Puzzo showed the jury how someone or something had ripped Doyle's flesh deeply from his wrists to his fingers.

The lineup continued when Jean Day, another sister, took the stand. Marie's mother heard the broadcast on the radio early Monday morning on her way home from her overnight shift. She quickly detoured to pick up Jean, and the two arrived on the Doyle's doorstep before seven a.m. Before they said a word, Doyle's mother gasped and covered her mouth with her hands.

"Oh, my God!" Jean recalled Rosemarie Doyle's reflexive reaction.

"Did you notice scratches on his hands?" Burke asked the witness to recall events Monday morning when the family gathered at the Iannuzzi's house.

"My father talked to him," Jean Day explained. "He was sitting on his hands, and then I noticed the scratches when he got off the chair."

Burke needed to deal with Doyle's marred hands if he was going to nail the target of his grand jury inquest, Paradiso, for the crime. "Describe the scratches."

"Across the top of his hands," Jean vividly remembered, "pretty good gouges. They were fresh, done within a couple of days."

"Do you know of any problems she [Marie] had with Dave?" The juror's question reinforced to the prosecution the reasonable suspicion pointing to Doyle.

"They were on the verge of breaking up," Jean confided. "She called me; told me they got in an argument. He hit her; tried to grab her by the neck."

Burke digested all the problems he had with his case. Jean had described the attire Marie was wearing and unambiguously described the missing stockings that her sister wore underneath the other garments. Jean pinpointed the time she saw fresh scratches, before relatives identified the body at the morgue Monday morning. Another damaging fact came in; the distraught sibling saw Marie's packed belongings when she and her mother arrived before seven o'clock Monday morning. She described her promiscuous sister to the police, and she knew there was trouble in the relationship with Doyle. Having already suffered through the unresolved murder of their brother, Richard Day, in 1975, the family was convinced that Doyle was Marie's killer.

Family and friends gathered at the Joseph A. Langone, Jr. Funeral Home bore witness to the boyfriend's drugged stupor during visitation on Wednesday and Thursday, before he took flight to New Jersey. Each witness, one after the other, described the turbulent and abusive relationship between Doyle and Marie. She had been dating another man while she lived with David under his parents' roof. Both of them used drugs, and there was another man in the picture. Regardless, Burke's cause was number 038655, the *Commonwealth v. Leonard J. Paradiso*, the Webster suspect named in an anonymous call.

The stories kept coming, and they were all eerily consistent. Close friends recounted a recent incident highlighting the violence in the couple's tempestuous relationship. Anna Marie Kenney raised her hand and swore to tell the truth.

"'David almost killed me,'" Marie's friend shivered, repeating the victim's frightening words. "'He strangled me; he scared me,' Marie said. She had long red marks on her neck."

"You saw them?" Burke asked as he mentally calculated how to handle Doyle's previous behavior.

"Yes," Kenney confirmed as she wrapped her hands around her throat for the jury to envision Doyle's fingers tightly wrapped around a throat still gasping to speak. "This was summertime, May or June, before she died."

Marie's best friend, Christine DeLisi, took the stand, too. Christine was at the Cardinale's Nest Bar on the last night Marie was alive. Marie told her family she was going to stay with Christine when she phoned them Saturday night. Her friend turned and asked her to wait until she returned in a half hour, and Christine watched as Paradiso held the door open for her friend as she walked out. DeLisi left about one before learning whether Marie ever came back or not.

"Had she ever stayed with you before?" the solicitor inquired, already knowing the answer.

"She stayed with me four to five days, the end of May or beginning of June." DeLisi sighed and wiped her tears before she went on. "She was screaming and crying David beat her up. She had strangulation marks on her neck, fairly red marks, and handprints around her neck."

Marie had landed on DeLisi's doorstep just weeks before boaters found her best friend strangled and discarded on the bank of the Pine River. Doyle's foreboding behavior was a warning family and friends apparently felt they heeded too late. Both Christine DeLisi and Anna Marie Kenney recounted the unemployed waitress had thrown her clothes in a trash bag and hurried to DeLisi's house for refuge. Distinctive marks stretched around her neck exposed Doyle's tight grip, and the frightened runaway cried out he had tried to kill her. Now the Suffolk County ADA had to whitewash a prior act of violence just weeks before a predator strangled the young woman and dumped her body in Essex County. Things did not look good for the boyfriend, but the unwitting witness handed Burke the nail he needed to hang his case on: Paradiso left the bar at the same time as Marie, sometime after midnight on August 12, 1979.

Inspector Arthur Cook, a detective with the Saugus Police Department, was among the first on the scene after two passing boaters discovered Marie's body by the river. The officer now sat on the stand. Cook recalled Doyle's lack of emotion when he viewed Marie at the morgue about nine a.m. Monday morning. From the morgue, Cook took the three men upstairs to answer some questions.

"What about his person?" the controlling counselor asked about Doyle's appearance on Monday morning.

"He had a scratch over his eye and another scratch under the eye," Cook noted, "and scratches on the back of one hand. The ones on the hands were not brought to our attention until a day later, by the parents."

"When did you first see those, the scratches on his hands?" The sly solicitor needed room to wiggle around the suspicious gaping wounds Doyle brandished.

"At a later time, in New Jersey," Cook recalled. "David Doyle was arrested breaking into suitcases in the airport. It would have been Thursday night, Friday morning." The officer described the suspect's erratic behavior to skip town before his girlfriend's funeral, and the officer's trip to Newark early the next week to interview him.

During David's absence, Cook interviewed his parents and pointedly asked about the scratches on Doyle's hands. Rosemarie had stuck close to her boy throughout the two days of the wake. Something was missing from the police report Burke had to fix before trial. He unveiled another explanation for the incriminating dug flesh on the back of Doyle's hands, but Doyle's mother said nothing about it to the police at the time.

"His mother said the scratches were caused by a motor vehicle accident two months prior," Cook explained, recalling the interview conducted on August 20, 1979. "In our opinion, the scratches were fresher."

"Did you ask him how he got the scratches?" the attorney dared to ask.

"He said he had a cat that did it," was the cop's problematic reply.

Cook noted the wounds on the obvious suspect's hands after New Jersey police arrested Doyle days later in Newark, and the officer traveled to the Garden State to question him. Sometime after the last visitation ending at nine p.m. on Thursday, Doyle took off, and authorities apprehended him with a pair of lady's panties in a brown paper bag. Cops arrested Marie's boyfriend stealing suitcases in the late hours of Thursday or early Friday morning, the day the Iannuzzi family laid their loved one to rest. Strange and undeniable behavior suggested Doyle's consciousness of guilt, but Burke did not want the jurors to see it that way. The one-sided presentation did not mention other names typed in Cook's reports, people who saw Marie alive when the bar closed. Therefore, the officer handed Burke the desired implication.

"Who was the last person that saw Marie Iannuzzi alive?" the counselor coyly asked to emphasize Christine DeLisi's account of when she last saw Marie.

"Lenny Paradiso," Cook answered without checking what he'd noted in his reports.

"You have the right to remain silent," Burke began reading Miranda Rights to the next witness.

David Doyle had a job by this time, and drove a bus for the transit authority at the airport. The location of his employment was convenient for the many undocumented meetings with the undercover cop who took over the case in February, 1981. The rehearsed witness acknowledged his anger and embarrassment the day of the wedding. Alcohol and Valium helped him cope with the rage festering inside, and he even admitted that he used everything short of heroin. Rehabilitating a prime suspect began in the cause Burke filed against Paradiso on March 5, 1982. Doyle was confused about times, and evasive with initial questions about the scratches on his hands.

"Did you have marks on your hands?" Burke asked about the interview with police after they left the morgue.

"The detectives asked me about that," Doyle answered. "We had a cat. He asked where they came from; that was all I could think of."

"Was she going out with anybody else?" the counselor inquired.

"Somebody named Fisher," the dejected boyfriend believed, but Doyle's concession lacked any familiarity with the other man his live-in girlfriend saw on the side.

The questioner addressed the suspect's abrupt departure for New Jersey, too. The state's delegated advocate passed off guilty behavior as an innocent retreat Doyle took to clear his head from the events of the past few days. The witness admitted he was high, but intended to return for the funeral. He suggested he paid for the ticket out of unemployment or his criminal activity dealing drugs. The bereaved boyfriend continued his illegal behavior, stealing from the bags on the carousel at his final destination, and gave a false name to the police who cuffed him. His pitiful excuse, he was waiting for a return flight, overlooked the fact the procession began at 8:30 in the morning, and cops had the crook locked up in Newark with the reported stolen ticket from LaGuardia to Boston in police evidence.

The fresh oozing wounds were a problem, but Burke probed for another answer. The state unveiled a new explanation for the deep gauges on Doyle's hands in front of the grand jury convened against Leonard Paradiso. The practiced story was not in police reports, and suspiciously, no one offered the explanation before this hearing. Burke's skills to discern the truth hit a low with this thin story.

"Do you remember marks on your hands?" Burke repeated.

"The detective said somebody saw me at the wake with marks on my hands." Doyle served up yet another unpolished excuse. "I got in a fight at one of the wakes. I was with Fisher and a couple of other guys. We were at a bar across from the funeral home after one of the wakes."

Doyle insanely suggested he was commiserating with the other man who had made him jealous, a man he had just labeled, "Some guy named Fisher." His mother had kept a close leash on her strung-out, baby boy during the wakes, but had not recalled this latest excuse when police asked about the scratches. Doyle was vague about other names, but creators inserted an alibi witness when the saga was embellished at trial.

"You have had bad fights?" the solicitor confronted the abuse.

"I would whack her," Doyle acknowledged with confidence, knowing he had friends at his back. "I would hit her. I have grabbed her by the neck and held her off, but never put a stranglehold on her."

Just days after Burke's deceptive presentation for the grand jury, crafters enhanced the strategy in play. On March 11, 1982, Trooper Carl Sjoberg, the officer usurped by Trooper Palombo on the Iannuzzi case in February, 1981, called Paradiso's parole officer and covertly spread the rumors generated from the anonymous calls made by Sgt. Tammaro's childhood friend.

"Paradiso is suspected in another Boston crime," Sjoberg indicated.

A sincere effort to seek justice for Marie Iannuzzi would have handed the cunning counselor an indictment against David Doyle on March 5, 1982, but the session he slated was against Paradiso. The cause number was unchanged, but the grand jury mysteriously morphed into a John Doe for the same cause number 038655 by the time Burke paraded in front of the jurors seated on April 5, 1982. "John Doe" now suspiciously concealed the intended target previously named in Burke's cause.

The determined prosecutor had several chances until he finally got what he wanted. On April 23, 1982, Candy Weyant took the fifth on the sage advice of her counsel, James Cipoletta. Flanagan's pupil was at it again on June 22, 1982, and finally brought in the hammers that would get him the desired result to the satisfaction of Joan's parents.

Trooper Andrew Palombo took the stand and used the authority of his position to sway opinions. His testimony revealed critical clues to the truth that escaped listeners at the time. Palombo's smile reflected off his badge as he told the jurors Paradiso was the driver that dropped the victim off at the bar. However, the lead officer had statements in his files from the Milano family to the contrary, and there were no known witnesses telling the trooper's same story. Questions then turned to where passing boaters found the body. Marie's lifeless form lay motionless behind Conley and Daggets, a shuttered up business. New owners renamed the previously vacated enterprise to Atlantic Lobster Company by the time the state reignited this case. The location was significant for the state's cause, because the parole officer's notes specified Conley and Dagget's as a place Paradiso had made deliveries.

The neophyte, homicide litigator described the young woman's attire. On the night of her murder, Marie wore a one-piece, red Danskin with a matching wrap-around skirt, but she wasn't wearing her pantyhose when observant passersby found the body. The seasoned detective slipped, but his testimony was not presented during the same session when Burke cajoled Marie's family and friends back on March fifth.

"In what order would these clothes have gone on?" Burke asked his investigative partner.

"The stockings would have had to go on first," the astute detective observed. The statement supported previous testimony where witnesses described the hose worn underneath other garments. The bodysuit had no snaps in the crotch, and responders photographed Marie's clothes intact.

The nail Burke selected to drive into his target was the fact that bar patrons saw the victim leaving the bar about one in the morning while Paradiso held the door. Burke led his witness to the conclusion the courteous man had been positively identified.

"On the sixteenth of August, 1979, photos were shown to Christine DeLisi in District 7," Palombo recalled from his case. "She then picked up the photograph and stated, 'That's the man that was sitting at the bar with Marie and walked out with Marie.'"

However, the lead officer's files said something different. Det. Arthur Cook was the officer that had shown Christine DeLisi mug shots, trying to identify who held the door.

"Christine mentioned Marie was a cock teaser with guys, and she knew this would happen to Marie someday." Cook's report detailed the interview with Marie's best friend. "Christine accompanied us to District 7. She picked out a couple of photographs only as people who looked somewhat like the person she saw leave with Marie."

Burke brought in the retired parole officer and cleverly examined his notes that the jury could not see. Paradiso called Victor Anchukaitis for a routine check-in on Monday morning.

"I will show you a document I have here," Burke said as he handed Anchukaitis his parole notes, "directing your attention to August 13, 1979."

The parole officer made two entries for the date in question; the first date was typed, but the second date was obscured with a hand-written date below it. The notes contained another entry in between with the typewritten date of August 15, 1979. The first entry, with a typed date, merely recorded Paradiso's standard check-in call on Monday morning with his parole officer. It recorded Paradiso had not heard from the new parole officer assigned to take over, but no mention of meeting with Anchukaitis later. The next notation, on the fifteenth, described the officer's follow-up to contact his successor, Jim O'Neil.

The public defender zeroed in on the third entry, a notation with the handwritten date out-of-sequence, with the witness. The supervising officer tread carefully not to lie under oath about Candy Weyant coming into his office to discuss the events surrounding the wedding over the weekend. He jeopardized his pension if the court knew he actually met his assignee and his girlfriend in a bar on Tuesday evening. Victor hesitantly went along with representations the prosecuting lawyer directed. Burke implied the hand-dated, out-of-sequence entry described the behavior of a guilt-ridden parolee divulging his connection to a murder victim before the public knew she was dead.

The desired illusion fueled the jury's suspicion. What the seated citizens heard was that Lenny drove Marie to the bar, was the last person seen exiting the establishment with the deceased, and that he had familiarity with the location where the culprit dumped the body. Burke further stirred the perception that Paradiso panicked and confided to his parole officer before anyone but the killer knew the victim was Marie Iannuzzi.

Burke convinced jurors seated during his inquest in June that John Doe was Leonard Paradiso. The fragmented and distorted pieces they heard was all the proof they needed to hand down a true bill on June 28, 1982. The indictment did not include the rape charge that the prosecutor needed to fit the profile being developed. However, Burke needed a reasonable motive to pin on his suspect. The vulnerability he attacked was Paradiso's prior record with a woman named Constance Porter.

The case was weak, and those in charge had to devise something more to bolster the obsession that Paradiso was guilty.

"What was Burke sniffing?" I thought aloud as I read the transcripts. "What did George and Eleanor know, or not know? Who was in charge?"

Things just did not add up. Something was missing. I had already probed into the CIA that molded George and Eleanor's thinking. The family had secrets, secrets I did not know. Was there something that happened before Joan disappeared? ITT, George's employer, was involved in the investigation, too. To the casual observer, it seemed the conglomerate was a caring support system for the bereaved parents, but they had a particular set of skills I did not understand.

CHAPTER 6

Chitelco

I fondly recall the Thanksgiving gatherings I grew up with in my Midwest hometown. The relatives were stuffed to the gills with Grandma's specialties, and soon fell asleep in front of the television with the football game flickering in the background unwatched. Later, as we put our coats on to leave, Grandma carefully packed leftovers, and our eager hands gratefully clutched the tasty morsels that underscored our blessings. Family passed bear hugs around with such loving vigor that they seemed to protect one another from harm. This warm, loving core was well rooted in my character, and freely extended to the new family in my life.

On that first Thanksgiving with the Websters in 1978, I quickly realized what a different kind of family they really were. George sent out an itinerary before Steve and I landed in New Jersey. My future in-laws had an itinerary for a family gathering, which contained details down to the most absurd minutia. George and Eleanor's background in the CIA was no secret, but the association seemed like a distant history when I met them. Their skill at over organizing family gatherings should have been a tip-off, perhaps, of the control agency employees assumed. George was now an executive with ITT in Nutley, New Jersey, and Eleanor busied herself with activities in their small, commuter community not far from Manhattan. Nevertheless, they were not too busy to make sure bedroom assignments and the tennis ladders were preplanned. George and Eleanor had even constructed a seating chart for the ride into the city.

The charm of the Webster men, however, clouded the obsessed concentration to manage events even down to the smallest detail. Attention subtlety turned to the performers who entertained and seduced the gathering, to sing along with the show tunes stroked on the ivory keys. The bear hugs I was used to were replaced with reserved pecks on the cheek, but flattery flowed like champagne and embraced every newcomer with a sense of belonging. George called all this "fundador," as if to mask his overbearing control with a cutesy word that would make it a bit more palatable, but no one questioned who was in charge.

The compulsive consideration to the slightest detail was on full display on October 12, 1982, when the Websters held a press conference to increase the reward money. The couple spoon fed reporters and handed out photographs of themselves taken before the meeting. The pictures were for any news outlet not in attendance and depicted Joan's parents in the same attire they were wearing that day. The savvy couple did not miss a detail, even down to George's same striped tie and the tasteful pin on Eleanor's lapel.

George never wanted to relinquish control. When searchers discovered Joan's remains in Hamilton, Massachusetts in April, 1990, George influenced the impression represented to the public. More than eight years had passed, and he was not convinced these were his daughter's remains, despite the positive identification on April 30, 1990.

"I'm cautious despite yesterday's announcement," George told the *Beverly Times* on May first. "I can't say for certain the remains are Joan Webster. I'm not saying they're wrong, but that sort of thing remains to be seen."

Most parents want closure, some might even be too eager to identify a body, but George was the opposite. It was not until he was confronted with an undeniable dental record match that he agreed the remains found were Joan's.

"The inmate, Robert Bond, could not have made it up," the victim's father told the anxious media three days later.

"Mr. Webster," the reporter raised his hand, calling out the next question, "Bond insisted Miss Webster was dumped in Boston Harbor, but her remains have been found buried here. Why are you so sure Paradiso confessed to the inmate?"

The room went silent waiting for the response. Eleanor fixed her icy glare on her husband, and the collection of microphones in front of him could have picked up his racing heartbeat. "No comment," George finally answered, and he refused to elaborate why he still believed Paradiso had murdered his youngest child.

The informant's statement no longer made sense to a rational thinker, but the family believed it. The power of their influence guided perceptions, and everyone tread cautiously not to topple their presumed fragile balance. They must know something the rest of us do not, was the accepted explanation for things that made absolutely no sense. These educated, intelligent people had stayed close to the case. They had a Norman Rockwell image of the perfect family, but George's control kept the focus on an increasingly irrational story.

The discovery of my daughter's distressing letter in 2001 gave me a nearly lethal dose of the family's control. The letter painted me as depressed and suicidal, and my child was feeling that way as well. The constant harassment, devaluation, and later alienation from my children did take their toll.

"I don't know how you get up every day," Carol Metzger soothed.

"Carol," I cried, "I'm human and far from perfect, but I don't know why I'm being treated this way."

"Were allegations of abuse made to you by my children?" I pointedly asked the girls' advocate, Sarah O'Brien.

"Yes," Sarah acknowledged. "Emotional abuse was the form of abuse."

"What do you consider emotional abuse?" I probed, desperately looking for answers.

"Invasion of privacy," Sarah revealed.

Nevertheless, the gut-wrenching letter accused her father, Steve, of hurting her. It made no sense for a loving mother not to be vigilant, and I had an enormous burden with conflicted images of the family I had trusted. Sarah finally had spelled out my offense, breaching the well-guarded privacy of the Webster family. Unfortunately, Sarah had no concept of what that really meant, and neither did I at the time.

My daughter was called to the stand on May 23, 2008, in a contempt suit I filed against the girls' father. She raised her right hand and swore to tell the truth, but her story changed.

"There are parts in this letter that I did not write," my child angrily accused. "There are things I believe were added in."

The testimony was perjured, and it was easy to prove, because copies of the letter were in two counselors' folders and reported to the police. The original letter, though, remained with Carol Metzger, who had failed to report it. Sarah O'Brien also failed to report the concerns, and she suggested I was emotionally abusive for violating my children's privacy. This horrifying evidence of a potential felony against my child compounded the concern; my daughter felt threatened to sit down and sort out the truth.

"No one will ever believe you," Steve's warning echoed. "They'll think you're crazy."

"Don't tell," was mandated from every Webster's lips.

Intent was gradually uncovered in my children's journals and online chats with their friends captured by the net nanny software. The intentional malice was obvious when I ended up in the hospital near collapse from severe devaluation.

"DONE DONE DONE DONE!" my oldest child trumpeted to her friends. "SHE'S GONE!

"My birthday is next week—but the party starts NOW b/c you-know-who is gone :-D!" her auto response posted online. "You've never seen me so happy!"

"Are you home alone?" Heather asked, concerned.

"I wanted to hang out with my dad," my triumphant daughter declared. "OMG, he is so happy!"

My instincts and ability to mother were systematically devalued by unverified accusations, controlled information, and the Websters' overpowering notion that my own children were none of my business. In the end, the family convinced counselors that my questions about the incriminating letter were violating privacy. The entire situation underscored the dysfunctional need for secrecy in the codependent Webster family. The accusations surrounding Joan's case had not unfolded for me yet to see how the stories surrounding the Websters' suspect had also changed on the stand. The pressure mounted on my child over what was in that letter and the corroborating documents discovered later. My daughter's testimony followed another pattern, too, uncovered in researching another powerful influence in Joan's case: George's employer ITT.

The family's need for privacy was nothing new. Steve was born in Washington, DC in 1953, and the word "whisper" was not in George and Eleanor's Webster Dictionary; their discussions permeated walls. About the time their baby boy began to communicate in real words, the couple left the agency and moved to Dayton, Ohio. George went to work for his father at Standard Thomson manufacturing airplane parts. Anne arrived in 1955, and the family was complete when Joan came into the world at 9:15 p.m. on August 19, 1956. George was set for life to provide generously for his family as heir apparent to his father's successful company. Apparently, it was not his calling, and a better offer lured him back East in 1957, before the girls were out of diapers.

The company that enticed him was International Telephone and Telegraph, a company that extended their expertise to the Websters when Joan disappeared. Sosthenes Behn founded ITT in 1920. Behn assured the company's survival during World War II with associations and dealings on both sides of the struggle. In fact, he was one

of the first American businessmen received by Hitler after the dictator took power. ITT's German holdings were all under the control of
the German government, including ITT's interests in airplane manufacturer Focke-Wolfe, a company that kept the Nazi's airborne during WWII.

The well-documented history raised questions about Behn's allegiance, a man who had his bets hedged. Regardless who won the war,
Behn was set to score big financially. Research and development was
a continuing objective after the war. Even though ITT's global holdings accounted for a respectable, but relatively modest, $756 million
in sales, George strangely left the security of his father's airplane parts
manufacturing company for the telecommunications division of ITT
in Nutley, New Jersey. George conducted his business under the lofty,
microwave, test tower, a landmark humorously nicknamed "Behn's
last erection," that cast shadows over his office. His skill and charm
eventually led to the position of planning and development for the
defense group, a positioning that conveniently aligned him with the
interests and budget of his former government employer.

Sosthenes Behn died in 1957, and George had the fortune,
good or bad, to be on the ground floor when the board tapped
Harold Geneen as the new Chief Executive Officer of ITT. The executive left his position at Raytheon in Waltham, Massachusetts; the
company was less than a half mile from RN Webster's corporate
offices at Standard Thomson. Geneen was a demanding man who
held the reins of power tightly. He charted a new course for the company, and expanded their holdings through acquisitions, turning ITT
into one of the world's largest conglomerates. ITT eventually
became so powerful and influential that it could wield considerable
influence, even contributing to the collapse of a weakened president.
This was the company that George Webster worked for, a company of
power and influence, a company unafraid of using its power to topple
government leaders.

By the spring of 1961, the threat of communism had crossed the
Atlantic and George's former employer, the CIA, was busy contriving
plots to eliminate Fidel Castro. Their methods of enlistment had no
boundaries. The CIA conspired with known mafia figures Johnny
Roselli, Momo Salvatore Giancana, and Santos Trafficant in failed
plots to assassinate the Cuban dictator. Though the public would
abhor such behavior, the CIA was more than willing to get in bed
secretly with unsavory elements in attempts to get a dirty job done.
The unbridled agency was the secretive instrument of the powerful
few on a course to manipulate populations and political outcomes.

No methods were off limits to achieve an objective. The only thing that mattered was reasonable deniability.

These tactics spread to George Webster's new employer, ITT, through the influence of board member, and past CIA head, John McCone, an industrialist from California. McCone left the private sector in 1961, when President John F. Kennedy appointed him to serve as the Director of Central Intelligence, and he became a key figure on the National Security Council. During his tenure with the agency and beyond, McCone's intrigues influenced the lives of millions and the futures of entire nations. The development of a greater intelligence collection was a primary focus for McCone at the helm of the CIA. He resigned his position in 1965, but remained a consultant to the CIA until 1970. After his resignation, McCone walked past the inscribed motto at Langley, espousing the virtue of truth, as he left the building and walked through the next door into the boardroom of ITT. The fit was perfect with a company described as vital to US intelligence and compatible with the focus he directed. Even at the most basic level, there were no better experts at bugging phones than the pros on ITT's payroll, but the skills only escalated from there. Now all the controlling players were in place.

The telecommunications division of ITT, George's division, had substantial interests in South America. During this time, political stirrings revealed the Chilean government disfavored the 150 million-dollar interest ITT held in the country's telephone company, Chitelco. By 1963, Harold Geneen was very concerned with the rising voice of Marxist Salvador Allende, a candidate who promised to nationalize the company. Geneen did not like to lose, and the wheels were in motion to keep Allende from gaining power. Geneen had the connections and made a seven-figure offer to the CIA to funnel money into Chile to oppose Allende. On record, the CIA declined the offer, but gave guidance and contacts for ITT to infuse the finances themselves.

The Committee on Foreign Relations in the US Senate released a report on June 21, 1973, that disclosed the strategy implemented between the CIA and the corporate conspirator they had gotten in bed with.

"Mr. Merriam," a committee member demanded, "are these recommendations accurate detailing the plan ITT followed?"

"Yes," the head of ITT's Washington office admitted behind the Senate's closed doors. "Mr. Broe contacted me to set up a meeting with ITT CEO Harold Geneen."

"Mr. Broe," one senator grilled, "do you affirm the testimony we have heard from Mr. Merriam?"

"Yes," the CIA Chief of Clandestine Services attested. "The report is accurate and the recommendations were good."

The recommendations in the ITT directive outlined the tactics deployed. The dictate spelled out how combined efforts with the CIA and the White House set the stage for ITT's concept of how to get a job done. The memorandum distributed through the corporation orchestrated the company's control in Chile. The ITT mandate read:

1. We and other US firms pump money into *Mercurio*. (This has been started.)

2. We help get propagandists working again on radio and television.

3. Assist in support of a "family relocation" center in Mendoza or Baires (Buenos Aires) for wives and children of people involved in the fight.

4. Bring what pressure we can on US Information Services in Washington. Start moving the *Mercurio* editorials around Latin America and Europe.

5. Urge the key European press, through our contacts there, to get the story out of what disaster could fall on Chile if Allende & Co. win this country.

Bernard Goodrich, an ITT public relations man, acted on the recommendations and had a meeting with the US Office of Information.

"Is there anything ITT can do as a private company," the messenger offered, "that the US Government can't do?"

"The company shouldn't do anything overt," USIA officials instructed. "We don't want anything that might be interpreted as intervention."

"You have my guarantee," Goodrich assured them. "Our people are well experienced in that field." They sure were. George's position in the division involved, his responsibility for the Defense Department, his CIA background, and a signed Form 368, all made him an asset to a company involved in such conspiracies.

The CIA deployed the classic methods in Chile funded by corporate America who were motivated by their bottom line, not political beliefs. These funds helped set up *El Mercurio*, an opposition newspaper spreading disinformation and propaganda in Chile. ITT contributed to more favorable political candidates, and the clandestine directive made the conglomerate a secretive player in the political outcome of a foreign government. Both ITT and the US Government had similar interests: to keep Allende from gaining power in Chile. For a time, they even succeeded.

Nevertheless, despite the CIA and ITT-funded opposition, Allende prevailed and earned the popular vote in a free election in Chile on September 4, 1970. The Chilean Congress selected him from the top two candidates in the election, and the new president swore his oath on November 4, 1970. The outcome did not please President Nixon, nor did it please Harold Geneen and John McCone at ITT. Both offices had the number to the reigning DCI Richard Helms, and the next wave of plotting and scheming began. ITT was a cover firm in bed with the CIA, and the company had players who knew the game. The White House devised Track I and Track II to undo the elections of a sovereign country. If they could not prevent Allende from being elected, they sought to undermine the election itself. Chilean citizens had freely voted for Allende, but they suffered under the cruel mandates imposed by the CIA and ITT to crush the country's economy. At the same time, these outside forces infiltrated opposing factions to move against Allende. Nixon's infamous Oval Office tapes revealed that the White House sanctioned these extreme measures. Stakes were high and patience to achieve the objective was essential. These things took time.

Jack Anderson, a Washington, DC investigative reporter, who was to the Nixon-ITT scandals what Woodward and Bernstein were to Watergate, revealed the scandal. The first sign of illicit ITT practices was discovered by a protégé of Anderson's named Brit Hume. Hume had gotten wind of a scandal early in 1972 when an envelope landed on his makeshift desk in the crammed kitchen of Anderson's office. The contents of the envelope exposed ITT's improper influence regarding an antitrust lawsuit brought against ITT by the Department of Justice. The nation's law enforcers suspiciously settled the antitrust suit because of ITT's contributions to Nixon's reelection campaign and the influence of their DC lobbyist Dita Beard. ITT Chairman Harold Geneen had filled Nixon's reelection coffers substantially, and the memo revealed the contribution was a payoff for a favorable resolution in the suit. Beard had a meeting with Attorney General John Mitchell to define Geneen's idea of what favorable looked like, and the DOJ announced the settlement she outlined two months later in July, 1971. Hume followed up with Dita, and he confirmed the authenticity of the memo in her smoke-filled kitchen while ITT officials shredded her files back at the office.

Dita was worried. Corporate officials secretly hurried their lobbyist out of town. She finally surfaced in a Denver hospital where E. Howard Hunt paid her a visit. The former CIA employee showed up at her bedside in the red-wig disguise the CIA had provided for his covert activities in the White House. The former operative's current position was on the President's Special Investigations Unit, but at the moment, he interceded persuasively with an ITT employee to discredit her memo. Hunt was in demand, but the nature of his assignments had not made the headlines yet. ITT's strategy was a smear campaign to discredit Dita as a mental case, a tactic to damage an observer I was uncomfortably familiar with. The tactic was not that successful as a propaganda tool, but was effective intimidation to influence a problematic witness. Members of Congress surrounded Dita in the sanitized room and heard sanitized testimony. The ITT employee changed her story, and told the senators she had not written or dictated the entire incriminating memorandum.

I had to put down the pile of reports and documents, and I reached for more tissues to wipe the never-ending flood of tears that blurred my vision. Everything I had encountered with the family paralleled what was in these pages. It hit hard to see the tactics George's company executed as routine. George's corporate model spread disinformation and propaganda through the press, hid and shred documents to conceal the truth, and worst of all, coerced witnesses to go along with a story. The patterns surfacing in recovered documents exposed the same travesty that denied Joan justice. The patterns also shed light on the torment my children suffered under the family dictate not to tell.

"There are parts in this letter I did not write," my child angrily accused, as if she were Dita Beard sitting in the hot seat with secrets to hide.

"Do you recognize this letter? I asked Sarah O'Brien, handing her the painful words of my daughter.

"Yes," the girls' counselor replied. "I have a copy of it."

"Do you have any doubts it was my child that wrote that letter?"

"No," she answered without hesitation.

"And what does the letter say about their father's behavior?" I insisted and locked eyes with the defensive family counselor that had unlawfully failed to report it.

"She wrote a statement at our request saying that he never..." Sarah excused.

Steve's attorney objected, but the deposition continued May 13, 2008, projecting the image Steve had manufactured to save his reputation. Sarah O'Brien had affirmed the letter, and she knew my daughter had written it. The girls' counselor attested what the letter said, but admitted she had not reported the written allegations to the proper authorities. Failure to report is against the law in our state.

Instead, my child was compelled to sign a statement that would certainly make her dad happy. Nevertheless, I was the one who was crazy.

"Do you think that these continued assertions of matters concerning Steve's sister's murder in the early 1980s, and these accusations of child abuse," Steve's defender redirected, "do you think that suggests Eve has mental problems?"

"I think it suggests something," the manipulated witness implied.

"No one will ever believe you," Steve smugly mused to himself as he nodded his satisfaction. "They'll think you're crazy."

When my tears finally subsided, I picked up the pages and continued to study. The patient, Dita Beard, feigned weakness when the questioning got too tough, but made a miraculous recovery three days later to assume her new position. Hume and Anderson stuck to their story and prevailed, exposing Nixon's hand in ITT's favorable settlement, and the president's hand in Geneen's pocket. George Webster was familiar, as a CIA and ITT employee, with the tactic of discrediting a person as a mental case, as he later did to me.

The antitrust suit was not ITT's only scandal, however. On April 5, 1971, stealth burglars ransacked the residence of the UN delegate from Chile, Humberto Diaz-Casanueva, in New York City. Culprits took only a few insignificant items, but riffled through his papers. A few days later, Javier Urrutia, the head of the Chilean Development Corporation and advisor to President Salvadore Allende, was the next target. After this break-in, a pistol was missing, but burglars left other valuables undisturbed. Again, operators shuffled government papers, the apparent interest of the intruder. Both Diaz-Casanueva and Urrutia were in negotiations at the time with American businessmen with financial interests in Chile. George Webster was in a key position in the telecommunications division, and ITT was high on that list. His company was secretly involved as a conduit for the CIA in Chilean affairs for most of the decade.

ITT dispatched bugging expert John Ragan and a member of ITT security to Santiago, Chile on April 28, 1971. For the next week, Ragan and ITT security represented themselves as allies sent to eradicate bugs from Allende's homes and presidential offices. The timing was suspicious, because it coincided with information gathering conducted by the US Government, the CIA, and ITT to undermine the Chilean leader. Master-bugging expert Ragan became better known later for tapping the Watergate plumbers and debugging services all the way up the ladder to Nixon.

Skilled and stealth burglars struck again on February 10, 1972, in the dwelling of Victor Rioseco, the economic advisor for the Chilean UN mission. The crooks again disturbed documents. Patterns emerged with similar break-ins around the country, but the culprits avoided detection.

Sometime on May 13, or 14, 1972, burglars left valuables untouched, but searched political files in the offices of the ambassador and first secretary at the Chilean Embassy in DC. Intruders staged another break-in in Washington, DC a couple of weeks later over Memorial Day weekend; the Democratic National Committee headquarters in the Watergate building was the target. Conspirators planted bugging devices and photographed documents, but the collaborators still eluded detection.

Reporter Jack Anderson moved through the concourse at Washington National Airport on June 16, 1972. He recognized Frank Sturgis and Bernard Barker arriving into town as Anderson departed in pursuit of another story, not realizing a piece of another swelling scandal was set to take place over the weekend. On June 17, 1972, authorities arrested five men at the Watergate headquarters of the Democratic National Committee during their second break-in. Newspapers reported similar break-ins for more than a year with consistent patterns. Burglars took few, if any, valuable items, but victims' papers were always disturbed. Anderson had crossed paths at the airport with two of the arrested participants.

The similarities between the string of Chilean break-ins and Watergate were eerie, but the direct connection between the two cases came a thousand miles away in Miami. In Miami, there was a pool of clandestine talent organized by E. Howard Hunt, the player ITT enlisted to get them out of a jam with Dita Beard. When the Senate recovered documents subpoenaed from the lockbox of White House counsel John Dean III, the classified documents contained a proposal for domestic espionage that included breaking into foreign embassies. Another White House counsel and Nixon aide, Tom Charles Huston, drafted the proposal for this action. The memorandum revealed their dissatisfaction with the government's intelligence gathering and recommended that other methods be used—methods that violated the law. The thrust of the plan was to increase the role of the CIA and Defense Department within the United States. There were plenty of denials, even under oath, stating the plan was not implemented, but the break-ins were now part of the factual record. Senators investigating Nixon's involvement in Watergate connected the dots further when they learned the Miami conspirators arrested at Watergate were also in town when burglars riffled Chilean papers at the consulate in DC.

E. Howard Hunt, Frank Sturgis, and Bernard Barker were among the seven men ultimately convicted for their part in the political scandal that brought down a president. The Watergate plumbers all had previous ties to the CIA, but their status as plumbers allowed the agency reasonable denial. Despite well-founded suspicions of White House-fueled, CIA plots, involving former employees and corporations, they kept their hand shielded just as magician John Mulholland instructed in his manual.

Senator Sam Ervin focused on the CIA's lack of cooperation during his Watergate investigation. Of particular concern was that DCI Helms withheld subpoenaed documents that included five letters James McCord mailed to the agency. McCord was one of the arrested Watergate plumbers and another former CIA employee. DCI Helms wrote a memo to undersecretary General Walters dated June 28, 1972, which raised the Senate committee's suspicions. The directive to Walters stipulated the agency's position on how to handle acting FBI Director Patrick Gray regarding the CIA's business.

"We still adhere to the request that they [FBI] confine themselves to the personalities already arrested or already directly under suspicion, and that they desist from expanding this investigation into other areas that may well, eventually, run afoul of our operations," Richard Helms ordered.

Director of CIA Security Howard Osborne testified in front of a House Intelligence subcommittee in May 1973. "Mr. Helms decided a series of letters sent to the agency from James W. McCord, Jr. should not be forwarded to the Justice Department."

Multiple Congressional committees and special prosecutors were probing deeply into CIA secrets and their possible involvement with the Watergate caper. The inquiries ran in tandem with the Senate Foreign Relations Committee's hot topic concerning the debacle in Chile, where the CIA hid behind the skirts of ITT in their clandestine affairs.

"Mr. Helms instructed me not to inquire into the agency's involvement with E. Howard Hunt, Jr.," Osborne disclosed to the panel. Hunt was a Watergate player, but also the persuasive conspirator that helped "refresh" ITT lobbyist Dita Beard's memory.

"A Watergate participant is also suspected of the embassy break-in," John Dean III confided to Gen. Vernon Walters. The chief White House counsel connected the dots to the undersecretary of the CIA, and he linked the Watergate plumbers to the scandal surfacing about ITT's participation in Chilean affairs as a cover firm.

"The testimony and documents indicate the intelligence agency followed the course it did," investigative journalist Seymour Hersh reported in the *New York Times* on February 2, 1975, "because of a fear some of its domestic cover firms, as well as its 1971 domestic activities on behalf of the White House, would be uncovered."

President Nixon got his DCI out of town and appointed Helms an ambassadorship to Iran. Teletypes, wires, and courier pouches bounced back and forth before Senate committees summoned former DCI Richard Helms to testify in front of their panels. It seemed everyone wanted to get the stories straight.

Nixon's paranoia led him to use the CIA in unethical ways, including domestic surveillance on private citizens such as Jack Anderson, a man on Nixon's list of enemies. Anderson's life was threatened, but Hunt declined to provide details, even under the Senate's scrutiny. Form 368 is a lifelong binding contract, so no Senate committee could compel Hunt or others to disclose CIA secrets, even secrets that violated the law. Watergate consumed the headlines while arguably more sinister presidential and CIA misconduct in Chile slid beneath public awareness.

In September of 1973, Joan began school with all the fun and anticipation of a senior's last year at home before taking on the world. She was the only Webster child still living at home, a home where she watched her father's Scotch drinking escalate. Every night George's guttural tones echoed through the house, breaking into Joan's silent studies across the hall. There was no way in hell George did not know what was going on at the office. Superiors distributed the memo for the legions to follow, and George pushed the pencil for the Defense Department's dollars.

Despite the problems, the Websters maintained the façade. When the phone rang, friends expected their presence at social gatherings, and George unabashedly provided the entertainment. Their public image was of carefree harmony; they put their best John Mulholland foot forward. Disconnected from problems, the family showed no hint of the stressors when they were in public and engaged friends in the "fundador" that made them popular on every guest list.

As Joan headed off to school that Tuesday morning in September, a military opposition, supported by the American government, headed toward the Presidential palace in Santiago. By the end of the day, while Joan cracked open her books for another evening of study, and George cracked the ice for a stiff drink, the crack of a gun ended Salvador Allende's life thousands of miles away in Chile. The coup d'état in Chile, known in some circles as the "other 9/11," was a ruthless rebellion supported by the CIA, ITT, and the White House to overthrow a democratically elected leader. The defeat of Allende paved the way for years of documented atrocities under the new regime of Augusto Pinochet, a brutal Chilean dictator brought into power by American intervention.

Richard Nixon resigned the presidency on August 9, 1974. Congress had an urgent need, after debacles such as Watergate and Chile, to explore just how our national intelligence agency operated its clandestine business. The Senate established yet another select committee to investigate the nation's intelligence activities. On January 27, 1975, the Church Senate Hearings began. They left no stone unturned, examining the CIA all the way back to its roots, the early days when George and Eleanor signed their contracts and developed their skills. Tactics used by the organization troubled the Church Committee, and they emphasized the agency employed the methods of the enemy as their own.

Congressional leaders uncovered practices that used control and brainwashing, and they determined the methods were illegal, immoral, and repugnant to any decent sensibilities. The committee established the clear relationship between the CIA and the Defense Department. Defense was the consumer of the intelligence product provided by the agency, and the department held the purse strings. The structure connecting the select groups exposed a lack of oversight and accountability, despite the fact their decisions were of great importance and consequence. The Senate committee found numerous conflicts with defined policy and law, but participants justified these abuses in the name of national security. These acts were not anomalies, but practices that evolved into the very fabric of the agency's clandestine behavior. Each DCI brought their own style and area of focus, but each was committed to the ultimate objective—and the ends justified the means.

The Senate committee's investigation hit uncomfortably close for George Webster. The relationship between ITT and the CIA had already been the focus of a 1973 Senate inquiry, but the review concluded before events escalated in Chile that put Pinochet in power. The Church Committee was investigating ITT again. George's very division went under the microscope for their complicity to save Chitelco. After exposing the web of connections within the intelligence community, the committee focused on exposing their non-government cohorts such as ITT.

The disastrous operation in Chile involved the CIA, ITT, and the White House. The operation raised such grave concerns it was selected by Senator Church's Committee for a case study of the CIA's collaboration with the private sector. Interrogators summoned witness after witness behind the Senate's closed doors. These sessions finally exposed the CIA's collusion with ITT to topple a democratically elected foreign leader. The DOJ had indictments ready, but reneged when some higher authority shielded ITT participants from prosecution because they worked on behalf of the CIA for purported national security. Our government censored participants' names from reports for fear of retribution in a climate still rife with kidnappings and assassinations. Ultimately, this level of secrecy meant there was a complete lack of responsibility and accountability for these actions.

George's desk was in the thick of the action. His background provided the required buttoned lip and familiarity with how the game was played in the circle of power brokers who presumed to play God. He had a well-established tenure with ITT when events peaked in 1973. George and Eleanor even traveled to South America in the 1970s on an ITT sponsored trip. Spanish rolled fluently off George's tongue, and the telecommunications division of ITT did not want to lose the Chitelco holding. He sat in the precise time and place, in a key position, and he had a desirable background to do the job of planning and crunching numbers designated for intelligence gathering.

The Defense Department was a key participant on the national security team with the White House and the CIA. George, with his knowledge and background, was in a particularly suitable position to wade the tide of these organizations. The Church Senate hearings brought the pieces together to expose the elaborate plot that placed unrestricted power in the hands of a few. It revealed the truth contrary to perceptions at the time, reality necessary in an open and moral society. Oddly enough, just a few short years after the Senate asked the last question, the ITT executive's daughter disappeared mysteriously from Logan Airport.

Microphones had barely gone silent in the Senate when I stepped into the family's crosshairs. George and Joan awaited our arrival at the quaint Tom Nevers Airport in Nantucket, and the charming family soon reeled me in. I recall thinking that Steve's parents were a little quirky, but I had no reason to connect any current events in the news to my unusual hosts. Like many Americans at the time, Watergate dominated my awareness, but ITT and CIA collusion were intrigues I knew nothing about. I was in the dark, naive about the intelligence world. I was oblivious until Steve broke the ice.

"Bill Kampiles is in jail awaiting trial for espionage," Steve whispered to his mother in the Websters' not-so-hushed tone.

"He used our names as a reference to get that job!" Eleanor huffed indignantly. She was livid. "How dare he take advantage of our hospitality here two summers ago!"

Steve and I had made a trip to Chicago the month before so Steve could visit Kampiles in jail. Both of them had worked for divisions of American Hospital Supply in St. Louis and became friends. I discovered George and Eleanor's early days in the CIA through Steve's disclosure to his mother in Nantucket. The Webster children grew up in this household and knew what to say and what not to say, and Steve had not said much. Eleanor's disproportional outrage seemed odd. Kampiles used their names on an application to an agency where George and Eleanor had not worked for more than two decades. What was so upsetting about that? However, I was new to the family and unaccustomed to the way things were hidden. A more damning connection was the undesirable awareness of their association to the agency on the heels of the Chilean debacle, and the Websters did not appreciate drawing any attention.

The CIA hired Kampiles as a low-level clerk, and the young recruit devised to advance his position as a double agent. The wannabe spy resigned his position and traveled to Greece in the early winter of 1977. His Greek ethnicity helped him fit right in, and the ancient language of the Gods rolled fluently off his tongue. Unabashedly, he arrived at the Soviet Embassy in Athens prepared to commit treason. He met with Soviet spy Michael Zavalis four times, and the schemer sold pages from the top-secret, KH-11 spy satellite manual for $3,000. Stateside, Kampiles boasted his access to the agency and hoped for a daring position. Now, at the height of the Cold War, Kampiles' defense attorney enlisted Eleanor's baby boy to testify as a character witness for his friend, a self-confessed infiltrator. Steve's testimony did not prevent Bill Kampiles from being convicted on six counts on November 22, 1978, and sentenced to forty years for espionage. Spy games were a world I knew very little about and was ill prepared to enter.

Just as I began to get used to the idea of being part of this strange family with CIA connections, Joan vanished. ITT, the same group that dirtied its hands in Chile, became an integral part of the investigation into her disappearance. The head of security, Jack McEwen, was the liaison with George and at his immediate disposal.

ITT CEO Harold Geneen had influence in the White House and
Nixon's hand in his pocket, and his connections with former DCI
John McCone meant his reach extended into the CIA. The company
used unethical tactics, sanitized testimony and altered facts, and the
media was their tool to spread disinformation and propaganda.

"The Websters have learned quickly how to sell their story," the
Harvard Crimson observed. They sure did.

ITT's resources were there for the asking when the Websters
required their expertise in the search for Joan. These people were far
from naïve, and this was far from the average missing person's case.

CHAPTER 7

Cousin Frank

"The counselors have suggested a break, Eve," Steve said one spring afternoon.

"What do you mean a break?" I asked.

"Take a sabbatical of sorts, just over spring break. You and the girls need some time apart," he explained.

It was true; it had gotten really bad. My girls' animosity toward me had reached a fever pitch. The girls spiced every conversation with provocation. Something terrible was troubling my children, but the root of the problems escaped my comprehension. The supposed advice, funneled through Steve, was to give me a short reprieve from the turmoil and put Steve in charge to act like a parent for a while. I reluctantly agreed. I did not really want to leave my daughters, but at the same time, I knew something had to change. We had to try something to mend this relationship, and if some time apart would do it, I was willing to try. The week had nearly completely passed before the phone rang.

"Mom, we caught Dad," my daughter calmly announced.

"You caught him doing what?" I wondered aloud.

There was a long pause on the phone, and then she said, "Me and some friends caught him with a woman, a young woman, probably half his age. She tried to jump over the balcony, but just ran right past us when she couldn't get down."

She recounted all this in the same matter-of-fact tone George Webster used at the Christmas gathering in 1981, stoic and nonchalant. However, I was horrified. Whether the counselor had indeed recommended this "sabbatical," I did not know. Regardless, Steve certainly took advantage of the time apart in a reckless and damaging way.

Another call rang in while I was still on the phone with my daughter.

"Eve, have the girls called you?" Steve asked on the other end of the line.

I did not answer. I knew what he was going to say, but I did not let him know the girls had already called.

"Anyway, the girls are going crazy—you know how they are. They've made up this story about me and another woman. You can't believe anything they say."

His techniques of deceit no longer worked on me, but that did not stop him from trying to desensitize the children. Two years after the incident with the young woman, I found the girls' journals detailing that night in Hilton Head.

"You're just imagining things," Steve lied as he pushed them out the door of the condominium.

"There's a woman in your bedroom; I saw her trying to climb over the balcony!"

"You're creating this like the whole harassment thing," their father pathetically blamed them. He completely blocked out the fact their "imagination" nearly ran them over trying to escape.

"You're lying!" my oldest accused.

"Girls, I have a 'big surprise' for you," he dodged, trying to replace reality with his distorted version of the truth. However, the girls caught him with his pants down.

The incident had a profound effect on my child. "I wanted to cry so badly, but I just couldn't," my youngest wrote. "Fuck my dad; you fucked up my life."

"I locked all the doors," Steve finally confessed as his "guest" nearly ran the girls over making a mad dash for the door. "I didn't want you to get the wrong impression."

They had the right instinct, but Steve did not want his nice guy image tarnished, and he lied through his teeth. I had counseling sessions lined up the minute they got back, but Steve's persona was so persuasive, distorting the obvious facts, that he had all of us confused about just what he had done. Somehow, I was still the bad guy.

"We walked in on my dad having an affair," my older child chatted online. "I'm not that upset, just shocked I guess. Don't tell anyone."

A strategy of divide and confuse, that became evident in Joan's case, was also a tactic used in the immediate family drama that played out with my girls. Steve shifted my youngest daughter to another counselor, Ari Gleckman, on December 6, 2004. It further fractured any avenue to the truth and any real help for my children.

"She's exhibiting a number of symptoms," the doctor said, describing my daughter's fragile condition. "The bottom line is that to the individual who is experiencing these symptoms, the world does not seem real. Their feelings do not seem real. Their thoughts do not seem real."

My input was blocked and eliminated reality to help my distraught daughter. Like his father, Steve was in control, and he fed the counselor the Webster version of the truth. This professional never verified the stories he heard, or analyzed other perspectives to get a handle on the source of her malaise.

"An effective psychologist should not sit and question the veracity of what is being reported," Gleckman pompously announced. "I absolutely believed her reports."

"What Cracker Jack box did this guy get his degree in?" I said to myself. "If his patient is struggling with reality, shouldn't he know what was, in fact, real?"

I struggled to hold together the pieces of a family that was falling apart. Steve had convinced everyone he was the victim. He performed a song and dance for Carol Metzger and Sarah O'Brien that his little escapade was just an innocent misunderstanding. When we retreated home, he refused to discuss it, and he announced he had not hurt my children, their friends, or me. Steve shut a door in his little mind; he was in complete denial and continued to sweep important issues under the rug. The girls and I were in incredible pain, but unable to reach each other through Steve's maze of conflicting perceptions. Though I could have offered plenty of insight into the situation, the Websters' pervasive image control was determined to silence me.

"Is brainwashing something you believe is possible?" I asked Gleckman.

"Oh, of course, it's possible to brainwash a human being," the manipulated advocate replied.

Just as they controlled perceptions of me, the Websters had worked endlessly to maintain their image in the media. In 1982, George and Eleanor journeyed once again to Boston and propped themselves calmly in front of the cameras. It was approaching the first-year anniversary of Joan's disappearance, and there were still no substantial leads out in the public. George and Eleanor were getting desperate, or at least appeared that they were. On October twelfth, they increased the reward money to $25,000 for any tips leading to Joan's whereabouts and $50,000 if this information led to the conviction of the offender. I had hoped that the monetary motivation would have inspired decent people to look and think a bit harder, and come forward with the clue to unravel the mystery. Money, though, has been the root of evil through the ages, and it is a temptation that dredges up the scum of the earth.

The day after the increased reward made the headlines, the phone rang at around one o'clock in the afternoon.

"Joan's alive," the caller said. "She's being held by two dangerous men in Boston." Then the caller hung up.

Eleanor immediately called local authorities, and the vigil lasted into the wee hours waiting for the anticipated next call. With no one calling, the police eventually left the Websters' home, but Eleanor summoned them back when the caller rang again at 7:40 the next morning. By this time, authorities had tapped the phones, and the FBI traced the call to a Laundromat payphone in Concord, New Hampshire. The Feds identified the caller as Harvey Martel, a known felon, and knew who it was by the time he called again on the fifteenth to arrange a meeting.

This meeting would not go exactly as Martel planned. Little did he know that the Websters had a string of resources at their disposal, including Jack McEwen, who led the team with all of ITT's know how at George's disposal, and Lt. Tom Dugan and Det. T. McLaughlin from the Glen Ridge Police Department. Participants called in US Attorney W. Stephen Thayer and Assistant US Attorney Maurice Flynn to examine the potential legal consequences facing the caller or any kidnappers holding Joan. When George and his team arrived in New Hampshire, the Concord FBI had a wired car ready. The G-men strapped George with a wire as well, and the operation was underway.

"Frank," George addressed Special Agent Barletto out of the Newark FBI office, "why don't you pose as my cousin to meet Martel in front of the state house in Concord. You'll be right there if there's any trouble." The former intelligence operative had a particular set of skills well suited for clandestine exploits, and he took charge of the group.

Martel had worked with a lawyer to carefully word his demand for the ransom, and the felon cleverly absolved himself of any responsibility in Joan's abduction. After meeting Martel in front of the state house, George, Frank, and Harvey pulled away from the curb. The trio traveled across the state line into Massachusetts with the FBI eavesdropping on every word. SA Barletto's finger was discreetly poised on the piece under his jacket and ready to pull the trigger if needed. The entourage motored to Boston, but when the group discovered that Martel had given a bogus address, the caper was over. Instead of driving to collect his reward, enforcers quickly gave Martel an expense paid trip to the Boston FBI office where he was fingerprinted and interrogated. Under the hot lamps, though, the hardened felon just zipped his lip; he did not explain the erroneous tip. In the end, the Department of Justice attorneys apparently could not find anything wrong with Martel's behavior and declined to press any charges, despite the fact that this was a clear case of attempted extortion.

The incident was as dramatic as any Hollywood script, and I recalled Steve's childish exuberance recounting the events of the day.

"I think there was a gun!" he excitedly proclaimed. "Dad was so brave. His training paid off, though, and he was able to keep his cool. Dad was in the CIA after all!"

It was not until May of 2006, after struggling with the family's behavior in the care of my children, that I started to look to Boston for answers that might shed light on my missing existence. I recounted the extortion incident in a letter to the Essex County DA's office, the office that held Joan's records. The dramatic episode, especially, was a point that always bothered me, because the man just walked away without penalty. Reporters never published the events in the newspaper, and several books discussing Joan's case missed the episode completely. The Harvey Martel drama should have heightened the DA's curiosity in the case. I had described an undisclosed fact about the decades-old mystery, but I did not have documented proof of my recollection at the time.

"The case file materials remain confidential, "ADA Dawley wrote back regarding the nearly twenty-five-year-old unresolved case. "Accordingly, I am unable to allow you access."

Who was he kidding, suggesting the case was still under review? Nevertheless, the extortion story sounded delusional without corroboration. It was easy to paint me as a nut case—too much butter on my popcorn at the movies—with a sensational scene of kidnapping and extortion, but nothing to back it up.

"Eve," the private investigator in Boston called with the news, "I have just had an envelope dropped on my desk from the FBI. It's four inches thick!"

The FBI had fulfilled the Freedom of Information request, and there it was in the voluminous stack of documents the Feds had released. Several reports detailed the October, 1982, joy ride Harvey Martel instigated. My recollection was right on the money; the spy-game George played out from New Hampshire to Boston was not my imagination.

"Steve, I want to ask you about an incident Eve's talking about," my brother began. "She talked about your dad being wiretapped and traveling around with an extortionist."

"I have no idea what she's talking about," Steve nervously replied as he gripped his phone firmly. "What, what timeframe?"

"Back when they were looking for Joan and all that," my girls' uncle clarified.

"I have no idea what she's talking about," Joan's brother craftily distorted. "Honest to God, I don't recall anything like that."

The inference was that I was delusional and needed help, but the FBI records and the Glen Ridge police had the ordeal well documented. I was not creating anything any more than my girls had when they encountered their dad in Hilton Head. His deceitful portrayal of my mental faculties with the ill-informed circles trying to help my girls had ruptured the family. If people listened and believed me, the letter to God threatening his reputation exposed a darker side. Now, the strategy widened, and he suggested I was not based in reality about his sister's murder to my family.

"What's her premise?" Steve continued. "What does she think happened to Joan?" He rhetorically asked the question, but he closed a door in his little mind to whatever I had discovered, confident no one would ever believe me.

Even though he denied my earlier request for information, ADA John Dawley had a second chance to demonstrate his office was sincere to find justice for Joan. I met with Dawley on May 20, 2010, to discuss Joan's case. By this time, nearly twenty-nine years had passed since Joan's tragic loss. I handed the FBI report, initialed by Director William H. Webster, to the prosecutor, the man currently delegated responsibility for the case, and the three troopers seated across the table. Oliver Revell, assistant to the director and part of the top echelon at FBI headquarters, was also on the routing list.

"We don't know anything about this incident," ADA Dawley indicated.

"Isn't this in Joan's records?" I wanted to know. "Why wouldn't you know about this?"

"I don't remember," the counselor dismissed. "I would have to go back and look."

I had just disclosed an event not known to the public during Joan's investigation. The authorities present all admitted no knowledge that this had occurred, and neglected to request copies for their files. What other things were missing from her files? I am not a lawyer, but it is simply common sense that any legitimate investigation requires gathering all of the facts.

Men who indicated they did not know George and Eleanor's background, but had only conversed with George on the phone, represented the state. It did not take much for me, by this time, to imagine what George had misrepresented about me to the custodians of Joan's files. Any thorough investigation into a cold case, or any case for that matter, should begin by understanding the dynamics of the victim's family, but this clearly was not their objective. The law, denying access to files in an open case, became an obstacle preventing an independent review of the unresolved mystery. These public defenders, with incomplete knowledge, were not going to uncover the truth with that approach. It was clear there was some other agenda, and I was confident the manipulated, new crew in charge was not going to miraculously solve the lingering mystery of Joan's murder. I concluded, after that meeting, authorities forgot their responsibility was to the victim. The result of their inaction covered up facts in Joan's case.

The Harvey Martel extortion caper was not the only exaction phone call in 1982. It was only a few days later that another call came in on October 25, 1982, claiming Joan was alive. This pretender described drug dealers holding Joan captive on a large, guarded compound in Maine. The authorities called the FBI in Bangor to follow up on the tip. The FBI had a large, guarded compound of their own at Moosehead Lake, a destination for training and the occasional retreat. It turned out to be another dead end, and the media missed another dramatic event. Information was controlled, and only George and Eleanor knew all the components taking place in the increasingly complicated case. The published reports all indicated there were no significant leads, no suspects in Joan's disappearance, and this was precisely the perception that the Websters maintained. It was certainly the impression they gave me. Meanwhile, the family and authorities kept the suspect fingered in an anonymous call under wraps. Quietly, law enforcement dug up dirt to use against Paradiso, and covertly spread suspicions to other departments involved in the search.

The roller coaster was an emotional drain, and my body shed another new life. I received a letter from Eleanor shortly after my second miscarriage at the end of October, 1982. Her four-page letter went on and on with all sorts of medical advice.

"Ask your doctor about this," Eleanor counseled, suggesting she had some medical knowledge. "Get a second opinion. You've really got to shop around with doctors."

Then she elaborated about the time when she stopped taking the pill. "I might add that my doctor is the best in our area, too—all the Jr. Leaguers go to him. He was the star of the residents at Cornell Med, boards, etc…"

I appreciated her seeming concern, but she clearly missed that stress was a major contributing factor for the miscarriages. Even after the months of the draining ordeal surrounding the disappearance of her daughter, there was no anguish in her tone. There was no mention of recent events, nor the peril of consorting with felons like Harvey Martel in the search of her youngest child. There was no mention of a suspect named Leonard Paradiso. In fact, Joan was not even mentioned until the last paragraph, and only then to describe the letter-writing project she had undertaken.

"I had Cherry and Barbara Mulhern here yesterday for three hours," Joan's mother touted. "I'll need to write at least one-liners on almost all of them."

The whole situation was disconnected from reality, and denied any of us the knowledge we needed to know in order to cope with the circumstances.

The day after she posted the letter to me, Boston players sent Leonard Paradiso's fingerprints to the labs in Quantico to compare with Joan's recovered belongings. The dutiful defenders of justice submitted the targeted patsy's records on November 5, 1982, at a time when they claimed they did not have a suspect. Paradiso's name had yet to be uttered by anyone outside of George's tight circles in Boston. Supposedly, authorities knew nothing about Paradiso in connection with Joan's disappearance at the time. However, under the radar, the group touted Paradiso as the prime suspect in Joan's disappearance. The fingerprint results were certainly a disappointment, because there was no match with Joan's recovered belongings, but probably not much of a surprise. Even so, Burke persisted in pinning the murder on the shell fisherman. Burke explained the lack of fingerprints with the illogical excuse that Leonard took time to wipe everything down before distributing Joan's body and her possessions all over town. He needed something to make it all fit.

My body rejected our efforts to have children three more times during the emotional upheavals and mind-boggling twists during Joan's investigation. Finally, blessings expanded the family in 1986 and 1987 when my daughters were born. I swore to God I would do everything in my power to protect them from harm, a promise I have never stopped trying to fill. Though she never lived to meet them, Joan's voice embraced the nieces she never knew when we spoke days before her fated flight. My pregnancy that Thanksgiving was meaningful to Joan, more than I could have ever foreseen. Her loving words of encouragement have stayed with me through the years, and brought me to the point where greater understanding of her loss needs to be shared with my girls.

CHAPTER 8

A Tale of Two Murders

"Are you Ms. Carson?" the man asked as he walked into the lobby with his phone plugged in his ear. "There won't be time for you to give your statement at the hearing today."

No one else had arrived, and I was sitting alone when Josh Wall breezed through the front door. The board knew I was coming, and I had forwarded a copy of my brief statement with the documents to support it. The victim's advocate had not compiled the list of speakers, so why was my name being crossed off before the open proceeding even began?

"I'll forego my comments," one of Mary's sisters generously offered, a selfless act of kindness. "Then there will be time for Eve to speak."

The advocate relayed the proposal to her supervisor to get Josh Wall's decision, but the answer came back with a firm "no" again. The hearing was supposed to be a forum open for anyone to speak, and I was properly certified with the Massachusetts Department of Corrections to be there. The powers that be muzzled a victim's right to make an impact statement.

Mary's family somberly filled the seats of the room in opposition to Bond's appeal for parole. Streams of tears and raw emotions were as fresh as the day twenty-nine years ago when they lost their loved one at the hands of a killer. They embraced each other and me with the same comforting hugs that I grew up with, and they were there in force to get through the day. However, I was the only one there to speak for Joan, but the suits in charge did not let the public remember.

The chains that shackled his hands and feet rattled as the murderer walked into the room under heavy guard.

"Raise your right hand," Massachusetts Parole Board Chairman Josh Wall instructed.

Lifting his right hand raised his left hand halfway; Bond looked like a puppet connected with strings. The restraints made for an odd, but necessary, image of a man swearing to tell the truth on April 19, 2011. The public hearing was Robert Bond's stage once again to demonstrate his skills of deception.

"I am guilty of killing Mary Foreman," the felon confessed. "I am guilty of making criminal decisions before, and during, and after her death."

"You've been sent to prisons all around," board member Roger Michel established. "You've had problems with enemies in prison. Do you want to say how you collected those enemies?"

"By testifying for the Commonwealth of Massachusetts," the con replied, "in murder cases."

The questioning stopped. Bond's one good eye remained fixed on the panel. Chairman Wall leaned over and whispered to his colleague, and the subject conspicuously changed when Michel continued. The man in charge erased the public's recollection of a chapter in Bond's history. The cases the board had just silenced were plastered all over the news for years. The board censored the cases of Marie Iannuzzi and Joan Webster.

"I'll give you one last chance," Michel resumed. "Do you want to tell me why you should be paroled?"

"The two crimes that was committed, that has no connection other than that the same person committed them." Bond disconnected himself as if he were talking about a third person. He was out on parole for the 1971 stabbing death of his girlfriend, Barbara Mitchell, when he shot Mary through the temple point blank. The felon idiotically lamented the two crimes were not related.

"Right," Michel said, and the whole board stifled their reactions.

Bond had another version of events for the night Mary died. The convicted felon claimed he and Mary planned to go out to dinner that night. The couple detoured into the cellar of Bond's seedy friend on Walnut Street in Dorchester. The house belonged to a drug dealer named Happy, and Bond's unsavory friend needed an urgent favor before dinner. Bond woefully described Mary's death as an unfortunate accident for which he was deeply remorseful.

"I was reaching up to hide Happy's gun," Bond insanely suggested. "Dust got in my eyes and the gun accidentally went off, hitting Mary."

Neighbors heard Mary's screams for help, and the autopsy indicated a straight on shot to the head. The offender battered Mary beyond recognition. The killer disfigured the woman so severely her own daughter could not identify the face she loved so dearly. She turned away from the mortician's table, then thought to look for the distinctive mark on her mother's arm. It was Mary.

Bond insisted that he never assaulted Mary, and she was his friend. However, the family testified the aggressor beat Mary earlier that summer, and a hospital report corroborated the fact. Robert Bond had beaten Mary so viciously, doctors admitted her into the hospital a month before Bond terminated her life.

Bond had tasted freedom courtesy of Governor Michael Dukakis's infamous furlough plan, a system of release for inmates and heavily criticized by its opponents as a "revolving door." During one of the convicted murderer's social outings, he met Mary Foreman, a community activist with six children. The con turned on the charm for Mary and persuaded her that he was a reformed man. The calculating killer shortened his own sentence for the 1971 stabbing death of Barbara Mitchell, and he missed roll call back at Walpole when the furlough was over. Even though he convinced Mary he had a changed heart, cops hunted him down and locked him back behind bars.

The compassionate woman visited Bobby in prison as part of her commitment as a community advocate. When his chance of parole came around, Bond feigned remorse, and he persuaded the board to release him from prison. Dr. Jekyll's good side soon morphed into the sinister Mr. Hyde when the paroled killer pressed the limits of the ill-fated relationship with Mary. Family and friends saw the good-hearted woman's terror; the evil menace to society terrorized and preyed on his victim. The abuse came to a tragic end when Bond lured Mary Foreman to the basement of his friend, a drug-dealer called Happy, on October 23, 1981. Bond lurked in the shadows.

The discovery traumatized the children that found Mary's lifeless body in the cellar. Witnesses placed the felon in the vicinity at the time of the crime. When police questioned him on November 11, 1981, Bond lied. He claimed he hadn't seen Mary that night. This gentle woman helped and befriended the killer until he gained parole. Four months later, she was dead. The murder trial began on December 9, 1982, and the jury quickly handed down a guilty verdict on December thirteenth, the fifth day of the trial. Large and imposing, Bond placed his hands on his waist and smiled broadly as the jury delivered their verdict.

Robert Bond was the state's star witness in the Iannuzzi and Webster cases, a fact Chairman Wall silenced, but the state's delegates promoted him as a credible witness back then. The misrepresentation facilitated the con's opportunity for a retrial, a second chance to ease the penalty for Mary Foreman's murder. The core team working with the Websters promised the willing rat that he could plead down to manslaughter. Suffolk County denied any such promises for the con's help in other murder cases, but Bond filed a motion on November 15, 1985, during the second trial, and he named the officials who made promises he relied on. Tim Burke, Sgt. Carmen Tammaro, Trooper Andrew Palombo, and "Bill" seduced the state's ignorant tool with assurances they had no authority to make.

"Mary Foreman's kids got up there and did what the district attorney told them to do," the cold-blooded killer lamented to the present parole board. "They came back in the second trial with what they was told to say, and I was shocked!"

"He rode outside the wake waving a gun," Mary's niece painfully remembered. "He threatened he was going to finish the rest of us off. This man doesn't have any remorse."

"I have come to the conclusion you are an extremely dangerous person," Wall scorned the petitioner. "After today, after hearing how you couldn't own up to certain things that you've done, I now conclude you're not only extremely dangerous, you're also extremely deceptive."

Newly appointed Chairman Josh Wall assumed his post after serving as the first Assistant District Attorney in Suffolk County. Ironically, he had been part of a panel in 2004 tasked with addressing, correcting, and preventing wrongful convictions in Suffolk County—the same office that represented Bond as a credible witness in their pursuit of Leonard Paradiso. Wall, a 1982 Harvard graduate, was also part of the collegiate community when Joan disappeared. Sadly, he now covered up the felon's involvement in Joan's story. His former counterpart, first Assistant District Attorney John Dawley, was now in charge of Joan's case, and Dawley acknowledged talking to the Websters. Who wanted to silence any voice speaking out for Joan's justice? It did not take much of a sleuth to connect the most logical dots.

"It's hard to think someone who is remorseful can be so dishonest," Wall emphasized about Bond while shielding the dishonesty of the unremorseful Massachusetts system that promoted Bond years before.

"Eve came all this way on behalf of our family," Mary's niece told the board. "We would have liked her to share her statement."

Bond was complicit in the state's case against Paradiso. How in God's name did that happen, and why? Why did the family believe Bond could ever tell the truth about anything? The family was labeling me delusional, but my judgment of Robert Bond's veracity matched the Massachusetts Parole Board's assessment. I already knew things that cast doubt years before, but George and Eleanor were promoting the ludicrous theory again through Tim Burke's fantasy, billed as "true crime." They were telling my children I was crazy, and in effect influenced them to believe a two-time convicted murderer instead of their mother. I knew too much, but not nearly enough, so I went back to the beginning.

Guards transferred the burly painter from Walpole to the Charles Street Jail on December 8, 1982, the day before the first Mary Foreman trial began. When the muscular black man arrived at the lock-up, inmates were causing a disturbance. Ray Morgan, a Boston private investigator who worked on Paradiso's case, recalled the jail was in lock-down with each prisoner confined to his own cell. Prison sentries locked cell door 68 firmly behind Bond before they processed Leonard Paradiso back into the facility. Overflow conditions had forced a temporary transfer to the Lawrence House of Correction on December 3, 1982, but conditions eased, and authorities moved Paradiso back to Charles Street.

The two men became acquainted in Walpole back in 1975. A jury convicted Bond of stabbing his pregnant girlfriend, Barbara Mitchell, and he was serving time for the murder. Seated peers found Paradiso guilty of assaulting Constance Porter in Amherst, but the shellfish merchant never trusted Bond; he never disclosed the reason for his confinement. At Walpole, the two men resided in the same block with some of the notorious wise guys and mafia that littered Boston's streets in the 1980s, but they were "misfits" who were never part of that group. Paradiso and Bond merely lived in close quarters in 1975; the state overemphasized the connection to their advantage. Fast-forwarding to the day the two inmates checked in to the Charles Street Jail, authorities seized an opportunity to advance their theories. Guards locked Paradiso in cell 36, floors apart from Robert Bond. Their paths never crossed on December 8, 1982, though ADA Tim Burke suggested they did.

While a suitable rat settled into the same facility as the state's prime target, George's circle strategized their next objectives. Jack McEwen, George's ITT conduit, arranged a meeting with a private detective and New Jersey law enforcement suspiciously coinciding with Bond's transfer. McEwen had met with Det. Tom Dugan for three hours on November 30, 1982, to go over the status and developments in the investigation.

"Detective," McEwen insisted, "we need you to be available on December eighth or ninth to meet with a private investigator the Websters hired."

Another player was cleverly positioned at the airport a few days later, but hardly by chance. A flight arrived on December 12, 1982, from Florida with a young, dark-haired woman onboard. Trooper Andrew Palombo moved with purpose down the concourse at Logan. The bearded, undercover cop spotted two young women returning home from a concert, and followed them. Neither of the arriving passengers recognized the unsavory looking character, but they sensed they were being followed. One woman turned abruptly to confront the intimidating presence behind them.

"What are you doing? Stop following us or we'll report you to the police," the dark-haired woman demanded.

"Don't worry. I'm an undercover officer," Palombo replied, and his badge preyed on their youthful confidence.

Palombo was convincing; he induced the girls to accept a ride. Now, there were two episodes of an undercover officer providing that service to women in Boston. Privileged parking made their exit from the airport quick and easy. Palombo decided to drop Deb off first in Quincy, then make his way back north with the young, dark-haired woman alone in his car. The conversation on the ride made Angela Paradiso uncomfortable; the trooper rambled on and on, making insinuations about her father.

"I'm going to make sure your father is locked away for a very long time. He attacks vulnerable, young women that remind him of you. Aren't you ashamed to have such a terrible father?" he continued with bravado.

Angela had not grown up with her dad, but was still unsettled by Palombo's vow to put him away. The driver shamed his passenger, and insinuated the memory of her sparked Lenny's alleged crimes. The intimidated passenger trapped in his car nervously listened. The encounter was too uncanny just to be merely a coincidence. Palombo did what an undercover cop does: covertly dig for dirt and have it ready to funnel through a suitable channel. Free rides were just a bonus. Personal tidbits leaked out of the sly inquisitor's bag of tricks throughout the hunt for Joan's killer. His timing conveniently coincided with the statement the Massachusetts State Police drafted with the stoolie, and like magic, cops came up with an authentic sounding confession—customized.

The suitable channel to sell the story was in place at the Charles Street Jail. Bond was just the right kind of rat to promote the state's story, and he had nothing to lose. Management reassigned the killer's accommodations to cell 31, opportunely near Leonard Paradiso in cell 36. Tim Burke really stretched the imagination, suggesting Paradiso arranged Bond's new suite himself, but if the Websters swallowed it, so did everyone else. Dukakis gave the prisoners a long leash, but the ADA's lame explanation defied common sense. Didn't prison officials control the animals' cages in Massachusetts? Paradiso abandoned all previous caution, according to Bond, and now trusted the felon with unimaginable secrets. In fact, Bond latched onto Lenny every time the warden unlocked the bars, and deviously cajoled the patsy for information the state wanted.

"Now, if you guys haven't said anything to him since you talked to me," Bond offered the police, "there's nothing that I can't get out of him."

So, what information was the state after? Law enforcement arrested Paradiso on July 6, 1982, for the murder of Marie Iannuzzi, and Trooper Andrew Palombo led the brigade. Sgt. Carmen Tammaro, Palombo's superior, paid his North End nemesis a visit the next day to solicit a confession about Iannuzzi before the judge arraigned the suspect. Tammaro's ploy failed, so the officer barged in on doctors the next day; they were treating Paradiso's attorney, James Cipoletta, at Massachusetts General Hospital. The lawyer rebuffed the repeated promises on behalf of his client and was stunned at the cop's tactic to intrude on his treatment.

Tammaro took another stab at a confession about three weeks later on August 1, 1982. The sergeant arrived in street clothes and paid his old North End rival a friendly visit. The cop was fishing and offered to help if Lenny confessed, but the desired admission was not for the Iannuzzi murder. The smooth-talking Tammaro glanced at Lenny's sparsely decorated walls and began asking questions. Photographs of the boats Lenny had proudly owned were in view of the pretender, and the captive audience quickly realized he was the target for something else—not for the crime he was charged with.

"You killed Joan Webster," Tammaro brazenly suggested as Lenny warily sat and listened. "You murdered her on your boat and then burned it."

Despite Tammaro's charm, the good cop ploy failed. Paradiso did not trust "Buster." Lenny was leery of his childhood acquaintance and suspicious of what Tammaro was up to that day. The dangled promise to help did not elicit any self-incrimination for the highly publicized crime or Marie's murder. The authorities had tried to connect Paradiso to Joan's case for almost a year, under the radar, spurred by the anonymous call to the Websters. The suspect stewed in jail for months with no whisper of a confession. As if by fate, Robert Bond arrived at the same lockup four months after "Buster" paid a visit, and the rat soon provided the "break" in Joan's case that suspiciously sounded like Tammaro's premonition.

Officials moved Bond to the facility in Concord on December 29, 1982, to await his sentence for murdering Mary Foreman. The chains on his hands and feet rattled when the convicted killer strolled back into the Suffolk County Courthouse on January 10, 1983, to hear the judge's punishment. Life was the justified decree for the dangerous menace to society, and the judge remanded the prisoner back to Walpole. Court officer John Gillen, "Gil," turned the key, caging the condemned man back in the holding cell.

ADA Tim Burke wrapped up another hearing in the courthouse the same day, and he quickly stuffed the Melendez triple homicide papers into his briefcase when he spotted Gillen in the back of the room. Burke had nothing to do with Bond's case, but Gillen escorted the zealous, young lawyer to the confined killer's cage. Reinforcements were there too, convincing DA Flanagan's protégé that Bond was their man. Burke and his cohorts dangled carrots for the condemned man to chew on.

"Bobby, we want to help you. We can help you get a retrial and plead down to manslaughter."

"What's Lenny been saying?"

"You know there's reward money for the Joan Webster case, $50,000."

A steady stream of law enforcement guardedly slithered in and out of the jail, but no one knew what they were scheming. Bond relentlessly prodded Paradiso for weeks trying to pepper the story with whatever he could get Lenny to say. The time had come for Bond to go on record. Authorities scheduled an interview for Friday, but Bond had some details to finish; things had to look legitimate before the devious group met again.

When the calendar flipped to Friday, Officer John Gillen escorted his unsavory charge into a small room at the courthouse again, and the snitch stared at the smiling enforcers. All ears perked up; they eagerly anticipated the stories they knew they were about to hear. Burke opted out of the inquisition, and the boys neglected to invite counsel to advise Bond. The band of "truth" seekers had the confidence of George and Eleanor Webster. The experienced intelligence couple was familiar with the methods of getting in bed with the unsavory to get a job done. Bond had not met them, but the "Man from New Jersey" sent people to see him.

Sgt. Carmen Tammaro interrogated the witness on January 14, 1983, and skillfully wove two, completely unrelated, murders together. Trooper Palombo, Sgt. Robert Hudson of the Boston Police, and Officer John Gillen crowded around the rat like a vice and stayed fixed on their boy. State Trooper Jack O'Rourke arrived late and had to catch up, but the tape was rolling to capture the tale of two murders. Boston had a history the enforcers had learned, and Bond was willing to help them do it again.

"That was the eighth," the felon calculated. "We had a couple hours outside, and he kept telling me. He kept talking. That's when he started running the whole thing down to me."

Questioning began with Marie's case.

"And then what happened?' Tammaro probed.

"He went straight to the Lynn Marshfield Road, or whatever it is," the con offered, "and this is where the sex and strangling took place."

The badges nodded satisfaction, but the envisioned crime contradicted DA Kevin Burke's explanation of why he handed the case over to Suffolk County. The Essex County DA surmised Marie was murdered somewhere else, then dumped in his jurisdiction.

"Like at first he told me he strangled her—Joan Webster," the snitch rambled, getting off track. "The last thing he told me was that he did it with a whiskey bottle, you know. I wrote both of them down, you know, so you can pick or choose whatever fuckin' one you want."

"Let's get back now," the sergeant reeled the con back to Marie's case. "He took her to the Lynn Marsh Road. He had trouble with her pantyhose."

"Yah," Bond agreed.

"Don't you know anything about the rest of her clothes?" Tammaro guided.

"No," the dense puppet fumbled.

"The other day you mentioned a wraparound skirt," the cop reminded the dim-witted tool of their previous meeting. "Did he say what she had on top of the skirt?"

"No," Bond struggled. "I'm going to say red."

"He says he slapped her when he tried to get her panties down," the guiding enforcer continued with the saga. "She rejected him."

"Yah, alright," the malleable snitch obliged, getting the story straight.

Bond did not have it down yet, but he infused details as if he had read police reports and the grand jury minutes. The scenario Bond provided suggested that Lenny left a wedding house party with his girlfriend and the victim. According to Bond, Paradiso drove, and he dropped the intoxicated passenger off at the Cardinale's Nest Bar. Supposedly, Lenny then took his girlfriend home to Revere and returned to the bar to hustle Marie. Witnesses saw Lenny leave the bar with Marie between 12:30 and 1:00 a.m.

Trooper Palombo was the lead cop on the Iannuzzi case after
some unknown authority shifted the case to him in February, 1981.
Obviously, Palombo had the police records at his disposal. The seasoned detective listened as Bond told his disjointed story; the undercover cop who dug up dirt, mentally compared it with the known
facts. Lenny and Candy both cooperated with police at the time of
the murder, and gave statements explaining they returned Marie's
belongings left in Candy's car. Both independently attested that they
watched Marie walk out of sight about one o'clock the morning of
August 12, 1979, and never saw her again. Nevertheless, Bond now
insisted Paradiso confessed he'd returned to the bar to hustle Marie
and was the last person seen with the young woman before her murder.

"Don't bother clearing the glasses, Marie," the bartender told
her. "That's Patty's job." Jimmy Cardinale was getting ready to close
and directed waitress Patty Capozzi to clean off the tables.

"I saw Marie in here at closing time, two o'clock," Patty Cardinale told police. "I'm not sure, though, if it was Friday or Saturday
night."

The bar's owner had seen Marie, too; she saw her an hour after
Bond's rendition placed her in Paradiso's car on the Lynn Marsh
Road. Police already knew the victim had been with a man named
Eddie Fisher on Friday night. Simple police work would have nailed
down the facts when Patty Cardinale last saw the victim. The detectives had no reason to believe Bond's story. It was clear from several
witnesses, more credible witnesses, that the story was concocted.

Regardless what the files said, Bond continued the story, and the
enforcers "believed" him. Bond described the victim struggling to
keep her pantyhose on. He described Paradiso as forcibly trying to
have his way with the unemployed waitress in a parked car behind the
shuttered Atlantic Lobster Company on the Lynn Marsh Road. When
she screamed, he choked her to death and dumped her body out on
the rocks; he slipped and fell in the process. Bond painted an image
of a monstrous crime, but gaffed like an actor unsure of his lines.

"He grabbed her scarf," the killer suggested. "This was after he
fucked her; he grabbed the scarf and choked her. That's the honest
to God truth."

"He killed her after everything was done?" the inquisitor continued.

"I'm going to say yah," the rat guessed.

The well-positioned inmate added a touch of realism to his tale
by suggesting Lenny had slipped on the rocks when he pulled his

victim out of the car and recklessly dumped her on the bank
Pine River. The boys in blue all nodded their awareness of th
conditions that night. The culprit hurried home where he cаɪɪ...
girlfriend, the felon continued, asked her to wake her mother, and
get her on the phone. In this sinister plot, the girlfriend took a cab
over to Lenny's place to get their stories straight, and consequently
became Paradiso's accomplice.

"Okay, now to get to Joan Webster," the sergeant shifted the
focus to the missing Harvard graduate student.

Even though a cab was the only plausible way of placing Joan in
the company of Leonard Paradiso, Robert Bond could not confirm
that Lenny actually drove one. When the question came up, looks
around the room prompted further clarification, and Bond elaborated his story. Presumably, police learned Paradiso was driving
undercover for somebody else, and the informant handed the cops
their own story.

"Now the way he told me, it was three weeks after he murdered
her he dropped some things off on the Lynn Marshfield Road," the
dupe tried to remember, "or the three weeks he was in Charles Street
when the police came and talked with him."

"He said they were in his car," Tammaro repeated the con's
account that Paradiso picked Joan up at the airport.

"He says he went to Pier 7. I'm going to say Pier 7. Now if he
didn't, you know, that's on you guys," the squealer punted to the boys
making the case. "I don't know and I really don't care where he kept
his boat."

Bond's version was even more incredulous when contemplating
the feat of acrobatics required boarding the vessel. This story had Paradiso forcing Joan down a wobbly ramp to a barge, and the pair then
leaping onto a bobbing craft in the dark. Bobby could not confirm
Paradiso used a gun, but he could not say he did not either; this left
enough room for the story to be embellished as needed. The authorities stretched their creativity to pin Joan's murder on Lenny already,
but they had to come up with a motive. Bond obliged and spewed a
ludicrous sequence that Paradiso proceeded to put the moves on his
prey in the small, dark, and cold boat. Apparently, Bond had not
been briefed on the weather conditions that night. The weather was
so blustery that evening, gusting winds spread flames that left Lynn,
Massachusetts in charred ruins, and the weather would have sent any
small craft on the water crashing against its mooring.

According to Bond, though, the conditions at sea were apt for
romance. Bobby alleged Paradiso made advances and poured drinks

for the sophisticated, young woman. The couple would have struggled to keep their balance on the rough waters, and booze would
have sloshed from the plastic cups in a setting that would not seduce
a dead fish. The suggestion that Joan said, "No," on a cold, dark Chris
Craft was the only realistic assertion Bond made in that stifling courthouse room. Paradiso's suave attempts at romance quickly became
sinister when Joan would not reciprocate. This was the story according to Bond's tale.

"You're going to make my hair stand on end," Tammaro pretended to shiver as he led the witness.

"He hit her when she refused to do anything with him," Bond
alleged, and the stoolie raised his right hand to point to the right side
of his head. "She had a hole right here from the whiskey bottle.
There was so much fuckin' blood. He took the boat way out and
dumped the body."

"Alright," Tammaro interrupted to make sure he had it straight,
"between sex and the whiskey bottle, which came first?"

"The whiskey bottle," the storyteller determined.

Of course, the melodrama was completely absurd considering
Paradiso reported the boat in question was missing months earlier.
The lawmen present in the meeting knew the craft had been scuttled.
Only Bond asserted that the boat was still afloat when Joan disappeared. Defying all logic and credibility, seasoned investigators
rejected everything they already knew and replaced it with their
snitch's version, conveniently explaining why there was not a body.

"Did he say to you if he weighed the body down at all?" Trooper
Jack O'Rourke questioned the plant.

"No," Bond fumbled.

"Or, he didn't say he didn't either," Tammaro quickly suggested
to help him recover.

"No, he did not mention whether he did or not," the trained rat
scrambled through the maze, and he left the door open for future
details.

"He showed you the picture on the wall," Tamarro reminded his
tool.

"Right," the convicted killer replied, and then recited the serial
numbers he had memorized.

"Does it look like there's any room to walk into the boat?" the
boys needed to know.

"I'm gonna say yes, because he got pictures inside of it," the pli-
able witness agreed. "You can see the booze inside."

The story had gaping holes, but the vagaries left plenty of room
for police to fill in the blanks as needed. It had to look like Bond's

moral code moved his conscience to come forward all on his own, but there was a snag in the plan devised at their previous meeting. Guards transported the eager contributor back to Concord after he met with the boys at the courthouse on the tenth, and he diligently wrote everything down. The letter was conveniently divided for the two separate cases. This strategy was helpful in court, but beyond the ignorant man's capacity for scheming. The collaborator addressed an outer envelope to his wife, Willie Mae. Her assignment was to mail the inner envelope on to ADA Tim Burke. However, the anticipated letter had not arrived in time for the day's meeting.

"I'm going to try and keep in contact with you," the sergeant advised, "to see if someone up at Concord held it up, if they still have it."

"I caught the deputy last night, Carter," Bobby explained. "'Jesus Christ, I don't think you really have a bitch, Bob,' he says. He says, 'You're talking about three days.'"

The date was January 14, 1982. The math was simple enough for even seasoned investigators to calculate. The letter was mailed on January tenth; it was mailed the same day Bond was sentenced, and the boys paid him a visit in his holding cell at the courthouse.

"If this letter comes in tomorrow, or something like that," Tammaro arranged, "we would like to, over the weekend obviously, go over it. You know, so the next time we see you we have the information."

"Why don't you take the number and he'll constantly call my home phone?" Bond offered. "I got it right there."

"Alright then," the collaborator plotted, "I'll have a dark (redacted). We'll be with Jack Murphy."

Bond dialed the phone, and the anxious sergeant arranged to try to intercept the letter they wanted with Det. Jack Murphy and another unidentified enforcer.

"You got to dial nine. You got to dial nine," the impatient sergeant instructed the dupe.

"Four three six six three eight five," the accomplice dialed. "Hey Monty, when a letter comes, you gonna get a phone call. Ah, if it's tomorrow, this er ah person gonna call you and er ah, hold the letter. He may come over; give the letter to him."

The key contacts with the Websters scheduled another meeting with Bond on Monday to go over the statement, and Sgt. Tammaro set up a polygraph that a man with no detectable measure of conscience would easily pass.

Bond had not met George Webster, but indicated the "Man from New Jersey" had sent people to see him, and ITT security arranged a strategy meeting in New Jersey at the same time Bond was moved to the Charles Street Jail. Three men were the primary instruments of George's operation in Boston: ADA Tim Burke, Sgt. Carmen Tammaro, and Trooper Andrew Palombo of the Massachusetts State Police. Bond asked his interrogators about the reward money, and Tammaro reinforced their discussion days before the recorded interview. Joan's parents offered money, and he had a reasonable expectation to claim it according to the badges in the room. Regardless, the felon was skeptical of their motives and nervous that he would have to change his name to collect it. Sgt. Tammaro made assurances, a particular skill he continued to practice, and suggested that Curtis or Kitrell, the inmate's sons, could intercede on his behalf.

The core group had a skeletal story promoted by Bond. Palombo opened the Iannuzzi files and compared the records to Bond's rendition with his neophyte partner, the duo paired at the Websters' February meeting. Marie's attire was a problem; autopsy photos showed the strangled, young woman fully clothed and her garments intact. She was wearing a bodysuit, with no snaps in the crotch, under the wraparound skirt, but Bond's version had Paradiso struggling to take her pantyhose off. The profile was of a sexual predator that lured his prey into his car. Medical examiners found semen in the promiscuous victim's body, but responders did not consider rape a motive at the time, and investigators ignored an obvious test. Rape was plausible, though, because of Lenny's past record of assault. Since Massachusetts did not consider it rape if the victim was already dead, the state's willing witness got the sequence in the proper order to pursue another charge. His story promoted what the authorities needed; he claimed Paradiso choked Marie after he had his way.

Trooper Rick Fraelich slipped on the rocks when he arrived on the scene, and interestingly, the same detail made the con's account more believable. On the downside, no phone records corroborated an alleged call to Paradiso's girlfriend, or cab records to validate that the couple got together that night to get their stories straight. Police had their own set of skills to work with the theory and fill in the gaping holes in the story.

Turning to Joan's case posed different problems. Lenny had at least been a suspect in Marie's case, but there was nothing to connect Leonard Paradiso to Joan Webster.

The fact that Lenny was a parolee and unable to get a hack license was a hurdle; the only plausible explanation for Joan to cross paths with this man was if he were driving a cab. Tammaro's leading questions did not elicit the desired response that Lenny drove one.

The only thing that remained was the notion of a phantom owner that would not come forward in the high-profile case for fear of losing his medallion. Apparently, Tammaro missed his big chance to make assurances again and encourage an important witness to come forward.

The prosecutor's devised motive required assault. Headroom in the cabin of the boat barely cleared Lenny's 6'2" stature, and the right-handed blow to the right side of Joan's head would have contorted the struggle. Regardless, someone convinced the seasoned detectives option two was the manner of Joan's death. Strangulation was the modus operandi for crimes piled on Burke's target, and Bond served up the alternative for the cops to choose. Instead, Tammaro envisioned a sensational crime from snapshots taped on Paradiso's cell wall and liquor bottles photographed on the shelf in the cabin. ADA Burke knew a picture was worth a thousand words, and he had support from the badges to cover his back.

Bond ended the scene with Lenny motoring his boat way out, dumping his bludgeoned victim into watery depths, and then returning his floating crime scene to the mooring. For the crafters, there was no difficulty suggesting a watery grave as long as there was not a body. Even though Bond said Lenny took the boat out two days later and sank it, the state had a problem with the suggested crime scene. Their suspect alerted the Massachusetts State Police, the Boston Police Department, and the Coast Guard on July 26, 1981, to be on the lookout for the missing craft. He then filed a claim with Liberty Mutual Insurance four months before Joan disappeared.

The enlisted informant was ignorant about Joan Webster's suitcase, although he did know it was in the possession of the Massachusetts State Police. I am not sure how Leonard Paradiso would have known that, but it is reasonable to conclude the state police did. Burke pulled out the FBI reports for the team to go over. Technicians meticulously examined the undisturbed bag officials shipped to the lab in Quantico, and examiners carefully listed Joan's recovered belongings. Magically, the enforcers, who feigned ignorance until Bond came forward in January 1983, sent Paradiso's fingerprints to Quantico for comparison with Joan's belongings on November 5, 1982—there was no match.

No one could bolster Bond's assertion that Lenny confessed. The cops suggested numerous names during the taped interview with the informer, but only one name ended up in the statement as a possible witness. Burke subpoenaed Paradiso's parole records on April 20, 1982; Victor Anchukaitis listed Peter Brandon's name and address. Lenny had moved out of his parole officer's jurisdiction, but he had a good relationship with the aging supervisor. Listing his friend's address enabled Paradiso to stay with the advisor he trusted. Now, creators wove Brandon's name into a murder plot. In addition, the snitch falsely suggested Brandon was the anonymous caller that fingered Lenny. Every tidbit showing up in Bond's statement cast suspicion on the circle closest to the Websters as the source of Bond's information, but no one could penetrate the inner sanctum. In George and Eleanor's minds, Paradiso was guilty, and records were safely out of reach from anyone futilely enlisted to help the beleaguered shellfish merchant the state was after.

The transcript was clear; the boys in blue expected Bond's letter, but it had not arrived. The tape was rolling, but there was not one single question or comment in the interview that referred to anything received in writing. It would have taken a divine vision to schedule the interview with Robert Bond on the fourteenth based on his letter describing a tale of two murders. Nevertheless, claiming the letter came first was the state's story. The suits signed the papers to move the state's star witness to Concord on December 29, 1982, and prison officials at his new facility summoned him into the office.

"Don't go forward testifying for the Commonwealth, Bob. They will double-cross you," a sage administrator warned. "They're not going to do anything for you."

However, Robert Bond did not heed the advice, and the state had the mouthpiece to promote their tale of two murders.

CHAPTER 9

The Bond Letter

I held my daughter's gut-wrenching letter in my shaking hands, trying to understand what she meant. In the best case, she misunderstood her father's inappropriate behavior, but in the worst, he had committed a felony against her. The stories and denials rolled off her lips and her father's, too, but there it was in black and white.

"He walked into the bathroom while I was taking a shower," my child explained. "He was emptying the trash, and I took it the wrong way." Steve nodded approval as he sat on the counselor's sofa beside her, defensive and playing the victim.

Steve and the girls clammed up and refused to discuss it any further. Gossip began to swirl to discredit the worry tearing me apart, and isolated me from the proper help we all desperately needed. Instead of talking to one another to straighten out the problems, my girls lashed out.

"You are completely crazy!"

"You are sick! You suffer from delusions!"

By May 2006, I had torturous difficulty sleeping; I went to see Dr. Larry Davis, a well-known psychiatrist in town. The qualified doctor conducted the MINI International Neuropsychiatric Interview and completed a physical with his evaluation. There was nothing wrong with my mental faculties, so why was my family so destructive to insist I was nuts? Dr. Davis noted a level of anxiety based on the real circumstances of severe alienation from my children and the fear of what may have happened to them. Loving families support one another if they think someone is broken, but not the Websters. They were trying to "break" me.

Now, I held another letter in my hands; a letter that had been secreted for years.

"Oh, dear God," I cried aloud as I read the pages.

The harder I pressed for answers in Boston, the more similar, nasty gossip swirled. These people did not know me or my experiences, but some invisible force distorted our personal, family struggles. These were the type of insinuations used to discredit someone with knowledge, and thwarted my pursuit of the truth about Joan. I had legitimate questions that other members of Joan's family should have been asking. There were questions that authorities should answer. However, I faced opposition at every turn. Instead of addressing the discrepancies I uncovered in Joan's case, hidden objectors instigated a smear campaign of false assertions and questioned my mental health and motivations. The family had dragged me down this vicious path before. The big guns came out with nasty, CIA-like tactics to spread destructive disinformation about me.

People clammed up as they did when the state served Lenny to the public, and players remained silent when searchers found Joan. The documents were easy to read, right there in black and white like my daughter's letter. Both the family and the authorities avoided facing the facts; they could not confront what the documents revealed, so it was time to shoot the messenger again. It did not matter what they said about me; it did not change what was in the record. Now I had another letter that was not supposed to mean what it said.

Like a magician's trick, confusion evaporated somewhere between the interview and the written statement. The letter finally produced coagulated the Commonwealth's version of events. Bond appeared incoherent, bumbling, and unsure of himself in the interview, but in comparison, he seemed to have mastered the written word. In the letter, his recollections were suddenly incredibly lucid. Items where Bond was vague and uncertain during the interview became clear. Examining the interview and letter together exposed the vast differences between the two, and the documents raised suspicions that authorities tampered or tempted the witness to fabricate a story.

Sgt. Tammaro, Trooper Andrew Palombo, and Sgt. Robert Hudson of the Boston Police Department met with Bond on Monday, January 17, 1983, to go over his statement while the Friday meeting was still fresh in their minds. The complicit witness miraculously had vivid recollection restored by time he got it down on paper. The boys ironed out the details Bond left up to their discretion, and it was obvious. Bond drafted the letter after the taped interview with the police.

"Bobby, I went to Pier 7 where I worked at," Bond transcribed the alleged confession. "My boat was there, because that's where I kept it."

"Bobby, I always kept a lot of booze on my boat," the con concocted from the pictures he had seen in the cell.

"Bobby, I had blood all over me and my boat," Paradiso allegedly confided to the rat. "She had a hole right here from the whiskey bottle."

Joan was still missing, so there was nothing to confirm anyone had committed a crime. No evidence affirmed the manner of death, and the modus operandi deviated from the profile the authorities were building against their prime suspect for other crimes. Strangulation was the pattern formulated in the profile and consistent with Marie Iannuzzi's death. Bond offered that option a few days before, but abdicated the decision to the enforcers. The cops had the leeway to choose whichever one they liked, and police picked a blow to the head with correct detail in the final draft.

"I took my boat 'way' out and dumped her body," the felon continued after chewing on the state's carrots.

According to Bond, Paradiso then told him, "The state police ask me about it. They told me I kill her in my boat and burn it up." Bond had just corroborated Paradiso's account of "Buster's" unofficial visit. The rat affirmed Tammaro suggested the boat—in August 1982.

The letter described a chilling account of a heinous crime. The written account unmistakably documented the blow to the head, followed by rape, and then disposal into the frigid deep. Only five men attended the Bond interrogation. Sgt. Carmen Tammaro, his subordinate Trooper Andrew Palombo, Trooper Jack O'Rourke, Sgt. Robert Hudson, and court officer John Gillen were the badges that corralled the witness. Who picked the blow to the head?

The state had their bases covered. Whatever the truth was about what happened "three weeks later," there were plausible stories created to explain it. As long as Bond's statement remained hidden, no one was the wiser.

"It was three weeks later," Bond recited the confabulated confession, "when I put some of her stuff in Saugus in the Lynn Marsh Road."

Joan's purse and wallet were the only items found in Saugus, and the tabloids had chronicled every event in the case. Maybe Bond did not read the papers, but there was no excuse for the police not to check their files. Overzealous enforcers obsessively tied the two, unrelated cases together. Anthony Belmonte found Joan's things on December 2, 1981, four days after she disappeared. The items were on the opposite side of the road and some distance from where Marie Iannuzzi's strangled body was found in 1979. Anyone following the story could have told the lead investigators Bond was lying.

"The state police told me," the snitch continued the fictitious Paradiso confession, "about three weeks after I was arrested for Marie's murder, they found some of J. W.'s things on the Lynn Marsh Road where Marie was found."

Charles Street Jail administrators facilitated Bond's incessant prodding of Paradiso by moving his cell near the state's patsy. The objective was obvious: gain Paradiso's confidence and have the rat get him to talk. Tammaro bent the rules when he stepped into the cell and planted the incredulous suggestion without a lawyer present to represent Lenny. When the time came, the ploy was child's play for the con to solicit preposterous subliminal insinuations "Buster" seeded four months before Bond moved in. Bond's written statement corroborated another account of Carmen Tammaro's visit on August 1, 1982, when the officer implored for an admission about Joan with a dangled promise of help.

"I'm being fucked for something someone else did," Bond spewed in denial. In his deranged mind, he was not the one that killed Mary Foreman. "What they got you in for, Lenny?"

"The police say I murdered Marie Iannuzzi," Paradiso disclosed. "All the evidence points to her boyfriend, David Doyle."

"They got to have something on you," the rat coaxed.

"The state police told me I killed Joan Webster on my boat and burned it up." Lenny shook his head at such nonsense, but he fell into a trap.

There it was, the so-called confession. Lenny knew the boat was gone, and he probably rolled his eyes in disbelief to repeat it. Supposedly, the cops knew nothing about a connection to Joan's case until after Bond's letter arrived. The authorities had their theory long before they ever met with Robert Bond, and my instincts gnawed away the illusion. Bond's letter exposed the real authors of the fictitious crime.

"BREAK IN JOAN WEBSTER CASE," was blazoned across the front page of the *Boston Herald* on January 28, 1983.

"The unnamed inmate," the paper reported, "informed Suffolk County Assistant District Attorney Timothy Burke in a January 4 letter of his conversation with Paradiso."

Trooper Andrew Palombo avoided giving details about the information to the *Boston Globe*, except to say, "Police believe it is 'very, very reliable.'"

"Now we have something we can really investigate," Sgt. Carmen Tammaro, who coordinates work on the investigation by the State Police, the Boston Police, and the Saugus Police, told the *Harvard Crimson*.

The media was an integral tool to get the word out there, and headlines kept people fixated on the state's theory. The public consumed an image of murder at sea. The story was sensational, to be sure, and there was nothing visible to dispel the notion. Although he was not named, spokesmen portrayed Bond as a man who still had some moral code to come forward. The DA's office asserted that Tim Burke received a lengthy unsolicited letter from the inmate on January 4, 1982. It detailed two murders Paradiso allegedly confessed to the man cleverly shifted near his cell. Apparently, no one checked the accuracy for the date of the letter. Burke was still waiting for the anticipated correspondence on the fourteenth when cops had the rat cornered in the courthouse. Bond mailed the letter on the tenth, and everyone in the room during the taped interview heard Tamarro's plot to intercept it.

At the same time Bond's allegations dominated the headlines, the phone rang in another office across the street from the Suffolk County Courthouse.

"The source identified Leonard J. Paradiso," the confidential caller told the Boston FBI office. "Paradiso is the person responsible for murdering Joan Webster and Marie Iannuzzi. The source stated Webster was taken by boat into Boston Harbor where she was killed and her body dumped into the harbor."

"News media in the Boston area published substance of above information," the agency reported on January 28, 1983. "Source of leaks is presently unknown."

The unnamed informant repeated what authorities pondered in the courthouse on January 14, 1983. The Fed's source repeated that Joan was onboard Paradiso's vessel, a boat reported missing months before the graduate student disappeared, and then swallowed into the waters of Boston Harbor. Five men listened to Bond's tale of two murders on January 14, 1983, and the papers quoted two of them the same day the FBI typed their report. Reporters quoted ADA Tim Burke, too, erroneously claiming the "break in the case" arrived days before Bond mailed it. Authorities feigned ignorance about the spawned theory until the snitch submitted the letter. It was not that difficult to figure out where the story and these leaks were springing.

Despite the disinformation fed to the press, the authorities still knew the theory had problems, and Bond's statement exposed weaknesses in the case. Bond declared witnesses had seen Joan leave the airport in a cab. The head of ITT security quickly hushed information that the young woman had been seen, and maintained the prevailing notion she vanished without a trace after waving to a friend.

The police knew a cabbie had come forward with the description of a bearded man, and Det. Corcoran personally handed the composite to Eleanor Webster. Instead of the truth, the proposed story lamented the plight of some phantom cab owner who could not come forward for fear he would lose his medallion.

Crafters solved the problem of a crime scene with the pictures taped on Paradiso's cell wall. The pictured boat set a perfect stage for the murder—no body. The con filled his report down to the registration numbers and bottles lined on the shelf. However, a bigger dilemma arose, because Paradiso reported the Chris Craft missing in July 1981, four months before Joan landed. The creators produced a crime scene that apparently did not exist at the time, but it offered a necessary explanation for not having a body. The state's star witness listed every agency that took reports on the missing craft, but there was nothing to bolster Bond's assertion that the *Malafemmena* was still afloat in November when Joan disappeared. He affirmed the body would not be on board, but incorrectly pretended that Paradiso took the boat "way out" to scuttle.

Facts and gaps muddied the waters, but defenders of the theory expected challenges and deflected any questions by conspicuously embellishing the account as the story developed. Bond failed to support the story that the accused used a gun to coax Joan down the wobbly ramp. He made no mention of the contents in the suitcase, and the badges looked elsewhere for weights to keep the missing body from floating back to the surface. Staging the murder at sea was convenient, because the theory presumed no one would ever find Joan's body. Murder at sea was a risky concoction, though, if Joan or her body ever turned up.

The core group thought every conceivable base had been covered or left with room needed to wiggle. Skeptics could not inject common sense, because information was controlled, and reporters marched to the state's story. Conflicts and errors were invisible. The final draft endorsed the idea that Paradiso hit Joan in the head with a whiskey bottle, and authorities irrationally abandoned the prevailing modus operandi developed for Leonard Paradiso.

Paradiso had lingered in jail since July 6, 1982, charged with the murder of Marie Iannuzzi. Regardless, the boys had not issued any warrants to find evidence to support the state's case. Now that they had Bond's story, the assigned team got busy filing papers with the court. Trooper Andrew Palombo swore in his April 25, 1983, warrant that Bond had taken detailed notes of his jailhouse conversations with Paradiso and turned them over when they met again. Both Palombo and Burke pledged to the court that the postman delivered a second, mailed letter on January 17, 1983. The letter Bond posted on January 10, 1983, may have reached Burke's office by Monday, or maybe the notes Bond turned over to Palombo on the seventeenth ended up on Burke's desk. Whatever letter they meant was irrelevant, because no one was going to see the correspondence locked in their files to clear up the confusion. Now there was a tale of two letters and the notes Palombo swore were in his possession.

I tried to digest all the conflicting things I had learned. What the family told me then did not reconcile with what I could read in the record for myself. On October 9, 2009, I sat across the table from Robert Bond with the private investigator I had hired, and the killer's skeptical demeanor told the whole story. He still regurgitated the same basic story. According to Bond, Lenny confessed to Joan's murder, and the cops were in the dark until Bond came forward. However, his memory lapsed when it came to the details, which suggested to me that he had been heavily coached and rehearsed in his earlier testimony. Bond disclosed that Trooper Andrew Palombo befriended his informant just as he had befriended David Doyle, the other suspect in Marie Iannuzzi's murder. According to Bond, the bearded, undercover cop corresponded with the jailed killer up until Joan's body rattled in 1990. The sage detective advised Bond not to change his story. Perjury was a capital crime, after all, and carried further consequences, jeopardizing any chance Bond had for parole.

"Don't change your story, Bobby," the felon recounted the trooper's advice.

Authority figures manipulated Bond from the start and never fully granted the hidden carrots dangled for his cooperation. The December 13, 1982, conviction for the murder of Mary Foreman was upended, and Bond did get another shot to ease his plight. Bond's accommodations were changed, and the two-time murderer avoided going back to Walpole. However, more significantly, unauthorized players representing the Commonwealth promised him a lesser charge of manslaughter. The bait was not a legitimate offer the state could make for his cooperation, and the authorities knew it. The state retried Bond's case, but the abandoned tool objected, because the judge failed to instruct the jury for a manslaughter verdict. Even Norman Zalkind, the skilled lawyer the state delivered for Bond, could not bring a better result, and the con was convicted again on November 23, 1985. George Webster, the "Man from New Jersey," kept his pen in his pocket, and Bobby lost out on any reward money.

The intimidating inmate stirred trouble with other prisoners wherever the Department of Corrections shuffled him in the system.

Bullying was his only means of survival. The inside scoop was that Bond had framed Lenny for the state and broke the code among inmates. In other words, he was a rat, and other inmates had it in for him. To survive in the prison system, Bond presented himself as the state's favored boy; he was an intimidating tough guy to keep others from messing with him. The buzz trickled out from prison that he participated with the state to nail Lenny, and the word followed the menacing pretender wherever he was caged. Tensions ratcheted up during the winter of 1987 when another surge hoped to put Paradiso on trial for Joan's murder. Inmates caught wind of the dirty dealing Bond had contrived with the state.

"He said he did set up one Lenny Paradiso, and the same thing could happen to me and my friends if we didn't watch out." Fellow jailbird Kenny Crawford detailed his encounter with Bond in a letter to Marie Altieri, another lawyer who took up Paradiso's futile fight for justice. Crawford resided in Connecticut at Somers with Robert Bond during the summer of 1988. "He also said he could get away with stabbing us, and that the state would make another deal with him because of the way he lied about Lenny."

Crawford and his friends recognized Bond was dangerous, just like the Massachusetts Parole Board concluded in April of 2011. I agreed with the board's assessment, but the Webster family labeled me crazy.

"In the summer of 1988, myself and several friends were involved in a stabbing in Somers." The correspondent confessed and explained why Bond's left eye was an unfocused piece of glass. "We were forced to act by stabbing him. The inmate stabbed was one Robert Bond."

Paranoia stared back from his one good eye as I challenged his story with questions in 2009. He was not forthcoming, probably because I was not forthcoming with the cash. Everything had a price, and I wanted something for nothing, so in his mind there was no reason to talk to me. I was not offering him anything. Nevertheless, admissions he made were revealing.

"The Man from New Jersey sent people to see me," the informant told the private investigator.

"The Websters came to see me in the winter of 1987," he said.

"The authorities showed Tony Pisa my notes," Bond revealed.

"Palombo wrote to me until 1989, or whenever they found her body," the con admitted, "and told me not to change the story."

Just before the publisher released Tim Burke's book in February 2008, one of the DA's offices concocted an illness for Bond and transferred him to Lemuel Shattuck Hospital. The story was that he needed surgery for prostate cancer, but this was news to the inmate; he had no knowledge of the condition and did not feel sick. So why was he there? The guards escorted Bond to a room on the eighth floor to the bedside of Leonard Paradiso. Doctors had the condemned man heavily sedated; their patient was in the last stages of bladder cancer. The gross misuse of taxpayer money funded someone's obsession to recruit Bond once again to wangle a confession. Unfortunately, for Burke's book sales, the cunning exploit failed to secure an admission from the incoherent, dying man. Paradiso maintained his innocence to the end. It was no surprise to me, or Bond for that matter, that his mysterious prostate surgery was never rescheduled.

Bond's testimony was never plausible, and even Burke himself discredited his heralded witness when the attorney's delusional book rolled off the presses. Now Burke's story claimed Paradiso had tossed the purse on the fateful night—not three weeks later. Burke twisted Bond's allegations again with his fictional premise Paradiso pitched Joan's belongings on his way to Hamilton to bury the body. According to Burke, Paradiso always took meticulous care not to leave any prints.

Something far graver disrupted my sleep. Bond's multiple-choice included strangulation, but the experienced enforcers settled for what turned out to be the correct manner of Joan's death. Many years passed before Joan's body emerged to confirm the massive hole in her head. The closed door sequestered only five men with the stoolie developing a story to explain Joan's demise. So, how did these men come up with the correct mode of death? The state had no body or credible witnesses to foretell Joan's condition. Guessing undermined a legitimate investigation, and earnest professionals would not resort to that practice. Without a crystal ball, there was no way for these men to determine the correct answer. That is, of course, unless someone in the room during the Massachusetts State Police interview knew what happened to Joan. It sure was not Robert Bond.

When I spoke with Bond, he was convinced I was there on behalf of the DA's office, and the next parole window was approaching. He would not say anything that would jeopardize that process. The killer had secrets locked behind his façade.

"I know so much about the Joan Webster case, I almost need immunity from prosecution," the state's star witness dangled. "I'm going to be up front with you; as long as I'm in prison you don't have a chance of cracking this case."

Finally, Bond was telling a morsel of truth.

CHAPTER 10

The Underhand

We journeyed to Nantucket in August of 2002, praying for an enjoyable vacation as a family, or at least I was. The girls and I took a detour to visit Pop Pop and Mimi in their new digs at White Horse Village, while Steve lingered behind. The drive was not pleasant; the girls were rude and distracting the entire time. Their efforts only intensified when we arrived on the quaint and foggy island. George and Eleanor had announced their intention to visit the island as well. When they arrived, George invited himself to dinner, that he expected me to prepare. Spaghetti and a big salad were one of my staples, and their places were set. I thought it was going well.

"Boy, I sure love your spaghetti," George said. Even Eleanor thought it was great. While the elders all sat there spouting their praise and thanks for the meal, my children were dumping the very same food in the trash.

"The food sucks!" yelled one of my daughters as they stormed out of the room. Silent tears filled my eyes, and the elders blissfully bantered, ignoring the total lack of respect. That August in Nantucket was my last family vacation.

By Christmas, tensions had reached a fever pitch. I warmly embraced George and Eleanor as they arrived for the holiday celebration. Nerves were frayed and it was stressful, but I was determined to hold onto the spirit of the season. Christmas 2002 was my last celebration with the family, but I was probably the only one who did not know it.

"We thank you, God, for our blessings this season. We are thankful for our health, prosperity, and family." George proceeded to lift his glass and toasted me, his daughter-in-law, as if I were merely the cook. I had been married for more than two decades, but George's insensitive salutation addressed me by my maiden name: Carson.

George and Eleanor raised their voices to God at the candlelight service, but I could not help seeing some irony in their adulation. After the service, Steve strangely assigned me to drive all the children home. The blizzard conditions were treacherous, but the intense heat fired off by the girls got me stuck in another kind of drift. Insults and accusations from the back seat flew all the way home, which only added to the difficulty of driving a car full of children in a harsh winter storm. When we arrived home, I asked the other adults to help ease the hostility.

"The girls are being very disrespectful," I said. "Please step in and correct them if they start up again."

"Everything looks wonderful, Eve," they all chimed, as if they had not heard my appeal. "You put on such a great spread. You're a great cook."

Familiar flattery for my holiday setting came from the senior lips seated at my table, giving me a false sense of security. The younger generation rudely interrupted the good feelings with their relentless hostility. The girls angrily stormed from the room, but there was no intervention from the adults once again. No one came to my defense. No one suggested to the girls that this was not the way to speak to others. My family blissfully ignored the antagonism as if it were completely acceptable behavior, and then they continued praising my culinary talents. Tears blurred my vision, and the silence was deafening.

"Why didn't you say anything?" I asked. "The girls shouldn't talk like that."

"Oh, well, no one ever treated me that way," Eleanor idiotically remarked—a ludicrous response from a mother who had raised three teens.

The adults administered no correction for the disrespectful behavior, and in effect they condoned it. Still, the adults kept showering me with compliments, though by this point I felt patronized and insulted by the barrage of praise. Their oblivion was disturbing; they were negligent, removing themselves from responsibility. They were the John Mulholland upper hand displaying accepted behavior with the flattery, while my recruited daughters had the dirty work of insulting me. Apparently, whatever my daughters said or did reflected what the whole family was thinking. I was glimpsing the underhand of the family.

George and Eleanor assumed a similar posture during the search for Joan's killer. They appeared to sit on the sidelines, and gratefully lauded Tim Burke and the Massachusetts State Police for their prowess. The subordinates visibly took the mantle and waged war against the target.

It did not take long for the Bond news to break before ADA Tim Burke lined up another session in front of the grand jury. He had obtained an indictment for Marie's murder, but needed a motive to seal the deal. Burke resumed his secret sessions on February 17, 1983, in the *Commonwealth v. Leonard J. Paradiso,* cause number 043033, for aggravated rape. He lined up some witnesses and was ready to go.

Burke had to hurdle the fact that Paradiso had an alibi witness the night Marie died, so Candy Weyant raised her hand first. Candy was with her boyfriend, and she witnessed Marie turn the corner toward Maverick Street and walk out of sight. She left the scene with Lenny about one in the morning, and the two never saw Marie again. Candy took the fifth on the advice of her lawyer, Walter Underhill, but that probably unfairly worked to the prosecution's advantage. Jurors are instructed that guilt not be implied when a witness exercises their Constitutional rights, but human nature takes over that there is something to hide.

The cocky solicitor trotted Robert Bond in next. The ADA miraculously produced a witness that was not available when he went before the grand jury on March 5, 1982, when he targeted Paradiso for Marie's murder. Burke guided the snitch to recall conversations Bond allegedly had with the suspect while the two were contained at the Charles Street Jail.

"This is what he was telling you?" the sly attorney asked for more.

"Yes," Bond eagerly offered. "He left the Cardinale's Nest, took his girl Candy to her home in Revere. He came back to the bar about eleven."

Bond had gone over and over the details after his interview on January fourteenth when his meeting with the cops was taped. The convicted murderer gave a convincing recitation of the crime that had confused him before. Conveniently, the order of events subtly shifted.

"He tried getting her pantyhose off," Bond regurgitated the massaged story. "He grabbed the scarf from around her neck and choked her. She passed out. He said he had sex with her."

"What was the order of sequence?" a juror astutely asked. "What happened first, the sex act before he choked her?"

"When he choked her, she passed out," Burke's witness explained. "He had sex with her, but then she came to. He grabbed her and tells me about how she is gagging, and her body jumped like hiccups."

The state was there to add rape charges and further their case. Lenny supposedly choked her with a scarf to a state of unconsciousness, then had his way with her. According to this story, the victim was choked not once, but twice. During the interview with the Massachusetts State Police the month before, Bond had only mentioned choking the victim once, after the alleged rape. This new version of the events was more suitable for the charges the prosecutor wanted to lay. A significant added detail furthered the cause. Strangulation was the state's promoted modus operandi, and consistent with other stories the boys lined up. A witch-hunt mentality gripped the city and the purveyors of justice.

"Did you write me a letter?" the deceptive ADA prodded. "When did you write that letter?"

"It was on December 23 to 24," the rat lied, "in that neighborhood."

A prearranged plan to mail the letter to Bond's wife was beyond the convicts' capacity for scheming. He supposedly placed an envelope inside one addressed to Willie Mae, and she was supposed to forward the inner envelope to Tim Burke. Nine days after Burke boasted the inmate's conscience moved him to squeal on Paradiso, he was still waiting for the "break" in the case to arrive.

Trooper Palombo took the warmed seat next, and his badge garnered the confidence of the seated grand jurors.

"I received information from an inmate in jail with Leonard Paradiso," the cop suggested.

"When did Leonard Paradiso go to his parole officer?" Burke slyly inserted.

"In the morning, Monday, August thirteenth," the officer answered without checking what was actually in his records. "The body was identified Monday, approximately 11:30 a.m." Palombo took Burke's lead to depict Paradiso deceptively, panicked and nervous, before the identity of the victim was known at 9:20 a.m. Monday morning.

It took another round, but Burke finally got the desired indictment. The grand jury handed down a true bill for aggravated rape on June 6, 1983. The landslide against the man the Websters suspected in Joan's loss was in motion.

I might have identified the underhand of the family a lot sooner if I'd had a clue what was really going on in Joan's investigation, but the family kept secrets. The Boston legal system of the early 1980s was rife with corruption. The case of the Boston Strangler underscored how an unscrupulous politician gave the public a false sense of security handling a high-profile case. An image spread through Boston, inciting the masses to condemn Albert DeSalvo, but DA Garrett Byrne vilified the wrong man.

This willingness to accuse the wrong person to appease public outcry did not stop with the Boston Strangler. DA Byrne tutored his successor, DA Newman Flanagan. Under the direction of Flanagan, the neophyte assistant, Tim Burke, directed the same stage with new players. The novice prosecutor had only been assigned homicide cases earlier in the fall of 1981, and now some authority transferred an unresolved cold case from another county into Flanagan's office. At the same time that case shifted, the state doubled up their resources, assigning a Suffolk County rookie to Joan's investigation. ADA Tim Burke was nothing more than a puppet delegated the duty of satisfying the public's demand for justice. Leonard Paradiso was just the man they needed to squelch that hunger.

Flanagan's office continued to operate unscrupulously until the Kenneth Spinkston case finally unmasked the illusion of integrity in 1991. A jury convicted Spinkston of murder, but the appeal uncovered misconduct by the state. Flanagan's office had a particular set of skills to handle exculpatory evidence and keep it from the defense. The man responsible was John Kiernan, the head of homicide in Flanagan's office between 1980 and 1988.

"PROSECUTORS CONFLICT OVER SECRET 'SLAY' CASE FILES," made the headlines of the *Boston Herald* on July 15, 1991. "At stake for Suffolk County District Attorney Newman Flanagan is the potential of legal challenges aimed at overturning hundreds of criminal convictions his prosecutors won from 1980 to 1988."

Cabinets behind Kiernan's office door hid the facts to exonerate Spinkston. The so-called "Kiernan File" contained information disclosing other possible motives and evidence, and it was suspected the tactic was routinely practiced in the DA's office. Joan's investigation, unfortunately, fell right into the duplicitous clutches of an underhanded system in Massachusetts, and manipulators delegated responsibility to public servants operating with dubious agendas.

Manufactured cases made the amiable politician Newman Flanagan's statistics look good to voters eager to see justice served quickly and efficiently, but his tactics just multiplied the number of victims. Other cases in the Massachusetts system surfaced too, but were uncovered too late to correct the rampant misconduct of the 1980s in Boston. The authorities circled the wagons when Essex County DA Martha Coakley rejected a review of the Fells Acre case and the travesty of the wrongful convictions from that era. Years later, when Amy Bishop pulled the trigger and killed three coworkers in

Alabama on February 12, 2010, her history revealed a case swept under the rug by Norfolk County DA Bill Delahunt. Bishop fired the shotgun that killed her brother in 1986 when she was 12 years old, but influence shielded the girl from accountability and psychological help. Massachusetts' legal system had been dysfunctional for years. Therefore, with an anonymous call at the height of the state's pretense of jurisprudence, an involved officer's friend threw Paradiso's name into the cesspool that was Boston's brand of justice.

Bloodied bodies had littered the streets in Boston for years. Organized crime held the city in fear, and infected the very departments charged with cleaning it up. Two competing factions left the community caught in their crossfire, and corrupted the enforcement of justice. The mafia ruled from the North End of Boston under the control of the Angiulos, while the growing opposition of the Irish Mob marched to the ruthless dictate of James Whitey Bulger in South Boston. On November 28, 1981, Joan Webster stepped into the chilly night air of a city at war and gridlocked with corruption. The cold climate of the season should not have been an obstacle in the search for the graduate student, but the climate of the policing agencies definitely provided an obstruction.

The FBI headquarters handed down the mandate of eradicating mafia influence across the country, but unfortunately their strategy reinforced the notion that the end always justified the means. The Boston office demonstrated unbridled power to manipulate events to their desired outcome, and Special Agent Dennis Condon was the first to bring informants under the protected umbrella of the agency. The notorious Whitey Bulger, a mobster and one of the FBI's most wanted men, and his associate, Stephen Flemmi, were desirable snitches to undermine mafia competition on the streets. Condon laid the groundwork for the plan on direct orders from J. Edgar Hoover. SA John Connolly, who admitted he admired the notorious "Southie" icon when he was growing up, solidified these plans.

Condon was a good example of the underhand in the Boston FBI. A few years before, he had teamed with SA Paul Rico on another exploit to dismantle justice and contrive a case. The FBI arrested four men for the murder of Edward Deegan. Important facts remained hidden in their folders, and they knowingly pressed wrongful charges against Peter Limone, Henry Tameleo, Joe Salvati, and Louis Greco for the crime. The Feds already knew Joe Barboza was the killer, but he was a protected informant who had cut some squealing deal to get a pass. The forces in charge obstructed the truth for more than three decades before the courts overturned the wrongful convictions and freed the two surviving scapegoats.

Ironically, Condon's career settled him in the seat as Commissioner of Public Safety and Superintendent of the Massachusetts State Police from 1978 to 1980, and he was undersecretary from 1983 to 1991. After he left the FBI, his new job placed him in charge of the Massachusetts State Police, a prime position to influence impressionable officers.

Unfortunately, the persuasive power of these informants could seduce and corrupt law enforcement. Bulger's control over the police was building in 1981 at the time Joan disappeared. The airport, a portal for drug trafficking and an exit for dirty money, was key for Bulger's operations. Therefore, having influence over the detectives assigned to monitor the airport was instrumental to Bulger's success. Another factor for Bulger's success was the influence of his brother, Billy, a state senator who pressured fellow politicians against making necessary justice reforms. Managing agents controlling Boston's office initialed the illicit methods the department deployed in the quest to take down the Angiulos' operations. Special Agent in Charge Lawrence Sarhatt and his successor Special Agent in Charge James Greenleaf affixed their approval for the methods used that protected criminal informants to eradicate the mafia, and their signatures approved methods in the quest for Joan.

New Jersey detectives placed a call to SA George Bertram in Boston on December 3, 1981, and the agent started a file. Personal experience was an advantage, and clued George Webster into how the agency could get a job done. However, years of misguided justice left the bodies buried before the Boston office toppled in disgrace. The intelligence group was in bed with the unsavory and exposed for their part in the pact with the mob. Numerous books have detailed the unholy alliance between the Boston FBI and organized crime that existed during the search for Joan. *Black Mass* by Dick Lehr and Gerald O'Neal, and *Betrayal* by Robert Fitzpatrick and Jon Land revealed the unfathomable level of deception that poisoned the system.

The Massachusetts State Police clashed with the FBI. Legitimate state law enforcement earnestly desired an end to the corruption and an end to Bulger, but leaked tip-offs undermined the continuous efforts to foil the mob leader, an FBI protected player. Insiders shielded plenty of rats to the peril of the public's safety. Troopers had set up surveillance of Bulger's front operation at the Lancaster Street Garage, and photographed a who's who of organized crime paying homage and greenbacks for his favor. Duplicitous Bulger publicly expressed his disdain for the drugs poisoning the city, but officers observed trafficker Frank LePere with a bag full of money at the garage, affirming Bulger's interest in the trade. LePere was a major drug trafficker that operated from Massachusetts to Maine, and anchored his boat south of the city in Marshfield. Profits from the illegal distribution financed a comfortable house by the ocean, and the amiable crook evaded legal consequence for years.

When legitimate law officers finally caught up with him, LePere worked a deal with US Attorney William Weld. In exchange for the evidence LePere provided exposing a corrupted official, Federal Prosecutor David P. Twomey, his sentence was shortened to a meager five years.

It was an era when you could not tell the good guys from the bad ones. The temptation of accessible drugs on the streets padded the pockets of players on both sides of the law. Some people responsible to clean up the streets conducted their own deals under the table before they walked into a courtroom to lock someone else up for the very same crimes. Others indulged behind closed doors, risky behavior if someone walked in, but drugs induced an invincible feeling that overrode their senses. The treachery had benefits for those who went along so long as they were not caught, and people on the inside had a distinct advantage.

Bulger was still at large when Tim Burke, then an eager, young recruit, drafted surveillance warrants to keep an eye on Bulger and get the bad guys off the streets. He hoped to plant bugging devices and eavesdrop on the criminal mind of a menace; he tried to listen in on Bulger's plots. Busting the notorious Bulger would certainly bolster Burke's fledgling career, but leaks spoiled his efforts. According to Burke, rats in the midst compromised every attempt to catch Bulger. People with other agendas always tipped off the mob boss to the impending traps.

DA Flanagan expanded Burke's duties, and the apprentice began arguing homicides in September of 1981. Experience was not a prerequisite for Flanagan when he dropped the Essex County cold case of Marie Iannuzzi on Burke's desk, or when the authorities assigned the rookie the high-profile case of Joan Webster at George Webster's Harvard meeting. ADA Carol Ball was already working on Joan's case out of Middlesex County, but Burke had the backing of Flanagan and Kiernan, so the controlling force suspiciously delegated the job to him. Teaming the malleable recruit with the seasoned officer on both cases created the image that no stone would be left unturned. Unfortunately, Trooper Andrew Palombo and ADA Tim Burke were set on a course that presumed a man's guilt.

Burke made a name for himself in the DA's office and later in his private practice. The more he spewed allegations in his obsession of solving Joan's case, the more his name was in print. The case definitely bolstered his notoriety and his career. However, Burke had nothing to support the premise that Leonard Paradiso was responsible for Joan's disappearance. Burke ignored the obvious facts in the Iannuzzi files, and justified misconduct in one case to project an image of guilt in the other.

His labors, however misguided, apparently paid off financially. Beginning in 1992, Burke signed land deals with the Early Bird Realty Trust, the LePere family trust, and bought a mansion by the sea and adjacent properties in Marshfield, Massachusetts. The house built with dirty, drug money now belonged to the very prosecutor whose failed warrants targeted the crime boss Frank LePere had paid off. Greedy landowners filed a suit in 1998 over a property dispute. The LePere trust and Tim Burke were among the plaintiffs claiming entitlement to a multimillion-dollar beach along the Massachusetts coast. More than fourteen years later, good citizens of the town are still fighting to keep the Rexhame Beach public.

The Joan Webster mystery enlisted the services and tax dollars of the Commonwealth on a level only surpassed by such cases as the elusive Whitey Bulger. Numerous state and Federal agencies participated in the hunt and were cajoled by George Webster, a bureaucrat with CIA training. The shady practices of the agencies involved were still hidden when Joan landed at Logan. Enforcers carried out their methods with precision when Joan disappeared. Each questionable technique demonstrated the excessively pragmatic mentality that the desired result was worth any method, no matter how unethical.

These players were supposed to be looking for Joan. Each had their own particular set of skills, and time exposed each of them for how they went about getting a job done. The combined forces of the FBI, the Massachusetts State Police, the Suffolk County DA's office, ITT security, and the CIA expertise of the parents could not find the answers for what happened to the petite student who landed in Boston. Those in charge derailed or discounted the sincere efforts by numerous others looking for Joan. The state never filed charges, and even Burke admits there was no real evidence connecting his suspect to Joan. A monster avoided detection, and denied this beautiful, young woman her bright and promising future. A line of defense still sticks to an implausible story that obstructs her due justice.

CHAPTER 11

Sinister Laughter

She had gone to the party against my objection.

As I came down the stairs, the pack of teenage boys went silent and scrambled to hide their bottles. It was a freezing February night, and the adolescent boys, waiting for the show, greatly outnumbered the handful of scantily clad girls. My daughter had feigned a Spanish assignment that morning in order to have the video camera ready for the main event. The teenagers transformed a plastic baby pool into a mud pit, a stage for the girls to wrestle each other for the boys' entertainment.

"You did not have permission to come to this party," I quietly said to my daughter. "Get your things; we're going home."

My mouth never opened on the twenty-minute drive back to our house, but my embarrassed child's tone escalated several notches every mile. She retreated to the computer when we got home, but the parental surveillance captured the manner my daughter rebelled against "no." The online chats were really my first sense of the gossip that swirled to undermine my parenting.

"Did you have an angry tone in your voice?" one of the male spectators asked online.

"Not at the beginning," she venomously replied. "She just hit me when I got home."

"Does she actually hit you?" Gabe asked.

"Ummm...yha..." she contrived. "I thought we'd been over this."

"She would have been mad at me," she apologized to the adolescent host. "She would have done the same shit to me (if you know what I mean), for another reason if I hadn't gone.

"Don't tell anyone," she insisted.

Over time, I heard myself labeled everything in the book. Plans were set out in detail in the basement closet the girls set up as a command center. The objectives, in the premeditated plot to force me out of their lives, pledged an allegiance to their father.

"Find things to use against Mom."

"Don't do anything she says. Only do what Dad asks us to do."

My sleep was constantly disrupted, loud music pounded throughout the house, and my children took every opportunity to provoke a fight. I was a prisoner of war in my own house. It was impossible not to be human and have moments of weakness. Twice, two and a half years apart, my daughter pushed me to the point of slapping her. In hindsight, God was thankfully monitoring any impulse, and restrained my reflexes under the unrelenting assault. The conditions were intolerable, no respite and no respect. Isolation and depression set in as I struggled to hold my ground and my sense of self.

It never occurred to me that the elders went along with the plot; to my face, they praised me as a wonderful mother. Nor, did I understand how wide the family's destructive brush was painting me with a monstrous image. When a parent revealed the false rumors the girls spread with their friends, Sarah O'Brien dismissed my concern.

"I haven't heard anything like that," Sarah responded as if she did not believe they would do such a thing. The fact that I had their accusations in writing was irrelevant in the counselor's opinion after hearing the girls' one-sided stories.

Nevertheless, my girls' journals opened the floodgates of the destructive forces working against me. One confabulated beating had me jumping out from behind a wall to pin my daughter's face to the ground. Grabbing her hair, I allegedly slammed her head into the floor repeatedly, and left her dazed and struggling to breathe. My daughter described sinister laughter in the horror she had played in her mind, a scene comparable to the unverified terror spewed by a woman in Boston named Patty Bono. This horrid pounding would have put my child in the emergency room and me, rightfully, in jail if it had really happened. No doctor or hospital records existed to verify the assertions she was spreading at school, and there were no injuries to question at swim practice each day. This never happened.

People whispered, but the mandate that punctuated the gossip was "don't tell," and silenced the feedback I needed to defend myself. I was being driven from my children with intentional malice and discarded.

As this nightmare spiraled out of control, Steve's words echoed in my mind: "We just want you to be gone."

The phone rang at the Saugus police station the day after the Websters increased the reward money in January 1982.

"I was scared to death; he threatened me if I didn't do what he asked." The female caller did not give her name to the desk sergeant taking the call. "I've known him probably as far back as I can remember. Officer, I just know he killed Marie Iannuzzi."

She described a horrifying assault that she allegedly suffered at the hands of Leonard Paradiso late in the summer of 1972. However, it was a decade later, in January 1982, when she placed the call to the Saugus Police Department and implicated a man she had known her entire life. Paradiso pushed his clam cart every summer for the North End festivals that filled the streets, and the neighborhood knew the boatman spent his happiest moments navigating Boston waters.

Everyone in the North End neighborhood knew the wholesale, shellfish merchant had been a suspect in the 1979 murder of Marie Iannuzzi, but Bono suspiciously waited more than two years to come forward. The caller replayed her alleged melodrama from the summer of 1972, but added nothing to support her insinuations about Marie's case. Apparently, she implied that if he did it to her, he must have killed Marie.

As soon as she hung up, she dialed the phone again and repeated Leonard Paradiso's name to George and Eleanor Webster.

"He said that he would throw me in the ocean," the unidentified woman sniveled to Joan's parents, "and threatened no one would ever find me. I think he has something to do with your daughter's disappearance."

Late in the summer of 1972, Lenny supposedly struck up a conversation with Patty Bono at the Jib Bar. The story continued that he convinced Bono that he did not feel well, and the notorious tease purportedly found herself parked in his car somewhere near the piers. Without provocation, Bono claimed the aggressor started beating her face and left a large bump from the gun he pressed to her head. According to the young woman, she was threatened within an inch of her life if she did not succumb to Lenny's advances. Water was a key element of the profile investigators were developing against Paradiso, and Patty obliged with a foreboding tale that fit the image. Paradiso ostensibly warned her that no one would ever find her in the ocean.

Conveniently, at least for the state, no one was around to corroborate her ten-year-old story. Bono apparently licked her own wounds instead of going to the doctor or the emergency room to mend the purported broken bones in her battered face, and she never reported the assault to the police. She happened to have another childhood acquaintance named Carmen Tammaro who brandished a badge. Instead of the law, Patty supposedly preferred for the wise guys, hoods controlling the North End streets, to settle her vendetta. If Bono was believable, thugs beat Paradiso to a pulp and warned him never to show his face in the North End again. Regardless, the amiable peddler continued shucking his clams year after year during the parades of patron saints.

A year had passed since Patty Bono placed her anonymous calls to drop the tin dime on Leonard Paradiso. Her uniformed friend from the North End, Sgt. Carmen Tammaro, interrogated a witness that told an incredible tale of two murders that craftily duplicated Patty's phoned accusations. Bond's revelations became the breaking news on every station and every edition hot off the presses on January 28, 1983. The story had remarkable similarities to other reports; Bono alleged Paradiso threatened to dump her in the ocean, and Bond said that was precisely what Paradiso confessed doing to Joan. It wasn't a surprise Bono was available for the state police when they appealed for anyone with information to call.

Two unreliable sources, Patty Bono and Robert Bond, had now fingered Paradiso for Marie's murder and Joan's disappearance. The cops in charge had a full year after Patty's calls to find things to use against Lenny and build a case. The objective to "find things" was easy for an undercover cop who worked with informants digging up dirt. In this case, his superior aided and abetted the story, targeting a familiar patsy he grew up with in the North End. A year after Patty's calls, leaks plastered Robert Bond's allegations throughout the media, and a confidential source called the same assertions in to the Boston office of the FBI. Hoping for a scoop, reporters sought their reliable sources: Palombo, Tammaro, and Burke. They were not disappointed; the trio rewarded reporters with a suspect on whom they labeled everything in the book. Reporters dangled the Websters' reward money in the next sentence of every story, and the phone began to ring.

Tammaro's subordinate, Trooper Palombo, was in charge of the cases and worked with the witnesses coming out of the woodwork. Patty Bono alleged a ten-year-old assault with nothing to back it up, but the boys had something to work with. Bono named two defenders that supposedly defended her honor.

"I went to some friends of mine in the North End, Willie Fopiano and Tony Rome." Bono provided names that now conveniently lived out of state.

Willie Fopiano was a notorious wise guy who had lived life on the edge before he was fifteen years old. He would have been a familiar figure coupled with Joanne White, the attractive waitress Fopiano dated, to a wannabe at the Jib Lounge. Willie and his cohorts were well known in the area, but Tony Rome, Bono's other supposed guardian, never made the named roster of hoods that hung out with Willie.

During the spring and summer of 1972, Fopiano had a target on his back. Gang wars left bodies littering the streets, and Willie packed a piece and laid low with his friends before his planned move to Las Vegas. However, Willie stepped in to defend the kids at St. Anthony's schoolyard from the menaces he detested, and an injury delayed his relocation. In May of 1972, Willie took on four drug pushers single-handedly, but the scuffle broke a bone in his right hand that needed immediate casting. Surgery followed in July, because the break simply would not heal, and doctors inserted a pin. "Undesirables" heeded Fopiano and the fellows he caroused with when they cleaned out the neighborhood, and there was no hesitation getting a job done. Willie detailed his own account of the times in *The Godson*, but there is no account of defending Patty Bono, or bothering with an amiable, clam peddler named Lenny Paradiso. He was too busy with problems of his own.

The ink had barely dried on the headlines when another rat, "Death Row Tony" Pisa, slithered from his hole to dial the Middlesex County DA's office.

"This guy Paradiso that's been on the news," Pisa told Middlesex ADA Tom Reilly. "I know this guy. He killed that Iannuzzi broad, and he killed that grad student."

Lines lit up, and ADA Carol Ball fed ADA Burke another unreliable source with an unverified story. Tony, otherwise known as Ralph Anthony Pisa, was well acquainted with Leonard Paradiso and recognized an opportunity when he saw one. A judge had sentenced Pisa to death for the September 9, 1969, murder of George Deane, but opportunity and chance ultimately whittled down his sentence to second-degree murder. Tony was a smooth operator; he played the system and learned the law in his caged world. He had filed seven motions of his own to redress his case, but Middlesex County opposed every appeal, and the court denied them. Pisa was a self-styled jailhouse lawyer, and fellow inmates turned to him for legal assistance. It just so happened, the con had helped Paradiso draft an appeal for the conviction of the 1973 Constance Porter assault. Pisa honed his skill and had the confidence of a population locked away with only their troubles to keep them company. The combination made him quite an asset, and a valuable employee to defense lawyer John Cavicchi. The inmate referred clients and drafted briefs.

Paradiso crossed paths with Pisa in Norfolk Prison in 1976, where the state incarcerated both men. The two prisoners worked at an off-site auto shop, a rehabilitation facility for the inmates. Pisa was still doing time when the parole board released Paradiso on May 10, 1978. Calendar pages turned to January 1983, when the Bond revelations saturated the news and Pisa recognized the clam peddler. "Death Row Tony" had the whole system pulling strings and petitioning on his behalf because of the unsubstantiated accusations he fed the salivating authorities about Paradiso.

Governor Dukakis's furlough program was at work again, and opened the door for a convicted murderer for Christmas 1979. Pisa enjoyed the warmth of the holiday with his employer, John Cavicchi, when there was a knock at the door. Leonard Paradiso handed his attorney a bucket of lobsters on Christmas Eve. Lenny had retained the lawyer for $500 in August 1979, when the parolee became a suspect for the murder of Marie Iannuzzi, the victim strangled and dumped on August 12, 1979. Cavicchi arranged a polygraph with a well-respected examiner in Boston on August 28, 1979.

"He passed the polygraph. In my professional opinion, Paradiso's telling the truth." Cavicchi, the attorney with a working relationship with Tony Pisa, tucked William J. LaParl's report in his files.

According to Tony, the two stepped outside Cavicchi's home on Christmas Eve, and Paradiso confessed to Marie's murder. Lenny allegedly begged Pisa to intervene with Cavicchi to handle the case. The jailhouse lawyer remained mum about the unproven admission until 1982, when the media perpetuated the presumed connection between Paradiso and Joan all over the news.

"Death Row Tony" knew his legal history well and dramatized his story with details from the John Webster murder case of 1850. The landmark case became an instruction manual of sorts for every criminal case since—including this one. The moment Dr. George Parkman was reported missing, suspicion turned to Harvard instructor John Webster, because he happened to owe Parkman money. A janitor found dissected body parts in Webster's lab, but even more horrifying and irrefutable was the partial jaw found in Webster's furnace; dental work was identified as Parkman's. A jury convicted Webster based on the circumstantial evidence, and the state hanged him within weeks of the verdict.

Prosecutors out of two offices envisioned Pisa pacing at the front of the courtroom and preaching his gospel. "It happened once; Paradiso messed up in the disposal of Marie, but as we can see, our good friend Lenny's hobby was well-honed by the time he encountered Joan Webster." The fact Pisa said he tutored Paradiso on the 1850 Webster case in October 1976, when Pisa helped Lenny with an appeal, was too subtle to raise suspicion. Paradiso flunked Webster 101 when he allegedly murdered Marie Iannuzzi, but went to the head of the class when he got rid of Joan.

The effect Pisa had bringing the 1850 Webster case into the public's conscious was subliminal; the public contemplated a victim with the same name where, coincidentally, there was not a body. Bond's whopper supposed the ocean swallowed Joan into its watery depths, and there was no chance of recovery or closure. ADA Burke was completely obsessed to prove Paradiso's guilt, and relentlessly pressed forward. The goal of condemning Leonard Paradiso for Joan's disappearance swelled without any human remains or evidence.

The 1850 case involved prominent, well-respected citizens, and the case waved the familiar name "Webster" in front of the public. In the highly publicized case, money was the root of the discourse between Parkman and Webster, and sensational events gripped the community. Webster denied any guilt and cast suspicions on a more vulnerable target—Ephraim Littlefield. Littlefield was the unfortunate janitor, the first person to discover the morbid scene in Webster's lab, and observed Webster's unusual behavior. Anonymous letters, dredged bodies of water, and wild speculation fueled a media frenzy.

The similarities between this case and Joan's were haunting, especially compared with the missing student's story now blazoned on every front page. Boston Harbor failed to claim either body, and dental records revealed both victims' names. Webster's confession came as a last desperate act to save his own life. The offender revealed he had struck a fatal blow to Dr. Parkman's head—Webster was guilty of murder. The reality of the 1850 landmark case came to the shock and consternation of the public, and Webster's wife and daughters suffered in silence.

"Death Row Tony" was only ten months from a parole opportunity when his fortune flashed across every New England television screen. The law made no guarantees he would ever gain a release, though luck and manipulation had dealt him the opportunity. He had finished his book manuscript, *I'll Prove My Innocence, Or Die Trying*, but no one bought into his story; then he saw another opening to get out. Tony brought his tale to Middlesex County in February 1983, and stood before the very same suits who previously argued against the felon's appeals to escape. Pisa portrayed himself as a man of conscience, and his thick moustached lip concealed any detectable twitch of deception as he carried on with his story.

On December 18, 1981, a payphone rang out from the bank of monitored phones at Bay State Prison. Correction officers probably heard birthday greetings from the family on a taped phone, but Pisa delivered a more demonic call for the state's case.

"Look, I'd been pretty sure we were talking about the 1850 John Webster case, not the recent Joan Webster case," Pisa told the public defenders. "He said they only found her purse."

Supposedly, Paradiso had communicated an implied confession about the missing Harvard graduate student in a way others could hear if they checked the recordings.

"Paradiso reminded me I had a family out there," the convicted cold-blooded killer shuddered. "He warned me to keep my mouth shut."

The clam peddler allegedly silenced the convicted murderer, threatening harm to his family and terrorized the felon more than the myriad of hardened criminals he lived with over the past dozen years. When Paradiso became the leading news story, Pisa could no longer keep silent, and he went on record professing his kindly concern for the women of Boston. Tony was sitting pretty.

Yet another pathetic squawker crept out of the woodwork soon after the public consumed the image of murder at sea. Janet McCarthy watched the evening news with her mother when Bond's supposed "break" in the case flashed Paradiso's image on the screen. Every news story reinforced the Webster reward for information.

Janet stuck her thumb out on July 10, 1980, for a lift to Revere.

"Need a ride? Hop in." The driver pulled away from the curb on Hanover Street in the North End.

"It was a fairly new, big, white four-door," Janet told the police. "I got part of the number; it was a dealer plate."

Janet escaped the driver's unwanted advances and flagged down a car on Winthrop Parkway.

"Can you take me to the police?" the frightened female asked the driver who stopped. Joseph Alvoarra, Jr. obliged the distraught, young woman.

Sgt. James Russo and Det. William Gannon noticed Janet had been drinking, and her account had some inconsistencies. A chubby, dark-haired man in his early thirties picked Janet up and drove to a spot past the last house on Winthrop Avenue. The young woman struggled with her attacker and managed to escape the forced advances. She scaled the white concrete wall to hail down a passing motorist. A good Samaritan took McCarthy to the Winthrop police station where dispatched Revere officers took down the report. Russo and Gannon observed the girl's messed hair and that her knee was bleeding.

"Take a look at the mug shots," the officers directed. "Do you see a picture of him?"

"Um...no, I don't think so." Janet studied the pictures, but could not find a face that matched her assailant.

"C'mon honey, you've gotta give us some kind of clue here—help us help you. Help us catch the guy!"

Unpleasant memories lingered of an unresolved night she was hitchhiking, and her festering desire to get even with someone, anyone, was sweetened with the promise of financial gain when Paradiso's picture stared back from the television set. The young woman's mother could not resist the siren song of the dollar bill, and called the number on the screen, 617-569-3777, the Massachusetts State Police Detective Bureau at Logan Airport. Trooper Andrew Palombo took control and interviewed another nail in the state's story. The open-ended incident was something he could work with, and he had a way of helping people remember.

Trooper Palombo filtered what he heard, but the incident was simply too distorted from Janet's confused account given under the influence. How could authorities possibly twist this into a clear recitation of Paradiso's guilt?

By time Palombo was done with the witness, the image of a terrorizing night emerged to hang another charge on the Websters' suspect. McCarthy was suddenly able to clearly identify Paradiso as the man who had picked her up in the summer of 1980.

"He hit me in the face four or five times," the young woman recalled for the zealous prosecutor. "I was cut down here on my mouth. My mouth was bleeding."

"Does this look like the car you got into?" Burke handed her a photograph of a two-door, yellow vehicle.

"Well, maybe," was her ambiguous reply. "I'm not sure; it was dark out."

The Suffolk County prosecutor listened intently when the witness came forward in February 1983. Janet's suddenly vivid memory fit with Burke's theory. According to McCarthy, Paradiso drove the first car that stopped when she was fleeing down the roadway. Minute details spiced her recollections even down to Paradiso's sinister laughter as he drove off into the night. The refreshed version had two men stopping to rescue the distressed woman stumbling along the roadside.

"They took me to their place in Winthrop to clean up," she devised, "then I called the police."

Spokesmen leaked the "break" in Joan's case to the public, and the speculation diverted the investigation to the unyielding waters in search of the missing graduate student. Three questionable witnesses, Bono, Bond, and Pisa came forward. They were the only witnesses that asserted Paradiso was guilty of both Marie Iannuzzi's murder and Joan Webster's disappearance. Willing participants working with Trooper Palombo and Sgt. Tammaro added fodder that fully supported Burke's ultimate modus operandi. The core group tagged Paradiso as a sexual predator who preyed on women, particularly those with long, brown hair, and enticed them into his vehicle. The women trotted out were generally hitchhikers or young women with promiscuous reputations, with the notable exception of Burke's obsession—Joan Webster. The press had a field day.

At the same time these lowlifes were surfacing to point an accusing finger at Paradiso, another witness went into hiding. Jean Day had dealt a heavy blow to Burke's case against Paradiso when she testified at the grand jury on March 5, 1982. The recollections about her stepsister's murder clearly pointed to the very suspect whom Trooper Palombo befriended. Trauma seared these events deep into her memory, and the recollections she told police implicated her sister's boyfriend, David Doyle.

Suddenly, headlines declared a "break" in Joan's case heralding the alleged dual-confession about Marie, and Jean felt the heat. The grieving sibling became a victim herself. A purposeful aggressor knocked on the door on a chilling day soon after the Bond story churned. Jean hesitated and remained silent, hoping the person would leave; she did not want to open the door after the harassing phone calls she had received. The visitor knocked again, then smashed in the locked barrier. The intruder terrified the murder victim's sister, pushing and shoving her to the ground. Swift kicks to the head followed the perpetrator's fists and broke bones in her face. The intimidating force delivered his warning, then left Jean shaking in fear. She picked up her toddler from day care the next afternoon and went into hiding.

"Paradiso has threatened Miss Day," Burke maliciously suggested. He broadcast the source of Jean's malaise was, of course, Lenny, who was sitting in jail. However, Jean confided her torment to a neighbor she trusted. A much different menace plagued the witness.

CHAPTER 12

In the Dark

"You need to turn off the music so we can talk," Carol Metzger, the family's counselor, requested.

"What?" Headphones stuck in their ears piped in the loud music, drowning out every word.

"The music! Could you turn it off for a bit?" the frustrated advocate repeated.

The girls perched themselves uncomfortably on Carol Metzger's couch and rolled their eyes in unison at her request. Their oath of silence rendered the counselor's efforts futile. The letter to God had escalated their rebellion. The wall between my terrified girls and me was impenetrable. My daughter never denied writing the letter; I suppose she thought that would be an absurd denial, but she vigorously reinterpreted the letter instead.

"It doesn't mean what you think it means," she said. She was backtracking, perhaps because she was embarrassed or confused, or perhaps because she dreaded repercussions from the family if she did not.

What was it, precisely, tearing our family apart? Counseling was going nowhere. There were no answers, so Carol suggested another professional to work with the girls. The heeded recommendation gave the girls their own space to open up and confide, at least that was the hope. Sarah O'Brien began her operation of untangling the web, but her methods fragmented communication channels even further, unfortunately.

The system was a disaster. The disjointed team communicated everything second hand, or sometimes not at all. Family counselors provided very little feedback, and I was kept largely in the dark about what transpired in their sessions. The dictate was that the girls would not speak to the advocate if she also spoke to me. With little accountability or information, this secretive method opened the floodgates, allowing the girls to spew anything without verification and the arrangement blocked a path for me to respond. The letter to God was a point of concern, and the author acknowledged, again, that she wrote it, but only with feeble explanations.

"She signed a statement, Eve," Steve exhaled. "She said nothing happened. Move on."

I wanted to believe that. Nevertheless, somehow, Steve portrayed himself as the victim while the three females in the house were all reaching desperate levels wanting to die.

My angry child faced me in one session. Tears were streaming down her flushed face.

"I can't believe you said that Dad killed Tillie! How could you say such a thing?" she yelled.

The accusation hurt her deeply, but it was not true. Steve painted himself as the victim again, making a false assertion of things I never said, and the girls took the posture to protect him. Tillie was a nine-year-old black lab who had been a strong, healthy dog. The vet put her companion to sleep only a short time before Tillie's condition appeared, and Steve struggled with grief. The vet put Tillie to sleep a few days after a sudden onset of bizarre symptoms that left the dog unable to stand. The vet ran extensive tests, but could not find anything conclusive. The black Labrador had an instantaneous loss of muscle control in her legs, and an enlarged rectum that appeared overnight in March of 1991. I accepted the vet's hypothesis of Myasthenia Gravis, lacking any other explanation for the healthy dog's sudden decline.

The profile constructed around Leonard Paradiso included rumors of animal abuse, but Joan's case had died down for a time and was the furthest thing from my mind. That kind of history is often foreboding behavior of an offender's future bad acts, so the allegations fit with the state's modus operandi for Paradiso. When bizarre maladies surfaced with the family pet, the insinuation hurled at Paradiso about torturing a cat was not something I was aware of. Now, Steve offensively planted poisoned seeds with my daughter, suggesting I accused him of killing a dog the vet had put to sleep.

I pleaded with both counselors' for help. Sarah O'Brien and Carol Metzger both recognized that the false accusations were very destructive, but failed to dig deeper into the vilification of a mother under attack.

"We had another dog that had a sudden onset of strange symptoms," I anxiously worried.

"You mean you think Steve did something to the dogs?" Sarah dismissed in disbelief.

"I don't know," I answered in all seriousness, "but I have the vet records."

The circumstances were similar. Minnie was a five-and-a-half-year-old, spayed lab that suddenly had an inexplicable enlarged vulva in August 2000, soon after her male companion was put down. Steve struggled with grief once again. The modus operandi crafted in Boston many years earlier was not an explanation I considered, that is, until Steve maliciously distorted my child's thinking.

An underhanded, invisible force drove a wedge deeper between my girls and me. I uncovered journal entries that raised more red flags about the distressing letter to God. I gave copies of the journal pages to Sarah; the entries corroborated the allegations in the letter about the girls' father. My child continued to sit in the hot seat to answer questions, but snitching was not acceptable in the family. The elders expected Websters to remain quiet about personal matters, to brush things under the rug, and never allow any embarrassment to come to the family.

"You're a whistleblower," Eleanor had coldly pronounced, "just like Cherry Provost."

My mother-in-law apparently did not like certain qualities in my character; it struck me as odd from a mother who still appeared to be looking for answers about Joan. She had watched my principled backbone to confront issues for years, but was not so happy to have it in the midst of the family.

Steve's ploy, shifting my daughter to a new counselor's sofa, widened the divide between my girls and me. Ari Gleckman took over the case under the pretense my daughter maneuvered the change. Sarah viewed the change of couches as stealing a patient, but was unaware Steve was the one who manipulated the shift.

"Ms. Webster came to me," Gleckman disclosed, "at the suggestion and referral of her father."

"I must be worth nothing," my daughter had numbly told him.

"An effective psychologist should not sit and question the veracity of what is being reported." Gleckman arrogantly ignored other input from those already involved with my family. He was easily swayed by the image of a hapless father.

"What do I do?" Steve lamented, throwing his hands up in the air.

"My heart goes out to you, Steve," the so-called doctor swallowed. "Eve is probably struggling with mental health issues."

It seemed obvious why Steve switched counselors; he clearly had found someone more sympathetic to his side of the story. The shift took place on December 6, 2004, before the divorce was final, but

Steve had named Sarah in the mediation agreement as the counselor he relied on for recommendations. What I did not know was that he had colluded with Sarah O'Brien during divorce proceedings to write his lawyer a letter, one that deferred to the girls whether they ever had contact with me. However, when Sarah was no longer useful to him, the girls' father covertly ousted her in favor of a therapist that Steve could control. The John Mulholland trickery paralleled Joan's case when the controlling force secretly shifted responsibility to Suffolk County.

Gleckman raised his right hand in a deposition on May 13, 2008, and swore to tell the truth. He was deeply concerned for my daughter; she was a troubled, young woman who did not know what was real. She struggled with disconnection, and she contemplated suicide from the trauma unfairly and undeservedly thrust upon her life. Aunt Joan was not a frequent topic, but my daughter's fear of the subject was an indicator to me that something was hidden.

"When she would bring that up, it was out of concern." Gleckman recalled the discussions with my daughter about Steve's murdered sister. "She was concerned that there might one day be a publication or legal matter that she could be drawn into, or forced to interact with her mom, something she wanted to avoid at all cost."

The subject of my daughter's felony allegations shaped the situation, and the newest counselor aped Steve's words in his defense. When my daughter shifted to a new couch, I placed a call to the so-called doctor. His rude and dismissive attitude reflected the distortions he had heard about me, but I informed him of my name change and a scheduled appointment. His lack of memory when I arrived was immediately rectified, and I was respectful of his wishes not to tape our session. Regardless, the meeting was twisted into one of deceit, suggesting I had tricked the therapist into the encounter. Remember that according to the plan, I was not supposed to talk to the counselor. I earnestly outlined my fears in a brief forty-five-minute session, and Gleckman stated he would tell my daughter I was a concerned and caring mother. The two communications were his only contact with me, and certainly not a foundation to play God in our lives. Our inability to solve the problem deepened my dread about what was held over my children.

News clippings filled our scrapbooks with the murder mystery in the family, but counselors had no concept of the extraordinary case. My daughter felt too much pressure to keep me alive, but the presumption was that the risk was from me. Gleckman rolled his eyes and gestured his shock over the outrageous allegations he had heard about me, but without detailing specifics. He admitted he

never verified what he'd heard, but proceeded to speciously pro-
nounce I had abused my daughter for years. Gleckman gave a disturbing performance, but the performance undoubtedly pleased my
ex-husband. I glanced across the conference room table during the
deposition, and Steve met my eyes with a cold, emotionless stare.
Image management required spreading false perceptions to discredit
any effort to deal with the terrorized expressions documented by my
children. Deflect the blame. Blame the victim. Spread lies, manipulate, and stall. These patterns had happened before when the family
pursued a suspect for Joan's disappearance.

During the intense search for Joan, the Newark FBI office and
the Websters strategized another angle, but they were not likely to
find Joan with this effort. The Feds collected information, at the parents' request, to submit a missing person Interpol Blue Notice. Joan
had been lost well over a year, but the collective intelligence thinking
lagged far behind. If a perpetrator abducted their daughter and
whisked her out of the country, any trail was now cold. It was not surprising the Blue Notice, initiated on February 8, 1983, didn't produce
any results, but it has left unanswered questions. Why was there a
delay? The notice finally crossed the wires on March 3, 1983, and
absorbed yet another Federal agency in the search for Joan, this time
internationally.

Robert Bond was the witness ADA Tim Burke needed to codify
the Iannuzzi case and move forward. The fortuitous coincidence, or
so it seemed, was that the felon also satisfied Joan's case. Burke
packed his bags with Joan's files and traveled to Quantico on March
28, 1983. SA Roger DePue had already outlined a profile based on
conjectured scenarios in April 1982. Now, headquarters sat down to
strategize with the zealous prosecutor to meet the goals in his case.

Police arrested Paradiso on July 6, 1982, on charges stemming
from the Iannuzzi murder. Witnesses piled up against him with dubious claims, and the press perpetuated the images authorities fed
them. However, it was nearly nine months later, and the team
neglected to issue any warrants to substantiate the allegations or further the case. Lurking in the back of their minds was an obsessed presumption Paradiso had torn Joan from loved ones, but they lacked
any evidence to connect him to the murder.

The grand jury had presented the conniving, young lawyer a
preview of the challenges he faced to convict Paradiso of Marie Iannuzzi's murder. Law enforcement had developed a statement from
Bond's convoluted recitation. The task now was for the department
to go out and "prove" the statement to be true, and find someone to

blame for Joan's loss. Having Bond's falsified statement placed blinders on the department, focusing their attention in all the wrong places, and leading the case astray for years.

First thing on the list under the Iannuzzi charges was establishing that Lenny was in town when Joan disappeared. Lenny had spent Thanksgiving in 1981 with the Weyants, made an appearance in bankruptcy court, and had metal splinters in his finger x-rayed at Lynn Hospital on November 30, 1981. Regardless, Trooper Palombo traveled to Maine to "prove" Paradiso was not in the Pine Tree State in between on Saturday night. Palombo also made several trips to the emergency room to check the film of the small particles embedded in Paradiso's left index finger. The team found things, chicken feed, and called it evidence to weave craftily into their version of the plot.

The same day Palombo verified his suspect was available, Tim Burke claimed he met the Websters for the first time. By his own account, Burke consoled the grieving parents on April 5, 1983, and told them about the new insights generated by Bond's testimony.

"I think Joan is lost to you," Burke wrote about their supposed first meeting in his book.

"Thank you for being honest with us," George said, according to the author. "Sgt. Tammaro told us you all felt there was little hope."

However, in his book, *The Paradiso Files*, he conveniently forgot the fact that higher-ups assigned him to the case in February 1982, at the meeting called by the Websters, or the frequent residence the parents took up at the Sheraton. Eleanor had sent clippings for weeks about the "break" in the case, and they were fully engaged in every aspect from the start. Burke's ludicrous contention was that he met the Websters for the first time in April 1983, and he depicted them as gullible parents drifting in the dark. Burke followed his ridiculous assertion, claiming the family abdicated Joan's justice, during their introduction, for the state's shot at Marie's.

The date was significant though, and it is likely the Websters had a meeting with the prosecutor that day for an update. The tenderfoot in Flanagan's office had just returned from a strategy meeting with the Feds in Quantico. A new ripple was about to emerge in pursuit of the man the Websters suspected, the name suggested in two anonymous calls made by Sgt. Tammaro's childhood friend. In addition, the collaborators needed a plan to meet the terms dictated by a convicted murderer in Middlesex County. The team heavily greased the wheels of injustice.

"Is there anything we can do to help Marie's case?" Eleanor asked, according to Burke, what the family could do. Maybe, there were things the state could not do that the Websters could, but they did not want it to look like intervention.

Paradiso helplessly bided his time behind bars for almost nine months on the Iannuzzi charges before the establishment got around to drafting a warrant. Trooper Andrew Palombo was in charge of the case, and he laid out the arguments to scavenge for things to use against Lenny.

"I am familiar with many procedures criminals use to avoid detection," Palombo told the court.

After safeguarded documents surfaced, an untended alternate meaning of his ominous statement became apparent. Corruption was rampant in Boston; the police routinely facilitated criminals to avoid detection. Palombo commingled the two cases he was charged to resolve, and Joan Webster became a part of the Iannuzzi case in documents filed with the court. Then he lied.

"On January 5, 1983, Assistant District Attorney Timothy M. Burke received a letter from Robert L. Bond," the bearded man falsely told the court.

Palombo went on to mislead the court that Burke had arranged a meeting between Bond, the Massachusetts State Police, and himself after receiving the inmate's correspondence. The warrant did not disclose the meeting on January tenth, the date the letter was actually mailed. The malleable ADA was absent when the "official" inquisition took place at the Suffolk County Courthouse.

"On or about January 14, 1983," the trooper swore in his affidavit, "the meeting took place at the courthouse."

Trooper Palombo swore, under the pain and penalty of perjury, that ADA Tim Burke received informant Robert Bond's letter on January 5, 1983. The lead cop sat in the crammed room at the courthouse on January fourteenth when his boss taped plans to intercept the letter they expected from Bond. The snitch admitted mailing the letter only three days before the taped inquest. The state constructed the foundation of their investigation on deceit.

The undercover cop who wrote the petition referred to two written documents: the letter Burke falsely claimed he had on the fourth or fifth, and notes Bond allegedly scribbled and produced days after the interview. The false, written statement miraculously cleared up the vague and confused elements of Bond's tale of two murders. The evidence the court relied on was shaped after the interview; enforcers met with Bond again on January seventeenth to go over the statement, and they ignored the information already in police files.

Palombo outlined Joan's case in detail in the warrant, but the trooper barely mentioned Marie at all. Even though there were no charges filed in Joan's case, Palombo sought "proof" to support her case instead of Marie's. The sly, undercover cop wanted to find a 50-millimeter shell, a casing, a plug, or a projectile; Paradiso identified the shell as the source of the splinters he had x-rayed two days after Joan's fateful landing. He told doctors the shell went off when he was polishing it on the grind wheel in the Weyants' basement.

"It went off like a cherry bomb," he said to the attending physician. The projected metal particles were, in fact, consistent with his explanation, not the state's. Nevertheless, a judge approved the warrant on April 25, 1983, and the boots goose-stepped to Revere in force.

The troops swarmed the Weyents' home where Lenny had a room. Palombo assigned Trooper Bill Johnson to look in the basement, and directed Sgt. Dave Moran to scour the first floor with Trooper Barrett. Trooper Flaherty, Trooper MacDonald, and Trooper Eastman all spread out on the second floor of the modest home. Trooper Eastman and Trooper Johnson migrated to the attic after they finished their first assignment. Meanwhile, Trooper Flynn and Sgt. Tammaro roamed from room to room sizing up the goods. The force made a thorough search. The haul included a 50-mm bullet, evidence that sustained Paradiso's declared source of the splinters, but the team twisted the find to suit the alleged crimes against Joan. Badges absconded boat paraphernalia along with manuals and flares, and they represented navigational equipment in the attic as apparatus from Paradiso's missing Chris Craft, the *Malafemmena*. The force took assorted photo albums and pictures, and they described any dark-haired women in the photographs as "looking like Joan." The team fueled the modus operandi that their suspect preferred dark-haired women like Joan, and the absurd notion was "proven" with the snapshots of dark-haired women in an Italian man's albums.

Searchers then seized a book on Lenny's shelf. *Maya: Monuments of Civilization* by Pierre Ivanoff seemed out of place in Paradiso's collection. The *Reader's Digest* book club offering published by Grosset & Dunlap was a large and heavy edition. It measured 9 3/4" by 13" and weighed more than eight pounds. The hardcover was a coffee table type book with many glossy, touristy photographs of Mayan ruins.

"One textbook was removed from the second floor," the lead officer reported to the court.

Maya had little or no value as an architectural reference or textbook, as authorities described it. The questionable theory was that Joan carried the cumbersome book in her tote with her fragile architectural drawings, and was working on a related project. Mayan step pyramids, like Chichen Itza, may have inspired stair-step seating, but had nothing else to do with the auditorium assignment Joan had, in fact, already completed.

The boys submitted the book repeatedly to the FBI labs. As one might expect, Lenny's print was found in Lenny's book, but to Burke's dismay, there were not any of Joan's.

"It appears Paradiso wiped everything down," was the official explanation.

Basic police work would have tagged the book as a white elephant that would have been hard to find. Ivanoff had several editions of his book offered by different publishers and released at different times. Grosset & Dunlap stamped Lenny's volume, and that edition of *Maya* was out of print in 1975. The boys in charge used the press to plant the suggestion Lenny had an item from the missing tote bag, but the hardback was out of print at least six years before Joan stepped on the plane.

The case slated for prosecution was Marie Iannuzzi, but the battalion of troopers rummaging through the house only sought and seized items they tied to Joan's case. Most items centered on Paradiso's boat, the suspected crime scene for Joan's murder, but the craft was the most problematic obstacle for Burke to hurdle. Paradiso filed reports that the vessel was missing on July 26, 1981, four months before the fated, young woman landed in Boston. He had notified the Coast Guard, the Boston Police Department, and the Massachusetts State Police, and he made a claim with Liberty Mutual Insurance that the insurer paid on September 29, 1981.

Paradiso did not list the missing boat or the insurance claim in his bankruptcy petition in August 1981, and Burke saw an opening. Burke strategized with the FBI in Quantico in March, and just a few weeks later he set out to deal with the missing crime scene he needed for Joan's case. Burke called the Boston FBI on May 3, 1983, as if he were doing his civic duty, and as if the FBI were just stepping into the case. Burke and Trooper Andrew Palombo hooked up with SA Stephen Broce, and endeavored to prove the boat was not stolen.

The personal crimes division added new case numbers that muddied the already murky waters. FBI files tagged so many file numbers concerning Joan that the defense was clueless to know where to look. There still were no charges in the Webster case; guardians would have denied any subpoena outside the scope. False information from the bureau's confidential source and exculpatory evidence remained hidden in an office that did not play by the rules anyway. The Feds now listed Joan as the victim in Paradiso's bankruptcy case.

"It is hoped that a successful bankruptcy fraud prosecutive effort by the Boston office of the FBI," the Fed's confidential report revealed, "will provide the leverage needed to gain the cooperation of Candace Weyant or Paradiso in the Webster and Iannuzzi cases."

The bankruptcy case was a smokescreen, a device to pressure Paradiso and his girlfriend. Other avenues of investigation were now available to the state for the Iannuzzi and Webster cases. A key element of the state's efforts was proving the reported crime scene, the *Malafemmena*, was not stolen. Authorities blurred the lines of jurisdiction grossly, and the two offices collaborated with the same objective from different angles. The endgame was to satisfy the obsession that Paradiso had murdered Joan Webster.

The timing seemed odd in the whole scheme of things, but apparently, Burke or his superiors were getting nervous about the dubious Iannuzzi case. The DA's office offered Paradiso a deal, though Burke came out later denying he would ever bargain with his suspect. The Commonwealth offered a lesser charge of manslaughter for Marie Iannuzzi's murder, but Burke's patsy declined. Burke rescinded the offer on June 2, 1983, just in time for another decision to break in the state's favor. Apparently, the boys were dishing out the same promises they were dangling for Robert Bond.

The grand jury handed down a true bill for rape on June 6, 1983, in addition to the murder charge an earlier grand jury delivered in June of 1982. Sexual aggression was the only palatable motive to suggest Paradiso had killed Marie, and the only conceivable thing to promote him in Joan's disappearance.

Burke walked into the grand jury again on July 12, 1983, to lay out his biased argument in a John Doe investigation for Joan Webster. The secret session was hushed to the press, but speculation swirled anyway. The hearing was yet another opportunity for Burke to get a preview of challenges he faced and hide exculpatory evidence in transcripts that Paradiso could not subpoena. The devious prosecution summoned Candy's parents to this rendezvous in court, but asked about the alleged call on the night Marie was murdered.

"No," Ruth Weyant attested. "My daughter did not wake me in the middle of the night. I did not speak to Lenny on the phone."

Bond spilled his story, too, but the defense could not move to discredit his statement, because the secret testimony was cleverly tied to another case. Candy took the stand and took the fifth on the advice of her counsel.

Burke's trickery had succeeded to pressure Paradiso's girlfriend, and he hoped to complicate her Constitutional right not to answer.

Burke was painting the witness into a corner and needed leverage to get her to talk. The conniving prosecutor was not done with her yet, because he desperately needed to discredit Lenny's alibi witness back in August 1979. In order to put her back in the hot seat, Burke convened another grand jury, and he charged Candy as an accessory in Marie Iannuzzi's murder. Burke worked every angle under the tutelage of Flanagan's office. The tricks enabled him to manipulate evidence and hide it from the defense. Lenny had the weight of a broken system against him.

Strategy Burke maneuvered, with the power of the DA's office, ultimately pressured Candy to give the refusal he wanted her to provide. She was the person with Lenny on the night in question, and the prosecutor had to nullify the alibi. Burke was back in front of the judge on July 27, 1983, and applied for a grant of immunity for the besieged, young woman pertaining to the boat and any matters surrounding Joan Webster. The immunity shielded Candy from any offenses charged by the state, but had no authority over the Federal investigation instigated by Burke connected to the bankruptcy charges, or matters related to Marie Iannuzzi.

Burke's sworn affidavit to the court spuriously asserted he received a letter from informant Robert Bond on January 5, 1983, detailing two murders. He had tried repeatedly to put Candy on the stand in grand jury hearings to elicit her information. Each time she took the fifth on the advice of counsel whether it was the grand jury examining the 1979 murder charges in 1982, the added rape charges in 1983, or the investigation of Joan's disappearance. Finally, Judge Liacos granted the motion, and Burke recalled Candy Weyant in front of Joan's John Doe grand jury on July 27, 1983.

"Where was the boat moored?" Burke asked Lenny's girlfriend.

"Did you help Mr. Paradiso strip that boat, the *Malafemmena*, on or about July 26, 1981?

"What happened to the boat afterwards?"

ADA Burke turned to point the accusing finger at his witness. "The boat wasn't stolen, was it?"

On the advice of her counsel, Weyant pleaded the Fifth Amendment and her rights under Article XII. She refused to answer if she knew Paradiso. The court had immunized the witness for this proceeding, and Burke wanted blood.

On the same date Burke was asking Candy questions about Paradiso and his boat, his FBI collaborator, SA Steve Broce, was filing a warrant in Federal court to search the woman's safety deposit box at the Haymarket Cooperative Bank. The agent asserted that the couple hid assets in the box, jointly rented by Paradiso and his girlfriend, not declared in the bankruptcy case.

"The confidential source indicated there was missing jewelry," SA Broce reported. "Jewelry is missing in both the Webster and Iannuzzi cases."

The tip had not come from Robert Bond; he knew nothing about missing jewelry. The public was unaware of Joan's missing gold charm bracelet, but no jewelry was missing in Marie's case. The amount of disinformation leaked to the FBI was piling up, and each piece added another clue to the informant's identity.

The court granted the warrant, and the G-men raided the safety deposit box the next day. The search yielded nothing to support the bankruptcy case being constructed, but did hand the state an item to weave deceptively into Joan's case.

"Miss Webster's former roommate was shown a black-and-white photo of the silk pouch seized from the safety deposit box," ADA Burke advised the Boston FBI office. "She tentatively identified the silk pouch."

"A small purse was seized by the FBI," Trooper Palombo leaked to the *Boston Herald*. "Webster's former roommate said it was identical to one Webster owned. The roommate chose the purse from the safety deposit box from an array of six to eight similar-style purses."

Joan was a dorm proctor at Perkins Hall and lived in room 316, a single room. The core group never revealed the roommate's name to the public, nor did the pair investigating Joan's case share it with the Feds, that is, if there was such a person. The photograph concealed the bright-red color, and detectives were derelict to follow up and find the true owner. Instead, spokesmen touted the red silk, jewelry pouch as Joan's to the courts and the press. The common item was part of a set, but searchers had not seized the box and the two other pieces in the raid of the Weyants' in April 1983. The impression circulated was that Paradiso and his girlfriend were in possession of things belonging to Joan, but neither search backed up the claim. Now, the Commonwealth had an out-of-print, coffee table book and a red silk purse Candy had given to Lenny to sheathe a prized shark's tooth. That's it.

Candy stood in front of Judge Liacos on August 11, 1983, and was arraigned on accessory charges in the Marie Iannuzzi murder, four years after the crime.

"Not guilty," the persecuted, young woman told the judge.

The dog days of the summer simmered into the fall, and the conniving counselor summoned the beleaguered, young woman before another hearing on September 8, 1983, in front of Judge Paul Connolly. She had taken the fifth answering questions whether she knew Leonard Paradiso or not. Their acquaintance was a vital element necessary in the Iannuzzi matter where authorities had filed charges against her, and the information was instrumental for the Federal bankruptcy efforts. However, Burke asked the questions in the grand jury for Joan where the harried, young woman had been given relief.

"I find you in contempt of court," Judge Connolly admonished Ms. Weyant. "You are sentenced to three months in the Framingham facility."

Weyant's attorney, Walter Underhill, gained a stay of Connolly's sentence of confinement from Judge Liacos, but the outstanding penalty still loomed over Candy's head. The judge had granted immunity already for issues related to Joan Webster. Regardless, Weyant was still vulnerable in the Iannuzzi case, and answering questions in the John Doe grand jury for Joan put the alibi witness in a quandary. Liacos suggested the state drop the Iannuzzi charges against Weyant.

The Feds marched forward with allegations of their own, charges the granted immunity didn't cover. There still was no legitimate evidence to connect Paradiso to a crime in Joan's case, and she was technically still just a missing person. Nevertheless, the prosecutor continued to blitz toward a conviction of Paradiso for Marie's murder. However, every other sentence came back to Joan Webster.

The underlying objective was obvious; Marie's case generated suspicion in Joan's. There was an apparent perversion of authority in one case; suspicion there satisfied an outcry for justice in another. The thought this was the brand of justice the state delivered for Joan's loss was appalling and made me sick to my stomach.

"Why?" I wondered aloud. "Who are they protecting?"

I picked up Burke's book and scoured the pages. The lawyer insanely published an account he billed as "true crime" when documents undeniably refuted his version of events. A legitimate case did not need the tricks and deceit. He was talking about the last moments of Joan's life. He distorted circumstances about a valued member of my family who faced a horrific death. Obviously, he was a protected player, and people in positions of authority had his back.

"Her shoes were packed in the suitcase with some pictures," Burke described in his published version of events. "That jives with what Bond told me. Paradiso told Bond they were stuck inside a pair of gray shoes to keep them from getting bent."

The couple Burke targeted had nothing of Joan's, but Burke's publication placed a pair of gray shoes in the possession of the Massachusetts State Police. The FBI did not list shoes of any color in the

Lark bag, and Bond only knew the suitcase was in the possession of the state police. The belonging could only have been in the tote, but law enforcement never recovered the tote bag. Therefore, the prosecutor at the center of Joan's investigation placed the cops on the list of suspects. The revelation led to a renewed search for the composite of the bearded man at the airport. Who gave Joan Webster a ride?

CHAPTER 13

Q38

The household fell silent. My daughters had encountered their father's infidelity, and his betrayal left us all feeling numb. Counseling sessions were little help, and Steve's charm and deceptive tactics confused everyone about what exactly he had done. I sat on the deck attempting to sort through the problem with my husband.

"We need to talk about what happened, Steve," I calmly said, but Joan's brother threw his hands up in rage.

"There's nothing to talk about, Eve." Steve refused to look me in the face. "You just need to get over it! I haven't hurt anyone!"

I'd had more than enough. I calmly stood up and looked Steve firmly in the eye.

"You need to move out," I said. "This isn't healthy. I'm willing to attend counseling sessions, but you need to deal with your issues."

The announcement stunned the girls when we told them. Despite the fact it was Steve who committed adultery, my children were more angry with me; they told their friends they wanted me to be gone. The next three days dragged on forever. I tried to assure my girls there was a capacity for forgiveness with the right help, but they did not respond well. Sleep did not come easy, and I lay in bed soaking my pillow. My youngest came in a few times through the night.

"Could I go to school late tomorrow?" she asked softly.

"You can stay home if you'd like," I replied.

"No, no, I'm all right," she said.

After I dropped her off and returned home, I found the bottle of Vicodin on the floor. She had taken pills through the night, but I did not know it at the time. I only discovered that later when she confided it on the computer. Before I could address the disturbing discovery, I was summoned to Sarah O'Brien's office. Steve was there and the two described the hysterical outburst that occurred at school. My child had walked into the school counselor's office and had a meltdown. The unified front, Steve and Sarah, omitted details from their feedback. The sensationalized upheaval had the entire school buzzing, and the tone was as if I had chopped up bodies and dumped them at sea.

"Your daughters are frightened of you, Eve. They're terrified," I was told.

They had rallied to find things, or make them up, to use against me. The hysteria took on the flavor of the infamous Salem witch hunts. I was baffled and distressed when the guilty party moved back in. I did not know what to do, so I went for a walk to clear my head. For hours I wandered with nowhere to go. Finally, I decided to call counselor Carol Metzger and crashed on her couch.

After the strain and trauma of everything that had happened, I admitted myself to the stress center, near collapse. Instead of expressing their concern for my condition, my children and their father were ecstatic about my absence. The family computers had parental guards installed that recorded activity, and the conversations, while I was at the stress center, were quite disturbing.

"Does your Mom know?" Fraiz asked out of concern.

"I knew it all along, anyway," my oldest calmly replied. "Yeah, I told her. My dad would've lied."

"I finally got a car!" The automatic response heralded my teen's good news. "My dad just went and bought a car, and didn't tell my mom, haha!

"PARTAY!

"OMG, he is so happy!"

Mom was finally out of the house. Steve was the happiest my oldest had ever seen him, and the good times were about to begin. The role model that influenced my children to devalue their mother was obvious. Steve's parental negligence was dangerously indulgent. My children knew the computer was monitored, and they used the opportunity for a constant barrage of devaluing harassment. These were not the loving hearts that I knew.

"I wish she would fucking disappear!" my youngest angrily hoped for.

This child told counselors she felt too much pressure to keep me alive, and hid Joan's scrapbook in the basement closet. Is that what she hoped for, that I would disappear? Still, Steve and the counselors offered no specifics for me to respond to, and I struggled to understand the animosity and fear that undermined my family. By this point, I was exhausted and near the end of my rope.

Nevertheless, I left the hospital with renewed hope and determination. Unfortunately, George and Eleanor descended on the house and made their rounds, exerting their influence with the counselors.

"We're worried about Eve," they somberly lamented to the counselors.

I'm sure they dreaded having to face me, but they mustered the words that I expected to hear, and demonstrated John Mulholland's methods to perfection.

"We all have to work together to get through this," Eleanor said when we briefly met back at the house.

Funny, her son had offended every female in our house, but I was the one under attack and uprooted. Eleanor looked me in the face with an icy glare that went right through me. They had witnessed the disrespectful treatment that had swept over my children and sat idly to correct it, even when asked. My in-laws had witnessed my principled backbone repeatedly over the years, but Eleanor was displeased that I blew whistles. The Websters always had the right words to say and indeed, I had placed a lot of trust in my family, However, their actions never matched their flowery rhetoric. The words were all doublespeak.

"I know they screamed and yelled at you," Sarah affirmed.

"Did they tell you they were breaking into my filing cabinets?" I asked.

"They probably did," the counselor responded, as if the Websters were pulling her strings. "This family is like spy versus spy here."

The metaphor the girls' advocate used was interesting, because she was unaware of the CIA background influencing Webster upbringing, and they deployed the same tactics on a mom from the Midwest. I found the family's treatment of me to be eerily similar to the enumerated CIA methods outlined in document OA 53-37, techniques to break down an enemy of the state. Sadly, the loss in our family had not ended with Joan's murder; the strife trickled down to the next generation. My children circulated sensational stories that paralleled the sensations surrounding Joan's case.

The feds and the state wanted to nail Paradiso, and used every method at their disposal to do so. After the core group identified the so-called culprit in January 1982, through a longtime acquaintance of Sgt. Carmen Tammaro, they pursued Paradiso using an unrelated case where he was a suspect. The crafty prosecutor defined the obstacles he faced through a secret and one-sided grand jury targeting Leonard Paradiso. However, things did not always go as planned. Testimony implicated another offender for the Iannuzzi murder prompting a prosecutorial trick, changing the grand jury case to a

John Doe. Let it be clear, they wanted Paradiso, and they disallowed any contrary evidence from consideration. His history made him particularly vulnerable to the gossip that swirled, and the authorities effectively used the media to shape perceptions. They had no real evidence against Paradiso, but they knew that he was a man they could pin a murder on—he had a record. A rat slithered out of the sewer to promote the state's case, and a string of witnesses was willing to sell their souls for some personal gain. Those who were not willing to testify as the forces ordained were pressured, coerced, and assaulted to manipulate the desired result.

Burke desperately wanted this conviction. He had the backing of DA Newman Flanagan's corrupt office, and could utilize John Kiernan's practice of hidden and duplicated files in the homicide division. Burke seated another John Doe grand jury to investigate Joan's disappearance, and once again concealed exculpatory evidence from the accused. A leak funneled false information to the corrupted FBI office, an office that secretly protected known criminal informants. Documents to the court boasted Trooper Palombo's insight how a criminal avoided detection. In other words, the trial was a sham. Still, ADA Burke faced hurdles and had to fill in the gaps to reach his objective.

Burke needed evidence of the crime scene. Tammaro was quite specific on this detail when he planted the seed with Paradiso, so Burke had to work hard to force the evidence to fit Tammaro's envisioned crime. The officer involved in Joan's case shrewdly suggested the story they had to coagulate on August 1, 1982, when the sergeant faced his childhood acquaintance from the North End in the Charles Street Jail. The pretender arrived in street clothes, bragging about his influence, and promising to cut a deal for Paradiso.

"I'm involved in the investigation against the Angiulos," he said. "You know, Lenny, you are friendly with Anthony Anko Angiulo."

Angiulo was a son of the mafia family the Feds plotted to topple. Paradiso knew exactly what "Buster" Tammaro was implying, and showed his disdain when his North End nemesis declared his involvement in the FBI's operation.

"The Angiulos and a lot of other guys in the North End are going to be arrested. They're being watched," Buster leaked. "There's a camera in the air conditioner above the Roma Pharmacy."

Paradiso sat silently and listened to the braggadocio before reminding Tammaro he was an Italian from the North End. Tammaro had revealed the bureau's devious methods to achieve the end, and a conflicting agenda with the state's objective to nail

Whitey Bulger. Burke had filed warrants to eavesdrop on the menacing Irish mob boss, but leaks undermined the efforts.

"They're bugging Angiulo's place," the indiscreet cop spilled. "When they get through with the tapes, the Feds will make it sound different."

History verified Tammaro's leaked disclosure that the Angiulos were going to be arrested. The unscrupulous enforcer, "Buster" to those who knew him, exposed the devices of authorities used to manipulate a case toward a desired end and his willingness to play along.

Tim Burke kept enhancing Bond's regurgitated story. He told the FBI lab that Paradiso entertained Joan on the still missing craft and bludgeoned her in front of the ship-to-shore radio in the cabin. He reported Joan bled heavily, but suggested Paradiso cleaned the boat down before he sank it. Bond described the excessive blood, but never hinted Lenny swabbed the deck when he went over the sequence with the police. The embellishment was complete fiction on Burke's part. The stoolie never mentioned the radio either; there was no equipment visible in the photos tacked up on the cell wall. The FBI lab received the radio, two compasses, and two depth finders Trooper Palombo had seized during the April search executed at the Weyants' home. It seemed as though Burke actually believed the manufactured story as he anxiously awaited results for the items submitted on August 5, 1983. The results were negative.

Taxpayer dollars financed the unprecedented search for the alleged crime scene. If there ever was a misuse of tax money, this was it. Bond's statement had enflamed public speculation that Joan took her last breath onboard the *Malafemmena*. Burke declared his obsession to find Joan's killer. His mania seemed to justify doing whatever it took to prove the man guilty of the graduate student's murder. Technically, the victim was still classified as a missing person. The informant's manufactured tale sent the search adrift in Boston Harbor. The claim was that Paradiso was diabolical and avoided detection, but he idiotically waited two days before taking his vessel out to sink it.

Divers scoured waters in several places to no avail. The Massachusetts State Police and the prosecutor's office offered a $5,000 reward to the public to find the lost craft. Of course, the reward notice never mentioned their suspect reported the very same boat missing on July 26, 1981, four months before Joan landed at Logan. Initially, the source of the dangled dollars was not disclosed even when reporters probed.

"We'd rather not divulge that." A state police spokesman declined to comment who put up the reward.

Nevertheless, things leaked out and the benefactor revealed, or so it seemed.

"Police offered a $5,000 reward for recovery of Paradiso's boat, the *Malafemmena*," the *Boston Herald* reported.

"After we got the tip," Sgt. Carmen Tammaro, who worked alongside Trooper Andrew Palombo on the case, told the *Lynn Daily Item*, "we put a wanted poster out for the boat."

"The Websters offered a $10,000 dollar reward for the boat," Burke published with the Websters' blessing.

Burke claimed in his book that the Websters had anteed up the cash. The trio worked closely with the parents. Bond said "The Man from New Jersey" had sent people to see him. Tammaro had envisioned the boat was the crime scene in August of 1982.

"I hear you painted the hull white," Buster cleverly suggested to Paradiso, "but you kept the boat."

Once Tammaro guided his snitch Robert Bond through the maze of two murders, he was the front man to put up the reward for the boat. However, authorities still did not know just where the boat was; Bond had not been that specific. He couldn't. With the appearance of thoroughness, Burke enlisted the assistance of a Massachusetts Institute of Technology professor, Harold "Doc" Edgerton, inventor of a sonar system, to help facilitate an underwater search. Even so, divers could not find the missing craft.

A confidential source began tipping the Feds as soon as the Bond allegations leaked in January 1983. The two officers involved in Joan's case, both assigned to F Barracks, commented for the papers when the story came out. Tammaro had exposed his involvement to the FBI, and his subordinate had friends in the right places, too. Palombo had stormed the high school gridiron in Lynn, Massachusetts with his close friend, Paul Cavanagh. Cavanagh was a G-man in Boston who assumed the alias "Joe Fitz" for his undercover infiltration of the mafia. Paul's supervisor, SA John Connolly, the infamous FBI handler for the notorious Whitey Bulger, eulogized his good friend after Cavanagh died in a small plane crash in Maine on June 19, 1990.

The connections were uncanny. The lead officer on Joan's case and his direct superior both had an inside track. These men knew how to manipulate justice. Conventional means of searching turned up nothing, so ADA Tim Burke enlisted the personal crimes division of the FBI. His scheme paid off with a tip on the boat. Suddenly, out of nowhere, a confidential source told SA Steve Broce where to look, and the agent passed the hint along to the wily assistant ADA three days later.

"On August 12, 1983, I received information provided on a confidential basis," Broce swore in his affidavit to the court. "Paradiso's boat, the *Malafemmena*, was likely sunk at its mooring area, Pier 7, in Boston Harbor."

After great effort to search for the boat with no luck, all it took was a couple phone calls to the FBI, and miraculously, the boat appeared. It pays to have connections; at least, it did for Burke.

The Massachusetts State Police knew all about the missing reports and the claim filed with Rodney Swanson at Liberty Mutual Insurance, but they still maintained the credibility of the recently convicted murderer with nothing to lose. After all, Bond was their key witness. Authorities also had the parole records; they clearly indicated Paradiso's practice to take his vessel out of the water for the winter in prior years. Paradiso would have stored his craft well before authorities alleged it was the scene of a murder.

"I took my boat out of the water for the winter," Paradiso had told his parole officer on November 3, 1980, during his regular office visit.

Regardless, the hunt was on, and collaborators sent divers into the waters all over Boston Harbor in search of the prize. The confidential source tipped SA Steve Broce to scour the waters at the very place where Paradiso moored his boat at Pier 7. However, the muddy bottom and continuous traffic kept waters churned and clouded visibility for the treacherous dives. The hunt seemed to be a competition of sorts between the Boston scuba team and the Massachusetts State Police divers vying for glory to find sunken treasure. It paid off; the frogmen struck the taxpayer's pay dirt on September 26, 1983.

Burke had the press jockeying for position on the banks along Pier 7. The spectacle was a media frenzy. Cameras flashed while reporters shouted over one another, trying to have their questions heard. Gawkers peered from restaurant windows, lined on the shore, and leered at the scene from boats in the water. The curious strained their necks trying to glimpse the Chris Craft break the surface, and held their breath to see whether Joan's bones would rattle.

"We don't expect to find a body," Burke said, keeping the expectations low.

"We are very glad they found this boat," George, the ITT executive, told the *Boston Globe* in a phone interview. "It's a step in corroborating an earlier theory."

Scuba teams meticulously scooped the mud away from the hull and slipped straps under the boat to lift it carefully from the floor at the pier. The process eliminated any suction that might bury evidence under more silt as an enormous crane slowly hoisted the boat out of the deep. The divers worked blindly in the dangerous conditions, but the *Malafemmena* was reborn on September 27, 1983, like a phoenix rising from the ashes.

She came up just as she went down. The hull was still blue, *Malafemmena* still painted in bold letters across the stern, and the serial numbers matched what Bond recited from the photograph. Burke touted his star witness, the only one to suggest the boat was still floating when Joan disappeared, but ignored the fact the craft was right where Paradiso moored it without any change in its appearance. Although the discovery suggested Paradiso was a dumb crook, Burke continued to press the ludicrous notion he had pulled off a diabolical crime. The image of Paradiso as a devious criminal that baffled battalions of seasoned investigators was inconsistent with the obvious fact that Paradiso lacked the intelligence to camouflage or move the boat.

Divers carefully brought up the small items they found underneath the boat. Items discovered included metal bolts and a seven and a half-inch cylindrical item they labeled as a possible bone. Anything recovered was included in an inventory of things to examine. Burke's supposed crime scene was then loaded on a flatbed, and taken to a warehouse at Pier 1 where it was kept under around-the-clock guard.

Trooper Palombo avoided media questions, and he quietly slipped away from his triumphant scene headed for Lynn Hospital. He knew the verdict was not in what secrets the craft would yield, but Palombo wanted another look at the x-rays of the metal splinters in Paradiso's finger.

The ink had not even dried on the warrant before the water drained from the raised hull. Palombo appealed for anything that placed Joan Webster on the registered MS9LP vessel. SAC James Greenleaf alerted the FBI lab, and a team arrived ready to scour the boat. The trooper ordered an inspection of the boat by the Marine Surveyors Group and forwarded it to SA Broce for the Federal bankruptcy case.

Investigators sealed their lips and kept results confidential; the sparse discovery was not the sunken treasure Burke hoped he would find. The haul produced no cinder blocks to aid in the sinking, or ties to use concrete bricks as weights on dissected body parts. Items onboard did not include liquor bottles as seen in the photos, nor were there several shards of broken glass as Burke described.

"Glass shards were found aboard Paradiso's boat," Burke broadcast to the *Lynn Daily Item*, "when divers raised it from Boston Harbor."

The first wave of evidence sent in on October 18, 1983, produced little of value, but Burke was resilient and kept technicians busy for months scouring the stream of crud. The booty included several plastic and Styrofoam cups, a flannel blouse, four plastic buttons, a hairbrush, and an empty can of Orange Crush. Examiners catalogued the location of each item as they found them on the boat, and then sent objects to Quantico for testing. Searchers found a bent, silver, metal hammer in the right side of the gunnel, a ledge around the top edge of the boat above the deck. That location made it more likely that the item had dropped into the water after the boat went down. However, if Burke wanted a murder weapon, this was the only option from what they found. The problem was, it had not been part of the story.

Another packet arrived in the lab on October 28, 1983, containing an item Burke described as a piece of green glass that possibly had a hair stuck to it. This time, the items were not properly cataloged where examiners found them, as they were with round one, but Burke waited anxiously for the link to prove Paradiso's guilt. The FBI lab described item Q38, Burke's so-called glass, simply as "debris." Beachgoers collect more sea glass combing the sands than searchers found near the suspected crime scene. The submission included no details about where Q38 was retrieved, and the lab determined it was worthless for testing.

The determined prosecutor had the vessel pulled apart and kept sending things in, but there was nothing to further his cause. Lack of evidence made it clear Joan never set foot on the Chris Craft, but it did not impede the march to prove that she had. The team kept their findings hush hush. There was no blood, no fingerprints, and not one strand of hair to place a victim at the scene of the envisioned murder. None of Joan's belongings surfaced with the alleged crime scene. Tammaro subliminally dropped the suggestion Lenny murdered Joan on his boat in August of 1982, but the cop neglected to find out whether the *Malafemmena* even existed. The boys had a free rein to represent evidence to suit, and no one had access to records to refute it.

Dave Williams examined the recovered craft on October 3, and again on October 12, 1983, and submitted his findings. The boat had a broken rudder, meaning it could not be steered. The investigative team overlooked this inconvenient fact and maintained their suspect dumped Joan way out in the ocean, though clearly, with a broken rudder, this was impossible. Two fittings had been unplugged and the toilet pulled from its base. The boys built their case on one fact: someone sank the *Malafemmena* on purpose, but there was no physical evidence to establish when it went down. The ambiguity allowed the crafters free to insert a date through Robert Bond.

Palombo's sometime partner, Sgt. Dave Moran, was part of the Massachusetts State Police dive team that continued to grope in the murky waters at Pier 7 for the next two months and collect all the refuse that had sunk to the bottom. Even the vacuum equipment they used did not suck up a single clue to link Joan with the boat, or to Leonard Paradiso. No evidence surfaced bolstering suspicions for the state's cause. Ironically, one of the items recovered was a poster: "RETAIN DISTRICT ATTORNEY NEWMAN FLANAGAN."

As humorous as this discovery was, the poster, like the rest of the items dredged from the murky waters, did not add to the state's case.

Burke still had to explain how Paradiso got Joan on the boat, but that was a difficult task. Bond's recitation omitted the obvious solution to force the young woman down the plank to the barge, the location where the suspect tied his boat earlier that summer. Burke and the seasoned detectives designed a scene that broke the pattern of a victim trapped in Paradiso's car, but the story gave officials a necessary explanation why there was not a body. Burke imagined Joan must have been taken there by force. It defied common sense for Joan to be there, but the obsessed counselor just explained it away by suggesting Paradiso forced her down the plank with a fake gun.

The diving teams found nil for two months, but Burke needed that piece of evidence to make the whole theory work. Magically, he produced another informant almost on cue; the Feds had the necessary source locked away in a Federal penitentiary for perjury. Tim Burke named John O'Donnell, a developer who had been renovating Pier 7, as the tipster that foretold an amazing discovery the legitimate divers all missed. According to Burke, O'Donnell fibbed on his grant application to renovate the pier and jailed for being a liar. The convenient fish tale, (O'Donnell's divers found a gun right under the surface where Paradiso had tied the *Malafemmena*) was certainly fortuitous for Burke's case.

"I didn't want to have anything to do with that, so I told them to toss it right back where they found it," O'Donnell allegedly told Burke.

An honest man would have turned the weapon in to police, and the less reputable man might have kept it, but to position it right where Burke needed to find it was all too convenient. The developer drew an accurate map, according to Burke, that pointed out the precise location to look. In no time at all, Officer Nick Saggese retrieved just what Burke wanted. There was no explanation how assigned divers missed the gun when they brought up the boat. Scuba teams still searching the waters snorkeled all around it, but they suspiciously missed it.

The realistic looking piece was a replica .357 magnum, the kind of item law enforcement confiscated off the streets and piled up in evidence rooms. Burke inferred the so-called evidence was Lenny's, and people bought it merely on the attorney's word. The FBI files made no mention of a confidential informant reporting a gun that Burke suspiciously found; even the developer may have been fictitious. Someone else was tipping the Feds with disinformation, but he was a protected player who knew how to avoid detection. This anonymity provided the perfect foundation for concocting and contriving whatever evidence the state might have required.

Even the sea will give up the bodies not meant to be there. Sgt. Tammaro set Bond up to give the right answer during the interview, but the dimwitted tool was not quick enough to give them what they wanted.

"You and I know if we dump a body over, eventually it'll come up," Tammaro coaxed. "Did he say if he did anything?"

"Nope," the dull fool missed his cue, "he just said he went way out and dumped her."

Jack O'Rourke asked the question again and emphasized there was not going to be a body. Not a single bone had washed onto the beach to give Joan back, and the boys had to devise something else.

The phone rang on September 29, 1983.

"Paradiso dated a girl named Charlene," the unnamed informer confided. "He lavished her with gifts of jewelry—jewelry from his murder victims."

The confidential source did not know the woman's last name, but he knew a lot about what she would say. She would be a valuable witness if the Feds could find her. Charlene had the information authorities were after. The team enhanced Paradiso's modus operandi to include stealing jewelry from his victims.

The phone rang again the next day, and agents throbbed with feverous anticipation from the startling revelation they heard from their secretive source.

"Charlene knows where Webster's body was dumped," the snitch tattled.

On October 3, 1983, a week after crews raised the boat, the FBI identified a potential witness on a tip from the confidential source. They anticipated the nature of her testimony as if they had a crystal ball, and again the core investigators hoped to seal the deal on Paradiso's fate.

"We've identified a witness, Charlene Bullerwell," SA Steve Broce updated the eager ADA making the case.

"A photo of a woman was confiscated back in April," Tim Burke breathlessly affirmed. "She's wearing an identical bracelet to the one missing in Joan Webster's case."

It seemed Burke and the confidential source had their stories together about missing jewelry. The missing gold charm bracelet was one of a kind and easily identifiable by the family. SA Steve Broce, and a second unnamed intruder knocked on Charlene Bullerwell's door the next day holding the picture they confiscated to find her. The written note on the back of the photograph read, "Lenny, who is one in a million. Love, Charlene."

By this point, I felt a little like John Le Carre's George Smiley, the character trying to smoke out the traitor that had infiltrated the "Circus." I mentally reviewed what the confidential source was feeding the devious Boston FBI office. The snitch leaked the Bond allegations that Paradiso murdered Joan onboard his vessel and dumped her in the ocean. The Feds got the tip where to look for the missing boat. A confidential informant provided the tip to find a gun right under Paradiso's mooring that the legitimate divers had mysteriously missed. The telltale told SA Broce there was missing jewelry in both the Iannuzzi and Webster cases, but the fact was Marie's killer did not take her trinkets. Now, this top-secret teller unleashed the dogs on a witness known only as Charlene. Paradiso supposedly lavished her with jewelry from his victims, and this unlikely woman knew where he dumped Joan's body, so the source said.

It did not take a seasoned sleuth to figure out who had the information and the opportunity, but Burke made it easy. The "crime-fighting" author connected the dots in his manuscript to his bearded, undercover partner investigating the crimes.

"You know the picture Andy found?" Burke's plot attributed the pronouncement to SA Broce in a seaside meeting with the ADA. SA Broce clued Burke in that the Feds had located a useful witness, as if the prosecutor didn't know.

"As a result of a related investigation in conjunction with several insurance companies," Trooper Palombo avowed to the court, "I obtained several photos."

The discreet cop divulged Charlene's identity to the Feds shortly after his trip to the emergency room to reexamine the x-rays of Paradiso's left index finger. Trooper Palombo affirmed to the court his involvement in an insurance matter regarding the boat. He stepped over the line and collaborated on the Fed's case, but the blurred jurisdiction escaped the court's scrutiny.

The redheaded housewife dated Lenny about a half-dozen times, and that somehow made her a valuable witness. SA Broce and his unnamed escort made promises to move Charlene and her son to another location in exchange for her cooperation to testify. The two men left with added fodder for two unrelated cases, but they scrambled the lines of jurisdiction inappropriately. Now, Burke had someone to suggest as the source of the tip to discover the *Malafemmena*, or at least that's what he published. He found this source a week too late, an inconvenient truth for his story, but still Burke added to the scorecard for the Federal case that the boat wasn't stolen.

The woman's story made sensational headlines, and a tale that bolstered Bond's fictitious statement that Joan rested at the bottom of the ocean. The boys inserted additional insurance that the body would not surface, though there was no physical evidence to verify such a claim. Bond fumbled when cops questioned him about weights; he was too slow to give the "right" answer. The cops wanted the point covered and kept the investigation focused on the harbor. Everything centered on not having a body.

"The last time in this state a murder case was successfully proved without a body was 1850," Burke woefully told the *Boston Globe*, apparently tutored by "Death Row Tony" in the Middlesex DA's office. "That case was the *Commonwealth v. Webster*."

The Boston FBI office was rife with corruption when Joan disappeared, and unethical practices derailed earnest efforts to find truthful answers. The crafty maneuver to reroute information to the ADA through an agent in the Personal Crimes Unit shielded the true source. Palombo and Burke were assigned together to oversee Joan's investigation, but the undercover cop abdicated the pronouncements to SA Steve Broce, his distracting accomplice. Divisive secrecy was an unnecessary ploy for a meritorious pursuit. However, these people all had the same objective of moving the Webster and Iannuzzi cases to the desired conclusion. The underhanded methods scattered pieces of the puzzle and diluted the truth. Palombo repeatedly solicited information from witnesses vital to the state's version. Stories contradicted documented facts, and sworn testimony changed on the stand. Bullerwell became another participant with a sensational account that made headlines without corroboration. It was not much of a surprise that Charlene's allegory filled the gap in Bond's rendition to keep Joan down.

CHAPTER 14

Across Town

One daughter was part of a group known as the "Drunk Bunch & Funk Patrol," and she boldly posted photographs of underage drinking parties and coed sleepovers online. *The Gawker,* an online tabloid, covered another exploit. The gossip column titillated readers with an alleged seductive interlude between actor Alec Baldwin and one of my girls. Dr. Suzy Block, a pornography peddler, posted pictures and identified one of my children on the salacious blog—fortunately, my daughter had her clothes on. This was how the girls' father had guided and "groomed" them. Steve excused and condoned the reckless behavior that put my children at unthinkable risk. I was mortified.

I struggled to bring these issues forward, trying to stop this continual devaluation of my children, but the family ran interference. I was a mother in pain, kept from my own children as the Websters defiantly claimed privacy.

Shortly after drug use showed up on my radar, an anonymous caller dialed my number. The unidentified scoffer left a taunting message on my voicemail, but I recognized the voice. The mystery vocalist set her mockery to music and ridiculed my genuine effort to get real help for my girls. I delicately broached the subject of drug use during a pleasant meeting with one of the girls, but she morphed a pleasant stroll with the dogs into a caricature of a mother on a rampage. One problem was obvious, the Websters wanted—and needed—to keep things a secret from Mom.

"Eve, I strongly suggest you cease this nonsense (libel/slander)," Steve e-mailed his rage and denials. "I have discussed this with them in the past and they are not doing drugs." He categorically rebuffed that there had ever been any drug use, though the photos and comments posted online were there in living color for anyone to see.

What was the truth? I was a mother concerned for her children. However, the dilemma was the family stigmatized me as a monster that harassed them with slander and libel. Steve was an enabler, making it very easy for my girls to access drugs and post their unchecked adventures online.

Miraculously, the waters calmed, and I met with Steve on January 27, 2007, to discuss the severe alienation and problems that had surfaced. He confided there had, in fact, been drug use, but he downplayed the concern.

"It's recreational, not major at all," Steve excused. "She's had some bad experiences and definitely experimented recreationally, but if you ever quote me on this, I'll never speak to you again!"

Steve condescendingly dismissed my concern, and my efforts to sit down with counselors about the well-being of my child were blocked. A child in distress using substances was risky behavior that could cause real harm, let alone illegal. The same tactic he used to manipulate my girls' thinking was then, unsuccessfully, tried on me.

"It's nothing like I think you're imagining it." Their derelict father dismissed a responsible mother's concern, and punctuated his denial with the Webster dictate, "Don't tell!"

"They don't trust you," he warned. "They'll never speak to you again."

"Why don't they trust me?" I asked, realizing he had driven the wedge.

"They don't trust what you'll do," he shifted the blame. "They're afraid you'll violate their privacy."

In other words, Steve did not want me telling the truth, making him look bad as a parent, or get appropriate help for my child. Telling the truth conflicted with the Websters' notion of privacy; that was the problem. The perceived threat closed off avenues to reunite and sort out the looming issues with my children. The cover-up mentality continued to endanger my daughters, and deny them the proper help and guidance they so desperately needed. Secrecy continued to facilitate the walk down a destructive path by more members of the Webster family.

Leonard Paradiso struggled with representation. Originally, when inquiries began and he was a suspect, Lenny retained John Cavicchi to help clear his name for Marie Iannuzzi's murder. However, the Websters' suspicions stirred the case up again after their February 1982 meeting. James Cipoletta was on deck next to defend Paradiso when he landed behind bars, and he was the attorney involved when divers recovered the scuttled boat. As the Webster case gained notoriety in the press, the team of Judd Carhart and Walter Prince stepped in to take over the high-profile situation. Yet, as the calendar flipped to the New Year in 1984, they, too, bowed out and left Paradiso defenseless.

Now, without representation, administrators moved Paradiso to Walpole to await trial. Trooper Palombo and Det. Jack Murphy of the Boston Police Department took advantage of this opportunity to try to get to their man. The two officers contacted Sgt. Easyrock at the prison and connived to meet with Paradiso under the assertion he wrote Burke and wanted to talk about the case. It would be an advantage to corner Paradiso during his time without counsel; Palombo and Murphy attempted to meet Paradiso twice: once on January 19, and again on January 22, 1984.

"Who's here to see me?" Paradiso asked.

"You heard me, Trooper Palombo. Come on."

The accused man halted Burke's ploy to sidestep the rules of engagement between a suspect and the police. The window of opportunity closed when the court appointed Stephen Rappaport to defend the targeted suspect on January 23, 1984.

Rappaport had his work cut out for him. ADA Burke quietly nudged Assistant US Attorney Marie Buckley to get going on the Federal bankruptcy case. The suit stalled after a vehicle accident sidelined Marie, but the case was moving forward now in tandem with the Commonwealth's case. The greased wheels turned again, and Buckley initiated another secret grand jury session on February 9, 1984. The hearings continued into March behind closed doors in the Federal courts.

The gray gloom and chill of the winter day shrouded the restricted grand jury on the fifth floor of the Federal courthouse. The redheaded, Revere housewife, Charlene Bullerwell, took a seat in front of the jury on February 16, 1984, and described the infrequent relationship she had with Lenny for a year and a half.

"I dated him approximately two or three times," Charlene explained to the jurors. "On and off; it wasn't on a consistent basis at all."

"Approximately how long did Paradiso keep in touch with you every once in a while?" the Assistant US Attorney asked.

"A year and a half, into 1981," the witness remembered. "The last time I saw him was around Christmastime, out shopping. It was hi and good-bye; that was it."

"Were you ever on his boat in 1981?" Buckley continued. "Can you describe it?"

"Twice," Paradiso's sporadic date replied. "I drew a picture of the boat for one of the FBI gentlemen that came to my house."

AUSA Buckley stepped into the topic that an unidentified squawker fed to the FBI. According to the confidential source, Paradiso lavished jewelry on the seated woman. Burke's story matched up; he told the Feds she was photographed in a bracelet identical to Joan Webster's.

"When did you stop seeing Paradiso?" the government's prosecutor continued.

"Right after the Christmas of '81," the redhead recalled. "He gave me a Christmas present, a live sea horse charm dipped in 24 karat gold."

"Do you still have it?" Buckley probed.

"No, he took it back to have a loop put on it so it would hang right on a chain," Charlene laughed to herself. "Anything he ever gave me, he took back."

The case Burke had instigated was to prove Lenny's boat wasn't stolen. Therefore, the piece Marie Buckley had to dig out was whether Paradiso had confided a scheme to his occasional date. The witness obliged and revealed a plot to scuttle the boat for the insurance money. Paradiso allegedly had suggested two options: out by the islands, or the harbor.

"Did Mr. Paradiso ever threaten you in any way?" Buckley pitched.

"Yes, when he talked about the boat," the woman in the photograph answered. "He turned around and said, 'If you ever repeat anything I have ever said to you, I will kill you.'"

"You understand these proceedings here are secret," the counselor assured. "There is no way of Mr. Paradiso knowing that you have been here unless you tell him."

Buckley was back in front of the secret Federal grand jury again on March 2, 1984, and questioned another witness outside the earshot of the salivating press. Trooper Palombo engaged Dave Williams to examine the boat after it surfaced. The marine expert examined fittings on the boat and the bill of sale for the navigational equipment that matched.

"Would there be particular types of connections?" Buckley asked about the wires and fittings the marine surveyor found on the vessel.

"You could not take one brand," Williams carefully explained, "and connect it to the fittings of another type of brand."

"So equipment would only fit into the fittings for that brand," the prosecutor clarified the point. "Is that right?"

"Yes," the expert definitively replied.

"Let me show you this document." The counselor asked as she handed the witness a bill of sale for the equipment insured with the boat.

"I would have to look up the model numbers," Palombo's marine investigator informed the solicitor, "but the items, Ray Jeff model 1400, a radio, and Ray Jeff model 5300, a depth finder, I assume, are manufactured by Ray Jefferson."

Coinciding with the Department of Justice's pursuit of the truth about Lenny's vessel, Burke staged a remarkable event. Burke hoped to establish a pattern, and paraded his witnesses in front of the press to describe terrifying allegations against his target. Palombo hopped between courts presenting his interpretation, drove the murder charges, and addressed the problem of the calculated crime scene.

George and Eleanor packed their bags and flew in Sunday night to take up residence, again, at the Sheraton. The Iannuzzi pretrial testimony began on March 5, 1984, and Joan's parents situated themselves near the back of the courtroom. Like bloodthirsty hounds, the media poised themselves in the courtroom too, to take down every word, or at least every word they could hear. The morning began with both counselors up at the bench.

"I don't want to further inflame the press by having all this out with Bond taking the stand." Burke represented his intentions to Judge Roger Donahue.

Motions piled up on Judge Donahue's desk. The prosecutor took advantage of the judge's apparent favor, and manipulated the case out of the spectators' range. Burke's scheme was to paint his suspect as a sexual predator with a litany of dubious contentions going back a decade. The prosecutor promoted Robert Bond as some priestly confessor hearing Paradiso's sins. However, the ADA hesitated to present him in the courtroom under the pretense of inciting the press. The defense had not seen Bond's affidavit, but read the leaked accusations saturating the news in all the papers. Keeping Bond out of the chair denied Paradiso's attorney a crack at him during the Iannuzzi pretrial. Rappaport pleaded to review the Bond charges and talk to the con himself. The question before the court was the admissibility of the dated allegations Burke trotted out. According to Bond, Paradiso confessed two murders, and Burke's obsession was to add the second one to the long list of victims. The problem was, the defense wanted to question the witness, too. Burke kept his ulterior motive backstage, though everyone knew this was about Joan Webster. The tactic stifled any challenge to the state's star witness during the pretrial hearings. Burke's recitation to the judge exposed what they were all after.

"Paradiso told Bond in a separate category of statements," the ADA subtly disclosed the clever ploy to segregate Bond's accusations. "In January–November of 1981, Paradiso picked Webster up at the airport."

Now it was Burke's turn to call a witness that had testified across town in the Feds' secret session; his intentions regarding the press reversed with this witness. Charlene Bullerwell raised her right hand in front of the reporters poised to take down every word.

"I dated Paradiso for a year and a half, on and off," Charlene told the court. "Eight times we went out."

"Now," Burke waded in, "what else was said that night?"

On one of their occasional dates, Paradiso was at Charlene's place confiding he planned to sink his boat for the insurance.

"Yeah, he said he was a hit man!" the woman broadcast as the reporters frenetically scrawled. "He said he would get a phone call from somebody who wanted to get rid of somebody else. He said he liked doing females better than males, because they were easier and more fun."

"What else did he tell you?" Burke asked as if he didn't know what was coming next.

"He said how he would get rid of them was to section their bodies and tie cinderblocks to them, and sink them in the ocean." The FBI's protected source had foretold that the redheaded housewife knew where Joan's body was dumped, and her testimony played right into the scheme.

"Did Mr. Paradiso make any remarks to you?" The coy counselor subtly redrafted the inference that came out in testimony across town. "Did he make any remarks to you about your mentioning what you just told us here today?"

"He said," Bullerwell tepidly glanced over to the prosecutor's table, "'if you repeat one word of what I say, I will kill you.'"

A chill passed through the room. An image began to develop of a cold and calculated monster that chopped his victims' bodies, tied cinder blocks to them, and sank them into unyielding waters. The alleged conversation took place in the summer of 1980, a year after Paradiso supposedly dropped Iannuzzi's body recklessly on the rocky bank of the Pine River. Now it made sense why the Websters made the trip to be there. The Iannuzzi pretrial was the setting to stir speculation in Joan's case. Charlene, apparently, was a daring, young woman. She described being on Paradiso's boat twice. Towards the fall of

1980, she spent the night on the floating slaughterhouse, and a second time with her son to go fishing. She admitted a consensual relationship with Paradiso, but her testimony was missing Burke's vision.

"Were you intimate with him at that time?" the defense counsel asked.

"Yes," she admitted.

"Was that by your own free will?" Rappaport continued.

"Yes," Charlene affirmed.

"He never beat you with a gun or strangled you to be intimate with him, did he?" Paradiso's advocate cross-examined.

"No," was the definitive answer.

I set down the transcripts for a moment, picked up my heavily flagged copy of Burke's book, *The Paradiso Files*, and turned to page 199.

"She goes out on the boat with him." Burke described a meeting with SA Steve Broce for his readers that represented the agent's chat with the witness. "They're naked, making out on the bed in the cabin, and all of a sudden Lenny pushes her against the wall and starts screaming at her, 'Shut up, shut up, and I mean right now.'"

"Lenny couldn't perform with her?" Burke connected his manufactured dots. "It sounds like what happened with Patty Bono, doesn't it?"

"She went on his boat another time right after Labor Day in 1980." Burke noted the berserk behavior he envisioned when Charlene and her son went fishing, apparently sometime after Paradiso's admission he was a hit man. "Nothing happens until they pull back into Pier 7. Some other car is blocking Lenny's Cutlass. He goes nuts and starts ramming the car until he pushes it out of the way."

Burke had billed his tome *The Paradiso Files* as "true crime" with the Websters' blessing.

The FBI found Bullerwell through a photograph, and two men descended on October 4, 1983, for a two-hour rehearsal. The woman was not a dejected lover lamenting a mad coupling onboard Lenny's boat. She never hinted a belligerent date ramming his car into another vehicle on the dock. Burke described someone on a rampage, but the terror was not in the factual records. The housewife did, however, suggest that her paramour made outrageous admissions during their infrequent romance.

"You had never repeated what Paradiso allegedly said to you prior to the FBI contacting you?" Rappaport astutely asked the witness. Unfortunately, he did not have the confidential FBI report for the bankruptcy case that indicated the Feds anticipated what Buller-well would say in advance.

"Do you remember how many agents came to see you?" the defense continued.

"Two," Charlene recalled. "They found me through a picture I had given to Lenny."

"Did they ask you if Paradiso had ever beaten you or assaulted you, sexually assaulted you?" Rappaport proceeded.

"Yes," the witness conceded. "I told them no, he had not."

"Did they ask you whether or not he made any admissions to you about beating people or killing people?"

"I was pretty well pressured before I gave the information out," Charlene disclosed, then warily scanned the faces at the prosecutor's table again.

Burke dug back in on redirect. He coaxed the witness to tell the court where Lenny had suggested he would sink his boat. Her more subdued recitation in front of the Federal grand jury swore Paradiso planned to ditch his craft out by the islands or in the harbor. However, practice makes perfect, and a discreet shift in her testimony reordered her recollection to match the location Burke's alleged crime scene was actually found.

"One option was out by the islands," Lenny's sporadic date obliged. "The other one was right there at Pier 7, where he docked his boat."

Court observers swallowed the bait, and the room echoed the noisy sound of reporters scribbling frantically to get the byline out. The scene eerily took on the image of *El Mercurio* a few years before, stirring ITT's premeditated chaos in Chile.

"FORMER GIRLFRIEND SAYS HE CHOPPED UP BODIES," filled the front page of the *Boston Herald*.

"HE TOLD ME HE WAS A HIT MAN," shocked readers in the *Boston Globe*.

"MY LOVER BOASTED OF MURDERS AT SEA," doubled the scandal in the *Boston Herald* on March 7, 1984.

Every paper tried to outdo the next with the titillating bylines. The front-page sensations ignited the public's outcry for justice, and of course no story was complete without the Websters' review.

"Our plea is that if anyone has information and has not come forward," George told the *Boston Globe*, "there is still time to do so."

"The $50,000 reward we had offered has since expired." Eleanor dangled the offer again after the anxious parents listened to the witnesses Burke promoted. "We are willing to negotiate."

Marie Iannuzzi was no longer the focus in the pretrial hearing slated for resolving her murder. Instead, Burke manipulated emotions that considered Joan Webster's fate.

Next, Janet McCarthy pledged the oath. Palombo worked with the witness on February 17, 1984, and reported that she had a vivid recollection of events. Her present story conflicted with details from the night it happened when police noted her inconsistencies. However, now she made it quite clear Lenny picked her up on July 10, 1980.

"See this gentleman right here, Trooper Palombo?" Burke motioned toward the hulking presence sitting at the prosecutor's table. "Did you go with him to the spot where you were assaulted?"

"I didn't even have to show him," McCarthy replied. "I know there was water after I jumped the wall."

"Can you describe that wall?" the prosecutor asked.

"It was a cement wall," the young woman described the scene, "just a white cement wall."

McCarthy had returned to the scene of the crime with Andrew Palombo, but he did not escort her alone. An unnamed partner accompanied SA Broce to pressure Charlene Bullerwell, and now someone returned the favor with another witness. An unidentified cohort rode along when Palombo drove the victim right to the spot where he needed Paradiso to be. Palombo took over the McCarthy case soon after she saw Paradiso on television and came forward. The incognito cop had remarkable skills restoring recollections that the confused victim could not describe that night.

An embellished account had Lenny pulling up to his escaped prey before driving off in laughter. This latest rendition asserted that Paradiso punched her several times in the face, but there were no visible signs or documented treatment for the supposed beating. Janet swore she and her mother had not heard about Joan Webster, or the reward the parents offered. Apparently, they lived under a rock while the rest of New England followed the drama. Subtle variations in testimony would not come out for another few days, but McCarthy unwittingly identified the authors of her allegations.

"Do you remember what kind of car it was?" the defense zeroed in.

"Yes," McCarthy confidently pronounced. "It was a yellow car. It was a big car. It had dealer plates."

Palombo took over the case and presumably read the initial complaint in the file. Regardless, he and Burke silently sat at the prosecution's table with discreet grins on their faces. Burke declared he did not want to enflame the press, but reporters scurried to phone their editors with headlines for the late edition, and the public's emotion continued to build.

Burke created an uproar before he swore the only legitimate witness in. A pregnant Constance Porter quickly gained the sympathies of the courtroom observers as she told her story the next morning. She was a student needing a ride to her home in Amherst. An earlier court believed her account that Paradiso picked up the young hitchhiker on September 28, 1973, in Boston. Police came across his parked car on a turnoff near Ames Pond, and found Paradiso in an incriminating situation with the young woman. Her allegations of assault added to the circumstances of the arrest, making the case ironclad. Paradiso protested he found her that way, but the September 1974 jury sided with her and delivered a guilty verdict. A jury convicted him of assault, but he had not raped the girl. Police found a weapon in his glove compartment after cuffing the suspect, but he never used it to threaten the young woman. Regardless, the ADA wanted the image of a gun in his possession. The prosecutor furthered the modus operandi of a quarry in Paradiso's car and violence committed near water. Paradiso served time for the assault and crossed paths with the unsavory sorts in bed with the Websters' team. Killers and cons were waiting in the wings to dump on the defendant.

The first claimant to portend a tale of two murders warmed the seat next. Only three witnesses accused Paradiso of both crimes, and the one who started the ball rolling now raised her right hand. Patty Bono knew the man seated at the defense table growing up, and she knew Sgt. Tammaro, the officer who coordinated the Webster effort. The North End woman talked to police to tittle-tattle about an alleged ten-year-old story, but there was nothing to corroborate her incredible account.

"I felt that I was going to die," Patty lamented.

"Now one other thing," Burke started, but checked his words. "Judge, may we approach the sidebar at this time?"

Burke wore a path to the judge's high perch and continuously dropped Joan's name into the Iannuzzi hearing. Some things had to be whispered in the court's ear without leaks to the press.

"I'll object in advance," Rappaport stated, weary of the state's persistence to draw Joan into the case.

"January 1982," the offense disclosed, "Miss Bono called the parents [George and Eleanor Webster] anonymously and told them that she had information pertinent to the Joan Webster investigation."

When questioning resumed, Sgt. Tammaro's childhood friend reluctantly dropped names to the court revealing her supposed defenders, but no one was available to attest her story was true. ADA

Burke took the information and used it to reinforce the image of Paradiso attacking a victim he had trapped in his car. The scene was always set near the water, and Bono moved the target close to Pier 7 where Burke determined Joan was murdered. Again, another woman feared for her life, and repeated Paradiso's unproven threats to cast her out to sea where no one would ever find her.

Patty Bono was the anonymous caller that tipped off the Websters and gave them a suspect to pursue. The North Ender was the first witness with a direct connection to George and Eleanor, and the prosecutor confirmed the link. Bono conveniently dropped the dime to implicate Paradiso of two crimes in January 1982. The woman's voice whispered a name to Joan's parents just days before the missing suitcase turned up in a Greyhound station—the bag turned over to the Massachusetts State Police. After the phone call suggesting a suspect, the Websters convened a high-powered meeting, and the Iannuzzi case, not Joan's, became the focus of the subsequent grand jury. The operation inextricably entangled the two cases, and the press irresponsibly promoted the story.

It is hard to imagine anyone would ever forget hearing such harrowing tales that the prosecution put on display, especially if they were sitting right in the room.

"Such information about Paradiso's past—and the knowledge that that background was not enough to keep him off the streets—preys on the Websters' minds." *Boston Magazine's* piece sympathized with George and Eleanor's plight.

"In the Iannuzzi pretrial—which we didn't go to," George says, "there were women coming forward to testify. And [Paradiso] talks about the next time he does it he'll make sure there's no body. If he'd been caught and convicted of some of these other things—this might never have happened to Joan."

During the interview in New Jersey, Eleanor added, "That's what I feel, particularly about the Iannuzzi case. If they'd really done their homework, thoroughly, in the jurisdiction where it occurred, it might never…" She stopped herself.

The third day of the Iannuzzi pretrial seated the badges, and Burke relied on human nature to trust what they had to say. Trooper Palombo affirmed he had reviewed allegations with Patty Bono and Janet McCarthy. However, his story deviated subtly from the version McCarthy had sworn two days before. The discrepancies wafted out the window.

McCarthy recounted before the court, "There was a plain, white, concrete wall at the scene of the assault, and Palombo drove me right to the spot without my direction." Her ordeal began late at night on Hanover Street in the North End after she had been drinking.

Unfortunately, no jury listened to the pretrial hearing testimony to compare the stories. The 16 jurors sat in judgment at the trial a few months later; they never heard the subtle contradictions. Burke preyed on human nature to place trust in a badge, and the team promoted their representation on the record in front of the press.

"Did you go to the area Janet McCarthy described?" the inquisitor asked his partner.

"I had Ms. McCarthy escort me or show me the direction to the best of her knowledge," Palombo stated with detailed precision. "We arrived on Bennington Street in East Boston. She directed me down Bennington Street to Beechmont Avenue. She then directed me through a series of turns, rights and lefts, until I came on Crescent Avenue in Revere."

Of course, Palombo executed a search warrant in this case on Crescent Avenue at the Weyants' home where Paradiso had a room. The booty recovered bolstered the state's speculation in Joan's case, not Marie's, but the saga continued.

"Ms. McCarthy brought me to Crescent Avenue," the trooper continued. "At the end of the hill, she directed me through another right and maybe a fork to the left. At the very bottom of the hill, she directed me onto an abandoned desolate road. She was very vivid in her recollections."

"Can you describe that particular area?" the moustached litigator pitched.

"On the left-hand side is a cement wall covered with graffiti." The enforcer took the sketchy encounter she described on the night that it happened and intentionally placed the victim in the vicinity where the suspect had lived.

The defense unknowingly made a point that refuted assertions leaked to the FBI, but the hidden contradiction was beyond the defense's reach, locked in FBI files.

"When Ms. Iannuzzi's body was found there was certain jewelry found on her," Rappaport stated. "Is that correct?"

"That's correct," the lead investigator confirmed. "Her jewelry was intact; that's correct."

The undercover cop facilitated Burke's intention to add another victim to the list, and testimony turned to the fate of Joan Webster. Long, dark hair seemed to link Joan to the other young women, and allegations brought Burke's audience to the edge of the water to ponder where the missing student was disposed. Then, Trooper Andrew Palombo entered Joan's picture as evidence in the Iannuzzi pretrial; it was a calculated scheme to add her to the list of victims Burke trotted out. The officer detailed the discovery of the *Malafemmena* for the court, but the boat had nothing to do with Marie Iannuzzi's murder. Unverified avowals forced Burke's pieces to fit without a single piece of real evidence to connect any of them. Trial by tabloid was moving the prosecutor's illusion forward.

Next up was a Palombo look-alike officer, Nick Saggese, a diver with the Boston Police Department scuba team. Authorities had already assigned teams to search the waters at the site of the boat's recovery, but the ADA directed his own exploration. Saggese plunged at the edge of Pier 7 where Paradiso tied the *Malafemmena* to the Erie Barge in May 1981.

"At whose request were you there?" the public defender asked.

"I was there at your request," the diver replied. "I found a gun. It was found directly below where the boat was."

"As the boat comes up," the defense cross-examined, "is there kind of a suction effect?"

"Not really," Saggese explained, "we had dug around the boat the previous night."

The frogman surfaced with what looked like a gun, an item everyone else had suspiciously missed.

Another impression was conjured while the diver answered Burke's questions; Saggese was part of the team that brought up the scuttled boat in September 1983. He stated, for the record, the divers found no navigational equipment on the sunken vessel. The statement was true, but Burke was constructing a misleading story a step at a time. Using the public's confidence in badges, he seeded false perceptions as his foundation. According to the state's vision, his suspect stripped equipment from the *Malafemmena* and stashed it in the Weyants' attic, but that was in July 1981. The distortion Burke plotted conveniently planted the so-called evidence where he wanted it found.

"Other than missing equipment," Rappaport delved deeper, "was the boat fairly well intact?"

"It was, sir," the officer earnestly answered, then added, "I think part of the rudder was broken off."

The testimony of the day predicted Joan Webster's fate left her in the depths of Boston Harbor. The presumed offender reported the alleged crime scene missing on July 26, 1981, four months before she disappeared. A diver involved in the recovery recalled the rudder was broken when the crew carefully hoisted the craft out of the water right where Lenny moored it. The Chris Craft could not be steered. Saggese acknowledged that Burke led the special investigation to add necessary evidence if Lenny forced the missing graduate student down the plank. Regardless, the media continued to promote the state's incredulous tale, and the intelligence-trained parents concurred.

Before that day's session adjourned, the players traipsed back up to the bench with attorney Walter Underhill, counsel for the state's next witness. Underhill had a problem he needed addressed. An outstanding contempt charge hung over Candy Weyant for taking the fifth during the Joan Webster grand jury. She refused to answer whether she knew Leonard Paradiso on the advice of her lawyer; at the time, the state had charged her as an accessory after-the-fact for Marie's murder. The presiding judge granted Lenny's girlfriend immunity pertaining to Joan's case, and Burke called Candy back to the secret session for Joan. The problem was that she was still vulnerable to the prosecutor's tricks for Iannuzzi, and the cases were inextricably tangled. Flanagan's pupil had craftily created a mess that entrapped Lenny's alibi for the night Marie died.

Boston's broken system heaped the weight of their dysfunction on the witness the next morning. Burke had already charged Candy Weyant as an accessory in the Iannuzzi murder, but immunized her to avoid the same charge for Joan. Candy began her testimony by taking the fifth, but Burke expanded his benevolence to the declared hostile witness to include immunity regarding Marie Iannuzzi. The court compelled the harassed woman to answer the litigator's questions, and disregarded the Federal indictment sought across town. The conniving prosecutor instigated the Federal probe, and orchestrated jeopardy for her wherever she did or did not talk. After all, she vouched for the subject of Burke's obsession, and she held the title for the boat where Joan reputedly took her last breath.

Burke methodically laid his groundwork. First, he established the couple had been together for thirteen years. Then, the ADA showed her the photographs Trooper Palombo entered into evidence of concrete retainers. The location, where Palombo directed an earlier witness and took pictures, was near the Weyants' home. Candy affirmed there were seawalls a few blocks from her house, but she did not know what was painted on the barricades. They were not the plain white cement walls McCarthy remembered, but walls decorated by local artists in the incriminating vicinity where Palombo guided the victim's memory.

"Do you recognize that car?" Burke smirked to himself as he handed Lenny's girlfriend a photograph. "Tell his Honor what color that car is."

"Yellow," she answered without hesitation. "His brother, Michael, had a yellow Caddy some time ago. I never saw this car in Lenny's possession."

Police confiscated the picture from Paradiso's albums when they raided the Weyants' home. The team transformed the large, white four-door Janet McCarthy hopped into on July 10, 1980, to match pieces that investigators could find to use against him. Burke undoubtedly hoped for an admission that the yellow car belonged to Paradiso, but unfortunately, the disappointment did not slow the accusations.

Anyone tuned in to the Iannuzzi pretrial knew this charade was really all about Joan. Burke's attention quickly turned to his construed crime scene, the *Malafemmena*, and Pier 7. Candy readily admitted she helped Paradiso strip down the boat in July 1981. The jurist ignored a simple fact; it made no sense for the suspect to strip a boat he intended to keep. In addition, the prosecutor's own witness, Nick Saggese, revealed the craft had a broken rudder.

"Did you help Mr. Paradiso strip a ship-to-shore radio, a Danforth compass, and a Danforth depth finder?" Burke described what enforcers confiscated from the attic during the April 25, 1983, search.

However, at the secret session across town in a Federal courtroom, two witnesses already confirmed that Ray Jeff made the missing apparatus; the two brands could not be interchanged. Witnesses in the tandem sessions disclosed two different things, but the public was only privy to the illusion the state devised. Those delegated to serve justice ignored the inconvenient fact that the boys did not retrieve the devices that matched with the resurrected *Malafemmena.*

"The boat wasn't stolen," the counselor accused, "was it?"

"No," the witness admitted.

"That boat was still above water November 28, 1981, when Joan Webster disappeared!" The ADA paused for effect. "Wasn't it, Ms. Weyant?"

She did not see it go down, but knew Lenny said it was gone on July 26, 1981. Candy's answer jived with everyone else the authorities had talked to, and reinforced that no one saw the boat after the date in July. Headlines doubled up the next day reflecting the prosecution's slant on two murders, and the Federal indictments handed up against Leonard Paradiso and Candy Weyant.

The only rat that bolstered Burke's confabulation was Robert Bond. He insisted Paradiso seriously confessed that he murdered Joan on a boat that evidently did not exist at the time. The convicted murderer waited downstairs while Burke appealed to protect him. Judge Donahue considered the motions again.

"I suppose at some time you better tell Mr. Rappaport who he is," Judge Donahue suggested.

"Judge," Burke whined, "he's afraid. He's been threatened by Paradiso. He's not going to come aboard and testify unless we can guarantee his safety."

"He can't testify out of the presence of the defendant," Donahue reminded the offense.

"Unless Paradiso waives it," Burke insanely suggested.

The likelihood of this burly weightlifter, who callously murdered two girlfriends, being afraid of Lenny was slim to none. Defense Attorney Rappaport pleaded for discovery.

"I just don't want to deny him that chance," Burke said in all fairness.

The insincere solicitor uttered the avowal in one breath, then moved for a protective order of discovery in the next. The accused has the right to confront their accusers, but the prosecutor was hoping the defendant would forego his right. Anxiety mounted, and the state's representative of justice offered an affidavit; submitting a sworn document would enter allegations into the proceedings unchallenged. Robert Bond was the key to the story, the device needed to pull the visions together. Despite the state's need for the con's rendition, he did not take the stand that day.

The court tagged Bond's affidavit as evidence item #15; the judge sealed and impounded the statement on March 13, 1984. Meanwhile, the discretion of the court upheld the right of free speech for the media, and reporters scribbled whatever they managed to hear. Burke piled on three more indictments against Paradiso to cover every possibility in a jury's decision. The defendant pleaded "not guilty" to the charges of assault and battery, intent to murder, and intent to rape.

The population devoured every morsel of scandal over the weekend, and they were ripe for more when the pretrial reconvened on Monday. Ralph "Death Row Tony" Pisa assumed the position in front of the court on March 12, 1984, and well rehearsed for Burke's deliberate questions. Pisa was the third witness to come forward alleging Paradiso murdered both women being fused in the Iannuzzi case.

"I show you this letter with an envelope," Burke submitted. "Do you recognize this?"

"Yeah," Pisa nodded, "this is the letter I received from Paradiso on October 1, 1977. He asked me to contact John Cavicchi. I had recommended him when Lenny was working on his appeal for the Constance Porter case."

Burke established the two inmates' acquaintance going back several years. The self-styled jailhouse lawyer referred Paradiso to his lawyer two years before Marie Iannuzzi died. When Lenny's name came up as a possible suspect in August 1979, he retained the advocate to help clear his name. Paradiso already had a working relationship with the lawyer when Paradiso knocked on Cavicchi's door on Christmas Eve, 1979.

The defense argued confidentiality with an employee of the lawyer Paradiso had retained in 1979, but the court quickly shot down the concept of privilege. Tony titillated the audience by insinuating that Paradiso had whispered his determination, "There won't be witnesses the next time." However, the self-incrimination supposedly happened when they coexisted at Norfolk years before some offender murdered Marie. When broadcasters plastered Paradiso's image all over the news, spiced with the Websters' appeal, Pisa finally crawled from his hole to turn state's evidence. The alleged admission sidestepped the obvious; the unknown killer recklessly discarded Marie Iannuzzi's body on the rocks by the Pine River, and Paradiso knew people saw him with the victim. The innuendo maneuvered the focus to the baffling disappearance of Joan Webster.

No one could verify the conversation Pisa claimed he had with Paradiso on Christmas Eve, 1979, but the furloughed felon said nothing to the authorities at the time. Paradiso felt pressure to take a lie detector or go before a grand jury, according to Burke's accommodating witness. The "heat" escalated Paradiso's discomfort, and he solicited help from the jailhouse lawyer. The facts were that Cavicchi arranged a polygraph Paradiso passed in August 1979, and there was no grand jury convened for Marie Iannuzzi until 1982, suspiciously in a different county. The first slated session, shortly after the Websters' high-powered meeting in February 1982, was the *Commonwealth v. Leonard J. Paradiso.* The parolee was disgruntled with Pisa because the convicted murderer had not returned Lenny's papers for the Constance Porter case. The illogical notion the clam peddler trusted him now was absurd, but court observers missed the subtle deception.

The prosecutor faced his stoolie as he moved into Joan's case. Both men wiped perspiration from their upper lips, but their thick moustaches concealed any detectable twitch of deceit. The state submitted no evidence of a call to the prison pay phones on December 18, 1981, that connected Pisa to the outside. No logs or recordings corroborated Pisa's assertion that Paradiso called him, out of the blue, on the felon's birthday, and blurted out an implied confession for Joan Webster's murder.

"They didn't find a body," Paradiso allegedly confided to the confined killer. "They only found her purse."

When Bond's statement broke in the news, "Death Row Tony" finally found his conscience, and he contacted Middlesex County. DA Scott Harshbarger replaced John Droney as the public defender, and controlled any objections that stood between Pisa and freedom. The convicted murderer first met with Tom Reilly, first ADA in Middlesex County, and Det. Lt. Tom Spartichino from the DA's Crime Prevention and Control unit that initially handled Joan's case. Within a month, Reilly brought in ADA Tim Burke from Suffolk County to go over the story, but all protocol was broken with what the con did next.

"The only way I would come forward is that I not receive the reward." On the surface, Pisa's motive to turn state's evidence sounded sincere. "I prefaced this with Mr. Reilly, along with Mr. Burke, along with Mr. Webster, along with every other person I've talked to."

Controlling forces obliterated all rules of proper procedure. Why was Pisa talking to George Webster? George and Eleanor now had assurances from a felon who was once on death row. According to Pisa, he did not want their money to testify about an assumed crime that hadn't been charged. What a nice guy.

A jury convicted Tony Pisa of first-degree murder in his joint venture with Roy White, and the judge sentenced him to death. He spent the first three years in solitary confinement. Pisa benefited from luck, and he studied the law to improve his situation. Massachusetts dropped the death penalty and his sentence reduced to a second-degree charge, opening the door for a parole. The Supreme Judicial Court upheld Tony Pisa's conviction, but nothing guaranteed a parole. The courts denied every previous petition Pisa submitted for a new trial, that is, until Tony had something the state wanted. A pardon was preferred to clear his record and clear the way to pursue law, but the top priority was to get out. "Death Row Tony's" pulse quickened on December 15, 1982, when Governor Ed King signed a new death penalty bill that went into effect on January 1, 1983, and suddenly nothing was certain anymore.

Pisa dialed the phone to the Middlesex DA and set the wheels in motion with his unverified tale. The cunning participant met in the Middlesex and Suffolk County offices, and he assured the "Man from New Jersey." First ADA Tom Reilly arranged for a polygraph with William LaParl, and Pisa predictably revised his version of the George Deane murder. Pisa submitted yet another motion to the court for a new trial on June 13, 1983, and Judge Elam took it under advisement. Enablers quietly shuffled the witness into a prerelease facility shortly before he took the stand during the Iannuzzi pretrial. Pisa was counting the days. He spun both cases Burke needed on March 12, 1984. Pisa knew Middlesex County would reverse any objections blocking his way out the door that Suffolk County held wide open for him.

Burke and Reilly interrupted Judge Elam's court the very next day, and threw every tenet out the window to spring Pisa. The lawyers conveyed a sense of urgency that the murderer felt threatened and requested a bail hearing on the spot. The courts do not grant bail to convicted felons, and a parole board determines a prisoner's release. Pisa found the idea of a change of confinement to be distasteful, and the suits seemed more determined to satisfy him than protecting the public, the job the state mandated.

"We, being the district attorney's office," Reilly told the Middlesex County judge, "we would review his case if and when he were to testify for the Commonwealth with respect to Mr. Paradiso. There have been threats made to Mr. Pisa."

"There is real concern for his safety," Burke chimed in.

The Suffolk County Assistant DA rattled off the "threats" witnesses had ostensibly received from Paradiso, and he bewailed the burden on the state to move them. Some authority arranged to move one man twice because of supposed threats against his life, but Burke claimed the danger, not Robert Bond. The zealous ADA also insisted steps were necessary to move a Revere woman who testified at the pretrial hearing. It was not apparent yet, but participants reneged on promises dangled for Charlene Bullerwell. The illusion that Paradiso threatened anyone from behind bars, just because Burke said so, justified two counties to beg for a convicted killer's release.

"It's based upon existing, real-life threats to this man's life," Burke shuddered.

"I don't feel that he is any threat to leave the jurisdiction," Reilly vouched.

Incredibly, "Death Row Tony" walked.

Judge Donahue denied Burke's attempt to include the harrowing tales of terrorized women at trial, but he had satisfied a primary objective successfully. An enraged public devoured every word, and stories fermented an increasing hatred for the target of Burke's obsession. Donahue delayed the start of the trial under the pretense that all the publicity would die down at some point. Regardless, the venue favored the prosecution—and their dirty tricks.

Joan Lucinda Webster
August 19, 1956 to November 28, 1981

January 5, 1980: Joan, George, Eve, Steve, Eleanor, and Anne Webster

Former Suffolk County ADA
Timothy M. Burke (Boston Herald
photograph)

Now deceased MSP lead
investigator Andrew Palombo

Former MSP Sgt. Carmen Tammaro
(Boston Globe photograph through Getty Images)

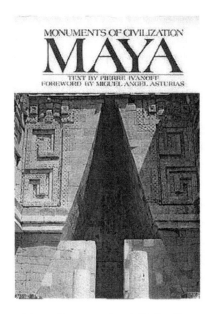

Maya: Monuments of Civilization
by Pierre Ivanoff

Maya publisher logo
Grosset & Dunlap

Joan Webster's
missing
gold charm
bracelet

Purse set belonging to Candy Weyant

Commonwealth witness Robert Bond (Boston Herald photograph)

Commonwealth witness Ralph "Death Row Tony" Pisa
(*Boston Herald* photograph)

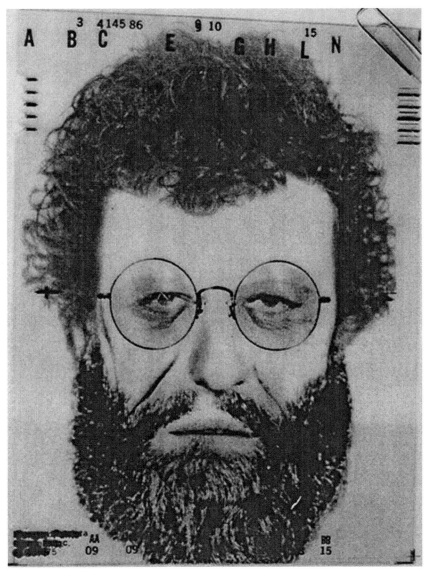

Composite of bearded man believed seen with Joan Webster at Logan
Airport on November 28, 1981. Image created in December 1981.

The alleged crime scene, the *Malafemmena,* raised at Pier 7 in Boston on
September 27, 1983. (*Boston Herald* photograph)

Joan Webster's remains recovered at Chebacco Road gravesite
in Hamilton, Massachusetts on April 18, 1990.

The right side of Joan Webster's cranium. (The mandible and maxilla are detached from the skull.)

Joan Webster's headstone located in New Jersey.

CHAPTER 15

How Offensive

"RETURN TO SENDER."

An impersonal stamp on the envelope was the reply. I had mailed a kind letter and a gift to my daughters, and all I got was this generic stamp. It's hard to express how painful it is to have mail returned in this frosty manner. I was cut off from my children. I had trusted the advice of a counselor, but I did not know at the time my trust was used against me; the counselor colluded with Steve to keep the girls away from me. I did not stop trying, however, though my kind gestures seemed futile, and the family still refused to explain why I was being cut off.

"Steve, could I at least have some photos of the girls?" I pleaded, but he ignored my request.

I tracked one of the girls down from an address in the school directory, but another name was on the placard, and no one answered the door. Was this an alias? The girls did not want me to find them, and their father didn't want me to have any part in their lives. Still, I wanted to connect with them somehow. One Christmas I placed a sign on their lawn.

"Dear Girls, Merry Christmas! Love, Mom."

Sadly, uncaring elders took down the sign in the middle of the night before the neighbors could see it. George's words in the *Boston Magazine* echoed in my mind. "We go through the holiday—but it's tough. You live with it all of the time." That is how he characterized the suffering after Joan's loss. They were empty words, the right sounding ones, but insincere from my experience.

Hand-painted boxes lovingly illustrated special moments in my girls' lives, but they rejected the Christmas gift even before they received them. Sarah O'Brien refused to extend my kindness, and told me they did not want them. A friend finally delivered the December gift to the house in July.

"Make her stop!" Sandy heard my oldest angrily protest.

"They are nice boxes," Steve said in front of the messenger bearing my gifts.

The hostility was irrational for an act of kindness and was completely confusing. Every kind gesture I extended inexplicably hit a painful nerve with my children. Why were these acts of kindness offensive? Sandy's observation of my youngest daughter's reaction gave me a glimpse of the control held over my children. She cried and walked out of the room holding her box. Deep inside, my children did not want this separation, but they could not make Daddy unhappy.

Each Christmas filled my heart with excruciating sadness, but I kept trying to reach out to my children. As the next Christmas approached, I knocked on the door clutching two little books. The panic echoed from behind the closed door, and my children quickly scurried into the basement. George sat in the green leather chair by the bookcase and tottered from Scotch as he stumbled to hide. Their Christmas spirit was pathetic. I knew they were there, but they still tried to disappear. Finally, I just left the books in the mailbox. The books contained the Websters' own words pleading for answers about what happened to Joan. However, the family chose to support Bond instead of other family that had lived through this with them. History repeated itself. Joan was murdered decades ago, and now the Websters had lost another family member: me. I had been discarded; I was dead in the hearts and minds of my children.

Looking back, my estrangement from the family was a long journey, a campaign as long as the conquest in Chile. It began before I discovered my child's terrifying letter and sought help. The family eliminated me with the clandestine precision of a CIA plot. A distressing factor gnawed at me. I was the only non-blood relative who was part of the immediate family when Joan disappeared. I had insight no one else had, and I could not reconcile the differences in the family's behaviors. On one hand was the image of bereft parents whose child was torn from their lives. On the other hand, the family ripped me apart from my children. I had to find the answers.

Sweltering heat enveloped the city as the gavel called the court to order for the *Commonwealth v. Leonard J. Paradiso*. Indictments charged him with the rape and murder of Marie Iannuzzi, though the many grand juries, pretrial hearings, and tabloid headlines presumed this was the tale of two murders. George and Eleanor Webster positioned themselves in the packed courtroom, certain that evidence in this trial connected the accused to the death of their daughter. Day after day, cameras snapped their stoic faces, and reporters quoted their reactions to the Iannuzzi case. The state had so successfully tied the two murders together that it seemed almost natural to people for the Websters to render their judgment.

Court convened on July 9, 1984. Opening statements laid out the state's ludicrous contention. Burke prepared for the case with the predetermined end and worked his way back into the crime giving mangled explanations to make all the pieces fit. The public screamed for justice, and Burke eagerly served up an answer for them—the end justified the means. Players distorted critical information, or withheld it altogether, creating the desired sensation. Collaborators promoted unverified rumors as fact, and the public unwittingly cheered the gross injustice. Authorities filed exculpatory evidence under case numbers that were out of reach to the defense. Paradiso's defenders could not find some witnesses, and other observers changed relevant testimony.

The defense responded with common sense. Advocates presented reasonable doubt; there was incriminating evidence pointing to another offender. Boston's particular brand of justice continued to play out in the press, and the citizens of New England eagerly awaited the outcome. Sadly, Paradiso received a trial by tabloid. The people in charge aggravated his justice with hidden agendas.

The jurors in the Paradiso case went on a field trip, or a view as the state called it. The excursion was a clever move by the prosecution. Jurors piled on a bus like schoolchildren and herded to the locales referenced in Marie's case. After the whirlwind tour, every brow perspired as jurors settled back into their seats in the stuffy, crammed courtroom. Burke called his first witness.

Father Aidan Walsh raised his right hand, and his clerical collar established the desired air of trust. The strategy was brilliant, a manipulative one, but brilliant nonetheless. First, Burke took the jury on a field trip so they would have a setting in mind when he spoke about it later, then he called a priest, of all people, as the first witness. In Catholic Boston, the word of a priest was taken seriously. Father Walsh performed the marriage of Michael Milano and Maureen Trotto on August 11, 1979, a wedding that the defendant had attended.

"Miss Iannuzzi was at the Milano's house party later that evening. She appeared to be intoxicated. The family seemed to be embarrassed by her behavior. Freddie, one of the groom's brothers, was interested in having some kind of relationship with Marie. Young

Fred Milano wanted to leave with her." The father testified the family wanted Marie to leave after making a scene with her boyfriend's cousin. "I offered her a ride, but Marie declined."

He continued his testimony, placing Paradiso at the Milanos' house that night. "I talked to him outside, briefly. They had a refrigerated truck to carry frozen fish or something, and I know they needed ice. They got ice out of the truck."

This subtle disclosure slipped corroborating evidence into the record that favored the accused if investigators had thoroughly checked at the time of the crime. Paradiso returned to the Milano's early Sunday morning to pick up clams kept in the truck. He delivered them with Freddie Milano, the subject of Marie's attention the night before. The priest's testimony added nothing to further the state's case against the suspect seated at the defense table, but the strategy had a subliminal effect. Though the specific words of his testimony did little to advance the prosecution's case, by starting with a priest Burke established a tone of honesty and brought credibility to all the other witnesses. By virtue of its connection to the father, the ploy made the entire case seem legitimate by association.

The next witness was Ruth Scully. She justified ADA Burke's intrusion into another county's cold case. As an employee of the Suffolk County DA's office, she drew diagrams used in presenting a case. Her graphics reinforced an old law Burke relied on to take over the case from Essex County, the office that had failed to press charges in the case for two and a half years. Boaters found the victim on the rocky bank of the Pine River not far from the Suffolk County line. The courtroom got a lesson in geometry as she explained the measurements taken with a sixteen and a half foot rod, and scale drawings. Essex County DA Kevin Burke stated he transferred the case because authorities believed Marie was killed somewhere else, then disposed in his county. However, ADA Tim Burke argued she was killed right on that spot. The taxpayer cash register kept ringing. ADA Tim Burke had another motive to be involved in this case, and Scully's testimony added nothing to support the notion that Paradiso committed the crime.

First thing the next morning, the ADA approached the bench.

"My next witness is very afraid to testify with the cameras and media," Burke fretted. "She's afraid because Paradiso has a lot of friends in the area."

"One of these days," Rappaport countered, "I'd like to hear who these friends are."

According to Burke, Paradiso was busy threatening everyone the state called to the stand. Despite Burke's efforts, Judge Donahue declined to restrict the First Amendment rights of the media. Par-adiso's court-appointed attorney, Stephen Rappaport, mocked all the elusive friends of his hapless client that Burke portended were the ready defense of the confined man. The prosecutor previewed Chris-tine DeLisi's testimony during the grand jury, and had the weight of his office to sway her recollection in front of the press. The dead woman's best friend took the stand next, and Burke massaged what the jury would hear.

Christine arrived at the bar about midnight and hooked up with Marie and Michael Kamer when she got there. The time she gave conflicted with the police report taken when events were fresh that stated Christine arrived at 12:30 a.m. The young woman left about one, presuming that's when the bar closed. In between, she danced with the victim and casually bantered with her friend. The camera-shy witness recounted that night at the bar and identified Paradiso as the man holding the door when Marie left.

"Wait for me," DeLisi recalled Marie's last words when she left the bar. "I'll be back in twenty-five minutes to half an hour."

When Marie asked her friend to wait, the young woman turned her limited attention to the door and watched her friend walk out. "He was holding the door for Marie." However, Christine had not waited long enough to know whether her friend returned or not. The defendant was the last person this witness saw with the victim.

As the defense took its turn, both counsels sidled up to the bench, as if no one would notice. Marie's best friend witnessed Marie's trepidation after an argument with her boyfriend, David Doyle. The terrified, young woman moved in with Christine for sev-eral days in 1979, and Rappaport narrowed the date to sometime in June based on multiple accounts of the episode. Doyle's foreboding behavior occurred about two months before an offender strangled the last breath from Marie. The defense wanted to pursue a line of questions to get the incident into the record.

"If there is other evidence of David Doyle's involvement in the death of Marie Iannuzzi…" the presiding robe decided, "but at this point in the case, I'm going to exclude the statement the victim allegedly made at the time."

Rappaport handed Christine a copy of her grand jury testimony to refresh her memory. The defense counsel wanted to know about the four or five days Marie came to live with her, a few weeks before her garroted throat ended up on the mortician's table. DeLisi's mem-ory fogged up; her response to the questions about the marks on Marie's neck conflicted with her grand jury testimony. Now she described them merely as scratches.

Her words stared back at her from the transcript, "She said David Doyle had tried to kill her."

"Ma'am, did you ever state," the attorney cross-examined, "she had strangulation marks on her neck, very red marks, and handprints around her neck?"

"I don't remember," the best friend nervously replied, as if one could ever forget such a traumatic event.

The woman lamented hardship in and out of the hospital, and told Rappaport she had suffered an asthma attack, cancer treatments, and was hit by a truck. Burke whined about the contradicting testimony entering the record, and the court played along. The judge absurdly ruled that the incident, an event that happened only two months before someone strangled the victim, was too remote for relevance in the case. About the only thing DeLisi was clear about at trial was seeing Paradiso's courtesy to hold the door as her intoxicated friend walked out.

Back at the bench, Burke dismissed the suspicions pointing to Doyle. "It's a hearsay statement."

The offensive prosecutor portrayed the prior incident as a fight just as anyone might have with a partner. Judge Donahue upheld his ruling; what Marie's friend witnessed and remembered did not count.

Christine's conscience tormented her, because her testimony was misleading. She confided to her friend, Dennis Albano, that she was badgered to testify for the prosecution against Leonard Paradiso.

"The state police kept calling me and coming to the house until I relented," Christine cried to Albano. "They said I would never see my child again!"

The coercive tactics hung over her head and mirrored the persecution Candy Weyant suffered. Authorities suspended the fear of prosecution over her head; they warned her that she could lose her child if she did not cooperate. Manipulators preyed on her vulnerability, a soft spot for any mother, her child. Coercion and harassment produced a witness that bolstered the prosecution's presumptions with subtly sanitized testimony. Her testimony at the grand jury implicated the abusive boyfriend as the culprit. On the stand during trial, however, she feigned forgetfulness and misfortune that distorted the real picture. The ADA's whining compounded the gambit that kept relevant information from the jury. A heavy underhanded strategy intimidated witnesses.

Burke lined up willing witnesses for months and had them stuffed up his sleeve. Observers saw Paradiso with Marie at the bar. Paradiso never denied his encounter with the victim, and in fact told police he was at the bar two times to return her belongings. The next witness bolstered a more sinister setup for the prosecution. Michael Kamer testified that he had played with keys resting on the bar in front of the victim. A tag hanging from the key ring said, "Day," the surname of Marie's stepsiblings. Doyle gave police the same name in New Jersey when cops arrested him on the day of Marie's funeral.

"He talked to her roughly half an hour or forty-five minutes," Kamer suggested.

However, the witness mingled with friends at the bar, not focused on the suspect's coming and going. Kamer perceived the interval between the first arrival and the second departure as one block of time instead of two, much shorter meetings. Burke projected the image that the defendant was at the bar the whole time. The impression from Kamer's testimony also contradicted the twenty minutes police noted in their reports at the time. The misrepresentation fed Burke's notion of an obsessed sexual predator hustling Marie at the bar.

Finally, the prosecution brought in a member of law enforcement. Trooper Rick Fraelick was one of the first responders on the scene after the call came in. He arrived at the crime scene and viewed Marie Iannuzzi's body on the bank of the Pine River late in the afternoon on August twelfth.

"There was a gate," the officer described the location. It was a two-section gate opening from the middle and swinging back to the other areas of the fence.

Conley and Daggets was a shuttered up business, and a fence barricaded access to the rear of the building where the body rested. The offender would have had to get out of the car to open the gate. Bushes had grown up on the front side of the fence, but the gate swung open toward the back. The explanation DA Kevin Burke offered, that the culprit killed Marie elsewhere, was more logical with the setting instead of Marie sitting patiently in a car while someone pushed the barrier out of the way.

"When I stepped on the rocks," Fraelick said, "I slipped for a moment."

Fraelick had slipped on the stony embankment as he edged down the slope to the discarded body. Strangely, this little morsel about the slippery rocks found its way into Bond's rendition of events purportedly confessed by Paradiso. The court secreted the amazing coincidence in Bond's statement in Exhibit #15, the sealed affidavit.

Fraelick's job was to determine whether there was evidence of foul play, and of course there was. He observed jewelry on the victim, a factor that ruled out robbery during the initial investigation. Rainy conditions left the victim's clothing wet, but the trooper did not know whether any tests were done. No lab analysis determined whether fresh or salt water dampened the garments. Rigor mortis had set in; the grim reaper's clock froze the young woman's hands in a clawed position. Her fingers had stiffened in the last desperate moments of her life trying to fend off a killer.

The trooper was a distinguished public servant. He was part of the team that conducted surveillance on the Lancaster Street Garage, the base where mob leader Whitey Bulger held court. Unscrupulous colleagues undermined the detective's dangerous work in squalid conditions, and tipped-off Bulger about bugging warrants. Trooper Fraelick was a first responder when passersby found this young woman's body. His job was to determine whether a crime had been committed, preserve the scene, and decide whether an investigation was warranted. The man was a true defender of the public's safety, and Burke used the officer's credibility to promote his agenda.

The state's designated hitter introduced parole records next. The prosecution called retired officer Victor Anchukaitis. The nervous pensioner pulled out his handkerchief and wiped perspiration from his brow, then swore to tell the truth. Attention turned to the entries Anchukaitis made in his notes on Monday, August 13, 1979.

"I received a telephone call from Mr. Paradiso," Victor recalled. "I'd say roughly 9:30-ish. He was scheduled to change parole officers."

The typed notes kept a running account of the parole officer's contact with his assignee. "Called—Waited for new PO to check him out. This PO gave subject PO's number. Subject said he would call."

"He said he'd like to come in and talk to me," Anchukaitis embellished the first entry to Burke's satisfaction. "He had something important to talk to me about."

ADA Burke inferred Paradiso had a dire situation to discuss, and planned to come into the office later that day. The nervous supervisor tried to recall whether the girlfriend came with him, and relented when Burke said that she did. According to the testimony, the couple came into Victor's office about noon on Monday, but according to the notes this did not happen as prescribed. The time distinction was important to the young lawyer's theory, because he alleged Paradiso disclosed his dilemma before examiners identified Marie's body. Anchukaitis read his entries, but with Burke's help, skimmed over some important details. The notation for August 13, 1979, only referred to a call without logging a time, and the entry only noted the change of parole officers. The next memo was August 15, 1979, recording the transfer request to the new parole officer, Jim O'Neil. Something obscured the date on the third entry, but a handwritten date, August 13, 1979, was added below it. Again, there was no time noted.

"I met Lenny and his girlfriend," he said, concealing the fact that he had actually met them in a bar on Tuesday, August fourteenth.

He struggled with his conscience and his recollections. Truthful testimony could jeopardize his pension, so he cautiously walked the fine line Burke cast to hook Paradiso.

"You're not exactly sure, or are you sure," Rappaport challenged, "that Ms. Weyant was with him?"

"To the best of my recollection, his lady friend was with him," Victor repeated without giving a definitive answer. His notes were right in front of him stating he met both of them, it just was not where and when Burke suggested.

"There's another notation in between the two we've been talking about both marked August 13, 1979." Paradiso's attorney suspiciously looked at the notes. "It's a different date. It's out of sequence."

"I don't understand that one at all, sir," Anchukaitis perspired in the sweltering heat of the packed courtroom. "Yes sir, it's out of sequence."

The next witness Burke had scheduled was causing a problem. He made it clear to the judge that he wanted her testimony in the record. The witness had graphically described how Paradiso got rid of a corpse, but Marie's killer had not chopped up her body or weighted it down in the ocean. The FBI's confidential source secretly squealed that this witness had vital information. According to the informant, she had knowledge of where Joan's body was dumped. The trial on the docket was Marie Iannuzzi, whose body rolled down a five-foot embankment to the edge of the Pine River.

"I suggest to the court that it is admissible, because it shows the same general pattern," Burke reasoned. "He doesn't bury them. He kills them and tries to dispose of them by putting them in water."

Donahue had already disallowed David Doyle's prior act, but irrationally, he was amenable to let Bullerwell squawk. The dictating robe was willing, but the witness was not. The anxious attorney ran to the bench, perplexed that his witness would not come into the courtroom. Charlene Bullerwell waited outside, and Burke bemoaned the presence of the press again, despite the fact they promoted his side of the story. The state panicked. They had a witness in the hall that refused to enter the courtroom. Finally, the judge summoned the witness for a lobby conference.

"I've had several seizures because of all this," Bullerwell lamented. "I'm on medication. I've had major brain surgery. I don't remember anything."

She had testified in the pretrial a few months before, but misfortune had wiped her memory clean. One had to wonder whether she compared notes with Christine DeLisi. Paradiso's supposed admission to his occasional date in 1980 came after two FBI agents pressured her to talk.

"They promised me they would move me, they would pack my things." Charlene had no problem remembering the promises made. "I got none of this. They told me my name wasn't going to get out. I got a check for two hundred dollars and moved myself."

Bullerwell's selective memory exposed the conspirators promising favors to get statements they wanted. Burke had appealed to Judge Elam to get Pisa out of jail with similar claims Paradiso was threatening witnesses. Paradiso was in jail and closely watched. Burke was the voice of looming threats. The Feds predicted Charlene's pressured testimony before she gave it, and it conveniently fit with the speculation churned about Joan.

"I will not go into that courtroom," the redheaded housewife adamantly refused.

Burke conceded, forced to move on to another witness. His failure to seat a key telltale on the stand only slowed his premeditated cause against Paradiso for Joan's murder. Bullerwell's conscience and selective loss of memory uncovered more evidence of a pattern, but a design that court observers could not see—coerced witnesses.

Essex County failed to indict the boyfriend when they first handled the Iannuzzi case. The authorities had an abundance of incriminating, circumstantial evidence that the killing was a crime of passion. Burke marched the first responders on the case to the stand next, but the heat must have dulled the jury's senses. Carl Sjoberg was the Essex County trooper originally assigned to the case until Trooper Palombo took over in February of 1981.

"There was a knot tied in back, behind her neck," Sjoberg described the scarf used to strangle the victim. "It was secured tightly about her neck."

Sjoberg conducted interviews in the first days after the murder. However, his reports did not reflect the testimony the rehearsed witness now suggested in court.

"What did Red Milano say?" Burke asked the practiced trooper.

"He said Lenny and his girlfriend took Marie home," the enforcer said without checking the files. No surprise, the answer fit into Burke's plot. The record at the time revealed the groom's father had asked Candy Weyant to give the inebriated, young woman a ride, and she obliged her host with no suggestion that Paradiso went with them.

Police officers spoke with both Lenny and Candy. Bond's story was that Candy went to Lenny's place after the murder, and the two got their stories straight. Burke needed that to sound plausible, and the trooper obliged.

"It was verbatim," Sjoberg offered. "It was almost word for word what Lenny had told me. It appeared to me as if it had almost been rehearsed."

Another witness affirmed there was jewelry on the body and ruled robbery out. It contradicted Burke and the confidential FBI informant's attempt to enhance Paradiso's modus operandi that Lenny stole jewelry from his victims. To Rappaport's credit, he went over statements Paradiso and Weyant made to police at the time. Line by line, he disputed Sjoberg's representation that the interviews were word for word, as if the couple rehearsed them.

"My interpretation, Counselor, is that their statements were the same. They used different words, but the content was the same." After talking to Burke, the seasoned investigator thought two people giving consistent accounts of events they both witnessed were suspicious.

The defense continued to grill the nervous trooper, and he was getting confused. "Had anyone scraped under Ms. Iannuzzi's long-manicured nails? Did you get a search warrant for the vehicle Marie got a ride in? Did anyone ask the examiner to test for rape?"

"No," the officer answered repeatedly.

Sjoberg had not noted the excessive nervousness he now described, and had not observed any scratches on Paradiso. Rappaport challenged the premise of guilty behavior. He pointed out that his client was a parolee answering questions about a murder victim the defendant had seen, so nerves were only natural under the circumstances. Burke dodged a key point with the witness because the defense overlooked a subtle point in the parole notes, and unfortunately, missed the state's possible motive to railroad Paradiso. Trooper Sjoberg conferred with the man's parole officer on March 11, 1982, about other suspicions, just days after the *Commonwealth v. Leonard J. Paradiso* grand jury began. By that time, Trooper Palombo had inexplicably usurped his colleague in the Iannuzzi case. Instead, Sjoberg's new role was as a messenger cleverly dispatched to implicate Paradiso in another Boston case—Joan Webster's disappearance.

Authorities planted the seeds months before Bond moved to the Charles Street Jail to wheedle a bogus confession. Through it all, the hypnotized jurors remained dazed in the presence of George and Eleanor Webster.

Burke had no shame trying to prove his case against Paradiso, and continued putting people on the stand that exposed an inept investigation. Next up was the pathologist who described the deficiencies his autopsy produced.

"The body was dressed in a red disco outfit, including panties, which were on the victim." Dr. Katsas described how the victim was dressed when she ended up on the examiner's table.

He described the ante mortem injuries, in other words, the injuries Marie sustained before she died. The victim had several small scrapes and abrasions on the face and neck, just above where the killer tightly knotted the ligature. The doctor was exacting down to the bruise on Marie's big toe, but the injuries were not consistent with rape. The postmortem injuries were more extensive, but of course the culprit dumped the woman down a rocky embankment. The cause of death was asphyxiation. The expert determined Marie had sexual intercourse sometime before her death, between three and eighteen hours before she died.

"As to whether or not she was raped," Burke infused his motive, "are you able to form an opinion?"

"I found no injury, sir," Katsas disappointed the state. "I found no injuries in the genital area of the body."

"Do you know whether or not any test was performed," the defense countered. "Was there a test to determine who had deposited the seminal fluid?"

"I have no report that the test was done, sir," Katsas acknowledged. "I would have known if it was done."

Examiners never scraped the long-polished nails, though Marie's clawed hands had frozen in the final fight of her life. The assortment of law enforcers never observed or noted scratches on the defendant, but hideous gouges had, in fact, been observed on David Doyle. Equally unbelievable was the fact the pathologist never conducted a test to determine who deposited sperm in the deceased's vagina; seasoned investigators neglected to ask. At the time, authorities did not consider rape a factor, though the young woman had been intimate with someone during an eighteen-hour window before she died. Police reports reflected the image of a promiscuous victim who lived with her boyfriend. Police knew Marie was with another man, Eddie Fisher, on Friday night, and they knew she slipped out of sight with Freddie Milano at the house party. The autopsy photographs showed the victim's clothing intact. The gallery, sixteen-seated peers, and Joan's parents all succumbed to the prosecution's lack of common sense.

"Death Row Tony," a con and jailhouse lawyer, confidently strolled into the sweltering room. The prosecutor faced his next witness, and both men wiped the sweat from the thick moustaches that covered their lips. Burke laid out the murderer's history for the court, but skirted a significant detail.

"When did you leave Bay State Prison?" Burke cleverly asked the unsavory sort he was secretly in bed with.

"I left there early, the end of February," Pisa said. "I went to Park Drive here in Boston, a prerelease facility."

"That move occurred after you spoke to Mr. Reilly, correct?" The defense cross-examined the witness about his conversations with the Middlesex County first assistant.

"Yes," was his telling reply.

The room had the image of a rehabilitated felon who was on his way out of the system, but they were not privy to the state's gyrations in front Judge Elam. Collaborators moved Pisa right along after he came forward to help authorities nail Paradiso. He escaped confinement after making assurances to George Webster and testifying at the pretrial hearing.

"He was talking about," the con carefully followed the prosecutor's lead, "if there were no witnesses, there would be no case. I explained that's not always true, and used the John W. Webster case of 1850.

Referring to this legendary trial allowed the state to insert the name "Webster" into the minds of the jurors. However, it was irrelevant to the proceeding, because the victim in the present case had been recklessly dumped, and witnesses had seen Paradiso hold the bar door for Marie.

"Do you remember the date in December 1981 when Paradiso called you?" the offense waded in deeper.

The attorneys trudged up to the bench once again. Burke mentioned the alleged call on December 18, 1981, attempting to bring the undeclared victim into the case. He cited Anthony Jackson's case as justification to get Pisa's prior testimony into the record. The claim was that Pisa thought a comment referred to the 1850 Webster case; it did not apply to Iannuzzi, as they found her body. According to Pisa, Paradiso confessed to another crime where police only found her pocketbook. The con gasped at the thought of the missing Harvard graduate student. Burke backed off with the risk of a mistrial, and the fumble deflated the couple from New Jersey.

The defense hammered the point that the felon had his own reasons to be there. Tony Pisa was interested in Tony Pisa, and his story had already paid off. He was already out on his own recognizance, and Middlesex County was favorably reviewing his case after years of objections. Nevertheless, Burke portrayed the killer's motive as altruistic, something a good citizen would do.

Burke and Pisa both stroked their thick growths again as they faced each other.

"Do you know what the penalty for perjury is in a capital case?" Burke asked, though neither man flinched.

"Life," was the reply, solidifying Burke's image of a sincere man.

Flanagan's protégé had his lineup well planned. Trooper Andrew Palombo took the stand the next morning to insert his badge between the two felons Burke relied on.

"I became involved in the Iannuzzi investigation," Palombo said. "It was approximately February 1981. I was at the home of Cornelius Weyant in 1982 to serve a secret grand jury indictment warrant."

The attorneys quickly made their way back to the bench. The secret session was a one-sided presentation that only represented the Commonwealth's version. Burke admitted to the judge that Candy Weyant had taken the fifth on the advice of her counsel, but he also revealed a deception he spread through the press.

"Paradiso, through his attorney," Burke disclosed, "indicated that if he was called he would take the fifth." Burke did not call Paradiso to the stand during the grand jury. The misinformation dispensed through the media, though, was that he had not cooperated.

Palombo cleaned up his undercover appearance for court, and the badge he brandished implied truth. He alleged Paradiso confessed after the officer cuffed him on July 6, 1982.

"He said he had been expecting this for three years," the trooper claimed, referring to Paradiso's arrest for the murder of Marie Iannuzzi.

The officer swore he wrote it down later that night, but in fact, Palombo did not get around to bolstering his assertion until three and a half months after the arrest. On October 20, 1982, Palombo supplemented Burke's files with the alleged contention that Paradiso had suggested his own guilt. The defense missed a golden opportunity to discredit the story. Trooper Bill Johnson, a dedicated trooper who honored his commitment to defend the public, witnessed the confession according to the clean-shaven cop now on the stand.

The unusual relationship between the undercover enforcer and the other named suspect subtly slipped into the record next.

"I've talked to David Doyle twenty to thirty times," Palombo answered nonchalantly.

"Do you have any notes of those communications?" the defense logically inquired.

"No, I don't," was the lead officer's ludicrous answer.

"Do you remember the sum and substance of those conversations?" The counsel wrinkled his forehead in disbelief. "You never kept one report?"

The seasoned investigator shook his head every time. "No."

"Doyle was a suspect in this case also," Rappaport reminded the cop, "wasn't he?"

"Not in my mind," the badge inexplicably denied. "No."

The true nature of the odd couple came out in court, but massaged for the jury's consumption.

"Doyle went so far as to come to me without me asking him, to relay information or things he had heard on the street." The undercover cop was describing the behavior of a snitch in a climate where Boston's "finest" protected their informants.

Palombo knew everything collected in police files; he was the lead on the case. Regardless, the trooper ignored every standard of proper procedure for a lead officer talking to a suspect. Moreover, the seasoned investigator went into denial that police considered Doyle. In his experienced opinion, the boyfriend was not a suspect. Those sitting in judgment overlooked the inept investigation the trooper described. Investigators never collected some evidence, and conveniently mishandled other evidence to the advantage of the state's case. An underlying influence entranced the jurors. Trooper Palombo's illogical rendition satisfied George and Eleanor Webster; they were convinced Paradiso had murdered their daughter.

Guards removed his shackles, and every eye fixed on the imposing convict's walk down the aisle to take the oath. You could have heard a pin drop, or a tin dime, as the state's star witness, the main event, settled into the chair. Sgt. Tammaro, SA Steve Broce, and Suffolk County First ADA Paul Leary cocooned the Websters in the gallery, knowing what was coming next. Conspirators had Bond well rehearsed, and the state was confident that practice makes perfect.

"It was show time," Burke mused to himself. (The attorney turned author described his thoughts in *The Paradiso Files* when Bond took the stand.)

Secrecy shrouded the authorities' movements when they worked the story with Bond, but Bond unwittingly slipped an important clue into the record.

"You were sentenced on January 10, 1982." Rappaport zoomed in on the gloomy day at the courthouse when the judge imposed his sentence on Bond for the murder of Mary Foreman. "Shortly thereafter, you had some discussion, did you not, with the state police as well as Mr. Burke?"

"No," the ignorant man revealed, "I had discussion with the state police the tenth of January. The initial discussion, the first one, was January tenth."

Tammaro referred to the prior meeting when they taped the con's tale of two murders on January fourteenth. The topics on the tenth included the Websters' reward money, the dangled promise of manslaughter, and Bond's escape from the Massachusetts Department of Correction's confinement back at Walpole. By the time the group met again on the fourteenth, Tammaro arranged to intercept the letter they expected from the rat that Bond mailed out on the tenth.

Rappaport did his best to get the witness to stumble. Bond had to focus very hard to keep events in order; it was a "who's on first" routine, but Bond eventually got his story straight. Then the star witness made a critical mistake. The creators had a refutable timeline.

"He left the Milano's home at 9:30. He dropped Marie off at the Cardinale's Nest," the pretender recited his lines. "He says he got back to the Cardinale's Nest after he took his girlfriend home. He returned to the bar around eleven o'clock."

The cross-examination revealed Bond's own contradiction on another crucial point: Marie's attire.

"Did Paradiso describe all the clothing she was wearing?" Rappaport asked. "Would it refresh your recollection, sir, if I suggested she was wearing black stockings?"

"Yeah, well I know that—no, no, no, no," the dim-witted stool stuttered. "I know that she was wearing black shoes."

The stockings were a key piece of evidence in the devised crime, and the coached witness went on to describe Paradiso's struggle with Marie to remove them. The original version of the so-called confession had Paradiso scramble to get rid of the girl's shoes and stockings before Candy saw them in her car.

The state had really dug up the dirt, a routine assignment for an undercover cop. The taped 1983 interview failed to provide an explanation about what had happened to the car. Nor did Bond mention the single cut hair the examiner found on Marie's clothing, or deep tire tracks found at the scene near the disposed body. Crafters went over Bond's statement on January 17, 1983, but the court sealed exhibit #15. Facilitators moved the rat to Concord on December 29,

1982, from the Charles Street Jail, and they cutoff the stoolie's contact with the state's target. Where did Bond get the added details to
enhance his story? The witness polished his act during frequent discussions with the core group working on Joan's case, and embellished
the story when the case came to trial.

Burke's star witness laid it on thick. Bond attested the culprit
burned the car ten days after Marie's murder, but of course there was
not a shred of charred evidence to prove it. The felon maintained he
told the police about tire tracks at the scene, claiming Lenny told
him. The con's chest swelled thinking he brought forward this information; he absurdly boasted the cops knew nothing about the evidence he revealed. In fact, it was unlikely Paradiso knew these details.
Testimony revealed Paradiso showed the fellow inmate pictures;
Bond described photos of two boats in the interview with the MSP.

"Now, in 1982," Burke added a new detail, "Paradiso mentioned
a hair. He thinks that's the only evidence the police have about him."

"That's what he said," the muscular man with the shaved head
agreed. "That's the only evidence that they had against him."

A technician in the police lab found the single cut hair clinging
to Marie's skirt when she examined the victim's clothing. Nearly five
years later, the state was still derelict to have the hair tested before the
case against Paradiso went to trial.

"They have no witnesses, no evidence whatso… other than the
strand of hair," Bond insanely implied.

"Mr. Bond, he told you on the morning of the fourteenth they
had no evidence?" Rappaport jumped all over the last statement.

"Yes, that was on the morning of the fourteenth." The state's
lackey alleged Paradiso's admission came the day after a jury convicted the deflated desperado for the murder of Mary Foreman.

"Did you turn around and say now they do, Lenny… me," the
defender skeptically asked. "Didn't you say, 'I'm their evidence?'"

"No, no, no," the practiced player changed the subject. "I said,
'Why jam the guy?' meaning David Doyle."

Lenny's counsel logically listed the evidence that pointed to
Doyle and asked Bond emphatically whether Paradiso caused or manufactured the known facts. Doyle and Marie argued the day of the wedding. The boyfriend knew about the other man, Eddie Fisher. Witnesses
noticed scratches on the back of the dejected lover's hands. The
boyfriend packed up all his murdered roommate's belongings. Family
members saw blood on the steps leading up to the couple's third-floor
apartment just days after the crime. Doyle took flight to New Jersey the
day of the funeral and gave a false name to the arresting officers. Every

incriminating point the defense questioned, Bond's answer was the same. Paradiso did not fabricate the evidence.

"He didn't put the scratches on David Doyle, did he?" Rappaport challenged the witness.

"No," Bond admitted. "I didn't say that he did, either."

"He didn't tell Doyle to run to New Jersey," the defense counsel continued, "did he?"

The witness was defensive, but attested Paradiso had nothing to do with the facts piled up against the other named suspect in the case. "I didn't say that he did."

Burke stood back up to rehabilitate his witness.

"When you said to him, Mr. Paradiso, 'Why jam him up?' meaning Doyle," Burke pried, "what did he say?"

"He just said, 'All the evidence points toward him.'" Bond affirmed something that should have been obvious to anyone with a lick of sense.

"It didn't bother him that he was going to jam Doyle up for a crime he didn't commit, did it?" The obsessed litigator exposed the premeditated bias that influenced the case.

"None whatsoever," the tool punctuated the state's supposition that Lenny devised to frame David Doyle.

"Did you have any conversation with Lenny when you left on the twenty-ninth?" the ADA asked to wrap up with the witness. "What did he say?"

"How do my alibi sound?" the star witness regurgitated. "I said, 'Sounds good.' I says, 'You ain't John Doe, you know.'"

The murder indictment finally came down after the state cleverly renamed the case before the grand jury. However, Burke kept his mouth shut that his quest began with cause number 038655, the *Commonwealth v. Leonard J. Paradiso* on March 5, 1982, soon after the Websters' high-powered meeting to assign him to Joan's investigation with Trooper Palombo.

The "Man from New Jersey" sat in the audience to see how the story played out and told reporters just what he thought.

"He [Bond] certainly made a good witness," the intelligence-trained father pronounced to the *Boston Herald*.

The *Boston Globe* captured George's quote, "In my opinion, the man [Bond] has no reason to make up a story like that."

"He [the witness Bond] has a fantastic memory." Joan's intelligence-trained mother applauded Burke's main event and swayed the public's opinion. After all, they were all in this together.

Lt. Harold Fulton of the Revere Police Department raised his hand to enter the stolen car report into the record. On September

13, 1979, the officer received a report for a stolen 1973 Buick LeSabre registered to Candy Weyant. The couple reported the vehicle missing a full month after the murder, not ten days when Bond said Lenny burned it. Police had never applied for a warrant to search the car. Candy never concealed the fact she gave Marie a ride, and detectives considered her boyfriend a suspect. The spin created an illusion that the defendant panicked and thwarted the evidence a month after the crime. Burke inflated the contention further through his star witness and suggested Paradiso burned it. With the defendant's history of vehicle claims, Lenny was particularly vulnerable to this sort of concocted story. The accused had filed several claims for lost or stolen vehicles. Some may have been stolen, or maybe some were lost by design to collect the insurance. Regardless, the premise fed into the Federal case Burke instigated concerning the boat, the trap Burke laid for Paradiso's alibi witness on the night Marie died.

The state promoted that two of Paradiso's vehicles were crime scenes, settings for not one, but two murders. The case on trial alleged the shell fisherman murdered Marie in the car he reported missing a month later, and Burke asserted an unverified theory that Paradiso burned it. In the case under the radar, Sgt. Tammaro deviously insinuated Paradiso burned his boat after killing Joan Webster. The sergeant baited the scapegoat on August 1, 1982, about three weeks after his subordinate arrested the patsy for Marie's murder. Bond affirmed the timing of Tammaro's meeting in his written statement, and reviewed the affidavit with both officers. With Eleanor's college degree in psychology and both parents' specialized background, one would think the couple would know their subliminal effect on the hearing; things brought out in Marie's case would fuel perceptions about their daughter.

The Charles Street Jail maintained inmate records, and ADA Burke called Larry Thomas to get them into the case. The prosecution wanted to establish that Paradiso returned to the Charles Street Jail from the Lawrence House of Correction on December 8, 1982. Administrators moved Lenny on December 3, 1982, because Charles Street was overcrowded. No one contested that guards locked Robert Bond in the same facility with Paradiso between December 8 and December 29, 1982, but the state made sure to prove it. However, the defense should have contested Bond's housing arrangements. The jury convicted Bond on December 13, 1982. Massachusetts law dictated that the felon immediately be remanded back to Walpole. Either someone with clout pulled strings to keep the stoolie nestled in close to the state's target, or Bond wasn't there when Burke said he was.

The former employee of the Suffolk County Sheriff's Department established visitation for the inmate on trial. Burke removed any doubt that Paradiso's girlfriend had visited Lenny in jail, and that the lawyers who took over the case, Walter Prince and Judd Carhart, visited their client beginning in October of 1982. The cunning counselor infused another name into the trial and introduced Elaine Covino to the court. Paradiso's friend had visited 18 times during the months he was imprisoned.

The plot thickened. Lenny's friend called him in the wee hours of August 12, 1979, looking for a little romance, according to the state's story. First, the culprit called Candy to come over and get their stories together. During that call, Paradiso asked his girlfriend to wake up her mother and get her on the phone to say, "Hi." Then another love interest dialed, begging for more. Why would Paradiso force himself on anyone when the state claimed women lined up at his door?

The defense neglected to ask the keeper of the records whether he extended a professional courtesy to the Massachusetts State Police to review the files. A routine request from colleagues would have provided the name that ended up in the Bond statement. Covino was not named in the con's statement, but she was described as the woman on her deathbed who could vouch for the accused. All Burke proved was that Lenny had a visitor. Nothing established the two had an intimate relationship at any time, and nothing corroborated a call Burke suggested during the wee hours on the day of Marie's murder.

The introduction of the seductive caller hid another motivation. Authorities tried to link Covino to the night Joan disappeared, and suggested another phone call. Instead of moonlight romance, Elaine suggested treatment for Paradiso's throbbing digit. Bond claimed the mope injured his finger murdering Joan. Superiors directed Trooper Charles Eastman and Trooper J. H. Flaherty to interview Lenny's friend on April 7, 1983.

"On August 12, or 13, 1979, did you call Leonard Paradiso?" Eastman asked.

"I refuse to answer that because I smell a rat," Covino instinctively challenged.

"Were you hospitalized in the Mass. General Hospital?" the trooper tested.

"In November 1982, I was hospitalized with a heart attack," Lenny's friend replied. "You know I was in intensive care, and I don't remember anything that happened."

"Do you know anything about Lenny in regards to Joan Webster?" the officers pressed.

"I was with Lenny when he noticed the boat was stolen," the woman affirmed. "It was either in July or August."

"During Thanksgiving 1981, did you see Lenny at all?" the boys continued.

"I saw Lenny either at my house or at Candy's," Covino acknowledged.

"How did he hurt his hand?" the coy cops queried.

"He did it down in Candy's cellar," she replied without hesitation. "As a matter of fact, Candy or Lenny called with what to do."

FBI SA Steve Broce took another crack at Elaine, at the state's request, and interviewed the skeptical friend again on July 11, 1983. Covino did not give the enforcers the answers they wanted, but it gave them something to work with. The illusion broadcast by Bond during the trial was that an unnamed woman could make a "deathbed" confession in 1982. It was not clear what she would confess, a three a.m. call the morning Marie died in 1979, or telling his friend how to treat splinters in his finger in 1981. However, the woman recovered and told them no such thing. The record keeper helped Burke insert the name of a friend, an occasional visitor on the log, who contradicted the state's story. However, she landed in the hospital right before Bond stepped into a cell close to Lenny, and that gave the boys some irrelevant information to prove. An undercover cop digs out information routinely, so it was not hard for the boys to verify some worthless tidbit and elevate Bond as a credible witness.

Trooper Palombo trotted back to the stand to confirm that he checked out Bond's statement. Burke proved, without challenge, that Paradiso paid attorneys with a car and a boat unrelated to Joan's disappearance. The trusted enforcer acknowledged that he found Elaine Covino, and somehow that bolstered the incredulous testimony of a convicted man with nothing to lose. That was simple sleuthing that proved nothing about either murder. Bond snubbed everyone's common sense with extraordinary detail that made the alleged confession ludicrous. Then the experienced officer in charge swept in to defend the outrageous claims. Camera bulbs flashed, providing images for the late edition.

The seventh day of the trial started with Rappaport's appeal to locate a witness. The unknown whereabouts of witnesses was a real problem, a frustrating one. The defense had trouble locating people, repeatedly. Finally, after much ado, an address was provided for Carol

Seracuse before the attorneys took their places back in the stifling courtroom.

The offense needed to tie up loose hairs in their theory, so they called Mark Grant from the Department of Public Safety Crime Lab. The state employed the chemist in the police crime lab for two years, but he hadn't been involved in the original investigation of Marie's case. The technician performed a rush analysis for the Suffolk ADA, and compared the single-cut hair, introduced through Robert Bond, to samples provided from Paradiso. Burke insinuated the defendant was paranoid the hair found on Marie's clothing would be his demise, but the follicle wasn't even tested until July 11, 1984, two days after the mock trial was under way.

"Were there enough similarities to form an opinion as to whether or not this was consistent with Paradiso's hair?" Flanagan's pupil foolishly asked.

"There were enough characteristics, in my opinion," Burke's expert concluded, "to say that it was probably not from Mr. Paradiso's head."

"It's probably not from his head." The prosecutor narrowly recovered, but dodged the fact that Grant also compared other hairs with the single-cut strand.

The witness had reviewed Kathleen Higgins' lab report, but the defense had trouble finding the original examiner. Burke suspiciously brought someone else in to make determinations about another person's findings. Not so strangely, he objected every time the defense tried to bring in evidence through officers and friends that took the stand when he could not seat a primary witness. Grant affirmed there was no evidence of seminal fluid on Marie's garments, but Burke had a senseless explanation for that, too. The offense guided the speculation that rain washed it away, or a salt-water rinsing removed any trace.

"I imagine if it was wet enough, washed off enough, it possibly could be washed away." Grant pondered the questioner's theory why there was not a trace of the alleged rape. "I suppose if it had been exposed to salt water for any period of time, it could have possibly washed off."

Burke asked the chemist to read from Higgins' report.

"The body suit was dotted with some dried vegetable matter and one short, dark-brown hair was found adhering to its surface." Mark Grant read into the record that there must have been selective rinsing of the deceased woman's attire if you followed the state's presumption.

Grant did not have time to type his notes. Rappaport picked up the examiner's handwritten record and pointed out Paradiso provided hair samples from various parts of his body. The lab technician compared all of them, but none of them was consistent with the hair. Nevertheless, according to Bond, the follicle stoked the defendant's paranoia. Dr. Katsas had no test results in the autopsy report, because examiners never conducted the tests. The pathologist never took scrapings from the decedent's clawed nails. Higgins never tested for salt water on Marie's clothing. Burke took advantage of the deficient inspection to imply a ludicrous notion: water lifted damning bodily fluid off the skirt, but left the vegetable matter. Chemists never typed blood groups for anyone other than Miss Iannuzzi. The prosecution enlisted Mark Grant at the last minute to examine the clipping, evidence ignored for nearly five years, and then asked Grant to explain another employee's findings.

The Suffolk County ADA wrapped up his case with a comrade out of the same office. Paul Connolly prosecuted Robert Bond in December 1982, for the murder of Mary Foreman and gained a conviction. The appeal came before the court on October 14, 1983, and the panel of judges set aside the verdict on January 19, 1984. ADA Connolly was on the docket to try Bond again and denied making any deals with the convict.

"Myself, nor anyone in the office, have made any offers of any kind to Bond," ADA Connolly stated.

The dirty tricks in the Suffolk County homicide division under John Kiernan were still obscured, and insiders were not likely to betray it. Connolly may not have known there were promises Bond relied on, but others inside Flanagan's system did. Human nature favored the prosecution. It's a natural tendency, believing in people delegated with the responsibility to dispense justice, and the suits on stage preyed on that confidence.

The attorneys had a well-worn path up to his Honor's perch by this time. Both sides whispered outside the earshot of the gallery again. Burke had a statement outlining the promises made to the sordid pretenders he put on the stand. The slithering solicitor wanted to slip it into the record and respond to Rappaport's request, a motion for disclosure of deals the state offered to the unsavory witnesses. The judge was willing, but the defense had called ADA Tom Reilly from Middlesex County to challenge a typographical error in Burke's offering. A word here or there changed the outlook regarding how Middlesex County handled Tony Pisa, but these subtle spins were invisible to the jury.

Rappaport bemoaned that yet another witness was missing, and wanted to enter grand jury testimony if he could not find her. Jean Day secluded herself and did not want to be found. The victim's step-sister had damaged the prosecution's theory and implicated the boyfriend. ADA Burke protested and griped that Trooper Palombo had looked for her, too. If the defense could not find her, the judge could issue a capias to bring her in, or consider whether to let Jean's grand jury testimony into the record. The tension ratcheted up another notch, because Burke did not want that to happen.

"Your Honor, at this time," Burke concluded, "the Common-wealth rests its case in chief."

Back they went to the sidebar.

"I have a motion for a required finding of not guilty," Rappaport submitted.

The request was a customary motion, but the judge decided the matter was for the jury to decide based on what he chose to give them. In our system of jurisprudence, there is a presumption of inno-cence until a jury of peers determines guilt beyond a reasonable doubt. However, Donahue's hushed response exposed the bias.

"They may well disbelieve Mr. Bond's testimony," Donahue judged. "I think the jury could conclude to a point beyond reason-able doubt that the defendant was guilty of murder. The evidence of rape was a little sketchy until Bond testified. I think on all of that, the jury could find he raped to a point beyond reasonable doubt."

The defense was up against a system that had already made up their minds, and held the power to direct that course.

"Mr. Rappaport, what you would ask me to do is disbelieve Bond's testimony." The presiding robe added his name to the list of supporters that either irrationally believed Robert Bond, or believed the Websters. "I don't think I can do that."

Burke was insulted. The suggestion that law enforcement had colluded with Bond hurt his feelings. There was plenty of reason to doubt the prosecutor's inference that Paradiso was the source of the rat's information. The Massachusetts State Police had the advantage of an undercover cop skilled at digging up dirt, and they dangled promises the felon relied on. The prosecution rested its case and fin-ished offending everyone's intelligence, at least for the moment. Now, the defense had a turn. Unfortunately, the monumental task of establishing reasonable doubt was dubious from the start with a judge that apparently lacked common sense.

CHAPTER 16

Childish Smirk

"I call David Doyle," the defense began.

There was something disconcerting about the way Doyle ambled casually to the seat. He carried himself with the confidence of one who knew he had the prosecution and friends in law enforcement at his back.

The couple had an argument the day of his cousin's wedding. David ripped his pants, and Marie offered to sew them. The party was shifting from the reception at the Ship Restaurant, but Doyle did not want to go. The disturbance escalated into a shouting match, to David's embarrassment, a raucous exchange on full display in front of his family and friends.

"She said I never wanted to go anyplace with her whenever there was parties," Doyle recalled. "My mother grabbed me by the arm and said, 'Let's go home.'"

"You lived together," Rappaport set the stage. "Do you know whether or not Marie saw any other men? Are you aware of a man named Eddie Fisher?"

"It's my understanding she was seeing him," the witness acknowledged.

The couple had fights, and the boyfriend admitted some of them were physical. The attorney focused on the incident that happened just a few weeks before the young woman was murdered.

"I put my hand around her neck, and held her off," Doyle said, making himself the victim. "I held her off from me."

The young man readily admitted he was a drug user, and he was often under the influence when the couple had fights. The poison scrambled his thinking and made his memory fuzzy. Then he described the house where they lived. Prior to a fire in September of 1983, the house remained just as it was at the time of the murder. A subtle detail came in that contradicted an excuse Burke offered for the suspected drop of blood, but observers missed it entirely. There were no changes, no work done, to the steps leading up to their apartment under his parents' roof.

Marie called her boyfriend later that evening to see whether she should stay somewhere else that night. He was still upset over the scene they had caused, and suggested sleeping elsewhere was a good idea. The call was sometime between 8:00 and 8:30 that night, but Doyle denied talking to her again. Drugs helped the loser escape, and admittedly left his memory blurred.

"Did you use any drugs that evening?" the interrogator asked.

"I don't recall," Doyle replied to his own advantage. He had remembered that detail for the grand jury on March 5, 1982, when the state targeted Paradiso to take the rap, but conveniently forgot it now in front of the jury.

Doyle just could not seem to get one point straight. He told the court the couple had a cat at the time, but Marie's sister had already testified that the cat had run away. The problem was, the testimony was buried in the secret grand jury records that this jury didn't see. The feline was the first excuse Doyle suggested to police for the scratches dug into both hands and around an eye. The alibi was all he could think of at the time. His memory wafted in and out as needed. Now Doyle remembered speaking to Jean Day on Sunday, something he could not recall during the grand jury. Uncharacteristically, he expressed his concern for his missing girlfriend.

Doyle shed no tears when he identified the body, and he said so, although he passed it off as being in shock. The wake was a blur, reinforcing all the witnesses who described him strung out on something. However, he was there all three times the family gathered.

"Specifically, sir," the counsel questioned, "do you remember whether or not you had scratches on your hands at the wake?"

"I might have," the other named suspect evasively hedged.

Attention turned to the boyfriend's behavior to take flight. He missed his beloved girlfriend's funeral because he was depressed, or so he said, and felt the need to get away. The first flight on the list was to New Jersey where cops arrested the bereaved man stealing suitcases from the conveyor, and Doyle gave them a false name. David Doyle's flight from the pressure was the exact sort of guilty behavior the prosecution suggested of Paradiso. He could not cope, and he drowned his sorrow in drugs and drinks, helping him lift off before he boarded a plane.

"I bought a round-trip ticket," Doyle asserted. "I was supposed to come back the next day for the funeral."

The defense got back to the night of the murder when the couple parted ways at the reception. "Do you know who Marie went to the party with?"

"She said she was getting a ride with Lenny," he stated, but he had been asked this question before.

"Do you know who Marie left with?" Det. David Martinez asked the detainee on August 17, 1979, the day of Marie's funeral. Martinez was an officer with the East Detective Squad in Newark, New Jersey, where Doyle was arrested.

"She left with my cousin, Freddie Milano," Doyle responded at the time. "They went to Freddie's house in Saugus, Mass."

"Do you know who took Marie home from your cousin's house?" Martinez continued.

"She got a ride home with a girl, who dropped her off at a bar called the Cardinale's Nest in East Boston," Doyle confirmed what little he knew.

"Do you know the girl's name who dropped her off at this bar?" the New Jersey detective interrogated further.

"No, I don't," was all the cuffed druggie could add.

The calendar pages had turned, and Doyle had a remarkable memory now. Of course, he met with Trooper Andrew Palombo twenty to thirty times.

"She said she was getting a ride to the party with Lenny?" Rappaport asked on direct.

"Yes," Doyle deceitfully answered, "Lenny and his girlfriend."

"And sir," the skeptical defense attorney queried, "it's your testimony that you never talked to Marie after eight o'clock on Sunday night?"

"No," Doyle answered without blinking an eye.

Having friends in the right places could certainly pay off. Authorities skewered Paradiso to take the rap for Marie; he was the Websters' targeted suspect named at the February 1982 meeting. It was not surprising the other suspect in the crime furthered the state's vision.

The manure was getting deep, and ADA Burke had to mentally pull on his waders before diving in to rescue the other culprit suspected by the defense. One of the Milanos introduced the two couples briefly at the restaurant, so Doyle and Marie barely knew who Paradiso was. The young man was embarrassed by his ripped pants and enraged when Marie offered to mend them, until his mommy pulled him away from the quarrel. It was a bit illogical to assume he took a deep breath during his outburst and calmly inquire who would give his unfaithful girlfriend a ride to the next party. Despite the absurdity of his story, he insisted she told him she would ask Lenny and his girlfriend. In the end, Doyle testified he did not know how she got to the Milanos.

"What happened at the wake, David?" Burke sympathetically stepped in deeper.

"I was there with Fisher, the other gentleman going out with her." The stench in the room must have dulled the jury's senses, hearing a jealous lover's ludicrous contention he shared a moment of grief with the other guy. Love was on the rocks, and unfortunately, so was Marie. "I went with him for a drink."

Everyone had described Doyle in a drugged stupor throughout the wake; he didn't know where he was. Regardless, according to the boyfriend, he and Fisher went across the street to a bar where an unruly patron would not shut up. The hot-tempered batterer was oddly calm as he replayed the bar scene with the other man, the guy who cavorted with his live-in girlfriend. Doyle supposedly picked up a barstool and got into a fight with someone else who would not stop talking.

"Was Eddie Fisher there?" The counselor inserted alibi witnesses to bolster the story. "Was Tony Leonti there?"

"Yes," he answered with the confidence that no one would betray him. "I think Tony was there, yes."

"And then some people started asking you about your hands after that?" the ADA continued to cross-examine.

"I had heard that people at the wake had mentioned to the cops that I had bruises and cuts on my hands." Doyle sighed in relief that lightning did not strike him down on the spot.

Burke manipulated the scabbed, oozing, raw-beef hands of a frequently arrested aggressor. A bar stool became the weapon of choice, but it did not match the dug flesh pulled from his wrists to his fingers. Burke was scrubbing as hard as he could. He guided the witness to explain Marie's packed belongings. Fuzzy memory miraculously became crystal clear; he packed all her things Monday night, and siblings arrived on Tuesday to pick out a dress. Then Burke whitewashed Doyle's paranoid behavior to take flight to New Jersey. The whole room felt sorry for the miserable misfit who felt so alone at the wake. He just wanted to get out of town for a while to clear his head. The poor soul intended to come back for the funeral he said, and he bought a round-trip ticket.

"I think it went from Newark to LaGuardia to Boston," Doyle misrepresented. "When I talked with the reservation, I needed it as early as possible, 7:30 or so."

The stolen ticket from LaGuardia to Boston, listed in police files, would never get him back in time for the 8:30 a.m. procession. He was in Newark, and he would have had to flap his own wings to get to the gate where passengers boarded the plane. While he was waiting for the flight taking off, the one departing in New York, that is, Doyle helped himself to the luggage on the moving conveyor in New Jersey and got busted. Inspectors Long and Cook, from the Saugus Police Department, had to tell New Jersey enforcers who he really was before traveling down to see him in an out-of-state clink. The officers recorded what ticket the thief had in his possession. The offensive counter Burke was spinning even wiped Doyle's habitual drug use clean.

"Why were you taking valiums?" the ADA asked the undercover cop's special friend. "What's the kind of pressure you were undergoing at this time?

The redirect emphasized the stretch of imagination to swallow Doyle's explanations. A couple hundred people attended the reception, and the couple only met Paradiso for a casual greeting, "Hi, how are you?" Marie did know some of Doyle's cousins, Freddie Milano for one, but supposedly went out of her way to suggest she might ask Lenny for a ride. Then Rappaport shifted back to the troublesome scratches.

"I didn't know where they came from," Doyle's selective memory fogged out again. "I didn't remember."

Doyle told cops at the time his cat caused them. Burke tried to redefine them as cuts and bruises, but the fact remained, the boyfriend's lame excuse was in the police record. The wounds did not match the excuse, and a witness previously testified the cat ran away a month before the murder. Fortunately, for the prosecution, Doyle met with Palombo twenty to thirty times, and miraculously the murder suspect remembered some fight. The offensive prosecution clouded the issue just when the scratches were seen, but Doyle had them, and the state had to have an answer.

"It could have been in the fight," the other suspect offered a multiple choice. "It could have been the cat."

Mommy took the stand next, and not surprisingly defended her baby boy. The protective mother overheard the discussion about Marie's ride to the Milanos. She was right there monitoring her son's fermenting anger after ripping his pants.

"She was supposed to go with my other nephew and his friend," Rosemarie confirmed the arrangement to ride with Freddie Milano.

David went home with his parents while his girlfriend went on to the party. Paradiso's name had not crossed David's lips to his attentive mother. According to Rosemarie, it was more than a couple of months before Lenny's name came up. The witness recalled her son went out for a walk for about a half hour, and swore he was at home for the rest of the night.

"My bedroom is right at the stairs," Rosemarie vouched. "My bedroom door is always open." Times varied between Doyle's recollection and his mother's, but it was subtle enough not to notice. According to Mom, her baby boy was in for the night about 9:30 p.m.

"Ma'am," the defense skeptically probed, "has David ever left the house, oh, in the last five years, without you knowing it?"

"No," Doyle's mommy replied.

Rappaport turned her attention to the damning scratches. Rosemarie had talked to the Saugus police soon after cops arrested her darling in Newark. Inspector Cook pointedly asked about the scratches on David's hands, after all, someone had just murdered his girlfriend, and he flew the coop on Jeffries Street. At the time, Rosemarie said the gouges, described as fresh, oozing, raw beef by an observer, were the result of a vehicle accident on June tenth or eleventh, two months before Marie died. However, something was in the water in Boston that evidently affected memory—authorities claimed it was Joan Webster. Rosemarie denied she gave that explanation to the police, but added another choice for the public to consume.

"I had told Cook, David fell at the MBTA station," the woman swore.

Maybe Doyle stumbled during one of his frequent undocumented conversations with the undercover cop working at Logan. Who knows? However, no one seemed to be keeping score. The tally was up to four explanations for the wounds Doyle brandished; none of them were consistent with the description of dug flesh from the wrists to the fingers. The fact was, witnesses saw serious wounds on David's hands. The truth does not change, but the story sure did.

When Rosemarie spoke to the Saugus police on August 20, 1979, the overly attentive mother, who monitored her baby boy with an open bedroom door, never mentioned a fight at a bar across the street from the wake.

"Do you know if David was involved in some kind of fracas at one of the wakes?" Burke cross-examined.

"I heard about it later on," she said, but never mentioned just how much later.

Paradiso waived his attorney-client privilege so his previous counsel could answer some questions. Judd Carhart affirmed his former client had relinquished a car and a boat in partial payment of fees. Burke belabored the point that Carhart never spoke with Robert Bond, the rat who came out with those details. The informant recited the attorney's resume when he talked to the police, and Burke inferred that Paradiso was the source listing the credentials for the con. Bond also forewarned the boys that the defense sought to deceive them and paint David Doyle as the likely culprit. Doyle was an obvious suspect, and there was undeniable circumstantial evidence against him brought out in the grand jury Burke convened against Paradiso.

"Did you ever make the statement, sir," Rappaport attacked Bond's assertion, "that you would be able to fool the jury?"

"No, sir," Carhart attested. The whole notion was silly with evidence already in police files. "I never made that statement."

The defense strategy to discredit the two convicted informants the state's case relied on fell miserably short, but it was the underlying agenda that sabotaged the effort. Rappaport seated two ADAs from Middlesex County, the office that handled matters with Tony Pisa. First, James Sahakian took the seat. He worked for DA Scott Harshbarger in the appeals bureau, and designated with the task to support Middlesex County's convictions. Pisa had filed motions with the court still under consideration.

"I was assigned to Pisa's case in September or October of '83," Sahakian explained. "I opposed all of them."

"Did your position as to those motions change at all as of March twelfth or March thirteenth, 1984?" Rappaport emphasized the date Pisa skewered Paradiso for two murders for the Commonwealth during the Iannuzzi pretrial.

"The Commonwealth's position did," the state's employee affirmed. "Yes."

The Commonwealth position for bail had eased while the judge considered the motion for a new trial. Sahakian pointed to his colleague ADA Tom Reilly and announced that Reilly was the advocate that came forward after Pisa testified on March 12, 1984. The ADA that hooked Pisa up with Tim Burke and George Webster lamented the killer's safety.

"As to the motion for a new trial, sir," the defense pointed out, "what is your position at this very time, right now?"

"I oppose it," the lawyer advised.

The Middlesex County public defenders were not about to admit special favors in court, so putting Reilly on the stand next was rather futile. Nevertheless, Rappaport gets credit for trying to halt the misprision.

"I believe I first met Mr. Pisa in February 1983," the first assistant in Middlesex County recalled. "Somewhere in that period of time there were motions for a new trial."

In other words, Reilly met the con in between Bond's incredulous accusations leaked to the press and Pisa's assurances to George Webster. The ADA defended the guarantee that suited Joan's father, and the state flanked their hind side with two cold-blooded killers. Reilly contacted Suffolk County and the Massachusetts State Police, the team investigating both cases already. The same core team that worked with Bond and other witnesses the state lined up checked Pisa out, too. Reilly was careful not to mention Joan Webster's name as part of his probe, but referred to things beyond the scope of the Iannuzzi case. Reilly, predictably, endorsed his investigation of Pisa was thorough. After years of defending the county's conviction, his office made a startling reversal. They came to a new conclusion about Pisa's involvement in the George Deane murder fourteen years after the fact.

"We made a determination that Mr. Pisa did not do the shooting," Reilly proclaimed.

The boys headed back to the bar. Burke had opened a can of worms, and the defense wanted to ask whether Reilly had done his homework about the Deane case. The judge apparently had the state's back, and he abetted any effort to discredit Tony Pisa.

"I'd like to ask him if he spoke to one Francis Dion," Rappaport appealed to the judge. "Pisa made a statement to him at the Clam Shell Bar in Beverly back in 1970, 'Not only did I shoot him, but I enjoyed doing it.'"

"No, no, no," Donahue scolded. "You can ask him if he spoke to the witness, but you can't quote what that witness would say."

It is fair to assume the statement appeared in police records or testimony under oath during Pisa's trial, but factual records or sworn statements were out of bounds in this courtroom. Reilly swallowed Pisa's predictable ploy to diminish his accountability in the Deane murder. Something underhanded was going on distorting real justice. The prosecution seated convicted killers and represented them as honest men, but cried foul when Paradiso's defender tried to expose there was plenty of reason not to believe them.

"Sir, as a result of your investigation into the background of Mr. Pisa's case," Rappaport tried, "did you ever speak to a Francis Dion?"

"Francis who?" Reilly ignorantly asked.

"Have you ever heard that name before?" counsel continued.

"No," the witness had to admit, "I have not."

"Mr. Reilly," Rappaport submitted, "it wasn't a very extensive investigation, was it?"

"Yes, it was," the public servant defensively protested.

The problem was not only that Mr. Reilly did not know Francis Dion, neither did the jury. They lacked the facts to evaluate Pisa's veracity. Reilly acknowledged the snitch conditioned his testimony on release from prison. The Middlesex office would reconsider their position on the motion for a new trial, too, after "Death Row Tony" appeared in court, that is. What a deal.

George Webster removed his glasses and closed his eyes to the misprision for the sake of his daughter. The mope George and Eleanor determined had murdered their child was defenseless against the underlying cause for the case.

The defense astutely called a cousin of the other culprit they suspected. Jimmy Milano cleared up the confusion Burke had caused about who gave Marie a ride after the reception. His brother, Freddie, and Marie both rode in the same car with him. His cousin diluted Doyle's self-serving contention that his girlfriend was going to ask Lenny. Jimmy knew Paradiso; the defendant had worked with his brother and delivered clams to their restaurant. The groom's brother observed the victim causing a scene at the house party, and his father wanted her to leave. First, Mr. Milano called a cab, but the obstinate partier would not get in it. He recalled Marie left the house with Lenny's girlfriend, Candy Weyant.

"Do you recall how late you stayed at the house that night?" the defense attorney inquired.

"Until about eleven o'clock," the eyewitness responded.

"Were there still some people left at the house?" Rappaport focused on the prosecution's mistake.

"Yes, there was," Jimmy knowingly affirmed. "There was my parents, my sister, and Lenny and Candy."

There it was. The wedding party thinned out and Jimmy called it a night about eleven p.m. on August 11, 1979. Marie was already gone, but the groom's brother corroborated that Lenny and Candy were still at the house when he departed. Candy told police she returned after dropping Marie at the Cardinale's Nest Bar, and a witness sat on the stand to confirm it. Bond testified Lenny tore through the streets and was hustling Marie a half hour away at the same time. According to Bond, Candy was nestled at home in Revere when Jimmy saw her with her boyfriend at the Milanos' home in Saugus.

Whom should the jury believe? On one hand, they had an ignorant felon facing life behind bars for two murders. On the other, they had an eyewitness at the party. Jimmy Milano's testimony placed suspicion squarely on his cousin's shoulders, and Jimmy knew it. If he were going to lie under oath, blood was thicker than water.

The story broke on the news early Monday morning. A young woman's body in a red dress had been found on the Lynn Marsh Road. Marie's mother was not the only person who heard the story on the news; Mr. Milano, the groom's father, called his sister, Rosemarie Doyle. After all, Marie lived under her roof with her son. When Jean Day and Mary Iannuzzi arrived on her doorstep, Rosemarie's immediate reflex was to cover her mouth and utter, "Oh, my God." No one knew who it was yet, but phones were ringing and speculation swirled.

Burke wasted no time to discredit the witness. Yes, Jimmy had been drinking at his brother's wedding, but said he was not a big drinker. He felt good, but he wasn't drunk. When police questioned the young man, Jimmy checked who had driven the victim. He had not witnessed his sister, Rosemary Sullivan, force the intoxicated guest into the car with Candy while Lenny nodded off at the party. Burke objected; it was hearsay. Jimmy had not observed loading Marie in the car firsthand. Unfortunately, Rosemary was out of state and the defense could not get her on the stand.

However, the prosecution could not alter one crucial fact. Jimmy Milano, Doyle's cousin, placed Paradiso at the Milano house at eleven that night—a time the state alleged, through Bond, that Paradiso was running every red light in East Boston on his way to get back to the bar. Jimmy Milano placed Candy Weyant at his parents' home in Saugus at the same time Bond asserted she was tucked in at home in Revere. The witness saw them. It is impossible to be in two places at once, but the Websters maintained that Bond was a good witness, and the controlling forces went along.

"When you left the house party," Rappaport redirected, "did you see Lenny?"

"He was there, yes," Jimmy attested.

"Was Marie still there?" the defense concluded.

"No," was the definitive answer from the eyewitness.

The chess game continued, and the defense put Det. Arthur Cook in the hot seat. As the defense emphasized all the witnesses the officer had questioned at the time of Marie's murder, Det. Arthur Cook reexamined his report. It did not take long for Burke to object and trot back up to whisper into the judge's ear. The brazen ADA instructed the defense how to question the witness, and Donahue played right along. Cook did not have a copy of his own report in hand, and of course, the state was determined to keep some of it out. Burke talked to the officer on numerous occasions about the case, and massaged interpretations were more likely to come in without a report to refresh his memory.

Regardless, Rappaport went ahead and handed the detective a copy of his running account of the investigation. Cook interviewed several people at the time with Trooper Carl Sjoberg, people who saw Marie back in the bar around closing time on the night in question. The defense then stopped its own direct about what witnesses had said to the officer, and approached the judge's bench yet again. Rappaport noticed some distractions going on in the courtroom. Tim Burke was making faces like some adolescent in junior high school.

"Well, Burke hasn't objected for at least fifteen minutes," his Honor defended.

"I know that," Rappaport said, "but he's giving me dirty looks. He's looking at me, you know, what are you doing?"

The counsel needed the report to refresh Cook's memory, and at the moment the inquiry focused on the prosecution's witness, Christine DeLisi.

"That's certainly not upsetting to your case," the defense suggested.

"Well, it depends," Burke asserted. "If you flush something out, that's not a problem, but if you start getting down to the nitty-gritty, then that's when it becomes a problem."

The nitty-gritty, of course, meant the witnesses that refuted Burke's contention that Paradiso was the last person seen with the victim alive. The secret sessions at the sidebar were revealing the problem Rappaport had defending his client. The ruling robe had already made up his mind, and Donahue predicted the verdict based on Bond's incredulous testimony.

In this case, times were critical when witnesses saw Marie in the bar. The defense did not contest the fact Paradiso held the door open for her and walked out at the same time between 12:30 and 1:00 a.m. on the morning of the twelfth. Paradiso and his girlfriend both provided that information independently. When cops asked them at the time, they had no knowledge of witnesses that saw Paradiso hold the door. Predictably, Burke objected to Cook telling the court what he documented in his report from other people in the bar that night. Police accounts and the autopsy report reflected that Marie was seen back in the bar around closing at two a.m.

"Sir, at some point your duties in the investigation ceased," the defense noted.

"Yes," Cook confirmed his removal from the case. "There was a jurisdictional dispute."

The case had stalled about a year after the Iannuzzi murder, and Cook was not the only defender usurped in the cold case. Higher-ups dropped Trooper Carl Sjoberg in favor of Trooper Andrew Palombo in February 1981. The undercover cop had an unusual relationship with suspect David Doyle, and he had many undocumented meetings with him.

The shift in jurisdiction was convenient for the district attorneys when an anonymous caller tipped Joan's parents that Paradiso was their man. The Websters then called a high-powered meeting in February of 1982, and the ball started rolling for an indictment against Paradiso for Marie's murder. Burke made up a story he had received a call from the victim's sister after she read the article about the Basilia Melendez case. The paper quoted Essex County DA Kevin Burke saying he shifted the case because it was believed Marie was murdered somewhere else, then dumped in his jurisdiction. Burke argued the opposite. Pairing Burke and Palombo on both cases was hardly a coincidence. The directors appointed Palombo to the Webster investigation soon after his boss's friend dropped the dime on Paradiso for both crimes. Sadly, what went on behind the scenes was invisible to the sixteen people seated in judgment.

The direct examination covered the facts with the initial investigator; the facts made David Doyle an undeniable suspect from the start. Cook identified David Doyle over the phone in New Jersey when the confined runaway gave a false name in Newark. The officer traveled to interview the detained quarry and noticed the scratches on his hands. The marks were inconsistent with the excuses Doyle and his mother suggested. A runaway cat did not cause the dug flesh, nor did a vehicle accident that happened two months before the scratches appeared. More importantly, no one mentioned a bar brawl to the investigator to add to his reports. In addition, Iannuzzi family members informed the authorities about the drop of blood they saw on Doyle's stairs. The investigation fell short of professional; there was no warrant for the Doyle house, and to Burke's relief, the suspected drop of blood never tested.

Both counsels resumed their familiar positions at Judge Donahue's bench. There seemed to be some confusion when police learned about the alleged drop of blood. Cook said he learned about it from Burke and testified he had knowledge of the suspicious spot during Burke's rendition of a grand jury back in 1982. Rappaport asked the court to mark a police report for identification intending to put the author on the stand. Donahue stalled and denied the request, but had other ways to handle the evidence when the time came.

The judge excused the jury for morning coffee while Constable John Roscoe Schifone took the stand. The due process server was there to enlighten the court about the defense team's difficulty trying to find witnesses. The exchange between Schifone and Rappaport began, but Burke quickly disrupted the questions to Rappaport's surprise.

"Judge, if I could interrupt to save some time," Burke announced. "Is this in regard to Jean Day? She was here, Judge, early this morning."

The defense had moved to enter the grand jury testimony if Day couldn't be found—Burke definitely did not want that to happen. Jean was the murder victim's stepsister, and her previous account thrust a dagger into the heart of the state's promotion that Paradiso was the culprit.

Dennis Slawsby, a private investigator for the defense, had escorted the victim's stepsister to a room to ask her some questions. He used accepted practice to review what the witness remembered first, before showing her transcripts of what she swore previously. Her account remained consistent with the grand jury testimony she gave on March 5, 1982, when Burke secretly presented the case of the *Commonwealth v. Leonard J. Paradiso*. Rappaport called the next witness while Slawsby conducted the interview down the hall.

"Carol Seracuse, please take the stand," Rapapport announced.

Carol Seracuse was a fellow patron of the Cardinale's Nest Bar. Marie approached the woman seated at the bar on the ill-fated night and asked her for a ride to Eddie Mack's. Marie recognized her as Andrea's mother, but Carol did not have a vehicle to usher the intoxicated, young woman to yet another drinking establishment.

"Do you have any memory of approximately what time this conversation took place?" The defense had another primary witness the court had to take care of.

"Not really," she evasively answered.

"Ma'am, I want to show you this document." Rappaport handed her the police report taken when her memory was fresh.

"Yes, I know. I seen it," Carol admitted, "1:30."

"No, Judge, I object to that!" Burke panicked. A time had slipped in placing Marie back at the bar well after Marie walked out while Paradiso held the door.

"Do you have any present memory of what time this occurred?" counsel tried again.

"I couldn't say," the witness shrugged.

Death froze the victim's clawed fingers in the last struggle of her life, and the long-manicured nails probably held the residue of her offender. Hideous scratches branded the other suspect, and the next witness described them during Burke's 1982 grand jury targeting Lenny Paradiso. Benjamin Puzzo was back on the stand for the defense, but Burke picked scabs to confuse the audience just how old Doyle's marks were when Marie's uncle recoiled from them at the wake.

"You noticed scratches?" the defense pressed.

"Scratches, yes," Puzzo confirmed. "They were bad, fresh scratches. They were wet, oozing, you know."

Burke kept bringing up a round-trip ticket as if it were the truth. The court learned, through Marie's uncle, Doyle was supposed to be a pallbearer. However, the jury did not know the procession was scheduled to start at 8:30 Friday morning. The lawbreaker was in jail in New Jersey, and police confiscated a stolen ticket from LaGuardia to Boston in his possession.

The obsessed prosecutor bloodied the proceeding with his offensive cross-examination. He explained away the wounds Puzzo had observed with diversionary tactics. However, the uncle made a very telling observation.

"Did you see any blood coming from them?" Burke asked.

"No, because he had a lot of mercurochrome, whatever it was, all around there," Puzzo said, revealing the gouges had been doctored.

Not one person was on record at the time of the murder corroborating Doyle's alleged fight. No one explained who tended the wounds Marie's uncle remembered. The classic denial, "I don't remember," was Doyle's testimony for the defenseless when asked whether he had those scratches at the wake. The topical antiseptic Puzzo described stained skin with a distinctive orange-red color and burned like the devil on raw flesh. The subtle disclosure that someone had treated Doyle's marred hands probably drifted right past the average person, but two of the spectators, George and Eleanor Webster, had special training to observe even the smallest detail.

The fact was, Doyle was severely scratched at the time, no scrapings were taken from Marie's fingernails, and the offense suggested four different explanations. The final draft for the case, an alleged bar brawl, was never reported to authorities when events were fresh. Suspiciously, Burke tested the excuse when he put Trooper Palombo's special friend on the stand in the 1982 grand jury that targeted the Webster suspect, Leonard Paradiso.

Apparently, Burke's assignment was to dull the family's suspicions about the boyfriend. The public defender diminished known facts and suppressed the instincts of those closest to the situation.

What the state did not like, Burke attributed to the family's raw emotions, distorted thinking, and ignorance of Paradiso. Tony Leonti admitted he was leery of the boyfriend during the wake, and he raised his right hand again, too. The grand jury convened two and a half years after Marie's death when family members vividly described their strong suspicions of David Doyle. Memory was more distant now, five years later, and the prosecution's influence confused the issues. Four members of Marie's grieving family, including Tony, stopped and whispered on the stairs up to the couple's apartment. The brother-in-law was more certain now they went to pick out a dress on Tuesday, which fit with Burke's twist. Tuesday was the day Tony noticed a drop of blood on the steps and Marie's packed belongings. The ADA wanted the jury to focus on Tuesday, the day after Doyle and Tony identified Marie at the morgue. The four adults who went to pick out a dress were positive at the time what the red drop was.

"It could have been a drop of paint, or blood, or something, dried up," Leonti speculated, but Doyle said there was no work done on the steps.

Tony was not on record recalling a brawl, but the other suspect named him as an alibi witness. Burke continued to guide Tony to bolster bafflement and doubt over David Doyle's scratches.

"At some point in time, during one of the wakes," Burke continued the whitewashing, "did you have occasion to go to a bar?"

"Yes," Leonti miraculously remembered five years later. "I think it was the 'Ninety-Nine.'"

"Tell the jury what it is you see, Tony," the ADA requested.

"David Doyle and the other guy, Fisher," Tony played along. "When I went in, they were just breaking up a scuffle that David had with another guy that was there."

Regardless, Leonti never recalled seeing the scratches, ever, even after the alleged fight. He was not the one who tended to Doyle's wounds, nor was anyone else in the bar if Tony was really there with Doyle. The facts remained; Doyle had horrible scratches on his hands, and there was a suspicious drop that four adults believed was blood. Witnesses saw both incriminating details shortly after authorities rolled Marie over with her hands frozen in the last desperate fight of her life.

The court took a recess before the afternoon session. Jean Day spent the morning talking to Dennis Slawsby, and he had a good sense of what the stepsister recalled. When the two left the room at 1:30 that afternoon, ADA Tim Burke and an imposing Trooper Andrew Palombo greeted her at the door. The two men escorted the elusive witness down the hall to an unknown location. When the trio reappeared, court resumed, and Jean Day swore to tell the truth.

"Before we even said anything, his mother said, 'Oh, my God.'" Jean Day recalled the moment she and her mother knocked on the Doyle's door early Monday morning.

The private investigator listened as testimony rearranged the story he heard that morning. The "heat" undoubtedly dulled the woman's senses. She could not remember the order Marie put her clothes on. Now, the suspicious drop could have been red paint. The stepsister acknowledged she saw Marie's belongings packed on Tuesday, but the testimony did not address what Jean actually saw and when. The scratches were there, but Marie's stepsister was now vague when she noticed them.

"It looked like they were done by his cat." Day contradicted her sister Kathy's testimony that the cat had run away.

"Ma'am," Rappaport asked, "when was the last time you had been at the apartment?"

"I think two weeks previous to her death," the witness threw a curve.

"Ma'am, do you remember talking to me about, oh, about an hour ago?" the stunned defense counsel queried. "That's not what you said to me outside."

Objections greased Burke's seat while Jean Day was on the stand, and he complained roughly every two minutes. However, this time the judge demurred, and summoned the attorneys to the front for one of his private sessions out of the gallery's hearing.

"Judge, forty-five minutes ago she tells me one thing," Rappaport suspiciously argued. "I'm sure her memory must have been refreshed by Mr. Burke, that's all."

"I don't like the suggestion that's inferred from the remark," Flanagan's defensive pupil pouted.

Jean had been in hiding until she showed up at the courthouse on the morning of July 18, 1984. An assortment of individuals had been looking for her on both sides of the case, yet no one could find her. Burke had a secret to share at the sidebar before his next line of questions.

"About a year and a half ago, Jean started making inquiries about Paradiso." The prosecutor's timeline coincided with the "break" in Joan Webster's case disseminated through news outlets, thanks to the leaks about Robert Bond's statement. "The following day her house was broken into. She received threatening phone calls to keep her mouth shut about Paradiso, and she was beaten. She was kicked in the face. She had a broken bone in her face here (indicating)."

"When did this happen?" Rappaport unknowingly inquired.

"I think it was about a year and a half ago," Burke shared. "I'm not—I'll find out from Palombo. He'll know."

"Wait a minute, Judge," the defense rejected. "My client was in prison."

"Her house was broken into; she was kicked viciously." The litigator inferred some mysterious connection to the defendant, hoping that somehow the judge could find a precedent to get this incident into the trial. "We've got pictures to show what happened to her."

The revelation stunk to high heaven. Where was the incident report, and why had the defense never heard it? Palombo seemed to know everything, including when this occurred, and the prosecution suspiciously had photographs proving Jean was assaulted. The secret remained at the bench, but as the cross-examination moved forward, another morsel came out. Jean denied any recollection she told the police about blood on the steps until much later in time.

"Two years later you still remembered it, and you told Officer Palombo?" Rappaport clarified.

"Yes, we did." Jean confirmed her incriminating disclosure to Doyle's special friend.

Jean Day independently recollected events surrounding the murder that morning and affirmed that her grand jury testimony was correct to private investigator Dennis Slawsby. Burke and Palombo then flanked her on both sides and guided her down the hall for a chat. When court resumed, suddenly she could no longer recall how her sister wore her stockings, and the order Marie would have put them on. Slawsby learned Jean saw the belongings packed early Monday morning, when she and her mother arrived looking for Marie, and nullified any relevance when people went back to get a dress for the wake. During her interview with Slawsby, there was no question when Jean saw the deeply gouged scratches on David Doyle's hands. She saw them Monday morning before the men went to the morgue. By that afternoon, she was not sure just when she saw them, and suggested the missing cat might have been the cause. Jean's vivid memory mysteriously evaporated after ADA Burke and Trooper Palombo led the victim's stepsister out of sight, and they had pictures of the intimidation that sent her into hiding. It defied common sense; the defense was derelict not to call Slawsby to the stand.

Jean was still distraught over the trial and confided in her neighbor, Louis Tontodonato. Police wanted her to testify at the trial of her sister's murder, but she did not want to testify the way they wanted her to. Because of her refusal to testify, her son, at the instigation of the police, was taken away from her. Then, Jean was arrested on charges unrelated to Marie's murder. She feared threats from the police, and went into hiding in Somerville.

"The police told me I would be sent to prison, and that they would see I lost custody of my son," the distraught mother sobbed to her neighbor. "I was forced to testify at the trial against Leonard Paradiso and gave false testimony."

Jean Day's experience with the authorities was eerily similar to the pressure described by Christine DeLisi. Both women were key witnesses, and both described the same persuasive tactics to gain their cooperation. Continuous legal harassment also overshadowed Paradiso's alibi witness, Candy Weyant, for the night in question. Strangely, it also struck a familiar chord with me, many years later, when the Websters suggested my children would never talk to me again. I was the one around when Joan disappeared, and I had a memory seared with the images of what happened, or at least what I was told.

"I believe when my patient would normally bring that up [Joan's murder], it was out of concern that there might one day be a publication or legal matter," my frightened child confided to her counselor, "that she could be drawn into or forced, if you will, to interact with her mom."

Burke bolstered two felons to convince the jury that Lenny had allegedly confessed to two murders, but the defense now seated an observer to David Doyle's alleged confession. David Dellaria swore to tell the truth and bared his pathetic drug addiction. He was engaged in the illegal behavior with his friend, David Doyle, when drugs and alcohol apparently dropped Doyle's defenses and loosened his tongue. When the story stirred in the neighborhood in the summer of 1981, police found and questioned Dellaria. He told them that Doyle said Marie got what she deserved, and that he knew the details of what really happened. However, fear gripped the informant—Dellaria was suddenly terrified of meeting again. He reported that Doyle assaulted him twice within inches of his life.

"He cracked me on the back of the head," Doyle's neighbor recalled. "They threw me inside of the trunk and took me somewhere. He said, 'I'm going to kill you and leave you right here, you rat.'"

The first time Doyle attacked Dellaria, a bike-riding druggie, Paul Leo, intervened to pull Doyle off. Not surprisingly, Doyle's hot temper flared again.

"On command, he had his two, big German shepherds attack me and pin me to the ground. He took out a knife about that long," the witness said as he held his hands out to measure the blade. "He put me on the ground and stuck me in the neck, and said, 'I'm going to cut your throat, you rat.'"

Dellaria somehow rolled from the knife's edge and escaped Doyle's grasp as the neighbors all watched.

"Did you do anything as a result of this attack?" Unlike Burke, Rappaport established it was not a recent contrivance. Doyle's rap sheet tallied his long list of problems with the police.

"I filed a complaint in East Boston District Court on attempted murder on Mr. David Doyle," Dellaria announced.

"Do you know whether or not David Doyle ever had a temper?" the defense asked.

"David Doyle is a crazy bastard!" The lifelong friend had no other words to describe his friend's bad temper. "Excuse my language."

David Dellaria had problems of his own, entirely apart from knowing Doyle. Tim Burke handled a prosecution against him for snatching a purse from elderly Sally Lemire. Dellaria found himself behind bars in October of 1982 at the Charles Street Jail along with Leonard Paradiso. He recognized Paradiso's name from conversations with Doyle, and he proceeded to give a statement to Lenny's attorney, James Cipoletta. Burke made short order of the defense witness mocking his condition at the time Doyle supposedly detailed the crime. Dellaria's addiction nullified his account of Doyle's confession, but the jurors apparently did not question Doyle's violent behavior.

Attorneys spent more time at the sidebar haggling conflicted positions, and less time allowing the audience to contemplate what witnesses had to say. When Marie's close friend, Anna Marie Kenney Orlandino, took the stand, predictable objections drowned her out. Marie had lived with her friend for a fair period of time, and Orlandino disclosed that she saw her friend get dressed many times. The witness knew specifically how Marie wore the very outfit she died in.

Burke was adamant; Paradiso had struggled to remove the seamed undergarment in his frenzy to have his way. Autopsy pictures showed her clothing intact, debunking the incomprehensible scenario Burke forced through Robert Bond. Anna Marie had first-hand knowledge how she wore the stockings. In addition, the witness could also corroborate Marie's turbulent relationship with Doyle. During the grand jury, she corroborated other testimony. She saw the strangulation marks that wrapped around her friend's throat.

"You haven't put David Doyle anywhere near Marie Iannuzzi." The judge chastised Rappaport back at the sidebar for the other culprit defense.

Donahue completely discarded common sense; a guilty party would try to hide his trouble. The gatekeeper of the evidence stated that he needed to mull over these opposing arguments before he would let testimony in. Then he adjourned for the day.

The next morning the judge wasted no time. Unfortunately, his Honor seemed to have already made up his mind, like George and Eleanor Webster, and was in the position to sway thinking. Attorneys met in Donahue's lobby. The judge pulled out his little evidence handbook and began landing blows to the defense. First, Dellaria's statement to Inspector Howard Long of the Saugus Police Department on July 16, 1981, was tossed, as well as the consistent affidavit he gave to Paradiso's attorney, James Cipoletta. The report Long compiled, detailing his conversation with Dellaria, included a few other things. Doyle had visible scratches on his face and hands in Long's office on the day examiners identified the body. Witnesses saw Marie Iannuzzi's bags packed before authorities knew the victim's name. Jean Day told police she observed blood on the fifth step leading up to Doyle's apartment. Finally, cops arrested Doyle in New Jersey with a stolen airline ticket.

Donahue followed his first cut by pitching the police report that documented Carol Seracuse's recollection at the time of the murder; her statement placed Marie back in the bar at 1:30 a.m. Relevant evidence was all sent to the trash. Five years later, Carol responded, "I don't remember." However, the judge disallowed the report filed when events were fresh.

Prior statements were on the block next. Christine DeLisi and Anna Marie Kenney Orlandino both witnessed strangulation marks around Marie's neck two months before her murder, and testified during the grand jury about their terrified friend. The wily ADA had sanitized Christine's testimony already. Now, the question turned to the present witness and the anticipated testimony she would give. Anna Marie corroborated Christine DeLisi's account from the 1982 grand jury. Both testified David Doyle caused strangulation marks around Marie's throat, an event that occurred shortly before the young woman met her fate: strangled and dumped on the rocks. Both friends heard the deceased woman's terror when she gasped to tell them David tried to kill her. Irrationally, the judge nixed input from another eyewitness and dictated what the jury would hear.

Rappaport had not been successful getting anything in the record rebutting the state's position that Lenny was the last person seen with the victim alive. Police reports differed with the prosecutor's premise, but it was up to the court's discretion what he allowed into the record.

"My position is, as a matter of fairness, due process if you will..." Rappaport pleaded in vain.

"Will you stop using that phrase 'due process,'" the judge snapped. "I try to give due process to everyone."

His Honor stifled Rappaport's limited choices for the futile defense. If Paradiso decided not to take the stand, his girlfriend, Candy Weyant, Lenny's alibi on the night Marie died, was the other possible option. Both were facing the Federal indictment Burke instigated; he had set the trap and had Candy cornered. The prosecutor insisted he was going to bring it to the attention of the jury if Candy did not take the stand. The devious ADA had a transcript he planned to use to grill the alibi witness—his secret weapon.

"Tim has informed me that he has the grand jury testimony of Ms. Weyant that he's going to use for cross-examination for impeachment purposes." The handicapped defender exposed the problem of concealed records. "He's willing to give it to me after her direct testimony. I would like to see it before I make the determination to call Candy."

"She's given her statement under oath in the grand jury," Burke haughtily declared.

"Isn't that part of discovery?" Donahue logically assumed the prosecutor competed fairly.

"No," the Suffolk County understudy rejected. "Her testimony there was narrowly limited to the Webster case."

The original agreement was for full and complete reciprocal discovery, but Burke was not playing by the rules. Donahue did not think the Commonwealth was obligated to share. There was no indictment in Joan's case, so Burke was the only one privy to the transcript. Neither Candy nor her attorney had one, and her counsel was not in the courtroom. The premeditated predicament favored the state's desired outcome.

Jimmy Cardinale was another possible witness discussed in the lobby who had given a statement to police. He had observed Marie back at the bar around the two a.m. closing, but the defense had trouble finding him. Cardinale was hostile and uncooperative with law enforcement. His father was murdered in the same bar that was now the focus of the trial playing out. The bartender on duty on August 11, 1979, resented the lack of police effort to help resolve the loss he had suffered. Again, the judge capitulated to Burke's repeated tantrums. Including any documents into the record casting doubt on his case was objectionable to the offense. Therefore, Cardinale's statement to police that he saw the victim at 1:45 a.m. missed the cut for the jury's consideration.

Anna Marie settled back into the scorching seat as spectators took their places in the sweltering hall of presumed justice. Burke continued to cloud the issue that focused on what outfits Anna Marie saw her friend dress in, even asking for precise dates. The victim had several disco outfits worn in the same way, and had dressed at her friend's place as recently as two weeks before the murder. Marie typically accessorized her outfits with a scarf, the adornment used as a garrote to suffocate her. The court disallowed further details of Anna Marie's prior statements. Those who sat in judgment did not get to hear about the foreboding violence when Doyle left imprints of his fingers around Marie's throat just a few short weeks before she died. The deceased uttered real terror to her close friends. Friends gave her refuge from her frighteningly violent boyfriend, but Burke effectively sanitized or silenced their recollections.

Rappaport called Kathy Leonti to raise her right hand, and another sister in the large Catholic family faced the room. Kathy acknowledged Doyle's mindset during a ride to the wake. On the way to memorialize the silenced corpse of his girlfriend, Doyle mused whether he should see other girls. Burke cross-examined Kathy to ease the initial suspicions of the family and passed Doyle's disconnected emotions off as confusion. Suspicion festered two and a half years after the murder when Marie's family testified before the grand jury in the *Commonwealth v. Leonard J. Paradiso*. The very woman Burke claimed drew him into the case, implicated Doyle back on March 5, 1982, but Burke had the advantage of knowing what to garble. The tactic of using the media to swirl images of the man now accused was reminiscent of *El Mercurio's* role in stirring unrest in Chile, but the propaganda did not roll off the presses until Robert Bond's allegations began to circulate in January of 1983. Before the undeclared victim became part of Marie's case, loved ones reasonably distrusted the boyfriend. Family was convinced—or possibly coerced—to ignore facts right in front of their faces, and instead, they joined the cause to crucify the Websters' chosen suspect.

Inspector Long was on and off the seat in no time. Officers that worked the case early on documented their interviews and observations that gave the Saugus police two suspects. The deflated defense counsel asked Long whether he questioned Dellaria, but already knew the judge barred the officer's report from the record. Long recalled his conversation with Doyle's friend on July 16, 1981, with Officer Charlie Gleason. The patrol car idled by the curb. Detectives picked up the known user to quiz him about the rumblings on the street—who murdered Marie. Dellaria had squealed on a friend from the Jeffries Point neighborhood, but the source's known addiction shaded his information with uncertainty. The seasoned investigator thought, but couldn't recall, when Doyle stopped being a suspect, because the officer was taken off the case. Trooper Andrew Palombo took the reins in February 1981, and talked with his friend Doyle twenty to thirty times in undocumented meetings.

Rappaport made the decision for Candy Weyant to testify; the defense had little choice. While Rappaport had the floor, and Candy repeated the events she told police at the time of the murder, the prosecutor impressed the jury with a strategy of his own. Paradiso's advocate stopped in his tracks, and Burke wiped the childish smirk off his face. The boys trudged back up to the bench.

"I detected some facial expression on the part of my brother," the exhausted defender complained for the second time. "I would hope it wouldn't distract the jury. I saw some laughter."

"Well, I wasn't aware of it," his Honor dismissed as if it didn't count if he didn't see it.

In order to provide the state with added advantage in the Iannuzzi and Webster cases, Burke prompted a Federal case for mail and bankruptcy fraud that included the boat. Burke successfully put Candy in a corner, then used the secret Webster grand jury testimony to discredit the defendant's alibi witness. Burke wasted no time; he asked the witness whether she had ever lied for Lenny.

"No, I haven't," Candy replied.

The cunning solicitor handed her a page and asked her whose signature was on it. He heard her admit it, but asked again for dramatic effect.

"Whose signature is that right there?" the prosecutor demanded. "Real loud please."

"It's my signature," the girlfriend humbly confirmed.

"I'll ask you again; did you ever lie to the police for Mr. Paradiso?" Burke accused. "Real loud."

"Yes," she honestly answered.

Burke badgered the witness to the verge of tears and repeatedly hammered the point that she had lied. Rappaport stopped the bleeding to approach the judge once again. He could not hear the disturbance, but sensed something going on behind him. Vultures circled in the courtroom and fed on the frenzy Burke was stirring.

"You were shown a document," Rappaport redirected. "What did that document relate to?"

"An insurance claim on a boat," the flustered witness stated, "that the boat was stolen."

"Was the boat stolen?" The defense counsel tried to recover, but his opponent had discredited the witness.

"No," Candy admitted. "I believe it was sunk."

The offense delved into Candy's testimony on previous occasions. Burke broached the 1974 case of Constance Porter. Anyone joining this case in progress would have mistakenly believed that the girlfriend bailed Lenny on assault charges, but Candy was not an alibi witness in the Porter case. She could not attest to the time in question during that trial, and had only been with Lenny earlier that evening. Regardless, Burke insinuated she lied for her man.

Flanagan's protégé punctuated the deceitful misrepresentation by handing Candy a report about the boat; the boat, of course, was Burke's suspected crime scene for Joan's disappearance. Even the sequestered jurors knew the speculation about the Harvard graduate student's fate, but collaborators locked away the FBI lab results that debunked the theory. Instead of disclosing the facts to try the case, the adjudicators nodded sympathetically to the Websters as they took their seats each day. The illusion in the courtroom was that Candy lied about the alleged murder scene in another case—Joan Webster's presumed ending.

"That boat doesn't involve simply an insurance fraud," the sly solicitor played to the crowd, "does it?"

"As far as I'm concerned it does," the young woman insisted.

"Ma'am, you're a future witness for Paradiso in another matter, aren't you?" The Websters' confidant toiled relentlessly to bring the undeclared victim into the case.

"Objection, your Honor," Rappaport demanded, but the presiding robe overruled.

The room was sizzling, and the gallery was restless. Whispers around the room reached a rowdy level, flash bulbs flashed, and reporters fell over each other to get to the phones. The judge excused the jury so he could question the defendant. Candy left the door wide open that might bring unfavorable incidents into the record. Paradiso was vulnerable to the accusations levied against him with his prior record of assault in 1974. He understood; he declined to take the stand in his own defense. Tim Burke humiliated Paradiso's girlfriend, the person threatening the state's case with the truth. The subliminal image of Joan sank in as designed, and her fate was the jury's last impression as the defense rested.

Burke had a couple more nails to hammer into the accused's coffin. The prosecution called two witnesses in rebuttal. Jean Day resumed the seat, and Burke revisited what appeared to be his favorite topic: what Marie wore on the night she was murdered. A red wrap-around skirt encircled the matching one-piece bodysuit, and Marie accessorized her ensemble with black stockings, black shoes, and a black scarf. The order of dress was integral to Burke's premise. Robert Bond described the alleged struggle to remove the pantyhose, but police recovered the body with her clothing intact. Anna Marie described how the victim put on her clothes, and so did Jean Day during the grand jury. The victim wore the seamed stockings under the leotard. Even Trooper Palombo affirmed the order of dress during a previous hearing.

"Underneath the skirt or underneath the bodysuit," Jean resigned to forget. "To me—the girl's dead. Does it matter what she was wearing?"

The stepsister was clear on that point the morning she spoke to private investigator Dennis Slawsby, but her memory faded quickly. Tim Burke and Trooper Andrew Palombo had escorted her down the hall. The thought of never seeing her child again loomed large, a vulnerability for any loving mother. The offensive force asked her how her sibling put her clothes on, and Jean said she did not know. Common sense escaped the citizens delegated the responsibility for a man's fate, and it suddenly made a strange kind of sense to them that a style-conscious, young woman would wear her hose over a bodysuit.

Det. Charles Gleason walked to the front of the room. The seasoned officer had worked in the East Boston area for several years, and knew both David Dellaria and David Doyle very well. Gleason was with Inspector Long in July 1981, and the officers picked up Dellaria to hear what he knew about the Iannuzzi murder. Burke scored a point; Dellaria's truthfulness was in question. Police knew Doyle's friend had indulged a drug habit for a long time. Rappaport countered with a point of his own, and the detective affirmed that Doyle's veracity was in question, too, because of the seamy drug world he navigated. As it happened, Doyle's unsavory business would make him useful to an undercover cop in the narcotics unit. The other suspect in Marie's murder told Trooper Palombo what he'd heard on the streets in a system where informants got a pass.

Back at the bench, Burke dangled a morsel in the pretense of fair play. The prosecutor revealed a letter dated January 11, 1984, that he received from Paradiso. The defendant forwarded a tip that someone had seen Doyle outside the Cardinale's Nest Bar at two a.m. According to Paradiso's letter, Doyle argued with the decedent in the dark morning hours before a stealth offender double-knotted her scarf tightly around her neck. Investigator Ray Morgan attempted to track down the lead, but nothing panned out. The accused offered to speak with Burke about it before the court assigned Rappaport to the case on January 23, 1984, but Lenny refused to speak to the messengers Burke sent. Trooper Palombo and Sgt. Murphy of the Boston Police Department contacted Sgt. Easyrock at Walpole prison on January 19, 1984, to relay their desire to speak with the inmate. Paradiso declined, but the two officers made a personal appearance at the prison in another futile effort on January 22, 1984. In an expressed tone of fairness, Burke entered the letter into evidence to show the state was not hiding anything—it was the state's idea of a fair trial for the wholesale shellfish merchant.

"I want to renew my motion for a required finding of not guilty," Rappaport concluded.

"I think on all of the testimony, there is sufficient evidence on the rape charge for the jury to find the defendant guilty beyond a point of reasonable doubt." Judge Roger Donahue's power manipulated what the jury considered and reflected his predisposition. "I think the same is true of the murder charge."

What had filtered through the bench left one impression. The evidence blocked at the bar and secrets tucked in other case files left quite another.

CHAPTER 17

Doomed

Steve's bad behavior ratcheted up the tension, and the in-laws soon booked flights to intrude more forcibly into our marriage. My husband displayed his obvious disloyalty in front of the girls, and then he cowardly lied to their faces. George and Eleanor swept in to influence professionals baffled by conflicting episodes in our house. After circling the block, their first stop was with Carol Metzger. The family I had lovingly embraced for two decades was now paranoid that I might be present. Their son's conduct was under the spotlight, and his enabling parents likened Steve's betrayal to the womanizing ways of George's father RN. They dismissed my spouse's reckless behavior in the sort of way you might say, "Boys will be boys."

"We've been happily married for years," they interjected, failing, of course, to reveal the pact of secrecy they vowed on CIA Form 368.

George was in denial. Steve obviously had hurt our family, and me, but George dismissed this as the innocent sort of behavior of an immature partner who was "just looking." I stepped on the porch with a forgiving heart, but resolved that my mate had to deal with his issues. That day was the last time Eleanor looked me in the eyes, but her frigid stare blocked out the pain I was feeling.

"We've all got to band together to get through this," she said. The words were right, if only they had been sincere. When gossip finally recycled back to me, I heard the erroneous insinuation I had been unfaithful.

The next stop plopped them on the couch at Sarah O'Brien's tiny, tucked-away office. Words rolled off their tongues with ease.

"We're really worried about Eve," they pined, though their insincerity did not take long to expose. However, the girls' confused advocate dismissed my observation.

Just days after the premeditated visit with the girls' counselor, my father unexpectedly lay dying. Not a single kind word eased my pain as my dad lingered near death for a month. When God called him home on July 12, 2003, not a single Webster was there to comfort me in my time of painful loss. They sent flowers, but the disconnection from real emotion was evident in the canned sympathy card. More than five months later, Eleanor finally composed a comment on the Christmas note she sent to my detached location, where I had been banished without explanation.

"He was such a good helper," was all she could muster.

She failed miserably to pay due tribute to a good and decent man's life, and ignored the joy of grandchildren my father shared with them. As the holiday intensified my anxiety over the separation from my girls, the Websters replayed the solemn Yule of 1981 with one less place setting at the table. Image control crossed another doomed name off the family list.

The state's burden was to prove beyond reasonable doubt that Paradiso had committed these crimes, but an unnamed victim loomed large in the courtroom. George and Eleanor Webster left town for New Jersey saying they did not want to influence the jury, but their presence during the trial left an indelible mark. Their authority had psychologically infused their judgment and entwined this case with the mysterious fate of their daughter. By tying Marie's murder to Joan's, they preyed on emotions that determined a man's outcome. Reporters scrambled to get their bylines to editors each day, and each day Joan Webster's plight was the leading edge of their stories.

The defense counsel told the judge he was feeling afternoon weary, but Donahue was ready to press forward. The judge proceeded, rushing into closing arguments that afternoon, another subtle advantage to the prosecution. The battle was over before it even began in front of the fatigued jurors, but Rappaport persevered to make sense of the chaotic melodrama.

"The defendant in this case comes in with the presumption of innocence," the defense reminded the room. "The defendant contended and did introduce evidence to show you that there was some other party, some other person in this case, who was as likely to have committed this particular crime."

Rappaport logically stepped through the case the jury had heard. The defense counsel noted some shrewd discrepancies. He remarked Christine DeLisi's recollection had changed from her testimony given at the grand jury on March 5, 1982, when her memory was obviously fresher.

"Her testimony is significant, as it has subtly changed since the grand jury," counsel reminded the court, "just as a number of other witnesses' testimony has subtly changed in this case."

The disadvantaged advocate pointed out significant details for the jury. Michael Kamer played with a set of keys on the bar in front of Marie. The name "Day" was on them; the same name as the victim's stepsiblings and the name David Doyle gave New Jersey police when they detained him. The parole officer's notes were out of sequence; a backdated entry recapped the discussion Victor Anchukaitis had with his parolee regarding this case. It might have helped the cause if Rappaport had pointed out the date was not typed into the running account, but obscured with a handwritten entry beneath it. Burke's embellished account that Lenny called in a panic to come into the office was not reflected in the parole officer's notes.

"Trooper Carl Sjoberg admitted it was fairly obvious that this did not appear to be a robbery." Rappaport's reminder contradicted the confidential source to the FBI that there was missing jewelry in the Iannuzzi case, but that little morsel remained hidden from the defense and the public.

Burke and Palombo simply smiled when Paradiso's defender brought up that point. They were fully aware that protected players swirled the image to enhance the defendant's modus operandi that he stole jewelry from his victims to lavish on girlfriends. Bullerwell never made it to the stand, but Tim Burke told the Feds she was wearing a bracelet identical to Joan's missing gold charms. The report said jewelry was missing from Marie Iannuzzi too, but the agent in the personal crimes division locked the report away in the corrupt FBI office's files.

The offensive team presented several irrational assertions that Paradiso had raped Marie Iannuzzi. The facts were simple. Authorities found her fully dressed with her clothing photographed intact. Burke had done a masterful job confusing everyone what had happened, but rape was not a factor considered at the time. No experienced authority ever requested tests to determine whether there was a criminal sex act violating the victim. Rape was simply the motive Burke needed to promote the case that consumed his thinking—Joan Webster. The most critical clue to what happened to Marie was the clawed hands of the victim, but no one bothered to scrape under Marie's long manicured nails. Her rigid fingers, frozen in the last desperate fight of her life, held the clue. One suspect had horrible scratches, and the other did not.

"Dr. Katsas said he distinctly remembered removing panties from the body," Rappaport described the inept investigation. "Trooper Sjoberg said, well, he never took possession of any panties."

The defense attorney emphasized testimony that witnesses saw Marie back in the bar at closing time, but the biased judge scratched the reports from the evidence that went back with the jury. Paradiso and his longtime girlfriend both offered information to the police willingly when asked at the time, and their stories were consistent. Subtle variations were not the exact pat answers Burke implied, but rather the accounts described the same event told from the two different perspectives. Police documented their investigation, but only selective reports went in with the jury. On the stand, their recollections resembled Burke's interpretations.

Rappaport addressed the credibility of the convicted killers Burke promoted. Motivation to help the Commonwealth in a high-profile case was obvious to any rational thinker. More importantly, Pisa and Bond's stories just did not add up.

"Ladies and gentlemen, consider their character," Rappaport appealed to their reason. "Consider whether or not their stories really mesh. What type of motivation do these people have to come and say what they had to say? That's what the government's case comes down to, whether or not you're going to believe Bobby Bond and Tony Pisa."

The hot topic during testimony was Marie's attire. What she wore and how she wore it was important in this case if the jury was going to believe Paradiso had raped her. The young woman did not have her stockings on when she was found, but the struggle the prosecution painted for the defendant to take them off defied reason. The prosecution suggested Paradiso's behavior proved his consciousness of guilt. Through Bond, Burke claimed Lenny burned his car to get rid of the evidence. However, the notion he panicked a month later defied common sense. Police never issued a warrant to examine the vehicle, though they knew that the victim had been in the car just hours before her death. Instead, a con suggested that there was blood, and the defendant destroyed the evidence when he allegedly burned the car later. This was not evidence but mere speculation based on the incredulous testimony of Bond. The state finally tested the single-cut hair after the trial began, but there was no match to the man seated at the defense table. The lab technician originally examining the clothing could not be found, and Burke enlisted Mark Grant to answer the questions. He compared the single follicle with hair taken from every conceivable part of Paradiso's body; there was no match to the strand that supposedly threw Paradiso into a panic.

"David Doyle told you he didn't know if he had scratches on his hands at the time of the wake." The attorney reminded the jury of Doyle's cloudy memory, but the advocate overlooked one witness who had observed the repulsive torn flesh stained with mercurochrome to fight any infection. Of course, Doyle was lying.

Doyle testified that he last spoke to Marie about eight o'clock the night of the wedding. He claimed he learned about Lenny and Candy giving her a ride from Marie. At eight o'clock, Marie was still cavorting at the Milanos' and flirting with Doyle's cousin Freddie. Candy did not give the inebriated guest a lift until ten o'clock, at the host's request, and Lenny waited at the house. If Doyle told police Monday morning about Paradiso, as it came out in testimony, he had to have had some sort of contact with his girlfriend later that night. Doyle's cousin, Jimmy Milano, placed the defendant and his date at the house in Saugus at eleven p.m. Paradiso could not have been racing through the streets of East Boston half an hour away.

Rappaport's arguments were logical and sincere. Certainly, there was enough reasonable doubt. Doyle was an enraged jealous lover who behaved strangely. The couple had a history, an abusive relationship, and they argued in front of numerous witnesses that day. The other suspect packed his dead girlfriend's belongings, medicated deep gouges on the back of his hands, stepped over the suspected blood on the steps to their apartment, and took flight to New Jersey in a drugged stupor. Doyle and his mother, Rosemarie, spouted four different excuses for the ripped flesh. This was not a multiple-choice quiz. Doyle's treachery was a given; he lied and gave a false name to the New Jersey police that cuffed him stealing bags at Newark Airport.

Burke's self-described style was to prepare by beginning with the summary and work his way back into the case. He salivated for months for this moment in time. Burke's advantage was that Candy's admission about the boat was still fresh in the jury's mind. He stood up and demonstrated the particular set of skills tutored in Suffolk County to wrap up a case.

"Think about the credibility of Candy Weyant's statements to police. You've seen her on the stand. What does she look like?" Burke's devaluation was a vulgar low. "And how did everyone describe Marie that night? Dynamite!"

Repeatedly, Burke demeaned the young woman. He was passionate and preyed on emotions. His closing envisioned a sordid scene of seduction at the Cardinale's Nest Bar. The offensive adopted something like the Webster philosophy, "Boys will be boys." Burke made the choice between a vulnerable, intoxicated, young woman with a great figure versus Candy waiting out in the car. The disgraceful mockery compared the appearance of two women, and suggested that the seductive temptation of an inebriated quean attracted

Lenny's attention. Burke insisted, however, that the plain girlfriend was home in Revere when Paradiso went back into the bar to lure the victim out into the night.

"Candy's not outside in that car," the ADA shamelessly supported Robert Bond's statement. "You know what his intentions were."

Candy Weyant's beauty glowed from inside; she held on to the truth, even admitting her own flaws, despite the state's despicable tactics. She still faced charges from the Federal indictment Burke had finagled; the strategy designed to pressure Paradiso and Weyant for the Iannuzzi and Webster cases.

"She was one of his alibi witnesses in a prior proceeding ten years ago," the pious prosecutor deceitfully stated.

The Suffolk County ADA replayed Bond's rendition of events in nauseating detail, and how the Massachusetts State Police tried to corroborate his story. Poor Mr. Bond did not want Doyle to be jammed up—wrongly accused as he was. The facts spoke for themselves, but Burke twisted the vision to suggest Paradiso was the one framing the boyfriend to take the fall. Unfortunately, there was no crystal ball to predict the outcome of Bond's retrial.

"Ask yourselves in assessing credibility, who really has the motive to lie here?" Burke distorted without disclosing his motives. "It's Candy Weyant."

According to Bond, Paradiso was running red lights when the groom's brother saw him at the house in Saugus. The con regurgitated the implausible scene that Paradiso struggled to take Marie's stockings off, and Burke embellished the tale with the image Lenny could have pulled them off through the opening of one leg. The fabric was stretchy material. Bond said Lenny burned the car ten days after the crime without an ember of evidence to prove it. The car, reported stolen a month later on September 13, 1979, was never found.

"What is true is what Bobby Bond told you," the entranced jurors heard the solicitor dictate. "No matter what you might think about Bobby Bond, there is still some sense of decency, even among cons. He is worthy of your belief. Candy Weyant is not."

The pious orator heralded Tony Pisa as a model prisoner who finally found the conscience to come forward. To listen to Burke, Pisa should have received civic commendations for establishing a law library at the prison and helping fellow inmates with their cases. Tony's record was reviewed, it could not be avoided, but poor Mr. Pisa had paid his penance. The fact is, "Death Row Tony" knew the system and worked it. He studied the law just as Burke did.

The Iannuzzi family suffered a horrible loss. They had grieved the murders of two family members and became victims themselves. The offense applied pressure to some and redrafted the instincts and observations of others. Burke pontificated they were wrong about Doyle; they made a mistake thinking he could have done this. David was just a miserable victim of circumstance and uncanny coincidences at the time Marie died. According to Burke, the Iannuzzis were simply ignorant of Paradiso, that is, until the Webster suspect was condemned through the press.

"And the harm Paradiso has done murdering Marie Iannuzzi is compounded by the fact that they try to pin it on David Doyle." Burke surmised that Lenny was the monster pointing the finger.

The ends justify the means, and Burke was obsessed with the idea that Paradiso had murdered Joan Webster. A conviction here, in his mind, would help "prove" the link between the cases. No evidence connected Joan's case to the defendant, but since Paradiso was a suspect in Marie's case, Burke had an avenue to obtain search warrants. The only so-called proof the boys dug up was craftily linked to Joan's case. In many ways, Marie's trial was just an exhibition match for the real game to come, the game of pinning Joan's murder on Paradiso. Though he seemed to be a doomed man, Paradiso would not break and maintained his innocence. The whole story played like a CIA plot—the state was in bed with the unsavory to get a job done. Authorities preserved reasonable deniability and thwarted any attempt to connect the pieces to discern what was real.

During closing arguments on July 20, 1984, a coy tactic crossed the lips of the charging barrister. Transcripts revealed the juvenile attorney's methods to gain a dubious conviction, and this trick struck a familiar chord with me. Burke fixed his glance on the jury, and he pointedly challenged the notion that they had just wheeled people in to say what they wanted them to say.

"Do you really believe that's what we're all about?" Burke remarked without flinching. "We just put people on the stand just to try to convict somebody, knowing that they're lying? You folks don't really believe that, do you?"

People are conditioned to trust authority figures, but Boston's abuse of power was not fully exposed when the ADA preyed on that confidence. The Websters had used this device repeatedly in our personal lives to squelch instincts that would have raised reasonable doubts. The twisted questions subdued dissent; the Svengali approach lured listeners to abandon their instincts and trust the authorities' judgment.

Recovered documents support that is just what Burke did, and current custodians vehemently guard the files denying access. The simple fact was if Bond was telling the truth, then many others were lying. He was a violent offender who waved a gun outside his victim's wake, but was exalted as a man who still maintained a code of integrity. People were lying; it is in the record, and Burke's self-serving tribute.

On page 91 of the published book Tim Burke billed as "true crime," the disingenuous litigator wrote, "In early March 1982, the first witnesses were called before the Suffolk County grand jury in the case *Commonwealth of Massachusetts v. John Doe*, the investigation into the murder of Marie Barbara Iannuzzi."

On the first page of those transcripts, there was another agenda revealed just before Kathy Leonti swore to tell the truth. The title read: 038655—Grand Jury, March 5, 1982—ADA Timothy Burke—*Comm. vs. Leonard J. Paradiso*—Murder-1st.

"The plain white envelope sat waiting on top of the radio between the tattered gray and the dark brown files." The author wrote about himself on page 121 of *The Paradiso Files* as if he had an out-of-body experience. "January 5, 1983 was a Wednesday. It was an average winter day following a standard New Year's holiday weekend. As the lawyer began to read the letter, though, his heart began to race."

However, the actual record said something much different. "I should have asked them guys this morning did they intercept the letter," Bond told the Massachusetts State Police on January 14, 1983, during the taped rehearsal. "I caught the deputy last night, Carter. 'Jesus Christ, I don't really think you have a bitch, Bob.' He says, 'You're talking about three days.'"

Bond went on with his story prodded by Sgt. Tammaro: "He took the boat way out and dumped the body, and brought the boat back."

Burke told the court Paradiso did not bury his victims; they were disposed in water, and Bond's submission, worked with the Massachusetts State Police, followed that premise. Joan's body had not been unearthed to dispute it. It is not my imagination, as Joan's paranoid brother would submit. The lies were in black and white, and this was only the tip of the iceberg.

"Dear God," I cried to myself. "If only I had known what was going on, so much pain could have been avoided."

The judge did his part and instructed the jury. The question of reasonable doubt is always an ingredient the citizens have to consider in weighing the evidence before them. Donahue reinforced his guidance with the 1850 case of John Webster. There it was again, an incredible device infusing Joan's memory into the trial. In that case, Webster did it.

Deliberations began on the afternoon of Friday, July 20, 1984, and resumed the next morning. The judge had filtered the evidence, and the seated peers lacked the facts they needed to make a fair judgment. Judge Roger Donahue stacked the deck and threw out the police records that bolstered the other culprit defense. Nevertheless, there had been a whole lot more going on that neither the jury, nor the defense team, knew anything about.

The participant Robert Bond asserted the "Man from New Jersey" sent people to see him. The jury was not aware that the Webster reward money enticed Bond on multiple occasions through the family's conduit Sgt. Carmen Tammaro. Bond's statement conveniently covered both murders. A dangerous criminal seduced with reward money and the promise of a new trial was hardly trustworthy. The promise of a lower charge of manslaughter in a new trial was not a promise the state could legitimately make, but the dangled pledge never reached the jury anyway. Palombo's superior guided Bond through his story, and arranged the polygraph to measure the veracity of a man without conscience and nothing to lose. There is a reason that polygraph tests are not usually admissible as evidence; people like Bond are so adept at lying.

Tammaro coordinated the various agencies in the Joan Webster case, and authorities suppressed the composite of the bearded man a cabbie believed he saw leaving the airport with Joan. His own subordinate, assigned to the F Barracks at Logan, sported a beard on frequent occasions. The fact was, the image looked nothing like the man they accused.

Bond's letter affirmed Massachusetts State Police met with Paradiso three weeks after his arrest for the Iannuzzi murder, but the disclosure was in part two of the affidavit, and no one could see it. Lenny documented the exchange he had with "Buster," a neighborhood nickname for George Webster's liaison. On August 1, 1982, Buster prodded his nemesis for a confession in Joan's disappearance, not Marie's, and planted the idea the young woman was murdered onboard Lenny's boat. He seeded his suggestion four months before he taped the rat at the courthouse tattling about contended confessions from Paradiso.

Patty Bono placed anonymous calls that implicated her North End acquaintance in both murders with an unverified ten-year-old allegation. She was not just any random anonymous caller, however.

She was the sergeant's childhood friend who contacted the Websters shortly before the parents' calculated February meeting in 1982. This was the same meeting where the powers that be assigned Burke and Palombo to the Webster mystery. The ball rolled quickly to a speciously renamed grand jury that produced a true bill for the murder of Marie Iannuzzi against the man now awaiting his fate.

Without the benefit of the background, the jury absorbed what they had. The first question jurors had late Friday afternoon was a distressing one.

"Is it possible to rape a dead body?"

The answer to this question would have made Bond's recitation of choking her twice significant for the charges. According to the law, it was considered rape only if the victim was still breathing. The forelady, Janice Leeming, presented the court with another question on Saturday when the sequestered jury resumed deliberations.

"We'd like a clarification on the difference between first and second-degree murder."

Jurors were to determine the degree of murder, but the rules defined that murder committed deliberately, with premeditated malice, was murder in the first degree. The jurors filed back out, but barely warmed their seats before they reached their verdict. At 2:04 p.m., they assumed their positions and responded to the questions of guilt.

"We find the defendant, Leonard Paradiso, guilty of murder in the second degree. We also find the defendant, Leonard Paradiso, guilty of assault with intent to rape Marie Iannuzzi."

Word reached the Websters and they were delighted. The Iannuzzi decision was as if they had received justice for their own daughter. An image emerged of their private celebration for the man they accused of murdering Joan. George no doubt poured a stiff drink. I knew exactly what their exuberance was like; I had seen it before, and experienced similar celebratory moments years later. I stumbled upon secrets and landed in the hospital under the weight of severe depreciation from the reticent family. Their devalued daughter taught them nothing, and the blade swung back cutting out another member of the family.

The proud lawyer and his sidekick strutted outside the building to a gaggle of reporters. Added innuendo spiced the latest editions about the condemned man. Guilty apparently unleashed some justification to add unconfirmed silage that fermented more hatred for the next round. Burke's obsessed witch-hunt was far from over in the name of vindication for Joan, but the foundation was firmly in place with the day's decision.

The parties all resumed their places on Wednesday, July 25, 1984, to hear the judge administer his punishment. The prosecution asked the court to impose a "from and after" sentence, meaning they would tack sentences one after the other and not serve them consecutively.

"The defendant compounded the horror of this case, the murder itself, by trying to create a phony alibi," the prosecutor indignantly pleaded. "As bad as that is, what he did in trying to implicate an innocent person through David Doyle is something the court should take into consideration in effecting the from and after sentence that we're asking you to apply."

Iannuzzi family and friends had incriminated the abusive boyfriend based on insight and strong circumstantial evidence. Legitimate enforcers considered Doyle a suspect from the time Marie died. The state went on and branded Paradiso as sexually dangerous, an evil man the state should cage for the rest of his life. Burke calculated the emotional effect of the body's disposal and insisted the judge throw the book at the condemned man.

"He tried to discard of the body like it was so much refuse," the prosecutor disdainfully sneered.

The defense held up a copy of the *Boston Herald* with statements made by members of the DA's team.

"There's a certain pecking order in prison," Rappaport appealed. "There's one offense a person may be accused of or convicted of; it's an offense dealing with offenses against children."

The attorney no longer expected responsible reporting from the press; they salivated for each salacious story. There was no factual basis for the rumors unleashed in the tabloids after the verdict claiming Paradiso used to hang at the bus station with child molesters. The insinuations were disgusting, but not surprising in retrospect. The gossip tied the state's desired culprit to a familiar location in the Joan Webster case: the bus station. The edition Rappaport held up only quoted an investigator close to the case, but other tabloids quoted Trooper Palombo making statements that day.

"A member of my brother's staff was talking to the press and made certain statements," the defeated defender announced. "This statement of Mr. Paradiso hanging around with known child molesters makes Mr. Paradiso a marked man in prison. The inmates at MCI Walpole are not going to be concerned whether it's true or not."

The papers were full of the unfounded accusations. Mouthpieces rehashed Patty Bono's unverified story as if it were fact, and kept the anonymous caller tied to the case. The authority figure described the doomed man's estranged daughter as an attractive, young woman with long, dark hair. According to the badge, this underlying pain caused Paradiso to hurt others. Trooper Palombo made the same insinuations that unsettled the passenger he picked up at the airport on December 12, 1982. Finally, the hulking officer, the driving force behind the Marie Iannuzzi case, now declared there was evidence to connect his target to the disappearance of Joan Webster.

Leonard Paradiso asked to address the court at the disposition of his sentence. Counsel understood that the defendant had that right, but Judge Donahue said he knew of no such privilege. Therefore, the besieged man remained silent and denied an opportunity to speak up for himself. Predetermined guilt was evident in the judge's decision, and he expressed his verdict at the sidebar before the jury had even gone out to deliberate the selective evidence he gave them. He adhered to Burke's request and heaped "from and after" sentences to lock Paradiso away for a very long time. He was a scapegoat, and was doomed right from the start.

The decision elated George and Eleanor. They had broadcast their certainty that this man murdered Joan. At the family gathering in Nantucket in August, they raved about Burke's prowess and the particular skills the lead investigator demonstrated to capture a killer. The core team dug up things to use against their suspect. As our week ended, Eleanor gave me the directions to the F Barracks at Logan.

"You have a long enough layover," my mother-in-law suggested. "You really must go meet Trooper Palombo."

I almost had to drag Steve kicking and screaming; he did not want to be bothered. Nevertheless, we made our way to the Massachusetts State Police office, across from the airport chapel, to meet him. He was a large, imposing man. He was clean-shaven that day and dressed in casual attire. His grip was firm, and his eyes penetrated, but his broad smile reflected off his badge and I was at ease.

"Thank you," I said, extending my hand. "Thank you for looking for Joan."

I had no idea what had really gone on, and it was far from over. The inner circle firmly planted a dagger in the out-of-reach center of Paradiso's back. The Iannuzzi case made the perfect hook to hang other charges, the nail to blame him for Joan, and the decision kept intruders out of the Websters' closet.

CHAPTER 18

Cutting Edge

"**C**an you fly up to Boston—ASAP?" Burke breathlessly requested. "Bring the charts with you."

It was November 26, 1984. Inspector Anthony Pascucci assigned to the Suffolk County DA pulled up to the curb at the airport. Lt. Tom Dugan of the Glen Ridge Police Department slipped into the car with the requested charts. Tim Burke had called that morning requesting dental records to compare with a partial jawbone that washed ashore. Dugan accompanied Pascucci to meet with forensic dentist Dr. Stanley Schwartz at Tufts University, but the comparison was negative for Joan.

Apparently, in Burke's mind, cinder blocks still weighted Joan in the deep blue of Boston Harbor, and no one but the killer knew any differently. The fixated litigator was stubbornly determined to prove that Paradiso had murdered Joan Webster on the recovered boat, despite the fact the FBI lab results conflicted with his inflexible premise. He submitted garbage from the bottom of Pier 7 for more than a year, but with no results to his liking. Burke hoped a new scheme would have better results, and the afternoon conference with Dugan put a new plan in place back home in New Jersey.

"We need for you to bring all property belonging to Joan Webster, in your possession, to Boston," Burke directed. "FBI agent Steve Broce is your Boston contact to obtain the case number for the evidence to submit to the FBI labs in Washington, DC."

SA Broce called the New Jersey detective on December 21, 1984, to go over the items the Glen Ridge police force collected from the house. Broce selected eight items that had a high probability of producing good prints.

"Let's send the miscellaneous photos and negatives, and the small deck of cards," SA Broce instructed. "Go ahead and include some of Joan's project folders. The Newark office can help you mark and pack the items to send to Quantico. They are to be submitted to Patricia May under latent print case number C-13738."

"Mr. Broce," the officer helpfully offered. "After examining the items, I think we should include the ski wax; it looks like there is a latent print."

Burke enlisted SA Steve Broce for the bankruptcy case. Federal charges were to prove the Chris Craft was not stolen, but they covertly provided added leverage the state didn't have—but badly needed—for Joan's case. Bankruptcy had nothing to do with what had happened to the bright design student, but that did not stop Broce from crossing lines. He became entangled, inappropriately, in Joan's case. The bureau spelled out the underlying motive in their confidential report that concealed Burke's bag of tricks. He enlisted the Feds to pressure the suspect, but the report, under the ruse of a bankruptcy case, was not disseminated outside the devious Boston FBI office.

"Mr. Pascucci, do you have the comparison card of prints? Pat May doesn't have it yet." The New Jersey detective tried to tie up the loose ends and get the package mailed. "I need Candy Weyant's address. Does she have an FBI number?"

SA Broce surfaced with his hand in Joan's case—but this fact simply was not visible where the saga played out. John Mulholland's tactics seemed to be contagious. Instead, Broce's involvement popped up in New Jersey where sincere law enforcement willingly did all they could. Another name resurfaced to facilitate with the transfer. SA Frank Barletto, aka George Webster's cousin Frank during the extortion drama, joined the cause to tag items and get them shipped out. Burke's objective was to match Joan's prints to the Mayan book from Lenny's shelf and force the dots in his case. Burke was not supposed to be a part of the bankruptcy case, and bankruptcy had nothing to do with Joan's disappearance.

"These items are being submitted by the Glen Ridge Police Department," the dedicated lieutenant submitted on January 8, 1985, "in conjunction with an open investigation involving the Massachusetts District Attorney's Office, Suffolk County District, and the Boston FBI Office, SA Steve Broce."

Tim Burke was insanely driven to lay the blame for Joan Webster's disappearance on Paradiso's back. However, every attempt to match prints came up negative. Joan's delicate fingers never clutched Candy Weyant's silk pouch, the one Feds confiscated from her safety deposit box. The graduate student's hands never moved along the rails of the suspect's submerged boat. Examiners stamped "no match" on every one of Burke's inquiries, so he dismissively rationalized that Paradiso painstakingly wiped everything down.

While authorities labored to manufacture a connection, Paradiso prepped for his next legal challenge. An insurance fraud suit was filed on November 28, 1984, regarding the paid claim on the *Malafemmena*—Burke's designed crime scene. The scheming continued in room 603 at the courthouse while another wave of legal wrangles preoccupied the inmate's attention.

The fixated public servant concocted a groundbreaking motion. He petitioned Judge James McGuire on December 16, 1984, to allow the surgical removal of a presumed splinter in Paradiso's finger. The state's star witness claimed that Paradiso injured his hand murdering Joan Webster. The emergency room at Lynn Hospital x-rayed the left digit on November 30, 1981, and sure enough, there were three, small metal splinters. Doctors checked the injury again on December 22, 1981, to reveal one fragment still embedded in his finger. Burke wanted to go fishing to dig the remaining particle out. Cops had recovered the ammunition shell that Paradiso maintained was the source of the fragments, and Elaine Covino corroborated other statements; she attested that her friend hurt his hand in the Weyants' basement. Regardless, the core group upheld Bond as the pillar of truth, and Burke set the wheels in motion for a cutting-edge expedition.

Judge McGuire heard the regurgitated allegations that had saturated the headlines during the Iannuzzi pretrial back in March. Judge Donahue disallowed the testimony during the Iannuzzi murder trial, just months before this new pursuit, but Burke served up the unsubstantiated claims to justify his cause to slice into flesh. The petitioning litigator promoted the object of his obsession as a predator with a history of sexual aggression. The Florence White incident reappeared, and the public defender spuriously asserted that Paradiso pleaded guilty. The grand jurors did not hand down a true bill for the 1970 assault and rape allegations, and the only offense left was unlawfully carrying a weapon. The weapons charge is what Paradiso conceded.

The ADA resurrected Sgt. Tammaro's North End friend next, the woman who tipped the Websters anonymously. She never reported the supposed assault in 1972, and never treated the purported injuries. Burke wove her contentions into presumed fact that bolstered the tale of Joan's demise. Patty Bono suggested Paradiso used a gun and threatened he would dump her in the ocean where she would never be found. Nothing ever affirmed Bono was telling the truth, and no one knew the offender buried Joan beneath the cold earth—the state's errant theory was distilling unchecked.

DA Newman Flanagan's office filed charges for Janet McCarthy's assault allegations, and the accused awaited trial. This judge had not heard the discrepancies from the police report filed on July 10, 1980, or Trooper Palombo's remarkable skill to help restore a vivid recollection that Janet did not have at the time. An assault with intent conviction for Constance Porter in 1974 was the noose that left the assailed vulnerable to every allegation the prosecutor threw out.

Burke refreshed the pressured testimony of FBI witness Charlene Bullerwell, the witness who balked at the trial. She conjured incredible images of a mob killer that chopped bodies before weighing them down into watery depths. The Feds' confidential source billed the occasional date as a witness who knew where the perpetrator disposed of Joan's body, and Tim Burke told the Feds she had a bracelet that looked just like the one missing in the Webster case.

The dubious Iannuzzi conviction, the juvenile jurist manipulated with his contorted faces, further nailed the image for the court to consider. The media had done its part selling papers that drove the public into a frenzy. The delinquent was pressing forward for Joan and the deemed interest of society, but it only served his own agenda—not justice for Joan.

The obsessed litigator's arguments continued with Robert Bond's allegations as the centerpiece of his vision. Once again, Burke touted the convicted felon was a reliable and credible source. However, the prosecutor twisted the killer's tale to suit, and the paired team of Burk and Palombo reversed the alleged order of events in sworn affidavits to the court.

"Paradiso raped her and beat her about the head with a whiskey bottle," Burke outlined in his brief. "Paradiso then took her body 'way out' and dumped it in the ocean."

"Bond said Paradiso told him he had taken Joan Webster from the airport to his boat at Pier 7," Trooper Palombo swore to the court in point five of his petition and gave a rearranged version of Bond's statement. "He forcibly had sexual intercourse with her, beaten her with a whiskey bottle, and taken her body 'way out' and dumped it in the ocean."

Palombo was sitting in the room when Robert Bond tattled the tale. Regardless, the men hypothesized their suspect raped Joan before he hit her with a bottle, then coldly dumped her into the sea. Palombo and Tammaro went over the story before Bond wrote it down; the blow had come first, according to Bond, but authorities knew the law determined rape was not accomplished on a corpse.

An undated photograph Bond saw at the Charles Street Jail showed liquor bottles on the boat, so Burked submitted that next.

Judge McGuire was still not convinced to let the team set out on their cutting expedition. He needed more, so Palombo supplemented the argument with another sworn statement in January of 1985.

"Among the many items located in the cabin area of the *Malafemmena*," the officer pledged under the pains and penalties of perjury, "there were several shards and bits of broken glass."

What report was Palombo reading? Q38 was the only item Burke represented as glass to the lab, and examiners never identified its location. The FBI lab described Q38 as debris unsuitable for testing; nothing else existed on the *Malafemmena* to support the state's representations. Players securely locked reports away that exculpated the accused, and the march to misrepresent and manufacture evidence continued.

Enforcers confiscated Danforth equipment in a search of the Weyants' house, but secret Federal grand jury testimony revealed Ray Jeff was the manufacturer of navigational devices missing from the predetermined crime scene. Erasing brand names from arguments in front of McGuire falsely implied the items were the same as the ones they were seeking.

Throughout the bitterly cold days of January 1985, Burke jammed his calendar with appearances. Sandwiched between his arguments to cut for clues was the disgraceful dance for "Death Row Tony" Pisa.

After Pisa started singing his unverified tune for Middlesex County in February 1983, suits set the convicted killer's good fortune in motion. The DA's office administered a new polygraph on April 28, 1983, where the con changed his story. He asserted he was not the shooter in the 1969 George Deane murder. The self-styled lawyer predictably laid the blame on his accomplice in crime, Roy White. Administrators shuffled the felon from Bay State Prison to the prerelease program at Park Drive. The rat settled into more comfortable accommodations just before he took the stand for the Commonwealth. Hence, Burke created the illusion that the convicted murderer was already on the path to freedom.

The day after the slick snitch testified in the Iannuzzi pretrial hearing on March 12, 1984, Burke and ADA Thomas Reilly barged uninvited into Judge Elam's Middlesex courtroom for an emergency bail hearing. After an affected rendition of how the killer was now at risk, Pisa walked. Tony had the benefit of Bond's notes when he told his story, according to the state's star witness. Bond asserted the moustached informant, greased through the system, saw the notes Bond had scribbled, and notes Trooper Palombo swore were in his

possession. However, authorities neglected that point in their presentation.

The New Year promised Pisa a new start. On January 3, 1985,
Suffolk County ADA Tim Burke found himself before Judge Elam in
a Middlesex County court again. Attorney Laurence Hardoon
escorted his date to the bar to argue the county's reversal to Pisa's latest request for a new trial. The duet had a hurdle though; a colleague
in the Middlesex office had filed a strong objection to Pisa's motion.

"On the evening of January 8, 1970, Francis Dion entered the
Clam Shell Bar," the DA's office recapped from the trial transcripts.
"Dion complained another man was going out with his wife. Pisa
offered to shoot the man for Dion, and further commented he had
shot a Watertown Arsenal guard. Pisa stated that shooting the guard
had not bothered him, and that the more he shot the more he
enjoyed the experience."

"The Commonwealth is hereby withdrawing its opposition,"
Hardoon irrationally contradicted his colleague. "It would now be in
the interests of justice for the Court to allow said motion."

The Middlesex County ADA indicated the state now believed
Pisa's new effort to disengage from George Deane's murder. The
rewritten history of the crime disconnected "Death Row Tony" from
pulling the trigger repeatedly that snuffed out an innocent life.

"The defendant has provided very significant assistance," the
enlisted Middlesex ADA explained, "in the conviction of one
Leonard Paradiso involving the death of a woman named Marie Iannuzzi. Further, he has provided assistance against the same Leonard
Paradiso suspected in the Joan Webster disappearance."

In other words, the killer, who made assurances to George Webster and would not testify unless he was out of prison, aided and abetted the Commonwealth in their witch-hunt of Joan's presumed
predator.

Pisa changed his plea, and his attorney Paul O'Rourke chimed
in to withdraw the motion for a new trial. Miraculously, the defendant
now only faced manslaughter instead of the adjudicated conviction
for first-degree murder. A jury might have viewed Pisa's new version
less favorably than the petitioners contriving to lessen the charge.
Judge Elam settled the matter right then and there, and the claimant
was sentenced to time served.

The decision stunned Deane's frustrated family; they could not
dissuade the court's determination to release the perpetrator back
into society. Too bad, the state compounded their sorrow and the loss
they lived with every day, but time served was the decision, apparently,
in the interest of Joan's justice.

Meanwhile, back in front of Judge McGuire's bench, Flanagan's pupil resumed his plea to slice and dice Paradiso's finger. Two splinters had worked their way out already, and the fragments were previously identified as metal. Medical experts took the stand and contemplated that the splinters might have been glass with a high lead content to show up on the film. In the event metal was found, Burke had covered that base with a fake .357 magnum mysteriously recovered from waters under Paradiso's mooring—a well-timed tip from a confidential source. Burke led the select divers to find what the legitimately assigned search teams missed. The solicitor offered no real evidence to justify his obsession to dig out the "smoking splinter" and herald a link to Joan's murder.

"The use of force to assure compliance may be reasonable if Paradiso refuses to comply with the warrant," Burke seconded Trooper Palombo's petition.

The public defender had the Websters' confidence to press on for their daughter. In the minds of the boat theory crowd, there was an urgent need to go after the particle. Paradiso's latest litigator, John Palmer, argued against the requested assault on Paradiso's person, but he was up against an unprecedented force.

"It might be the only physical evidence connecting Paradiso to the killing of Joan Webster," Burke passionately prayed for the court's favor.

The subtle disclosure was rather telling in light of everything spread in the papers. The boys said they had Joan's textbook and a silk purse where she kept her pearls. Burke told the Feds Lenny's occasional date, Charlene Bullerwell, wore a bracelet, a bangle identical to Joan's one-of-a kind, in a photo the team absconded. Authorities knowingly misrepresented evidence, claiming there were several shards of broken glass on the recovered boat. Burke only submitted debris maintaining there was a hair attached to it. The lab reports were all disappointing from the prosecutor's obsessed point of view, but McGuire was not privy to the findings.

"The need is especially great because Paradiso efficiently disposed of the victim's body." The petitioner's assertion was uncontested because Joan was nowhere to be found, dead or alive. "By taking her 'way out' and 'dumping' her in the ocean Paradiso made sure that, as he threatened Patty Bono, 'No one would ever find her.'"

While the tabloids chronicled Burke's bloodthirsty demands, a federal jurist discreetly filed a ruling across town. On January 21, 1985, Judge Robert Keeton, a district court judge in Massachusetts, changed the venue for Paradiso's bankruptcy case to the district court in Rhode Island. Media attention persuaded the magistrate to

remove the proceeding from the spectacle in the state courts, presumably in the interest of justice. The bankruptcy suit, like the insurance fraud case, focused on Burke's alleged crime scene, the
Malafemmena. The shift dissected critical elements of Joan's mystery
from the conceived plot and the public's awareness. The underhand
of the Webster investigation could pull strings covertly without a complete disclosure of the facts. Meanwhile, the state court pondered cutting flesh in front of the ravenous press spurred by Burke's argument;
Paradiso dumped human bait in the harbor.

On February 13, 1985, Judge McGuire swallowed the prosecution's whale of a tale and ordered an x-ray of the digit. He completely
disregarded the fact Paradiso had not been charged with any crime in
Joan's case. In his ruling, the state's disinformation had festered into
presumed fact.

"There was testimony from a named witness that Joan Webster
was raped and murdered. I find that the informant is reliable and
credible," Judge McGuire inexplicably concurred. "Should Paradiso
refuse to cooperate, the Commonwealth would be warranted in using
reasonable means in forcing compliance."

Paradiso was busy dealing with the insurance fraud suit in
Rhode Island when the order came down. Burke's Valentine dinner
got cold waiting for the fervent litigator to delegate the orders to Cor-
poral Marty Headd of the Massachusetts State Police. The direction
followed an exhausting day of activity. Headd drafted correctional
officers at Walpole to execute the court order and radiate the
inmate's finger. The official version reported back to the court insinuated Paradiso was not too willing, but the badges were empowered
with a free rein to use force. Paradiso objected to the invasion of his
person to satisfy Burke's mania, but he was far too outnumbered to
defy it. Burke summarily dismissed Paradiso's complaint of mistreat-
ment, and no one was likely to check. The state's wagons circled to
protect their own.

The emergency room took pictures of Paradiso's finger on February 15, 1985, justified by the illogical story of Robert Bond. Burke
smugly pronounced that force was necessary. The hunter never suggested the presumed broken glass lacerated Lenny's hand, and no
mention of bleeding or stitches. X-rays showed no broken bones or
bruises, injuries more consistent with the butt of the suspicious fake
magnum. Burke's medical acumen was laughable; this analysis
required only the minimum of common sense like David Doyle's mercurochrome stained gouges.

Instead, the medical evidence from November 30, 1981, showed
three, deeply embedded metal splinters, consistent with shavings

sparked from a grind wheel as the accused had described. The determination to go fishing with a scalpel rested on what showed up on the film. It would take several weeks before evidence of maltreatment surfaced. Unfortunately, for the accused, it surfaced in another judge's chamber across the line in Rhode Island.

While the drama continued trying to create a connection to Joan, a ruling went largely unnoticed. A court clerk read the verdict; due process acquitted Leonard Paradiso of insurance fraud for the loss of his boat. Leonard Paradiso reported the *Malafemmena* missing on July 26, 1981—four months before Joan's fateful flight.

Presumably, Liberty Mutual did their due diligence to investigate the claim before they paid for the craft's loss on September 29, 1981. Divers recovered the vessel in waters right beneath the Erie Barge mooring where Paradiso previously tied his boat at Pier 7. The hull was still painted blue, and registration numbers were intact. The unaltered appearance made it rather hard to swallow the idea that the insurance investigators missed it if it was still floating in November as alleged. Burke produced nothing to suggest his suspect anchored the boat anywhere else before the hull surfaced by the mooring and produced his speculated crime scene.

Not a blessed thing showed on the film to further the calculated condemnation. Burke never got the opportunity to scar his prey physically, but the setback did not slow his accusations. The dejected counsel sought another court order on March 20, 1985, from Judge McGuire, to allow a doctor to examine Paradiso's finger. The zealous ADA alleged the closely watched inmate had devised to extract a presumed microscopic sliver himself before Burke could cut. Medical Examiner Donald Dixon examined Paradiso's left index finger in Suffolk Superior Court later that day.

"There appears to be a puncture wound on Mr. Paradiso's finger," the willing doctor obliged.

No one explained what instrument the captive could possibly access to perform his own microscopic surgical procedure, but players swirled destructive inferences in the press. Reporters' familiar sources added layer upon layer to the story to suit and prolong the witch-hunt without any real evidence.

On March 28, 1985, jail administrators strangely summoned Paradiso to the hospital for a dental appointment that was not scheduled until April. An inmate approached Lenny with familiarity. Anthony "Big Sid" Manni had started serving a sentence of eighteen to twenty years for cocaine, plus forty years in the Federal system. The whispered warning Manni delivered alleged that Sgt. Carmen Tammaro was making promises again if the inmate could come back with a confession from Paradiso.

"Gee Lenny, what are they doing to you?" Manni wondered. "Sgt. Tammaro and the MSP are going to frame you anyway they can, and dishonor you in the community."

Every edition off the presses reinforced "Big Sid's" charge that authorities were dishonoring the accused in the community. Paradiso was not about to confide in a caged prisoner, even though the inmate disclosed the dangled enticement Tammaro offered—dismissing Manni's charges. However, facilitators intended to ease the drug dealer's confinement already; a transfer was in the works to move him to MCI Concord, the same medium security facility where the boys shifted Robert Bond. There was no declaration of guilt; Paradiso maintained his innocence for both the convicted and contrived crimes.

Why did these public servants go to such extremes? The Iannuzzi case had gone cold long before Burke stirred it back up. The litigator used every dirty trick in the book to gain a conviction in that case when the evidence obviously pointed elsewhere. Such conspiring produces a desired result that is not always consistent with justice. The uncovered misprision was a dead giveaway that they were never looking for the truth. The prosecutor set a frightening precedent trying to cut into a man's flesh, and with the court's blessing they used force. The methods sounded like the Gestapo. Deviants loitered behind every corner waiting to trick a confession, and Sgt. Tammaro covertly lurked there with them. Why did these public servants go to such extremes? One name was broadcast in the headlines daily—Joan Webster.

CHAPTER 19

Across the Line

A picture hanging in the locked closet in the basement fueled the operations my daughters plotted. On first glance, it was an image of an enraged lunatic, but it was not what it seemed. The photograph confused me when I found it; clearly, it was part of the detailed plan to find things to use against me.

The time and place of the photo was immediately identifiable, but my children used it to portray something far different to shocked friends they showed it to. The picture was taken during festivities for my youngest daughter. Party lights were strung on the deck of our house for my child's thirteenth birthday celebration. Enthusiastic adolescents ruined the string after only one use, because they broke bulbs in the strand. Loretta Kroin helped chaperone the party jointly held for her daughter, Makaela, and the photographer captured her ringed finger in the shot. As a disc jockey blasted tunes on our back deck, I started to sing in unbridled celebration. The snapshot was not very flattering, but taken at a moment of innocent revelry. Now, however, my daughters distorted the image to convince others I was some kind of deranged monster.

"Look, see, this is how she is! She's crazy! Look at this photo."

Family counselors did not have the whole picture and swallowed the impression designed for them. I stood alone behind the line that divided me from my children, and misinformed people advised me not to step across it. I was absolutely frozen in my tracks trying to parent; I was terrified my children would cause harm to themselves.

Flashing bulbs and frenzied correspondents were notably absent from the mundane court proceedings that began in April 1985. The case on the docket was a bankruptcy fraud case, which could not boost tabloid sales nearly as much as images of chopped up bodies murdered at sea. Nonetheless, pieces of the Joan Webster mystery were buried in records of the case. Truth remained as hidden as the body of the young graduate student. The scene shifted again to Rhode Island where Assistant US Attorney Marie Buckley continued the complex operation. The *Malafemmena* was the centerpiece of the Feds' case. They hoped to prove that the boat had not been stolen. By this time, Steve Rappaport and John Palmer had both begged off Paradiso's defense, and Owen Walker, Esq. assumed the seat despite the defendant's objection.

Buckley set the stage during the Federal grand jury that ran in tandem with the Iannuzzi pretrial. In this case, pressured FBI witness Charlene Bullerwell held back the bombshells. The shockers came days later when Tim Burke's session convened in front of the press. During the Feds' grand jury, Charlene focused on where Paradiso might sink his boat. Mary Morris was another paramour who uncomfortably took the stand to speculate about where her occasional date hinted the craft might go down. Peter Petruzziello sold the Chris Craft on May 3, 1980, and records showed Candace Weyant was the buyer. Trooper Palombo made an appearance in the grand jury too, using his brand of persuasion. His theory that Paradiso sank his own boat convinced the grand jury who trusted his badge. After the recovered Chris Craft dried out, Palombo enlisted a marine expert who determined the cruiser had a broken rudder. The bothersome fact remained in the files, as participants fed the public and press the notion that Paradiso steered his boat way out into the harbor to dispose of Joan's body.

Spring did not bring renewal for Paradiso. The court assembled a jury in Judge Bruce Selya's courtroom on April 4, 1985. The barristers hammered out procedures with the judge, and the defense submitted exhibit D for identification. To Walker's credit, he tried to expose the duplicity that had played in another courtroom across the line in Massachusetts. Paradiso's new advocate handed the judge Bullerwell's sensational tale of chopped up bodies that Burke had wheedled out of the pressured witness. His sensational powder keg exploded after the much tamer Federal grand jury testimony helped AUSA Marie Buckley garner an indictment. However, Bullerwell was not on the list of witnesses the Department of Justice intended to call.

"Your Honor, if you please," the defense counsel informed Judge Selya in chambers. "Mr. Paradiso has something he would like to address the court about. I'll find out what it is."

Paradiso requested some medical attention, but there was no ongoing treatment or the need for treatment forwarded from Massachusetts. The hour was already late in the day, and the attorneys had not given opening statements yet. The judge said he would hear more on the matter at the end of the day.

The jurors in Rhode Island finally settled into their seats at a quarter till three. The time had come to deal with Burke's declared crime scene. AUSA Buckley did her part and laced her opening statement with a strategy that left an impression Burke and the boys were after.

"Basically, this case is about lying," Buckley opined.

The defendant signed and dated the bankruptcy form on August 18, 1981. Paradiso filled in his answers and declared he had no assets beyond a ten-dollar bank account. The allegation was that he lied on that claim. However, the prosecutor argued assets were hidden, a very different crime, an offense the government did not charge in the indictment.

"We expect to show you that Leonard Paradiso was the true owner of a boat that was in somebody else's name," Buckley promised.

Buckley conceded that the items in question legally belonged to somebody else, yet she claimed Paradiso lied. The presumption he lied was nothing more than her personal opinion. Walker waited for her last opening breath before a colloquy at the bench. Unfortunately, the presiding robe denied the motion for an acquittal despite the prosecution's admission that Candy Weyant was the owner of record. Candy had not filed the bankruptcy form that the court considered. Walker opted out of any opening remarks, and the prosecution moved to call their first witness.

Deputy Clerk Arthur Capozzo verified the bankruptcy petition submitted to his office on August 26, 1981. Joan Webster left the warm sandy beaches of Nantucket for the ivied brick walls of Harvard when the petitioner filed his bankruptcy claim. Paradiso had not listed the boat that he reported missing on July 26, 1981, nor the insurance compensation for the loss. Liberty Mutual Insurance had not paid the claim out when the defendant filed. The prosecution insisted the accused man made false statements on his form, but the AUSA failed to charge him with what she seemed to be after. Walker objected and counsels made their way to the bench.

"They haven't charged him with a charge of a concealment of assets. That's a crime in itself," Walker argued the prosecution's lack of sense. "They have picked out certain statements, which in fact are answers which are true under any theory the government presents."

Leonard Paradiso was clean-shaven and pressed in front of the bench when the court discharged his bankruptcy on November 30, 1981. Capozzo confirmed he had to be there for the proceeding. Robert Bond had convinced the seasoned force across the line that Paradiso was swabbing the bloody deck of his boat that day before taking the crime scene way out to sink it. The churning story had him murdering the diminutive student on the vessel two days before the bankruptcy court reviewed his petition. According to Bond, the cunning shell fisherman hid a diabolical crime the same day the court relieved his debt.

The government called Philomena Cipione to the stand. She was an executive with the Haymarket Cooperative Bank, the bank that contained safety deposit box 59 jointly held by Paradiso and Weyant. FBI SA Steve Broce searched the box on July 28, 1983, but the invasion produced nothing of any probative valuable for the Feds' case. A roll of Susan B. Anthony dollars was hardly a "stash of cash" secretly secured in a bank vault, but collaborators portrayed a silk pouch as something Joan kept her pearls in to the media. The sheath was part of a three-piece set, and the complementary items remained boxed in owner Candy Weyant's drawer in Revere.

"The account 2-7662 reads Candace Weyant," the bank executive identified Candy's savings account, "only Candace Weyant."

"But it's in trust for Paradiso?" Buckley asked.

"Yes," Cipione affirmed, "if anything happened to Candace Weyant, the balance in the account would go to the beneficiaries."

Weyant's savings account at the bank was shrewdly shaded as suspect, because her boyfriend and his daughter were named in trust. Lenny could not waltz into the bank and withdraw any money. Paradiso was not on the account and had no access to it, but the prosecutor implied devious intent in the arrangement that was more or less a short form of making a will.

The court wound down for the day in front of the jury, and both counsels retreated to the judge's chambers to haggle over the fine points determining what evidence could come into the record. Paradiso appealed to address the court, but the defense counsel had to relay his complaint.

"Your Honor, it has to do with Mr. Paradiso's broken finger and the pain that he is in," Walker reported. "He did not sleep last night because of that pain."

Selya ordered treatment for Paradiso's broken finger. He delegated Marshals Wyatt and Graham with the duty of getting the throbbing digit checked out and report back to the court.

The jury went home, but Judge Selya kept long hours, and there was more work to do with the two lawyers at the courthouse. The court reporter typed while the trio reviewed documents to determine just what could go into the record, and Mr. Burke had apparently been very helpful. If Buckley could not submit an affidavit considered hearsay, she had Iannuzzi trial transcripts copied to sidestep standard procedure. What she wanted was Candy Weyant portrayed as Paradiso's agent concealing assets. Buckley thought she could wrap up witness testimony the next day, and the public servants concluded for the evening.

First thing Friday morning the lawyers were back in chambers.

"The physician has recommended that Paradiso's finger be x-rayed," Selya advised both attorneys. "Mr. Paradiso, interestingly enough, told the physician at ACI that he had seen a doctor at the Massachusetts State Prison who recommended that the finger be rebroken and splinted."

The little morsel of information was interesting, indeed. Further examination of the throbbing digit exposed the heavy hand enforcers had used across the state line. The jail scheduled medical attention for the aching finger at noontime, throwing the dismayed prosecutor's timetable off.

Rodney Swanson was the claims manager for Liberty Mutual Insurance that held the policy for the 1972 Chris Craft. The record showed the vessel was last seen at eight p.m. tethered to the barge at Pier 7 on the twenty-fifth, and the discovery it was gone was made the next afternoon. The policyholder, Candace Weyant, reported Burke's alleged crime scene, the vessel suggested in the November 28, 1981, disappearance of Joan Webster, missing on July 26, 1981. Divers resurrected the missing craft right where Paradiso moored it; no real surprise. The couple filed reports with the Boston Police Department and the Coast Guard, alerting officials to be on the lookout for the twenty-six-foot, blue-hulled cabin cruiser. Swanson's testimony revealed subtle clues detrimental to ADA Tim Burke's supposition next door in Massachusetts, but trapping the Webster suspect was a divisive operation. Participants kept pieces of the puzzle miles apart.

"Insured said they belonged to Beachmont Yacht Club," the claims adjuster read from the written account. "The boat was stored there during the winter."

The tidbit was consistent with Victor Anchukaitis's parole notes that recorded Paradiso's practice to take his craft out of the water when winter weather swept through New England. If the boat in question was afloat at the end of November, when Joan disembarked Eastern flight 960, it would have been sheltered miles from Pier 7 out of the harsh elements. Paradiso had stored this very craft on November third the previous year. One document after another reinforced that Paradiso had not lied on his bankruptcy form as the government charged; items legally belonged to his girlfriend of many years. The couple made no effort to conceal Paradiso's interest and use of the boat, but Candy purchased, insured, and registered the craft.

"And in whose name is that registration?" Buckley asked the claims agent regarding the boat.

"Candace Weyant," Swanson attested.

Buckley handed her witness another document to examine. The exhibit was a bill of sale for marine navigational equipment covered with the boat. The insurance claims agent reaffirmed that Ray Jefferson manufactured the equipment indemnified with the sunken boat. The Massachusetts State Police confiscated Danforth equipment when they ransacked the Weyant home on April 25, 1983, under the cover of an Iannuzzi warrant. Buckley already knew, from the marine expert Palombo requested, that the different manufacturers were not interchangeable. The discrepancy was invisible to this jury and irrelevant for the case on stage for bankruptcy. However, it was a critical element of the hyped theory influenced for Joan's death. The pieces did not fit if all the facts came out in one place. Liberty Mutual paid the claim to Candy Weyant for the loss of the boat and equipment on September 29, 1981.

Court recessed early so Paradiso could have his broken finger x-rayed, the examining doctor's recommendation from the day before. The film showed a prior fracture that had deteriorated.

"It has been reported to me that same treatment, splinting of the finger, had been recommended six weeks ago at the Massachusetts State Institution and refused by the defendant." Judge Selya's announcement to the attorneys meant very little in Rhode Island, but the calendar matched up with the Bay State's free hand to use force—Burke had an obsession to dig out a splinter.

Cracked bones were not consistent with the denials spewed by the pupil in DA Flanagan's office, and Tim Burke dismissed contentions the accused was roughed up. Necessary treatment for the defendant's medical condition delayed the present prosecution to the consternation of AUSA Marie Buckley.

"Marie," the sage judge observed, "you look like you want to cry."

"Everybody has had a broken finger at some point," the government's advocate whined. "It just isn't that big a deal."

"We know that he is in need of some medical type of treatment," Selya pointed out.

"Do you think this is a selfish question, just in the interest of trying to arrange my schedule?" the persistent prosecutor suggested. "I think I told the court I was supposed to fly out of here. Do you think we could arrange to have a session on Easter Sunday?"

A prolonged Good Friday wasn't in anyone else's interest, nor was conducting an Easter egg hunt in court. Buckley held back tears not realizing Burke, who had prodded her to get moving on the case, was the predator who insisted on the use of force that caused her dilemma. The judge dismissed the jury for the day and instructed them that the case would resume at nine a.m. sharp Monday morning.

The registration on the *Malafemmena*, visible when the crane hoisted the hull from the floor of Pier 7, was 9-LP. The number was the marine equivalent of a vanity plate and registered to Leonard Paradiso. Dante Mayano faced the courtroom, described the procedures to register a boat, and he showed the two-part card required to get a valid license. The government questioned the record keeper from the Massachusetts Division of Marine and Recreational Vehicles, and slyly submitted a document that was not in his files.

"There are two licenses for the boat in question," the defense counsel objected. "They're not part of Mr. Mayano's records. Miss Buckley didn't seem to know exactly where they came from."

"I got them from the district attorney's office in Suffolk County, Massachusetts," the AUSA haughtily justified.

"What do you have remaining in your file then to show who has this little card?" Buckley resumed with the witness.

"We should have this," Mayano indicated their copy. "I think the district attorney has kept some of them, because that was, I was out sick, and they came in and took the records, which they weren't supposed to be let out of that office."

Sleuths had removed records that should never have left the premises, and the prosecutor submitted an extra laminated license that brandished Paradiso's name. Trooper Andrew Palombo strolled into the Registry, and solicited records in July 1982 under the ruse of the Iannuzzi case the state had charged. Collaborators conveniently proposed, through deviant Robert Bond, that the vessel in question in the bankruptcy case was the scene of a murder. Sgt. Tammaro guided the con's recitation on January 14, 1983, together with Trooper Palombo. Now, Marie Buckley handed Mayano a slip to identify the registration for the same boat, but Walker astutely objected.

"He [Mayano] doesn't know where they came from," defense counsel argued.

"It corresponds in every way with the name and license number, and everything else on there." Buckley asserted the witness could affirm the slip was the part torn off the form for the applicant. "It's then laminated, and an official seal put on it."

"I'm going to overrule the objection," the judge absurdly decided.

The witness identified exhibit 7-B as valid license number 683702 issued to Candace Weyant on May 6, 1980. A valid license required a director's seal, the director's signature, and the financial number, and all items were appropriately present on the document. The clerk in the registrar's office affixed the seal and the number by machine, but the office did not laminate the license. Then the government handed Mayano a second license with a significant difference.

"Is that card issued by your office?" Marie asked, not knowing the answer.

"Yes, it is," the witness confirmed. "It has the director's signature. It does not have a financial document number. It is not valid."

"What do you mean by financial document number?" the flustered prosecutor scrambled.

"That same one, as the other card, is written," the record keeper explained. "It's the same financial number, but it's written in by pen and on exhibit 7-B it was done by a machine."

"Is the seal on that a seal stamped by your office?" Marie confirmed this license was created in the marine office.

"Yes, it is," he affirmed, but he did not have the records to support it. The documents had suspiciously walked out the door.

The standard procedure required a financial number imprinted on the layered card by machine, and a director's seal to make it official. The seal was affixed, as well as the director's signature, but the number on the invalid license was handwritten to match the real one. The office did not provide the laminating service for the single slip handed back to the registrant after paying the ten bucks, but both facsimiles had been sealed in plastic. One was valid and one was not. The government moved to enter the second license into evidence, but the defense strongly objected to the suspicious production of a fake ID admittedly from ADA Tim Burke's office.

Further tricks swayed the judge on the admissibility of the phony license, and it was clear things were not going to go well for Paradiso.

"Count six has now been identified as not being a valid official document," Walker protested. "That makes it objectionable."

"He has identified it as a document issued by his office," Buckley pointed out. "It has the official seal, and so forth."

"Is it your plan to have testimony from the handwriting expert?" Selya asked. "That might make a difference to me."

"They were supposed to make any discovery available." The defense reminded the court of the rules of due process. "I haven't been given anything that indicates the handwriting expert has ever even looked at this item."

"I got these the night before we started trial," the Department of Justice's mouthpiece excused. "The handwriting expert came into town after Friday. I had him examine this, and there is no written report on this, but he will say that is the signature of the same person."

All the secretive last-minute maneuvers were news to Mr. Walker. Perhaps, if he had known "Buster's" admission to Lenny, "When they get through with it, the Feds will make it different," he might have had a stronger argument to persuade the court. The Boston FBI office handling this case was up to its eyeballs in dirty business, but of course, at this point they still avoided detection.

Victor Anchukaitis raised his hand next, then walked the tightrope trying to tell the truth. Both sides had stipulated to terms not to disclose the relationship the retired parole officer had with the defendant, but that the witness spoke with him on a regular basis as part of his job up until February of 1981. He knew nothing about Paradiso's financial affairs after that time. Victor added little to the discussion. He affirmed the defendant's employment, but the dates were irrelevant to the present proceeding. In addition, the retired parole officer heard the shellfish peddler's pipe dreams for the future. Victor saw the boat and assumed from discussion it belonged to his charge, but nothing verified the defendant's ownership contrary to the established record.

The United States seated Carl Raichle, a former New York City cop now employed by the Postal Inspection Crime Lab. The government submitted handwriting comparisons for analysis back in March of 1984, and the witness compared signatures to known samples using the tools he had in his lab. Paradiso inked his signature on the bankruptcy petition and records for the safety deposit box at the Haymarket Cooperative Bank. Paradiso signed his name on those documents, there was no dispute, and the defense obtained the findings through discovery.

When Raichle arrived in Providence to testify, the government slipped a mickey and had the examiner draw a spontaneous conclusion on the invalid license. The third piece of a two-part card got a cursory review after his arrival in Providence. The rush job lacked the benefit of the lab, or the magnified scrutiny that Paradiso's other signatures received. The former cop could not compare the pressure applied to sign the license to other known signatures, because someone laminated the cards. No two signatures are identical, even from the same person, but the examiner did not have the time and tools to check. Raichle concluded, in his opinion, the signature was that of Leonard Paradiso.

An objection fell on the deaf ears of the court, and the judge allowed Dante Mayano to retake the stand. Insanely, the ruling jurist permitted the record keeper to enter the suspicious card into evidence for the jury to consider. The idea Paradiso had the influence to have the office affix a seal on a blank document that he could fill in as he pleased defied common sense. It bore the seal, but was not machine stamped with the financial number it needed, and Suffolk County and the Massachusetts State Police had conveniently raided the documents needed to support it. The dirty little secret, uncovered in records that were not available during this case, was that Trooper Palombo waltzed into that office to check the records in July of 1982. Unfortunately, that revelation appeared later in appeal records for the Iannuzzi case.

Marie Buckley had more up her sleeve while Mayano sat on the stand. She asked the keeper for all his records back in March, but now pulled out a new document listing the history of the registration 9-LP.

"I've never seen any of this stuff before," Walker complained. "We were entitled to have it a long time ago."

"I have just seen this for the first time this morning, your Honor," the prosecutor nonsensically claimed.

Yes, it was Paradiso's registration going back to 1967 and renewed over the years. The plate was transferable to other marine vehicles, or to other persons. It was not surprising the registration was on the Chris Craft legally owned by Candace Weyant, the defendant's longtime girlfriend. There was nothing illegal or sinister about that.

The judge motioned for the clerk to close his chamber door and nodded for the attorneys to take a seat. The fractured pursuit to condemn Paradiso for the murder of Joan Webster aboard the *Malafemmena* was uncovered in the conference with his Honor discussing the bankruptcy charges. Each player only knew his or her own part, but creators segmented the process with the precision of a CIA operation to block an avenue to the truth. Selya was not aware what his court's decision would imply in the hands of authorities across the line. The lawyers discussed the counts in the indictment with the unwitting presiding black robe.

The Federal case laid four charges on the table against Paradiso. Count A charged the accused with deception for a bank account at the Haymarket Cooperative Bank. Despite the bank's rules and regulations defining Candy Weyant as the sole owner of the savings account, the prosecution suggested it was in name only. Speculation the defendant controlled funds for the couple and made sinister transfers weren't supported with any real facts. A second count asserted a GMC truck was not listed as an asset on the bankruptcy form. Candy Weyant registered and insured the truck in count B. Paradiso used the truck reported missing on April 26, 1981, but the insurance claim was paid to Candy, the titled owner, on January 11, 1982. Employment was vague in the hearing. If Paradiso lied about having a job, the government failed to produce substantive proof he was collecting a paycheck, or earning income on his own for count D. Self-employment does not mean the man made any money, and he claimed to be going under.

ADA Tim Burke waited anxiously by the phone for a verdict on count C, the indictment that Paradiso lied about the boat when he filled out his form. It was not listed as an asset, and the claim was not paid when Paradiso filed for bankruptcy, but Burke floated the illusion that the boat was bobbing in the water in November of 1981. Officials looked for the 1972 cabin cruiser going back to July 26, 1981, when Paradiso alerted authorities, but not a single witness ever caught a glimpse of the vessel before it was raised near its mooring on September 27, 1983. Two unplugged fittings and the john pulled from its base caused the ship to sink to the bottom. However, nothing camouflaged the features for someone to spot the boat if it really still existed as claimed.

"I am very concerned about Mr. Walker's arguments that since the evidence in this case is uncontradicted," the judge concluded, "whoever owned the boat and the truck prior to August of 1981, that by August of 1981 both of those assets were long gone."

The undisputed evidence showed the craft was long gone by August 1981 when Paradiso filed for bankruptcy, months before Joan Webster landed at Logan. In other words, the rumored murder that captivated the masses across the line in Massachusetts, that George and Eleanor fervently believed, missed the boat, literally. "Basically this is a case about lying," the government prosecutor said. The real dilemma was just who was doing the lying.

"All that the owner owned was some type of claim for insurance proceeds, rather than what this indictment charges." The judge was rightly disturbed by what was going on in his courtroom. "I'm very concerned about that."

Buckley continued her argument that Paradiso controlled the couple's assets. The assets were his, she declared, even though Candy was the owner of record in a title state. Therefore, Paradiso had not lied on the bankruptcy filing, the criminal conduct the government charged. Common sense that Lenny would be left with nothing if discord split the couple just was not enough to look at legal ownership.

"There's no count here for concealment of assets," Selya pointed out again. "If a jury believes as evidence and concludes Candace was a straw for the defendant, an indictment could have been laid."

Despite the judge's conflict, he rendered his decision to hand all four charges to the jury for their consideration. All hope was now gone for Marie Buckley's continued education at the Department of Justice conference in Denver. She begrudgingly resigned that she had to return the next morning for her closing arguments to the jury.

"Your Honor," Walker said without calling one witness, "we do so rest."

Marie poised herself in front of the jury and adjusted her glasses. "This case was all about lying to a court of law."

The slight of tongue was so seamless it held the jurors entranced. Despite all the legal documents to the contrary, the counselor argued everything belonged to Lenny; he was in control. She spindled a story. Candy could withdraw large sums of money from her account and placed cash in the safety deposit box where Lenny could get it. The conspiracy was mere speculation.

"He told everybody it was his boat," the AUSA insisted. "He went and got a license for it in his name."

The litigator had indeed exposed a lie, but it was not Paradiso's. The fake ID came from the Suffolk County DA's office. The marine office stamped the required emblems on the registration card, but the number was handwritten to match the one that was valid.

"It's about lying to the court," she repeated.

Deliberations were brief. Selya excused the jury at 12:20 p.m., and the selected citizens took time for a bite of lunch. They were back in their seats with a verdict at quarter past three on April 9, 1985, the fourth day of the trial. Jurors found Paradiso guilty for counts A, C, and D, and the judge tacked more years to Lenny's life behind bars. The defense appealed for a retrial as soon as the jury left the room, but Judge Selya did not waiver from the decision. Despite the deficient government charges, which failed to encapsulate what the prosecution debated, observers decided Paradiso was guilty of crimes never charged, and he had to pay for it. The AUSA effectively established the defendant had a relationship with his girlfriend, Candy Weyant, not really much of a surprise. Bank regulations were tossed out the window to define who owned an account, and it was somehow determined the man was gainfully employed. Seated peers excused one vehicle, but not the other, though Candy purchased and registered both of them. Bragging the boat was his, together with the counterfeit identification the Massachusetts Suffolk County DA's office produced, apparently convinced the jury that Paradiso should have listed the waterlogged craft or the insurance claim as an asset when he filed. The government had no evidence the boat existed when he filed for bankruptcy. However, those seated in judgment in Rhode Island were oblivious of the fish tales making headlines in another state. They did not have the whole picture, and swallowed the image designed for them.

Burke's heart pounded when the phone rang in room 603 at the Suffolk County Courthouse, and his tense muscles eased into a childish smirk. The facts showed the alleged murder scene did not exist when the Harvard graduate student deplaned in Boston, but the inconvenient truth did not faze ADA Tim Burke's obsession to prove it. The verdict was not exactly a victory that supported Burke's theory, but it was something the boys could work with. This case was about lying. The Websters had confidence in Flanagan's boy, and players fueled the illusion further that the alleged murder scene was available on November 28, 1981.

The numerous disjointed and disconnected proceedings established the boat wasn't stolen, but sunk at Pier 7 by the beleaguered shellfish merchant. The state lacked any evidence the boat floated any time after July 26, 1981, but had facts to the contrary. Existence of the *Malafemmena* in November 1981 did not matter for the case the government framed, and the Federal jury determined that it was not important for their deliberations. An agenda in Massachusetts motivated the march to pile on and find things to use against Paradiso. Illusion, distortion, and deceit incriminated him for an impossible crime on board a boat that did not exist at the time.

At the time, no one knew where Joan was. Nevertheless, the revelations in Judge Selya's courtroom debunked Tim Burke's contentions; the boat was long gone before Joan disappeared. The obsessed prosecutor instigated the federal case. Soliciting SA Steve Broce from the devious Boston FBI office provided the team with additional resources for the Iannuzzi and Webster cases. He prodded AUSA Marie Buckley and supplemented her case with suspicious evidence. Burke distorted the findings to suit the hyped story of Joan's demise. He knew the details of this case.

The former ADA buried the truth deeper when he published *The Paradiso Files*. "On November 1, 1985, Paradiso was convicted in federal district court for submitting a fraudulent bankruptcy claim involving the theft of the *Malafemmena*. Judge Richard Sterns imposed a ten-year sentence."

Simple fact checking exposed Burke's tactic to cover the tracks. The case concluded on April 9, 1985, in Judge Bruce Selya's courtroom in Rhode Island. Only one name in the federal court system, anywhere, past or present, compares to the jurist's name Burke infused. Judge Richard Stearns is a federal district court judge in Massachusetts, appointed by President Bill Clinton in 1993. The judge, recently removed from the present Whitey Bulger case, ascended to the bench in Massachusetts eight years after Paradiso's bankruptcy case concluded in Rhode Island. The prosecutor turned author powered a chainsaw, revisionist history, without even a spell check of Stearns' name. Severed limbs of disinformation decay on the path denying Joan's justice. As Marie Buckley said, this case was about lying. It sure was. Burke's false representations covered up the brutal murder of an innocent victim, a member of my family.

CHAPTER 20

Giveaway

My hands trembled as I dialed the phone. I struggled to gain my composure, took a deep breath, and tried to get the words out.

"Steve, the doctor said I am going to lose this pregnancy," I sobbed just a couple of days before Joan vanished. "Please come home. I need you."

"I still have some things I have to get done; I'm sorry," my husband told me. "I'll be back as soon as I can."

"Can you come home yet?" I begged a couple of hours later.

"There's an office basketball game tonight," Steve prioritized. "They need me so they have enough players. I can't let the boys down."

Steve shied from responsibility and his inability to cope with grief. My immature partner opted for "fundador" rather than deal with the sadness, and I went next door to cry with the neighbors.

I asked the doctor whether I could wait until the next week, after the Thanksgiving weekend, for his procedure to expel the blighted ovum. However, I did not make it that long. Nature took its course, and the doctor admitted me into the hospital on Saturday, November 28, 1981. I was heartbroken.

Loss plagued the Webster family. Throughout the emotional roller coaster of Joan's case, I suffered five miscarriages. As my heart sank deeper with every loss—with every life taken away—I felt God had forsaken both my family and me. At last, on a beautiful Sunday morning in May 1986, God granted the joy of renewed life; my first daughter was born. The miracle of life strengthened my faith again on another radiant Sunday in October 1987. My heart was filled with joy, pure and unconditional love, blessed with two of God's angels. Once again, love and laughter filled Webster households.

I lifted my prayers many times every day to keep my precious daughters safe and secure. The lessons learned in the horror that had befallen the family was both proof—and a warning—that real evil did exist. By all appearances, the Webster family supported my need to keep the next generation safe. However, disinformation regarding Aunt Joan had me watching for peril in the wrong direction.

The weather was unseasonably cool, and cloudy skies drizzled on the gathering at Gund Hall in Cambridge on May 28, 1985. To make it back for the dedication at Harvard, Steve and I flew the red-eye from San Francisco in the middle of a United Airline strike. It did not matter; the important thing was that we were there. We were there as classmates lovingly remembered Joan with a garden in her honor, outside in the courtyard where she had often spent time absorbed in her studies.

"I can't believe you insisted on coming," Steve muttered again.

I was exhausted from the overnight flight and worried about having gone against my fertility doctor's orders—and now this. My spouse was incredibly childlike and annoyed by commitment if it was not going to be fun.

"Steve, your sister meant a lot to me," I insisted. "We need to be here for her and for your parents."

The California visit with Joan's old boyfriend, Walter Johnsen, had us flying all night and reflective of the lives Joan had touched. The damp dreary day was warmed by the packed room of gathered friends, and they tempered Steve's aggravation.

Our departure for home crossed paths with a letter arriving at the Boston office of the FBI. Chief Richard Steiner at Interpol in DC wanted an update dated May 31, 1985. Resources around the world had been on the lookout since March 3, 1983, for the design student who vanished from Logan on November 28, 1981. The time lapse to get an urgent Blue Notice filed, at the request of the family, magnified the negligence; George and Eleanor did not notice she was missing for three days in the first place. By the time the family requested this notice, they already had their sights fixed on a target pegged by an anonymous caller early in 1982. The papers had plastered sensational leaks about an alleged jailhouse confession before the exceedingly belated notice ever crossed international wires. Steiner wanted to know whether developments justified canceling the alert.

At this point, nobody could confirm her passing, so Joan Webster was still technically a missing person. Wild speculation conjured visions of a chopped body sunk to the depths, but no real evidence supported the tale. Investigators pursued leads that abruptly halted in dead end after dead end. The diversions effectively used up the resources that might have actually uncovered the truth.

The media did not let up and continued to sully Paradiso's name as the offender who dumped Joan in the ocean. He filed a suit for defamation, but the smear campaign had ruined his reputation so badly that a judge threw out the case. There was no presumption of innocence in the Bay State's particular brand of justice. The puppet press kept Joan's case alive at every opportunity—it sold papers. Reckless reporting continuously pointed the unbending finger at the suffocating inmate. Eleanor sat down to write a letter when prison administrators transferred the parents' prime suspect to a medium security facility in Norfolk in July of 1985.

"He is a vicious, amoral individual. We demand an official explanation for this travesty, which has taken place less than a year after his conviction for murder." Joan's mother expressed her outrage to the *Boston Herald.* "I fear that Paradiso might escape from a medium security facility or be killed before our case is adjudicated."

The presumption of guilt was their opinion with no real evidence to support it. While the family maintained the expected upper hand tutored by John Mulholland, the underhanded inner circle, responsible for justice, mulled over the "evidence" they had. George and Eleanor's liaisons told Interpol, the Federal agency in the Department of Justice, that their services were no longer needed.

"We have the *Maya* book found on Lenny's shelf, you know, the textbook."

"Don't forget the silk pouch we found in the safety deposit box."

"Charlene Bullerwell knows where Joan's body was dumped, chopped and weighted down in the ocean."

"Oh yeah, don't forget she had Joan's bracelet on in that picture we found in Lenny's albums, the ones with pictures of dark-haired women."

"Robert Bond was like an unrelenting human video camera giving us graphic details of Joan's murder."

"Yeah, that's good; he helped us convict Paradiso for Marie Iannuzzi's murder. Paradiso is a sexual predator; there's Patty Bono and Janet McCarthy."

"We couldn't get that splinter, though, the only physical evidence that would have connected him to Joan's murder, but that mark on his hand looked like a puncture wound. That's enough to convince me."

"The boat was recovered, and a jury didn't buy that it was stolen. Anyway, Candy admitted it wasn't stolen in front of everybody, ha ha ha."

"We just don't have Joan's body. Without a body it's tough to go after Paradiso."

The memo addressed to the Director of the FBI had a changed subject line to reflect Leonard Paradiso as the subject, and Joan Webster his victim. The two names irresponsibly fused in the tabloids were now headed for DCI William Webster's desk, irrevocably bound together with unfounded conclusions. On July 24, 1985, officials committed in writing that there was sufficient evidence gathered to cancel the Interpol Blue Notice and withdraw resources from the search. However, all they had was chicken feed, an intelligence term for worthless information.

"The consensus of investigators in Boston is that sufficient information has been developed indicating that subject PARADISO murdered victim WEBSTER in November 1981." An assistant retyped the memo on the Department of Justice letterhead, Federal Bureau of Investigation, making it all very official.

The public branded the named perpetrator as a convicted murderer thanks to the gyrations of a zealot assigned to argue the Iannuzzi case. The case followed the patterns found in wrongful convictions in Massachusetts that were later exposed. An-out-of-state jury, armed with suspiciously produced evidence, determined that in the summer of 1981, the accused had lied to the court about a boat that was long gone when he filed. Authorities promoted an out-of-print coffee table book as a textbook belonging to Joan. They added a red silk, jewelry pouch separated from the rest of Candy's set for good measure. The confidential source, that Tim Burke identified as Andy, whispered that Charlene Bullerwell knew precisely where the killer dumped Joan's body. Burke played along and suggested that Bullerwell wore Joan's distinctive bracelet in a photograph the cops had confiscated. Obviously, this was the information developed by the core group: ADA Tim Burke out of DA Newman Flanagan's office, lead investigator Trooper Andrew Palombo, his superior Sgt. Carmen Tammaro, and SA Steve Broce out of Boston's shady FBI office. Perhaps the determining factor to draw back resources on the case was the inexplicable fact the Websters concurred.

The team regurgitated the same incredulous story they enticed Robert Bond to spew for two murders while they ignored conflicting facts collected in the files. Splinters spiced the story, though the predator never had a chance to sharpen the knife. Spokesmen fed propaganda to fervent reporters and incited the public's opinion. Lab reports nullified accusations, but participants safely locked them away where no one could see them. State, local, and Federal authorities hot on the trail predetermined the shell fisherman's guilt and shut down Federal assistance to find the lost girl. The Boston office closed the file and shut their eyes to look any further. The hubris behavior of a tight-lipped circle fed a story without facts; they cowered behind a mask of authority.

As the summer months faded into the brilliantly colored autumn in New England, some changes were in the works. First, the Websters hired former Middlesex County Trooper Bruce Latham to investigate the case further. Then, the state signed a contract handing the obsessed ADA Tim Burke a big client. The plum assignment helped ease him out of the DA's office and start a new practice. If the case remained open without charges, it was easier to guard the records. Burke associated himself with the Massachusetts State Police and fancied himself an investigator. The golden boy, who successfully promoted a mind-boggling theory, left Flanagan's office in September of 1985 to hang his shingle in private practice and represent his new client: the Massachusetts State Police.

Elle Gates opened the door to the barren office and carried in her own typewriter. Burke had called the pool for a secretary, and the former Middlesex County DA's assistant was high on the list. Back in December of 1981, when the investigation was still fresh, she worked on Joan's case under ADA Carol Ball. Elle pushed aside a box labeled "Joan Webster" to set her keyboard down on the desk.

The experienced assistant was suspicious about files improperly removed from the DA's office, but her honest ethics overrode her curiosity to examine the contents. Files or copies were supposed to remain in the district attorney's office in charge of the case, and the next person on the DA's list should take over. The state's responsibility was now in a carton across town, a maneuver similar to Dita Beard's shredded files. What information had Burke removed and why? Technically, he was no longer on the case. Even if the DA brought him in as a special prosecutor at some point later in time, he had no legitimate authority to keep the confidential files in his office. Now, anyone trying to fit the puzzle pieces together lacked vital information contained in Burke's box.

The discreet assistant had witnessed the underhand of the system; she knew the influence of Boston's organized crime. Power was seductive to those with the right connections, and Boston's stealth inner workings were out of control. Elle silently witnessed the next stage of Burke's compulsion in the hunt for Joan's killer.

Burke held court in his office with a confident air of self-importance. Elle soon knew the frequent visitors to the office and passed them right through Burke's open door. The very attractive ADA from Suffolk County had no known business with her former colleague, but Marcy Cass paid regular visits to the lawyer's new digs. Anthony

Pascucci was on the state's payroll as an inspector for the Suffolk County DA, but ran errands for Burke on the taxpayers' dime. Payroll was tight, but Burke managed to send his gopher out for a case of beer while he greeted the next guest that passed through the portal. The investigator was there so often, one might have thought he worked for Burke. Trooper Andrew Palombo was a familiar face in the attorney's new quarters. The hulking, undercover cop looked like a Hell's Angel walking in, but he eased the assistant with the broad smile that reflected off his badge. These were clearly the people to trust.

George and Eleanor Webster broke with the norm. The Commonwealth's obligation was to pursue justice for Joan, but no prosecutor assumed Burke's position to carry on with the case in Flanagan's office. When the influential couple walked in, Burke sat up straight, wiped his nose, and turned off his television set. The couple had a way of drawing people in with soft, invisible, pleasant tentacles of their personality and power. There was no question, they were in charge; they had a way of discreetly manipulating others to act—I was all too familiar with their maneuvers. George and Eleanor's influence and connections could have engaged the best minds to unravel the mystery of their daughter's disappearance, but they relied on Tim Burke. When the Websters called an important, high-powered meeting that February day in 1982, Burke was merely an undistinguished fledgling. Nevertheless, he got the assignment for the investigation bizarrely commingled with the Iannuzzi murder. Now, the couple abandoned the DA's office for the litigator who found things to use against the suspect implicated in the anonymous call placed by Tammaro's childhood friend. It was not clear who persuaded whom in this unusual pairing.

The key players had repeated conjecture and unfounded allegations so often by this point in time, it had morphed into presumed fact. Authorities locked reality in cabinets that could not be reached, or in cartons across town in Burke's new digs. The parents of a long-missing child reveled in Burke's tactic to pile on the accused and turned to him after he left Flanagan's office. Each new piece complicating the puzzle went to the lawyer the DA cut loose, and Elle filed them away in the cardboard box with Joan's name. Participants stashed additional information coming in from the family, whether it was useful or not, in Burke's office. It is impossible to say whether the DA's office ever saw it; they are not talking and they guard the state's files.

The burly weightlifter faced a jury again. The cooperative snitch appealed for a new trial arguing three points. Mary Foreman's confidante Fatimah Payne had testified about the threats Bond had made.

Payne saw Mary's black eye and talked to her close friend daily before Bond shot his prey point blank through the temple, but the new judge ruled Fatimah's observations were hearsay. Bond believed questions about Fatimah's religion prejudiced his case, and he complained the judge did not instruct the jury for manslaughter. The latter two excuses fell short for the con, but the terror retold by the victim's friend effectively reversed the murder conviction. The irony was two colleagues in the same office deployed different tactics to achieve their objectives. ADA Connolly attempted to get Fatimah's account into the record, but Burke had maneuvered to keep Christine DeLisi's account out. DeLisi's recollection was a spoiler that cast suspicion on David Doyle, but Burke sanitized it for the jury's consumption.

Jurors seated during the retrial convicted the state's star witness, Robert Bond, for the murder of Mary Foreman again, and the disgruntled snitch filed a motion. Unauthorized pretenders had promised manslaughter that carried a shorter sentence, but the Suffolk County DA's office denied there was any such plea deal. In a revealing attempt to dig himself out of this mess, the screwed rat named the four sweet-talking officials that wooed him, but none of them had any authority in Bond's case. The enforcers were after the story, and the ends justified the means to get it. Bond signed his sworn affidavit on November 15, 1985, naming the representatives he relied on.

"I have been told on numerous occasions by the following representatives of the District Attorney's Office… " Bond swore in his statement. The star witness listed the pretenders he relied on: "1. Tim Burke, 2. Andrew Palombo, 3. Carmen Tammaro, 4. Bill (last name unknown)."

ADA Tim Burke, Trooper Andrew Palombo, and Sgt. Carmen Tammaro had conveniently crossed paths with the squealer, a rat now dissatisfied with his outcome, and they guided him through the tale of two murders. "Bill" was the fourth name exposed for promises not kept, and suggested "Gil" or John Gillen, who was present with Bond on January 10, 1983, in the courthouse. Court Officer Gillen also escorted the killer to the Massachusetts State Police interview on January 14, 1983, conducted by Tammaro. Bond had not met George Webster at the time liaisons dangled promises, but according to Bond, the "Man from New Jersey" had sent people to see him.

"I have specifically relied on the representations of above-mentioned representatives of the District Attorney's Office, to my detriment," the state's star witness grumbled.

"Death Row Tony" Pisa fared much better in his deal. By the spring of 1985, he was running for selectman in Middleton, but lost his bid to fit right in as an elected politician. Amazingly, Pisa came in third in a field of five with 209 votes.

As the calendar moved into 1986, Judge Roger Donahue rejected two motions for a new trial. On February 13, 1986, and again on July 1, 1986, he upheld the exhibition of injustice played in his courtroom without hearings. The same judge who had presumed a man's guilt based on Bond's "credibility" shot down Paradiso's motion for a new trial. The same higher authority had selectively edited the evidence he sent back with the jury. Two days after the last rejection, Paradiso filed a notice for appeal, hoping to get a just review in the system that guaranteed it on a murder conviction. On July third, Suffolk County was on notice that their target was challenging Burke's outcome for Marie Iannuzzi, and the case suspiciously shifted from Essex County.

Burke lurked in the background as his former colleague hammered another nail into Paradiso's coffin during the Janet McCarthy trial that began on August 13, 1986. Her account to the police on July 10, 1980, was a confused and inconsistent allegation of assault. Opportunity surfaced in January 1983 to get her revenge. The media plastered Paradiso all over the news, and the Webster reward money flashed before her eyes. Trooper Palombo took the woman in, and he filed his report with Tim Burke after he interviewed the complainant on February 17, 1984.

"During this interview and several prior interviews conducted by this officer and Tr. John Kelley," Palombo recorded. "Ms. McCarthy was able to provide an extremely vivid and accurate presentation of the facts surrounding this assault and also a very detailed description of the alleged assailant and the vehicle used by him."

The same officer that met with Marie Iannuzzi's boyfriend, David Doyle, worked with this witness too, on several occasions. A new public prosecutor dramatized the night of terror, described in the Iannuzzi pretrial hearing, in front of a jury. Janet alleged Paradiso was the offender with certainty. Suffolk County ADA James Larkin, another one of DA Flanagan's understudies, faced off against Frank Bruno, the next attorney in line to defend a marked man.

The Commonwealth's concept of justice played the citizens seated in judgment for a desired outcome, and the prosecution utilized the John Kiernan secret file tactics. Bruno moved for a mistrial, because the state did not disclose information about the license plate number, taken at the time of the incident, before trial. Flanagan's protégés clearly knew all the tricks and concealed the fact that they knew there was another suspect considered in the case.

Badges battled for the jury's confidence. Revere Lt. James Russo and his partner Det. William Gannon filed the initial report, but their testimony conflicted with Trooper Andrew Palombo. The Revere officers were usurped in January 1983 when the state police took over the investigation. The shift, coincidentally, coincided with the sensational Bond story leaked to press, and the victim's mother spotted Paradiso's picture on television underscored with the Websters' tempting reward.

"We observed Miss McCarthy had been drinking and noted some inconsistencies in her statements." Det. Sgt. Russo reported his findings in the report that shifted into Trooper Palombo's all-too eager hands.

Their firsthand observation noted Janet's hair was messed up, but the dress was not torn, and the only visible injury was a bleeding knee. McCarthy's rendition recited something much different after Palombo took charge. The story she swore to in court lamented repeated blows to her face and a torn frock as the assailant tried to rape her. After her daring escape, she alleged Paradiso was the first car to stop, and he wickedly laughed as he drove off. The woman was disheveled when the two Revere officers noted their observations. However, this version of events claimed two unnamed Samaritans took McCarthy to their place so she could pull herself together.

"She flagged down a vehicle operated by one Joseph Alvoarra, Jr. who drove the woman to the Winthrop Police station," the detective recalled.

The original report never mentioned a detour to freshen her appearance, or Paradiso's sinister laughter as he supposedly left his victim in his dust. Prosecutors never placed Paradiso at the scene except by unverified innuendo from McCarthy after Palombo miraculously helped restore her vivid memory.

"The alleged assailant was operating a big, white car, four-door, fairly new with a dark colored interior." Revere officers recorded the details on the night in question.

"He was driving a yellow two-door car that night," Janet McCarthy Tibolt alleged in court.

"Registry records will show my client owned a bronze, four-door Cadillac in 1980," defense attorney Bruno told the court. "The registry limits the number of colors on a registration certificate, and since bronze isn't one of them, yellow was checked. He sold it four months before the alleged incident."

During the Iannuzzi pretrial, the now married witness had changed her tune; she said the car was yellow, consistent with a photograph Palombo confiscated from Paradiso's albums. The car of changing color, with either two or sometimes four doors, failed to match anything the defendant owned at the time in any form they described. Trooper Palombo smiled at the fourteen-seated peers and supported McCarthy's revised version that circulated during the media blitz in March of 1984.

"I thought I was going to die," McCarthy trembled in front of the jury.

"There is no doubt Paradiso is the man who attacked Janet McCarthy Tibolt," ADA Larkin closed. "Why else would the victim come in here and relive her night of terror?"

"The prosecution's case stinks to high heaven," Bruno rebutted. "They failed to place Paradiso at the scene of the crime."

When the judge handed the jury the case, reporters swarmed outside the courtroom, and the Websters' core group further maligned Paradiso's image. In reality, they had nothing more than their obsession.

State Trooper Andrew Palombo, chief investigator in the Joan Webster case, described his prime suspect. "Paradiso is a serial killer who preys on young brunettes with brown eyes. He may be responsible for seven murders going back to the 1970s."

New names dropped into the public's perception, and the state dusted off their unresolved cases. An irrational witch-hunt mentality labeled the besieged target as a serial killer without a shred of real proof to connect him to any of the crimes. Serial killer—of quahogs perhaps—but no genuine evidence justified the accusations planted in the tabloids. The byline that continued to sell papers promoted Paradiso as the prime suspect that crossed paths with Joan Webster.

The decision came quick, and the jury found Paradiso guilty on two of the three counts. Assault and battery and assault with intent to rape added to the lengthening list that snowballed from the Websters' February 1982 meeting. Suffolk County ADA Larkin mimicked Burke's pleasure; the predecessor hunting Paradiso probably smirked with satisfaction. Larkin quietly slithered to the defense table before Judge James McDaniel imposed his sentence and prodded Bruno and his client to talk about Joan. The weight of the state had not broken the resolve of the clam digger into confessing a crime he could not have committed. The judge tacked on eighteen to twenty years on August 15, 1986, to be served after and beyond what was already dealt.

Joan's continuing drama dominated the news and overshadowed a newly released volume with insight into the lingering mystery.

Dave Moran published a book titled *Trooper* in August of 1986 high-lighting the state trooper's experiences on the job. Moran sometimes partnered with Andrew Palombo, and the two officers co-owned a sailboat. Shared confidence between two state troopers bolstered the reliability of the meeting he recorded. Moran described the Web-sters' high-powered ensemble in February 1982 when some authority assigned Tim Burke and Palombo to Joan's case.

Palombo prodded his friend to dive one more time near the pier. The lead investigator had dug up the tip, the tip a confidential source whispered to the FBI office, where to look for the missing boat. Moran unmasked the Feds' protected informant.

"The guy that runs the dry dock at Pier 7," Moran wrote about the undercover cop's disclosure, "he hit something when he was low-ering the dry dock floor."

Moran participated in the search warrant executed at the Weyant home on April 25, 1983. He was a Massachusetts State Police diver scouring the dangerous murky waters at Pier 7 for the suspected crime scene. The perilous work in churning waters clouded visibility even on sunny days. Moran trusted his fellow officer and friend; Palombo convinced him that Paradiso was a guilty man responsible for Joan Webster's disappearance.

"Andy Palombo even got our trooper crew to dive around Pier 7 again with a device like an underwater vacuum cleaner," the dedi-cated enforcer published in *Trooper*. "Two months of underwater work sifting all the harbor silt around where they found the *Malafemmena* brought new meaning to the word patience. Still, nothing was found that would corroborate the evidence against Lenny the Quahog."

Assigned divers found nothing after the boat came up to further implicate the suspect in Joan's disappearance. However, Burke suspi-ciously produced a fake gun in the water right under the boat's moor-ing on October 20, 1983. The sanctioned searches before, during, and after the "find" yielded nothing but garbage that congested FBI labs.

The state always rationalized why there were no charges against Paradiso in Joan's case—there was no body. The counselor lacked real evidence too, and the tenuous conviction for Iannuzzi was para-mount to shield the creators. If that fell apart on appeal, the whole story connecting the prescribed culprit to Joan was on sinking ground. In November of 1986, Flanagan called Burke in as a special prosecutor to close out the fifth year of the missing graduate stu-dent's saga. Suffolk County ADAs Margaret Steen Melville and Ellen Donahue joined forces with Paradiso's primary legal predator to squelch the convict's resurgence to get a fair hearing. They rehashed the same stories in their briefs as if they were true. Apparently, in their minds, the conviction justified proffering the unverified accusations presented during the Iannuzzi pretrial as fact. The presentation followed Burke's self-described strategy to begin at the end-point—working backwards.

Elle made swift strides across Quincy Market to the courthouse where Burke, the special prosecutor for DA Flanagan, was on stage. She quietly whispered in her boss's ear that sadness had befallen his family.

"Mr. Burke," his assistant whispered, "I'm sorry to tell you Mrs. Burke has had a miscarriage."

Sympathetic colleagues nodded somberly when the litigator excused himself to be by his wife's side during their shared loss. With a tally of five miscarriages, this grief was familiar to the Websters throughout the ordeal with Joan. Burke's departure to be where he belonged was a strange contrast to the indiscernible model of the family he strove to impress. Words of condolence often flowed freely to those they barely knew, but when it was one of their own, the Websters simply wanted to "move on."

Burke consoled his wife and then went back to the task at hand, keeping Paradiso behind bars without his due process. Constant reminders in the paper kept Joan's plight fresh, and the Websters' somber expressions influenced opinions of the shell fisherman's guilt. George and Eleanor remained resolute that the man was Joan's killer and maintained confidence with the DA's specially appointed solicitor. The court deprived the accused of any chance of a fair trial rejecting an appeal for the Iannuzzi murder. Dissected facts hidden in assorted files around town conflicted with the state's theory, and the skilled practitioner's slight of tongue wove his fiction. However, as hard as the boys tried, they still could not come up with enough conjecture to charge Paradiso with Joan's presumed murder.

Elle answered the phone and recognized the voice of the Suffolk County first assistant DA Paul Leary. Using guarded words, Leary urged the assistant to put her boss on the phone immediately. The tension was evident on the flushed face of her boss, and the increased volume was a dead giveaway that the young lawyer had screwed up. The generous litigator apparently rewarded an ally that spent more time hanging out in Burke's new office than on the job investigating for the county. Styrofoam cups, a can of Orange Crush, and everything down to loose nuts and bolts went to the FBI labs. Every attempt to link the sunken vessel to Joan came back negative. Therefore, the bungling attorney allegedly seized an opportunity to benefit a friend before the year 1987 ended. As evidence, the *Malafemmena* was useless, but Joan's case was still open, and this was Tim Burke's alleged crime scene. Leary was livid over what he had heard; Burke apparently gave the boat away and handed the keys to the crime scene to Anthony Pascucci.

On July 6, 1982, Trooper Bill Johnson accompanied Trooper Palombo to cuff Paradiso for the murder of Marie Iannuzzi. On September 25, 1987, Johnson encountered the elusive mob boss James Whitey Bulger at Logan Airport. Whitey tried to slip through the gates with a bag full of money, and the alert cop got into a scuffle to detain him. The Irish mob boss of the Winter Hill Gang slipped away once again. The FBI's protected informant wielded a corrupting influence over the Boston system, but Johnson upheld the oath of his public service. In the months to come, colleagues shunned the honorable trooper, and superiors degraded his stature. Whitey's brother Billy presided over the state Senate, and a movement was afoot to cut the pay of whatever top-level law enforcement got in the way of another agenda.

During 1987, Gareth Penn injected his theory once again. The Mensa published his calculations in *Times 17* and conjectured that Harvard professor Michael Henry O'Hare was the notorious Zodiac killer. According to Penn's estimates, the trail ended with Joan in Massachusetts. His book described his contact with George and Eleanor Webster; a fact confirmed in FBI files. The parents dallied with him for some time and strangely disclosed the family's dissolution of RN Webster's estate—private family matters. Egged on with an aerial photo and a Crimson Travel American Express authorization slip, mysteriously provided by Eleanor, Penn followed his premise.

The couple lost interest in the Zodiac theory and dropped the Mensa's speculations. They had now firmly established themselves in the camp that pegged Paradiso as the guilty party, and Burke became a mouthpiece to berate the author. The Websters ignored Penn now, but someone ordered a copy of his book in the small neighboring town of Bloomfield, New Jersey. Their names were in print, and the author linked their daughter to the notorious unresolved crimes. The public's fascination and curiosity with the bizarre tangent in Joan's baffling disappearance spurred the media to pick up the story again.

Penn's speculations stirred a renewed interest in his theory about what had happened to Joan. Reporters asked the inner circle for their comments on the nightly news, and as 1987 ended, the missing Harvard graduate student remained a hot topic. The two competing theories certainly guaranteed high ratings.

"If she did go on that boat," Palombo opened a sliver of doubt. "She was attacked by Paradiso, and she was murdered on that boat, and her body was disposed of from that boat."

It was not clear why the trooper said, "if" she got on the boat. The team could say whatever they liked because the FBI lab results debunking that notion were secret. The slip was the slightest clue that maybe this was not what happened to Joan. The other core players did not make that mistake.

"He's got her onboard his boat, sexually assaulted her, killed her," Burke feverishly replayed. "Then took her body out in the Boston Harbor area, sunk her body, and then brought his boat back into the Pier 7 area and cleaned it up and sunk it two days later."

"He's almost like a serial killer," George aped Palombo's portrayal for WBZ channel 4 in Boston. "I think he's completely amoral."

Burke and Palombo reinforced Leonard Paradiso was the prime suspect, and the Websters continued to nod their agreement. Repetition perpetuated the notion that Joan was lost forever at sea, but anyone privy to the inner workings of the investigation had to have serious doubts. Nevertheless, there were concerted efforts to move forward, and Robert Bond was approached two or three times to testify once again. Bond remembered the warning from the official at Concord that the state would screw him if he ever complied. The con was not that bright, but still had a bad taste in his mouth from the betrayal after the Iannuzzi trial. Bond capitulated once to no real advantage, but the team had laid a foundation to pile another case on the Webster suspect.

If the concept to try Paradiso for Joan's murder was going to move forward, the inner circle needed Bond's testimony. While the latest reports reignited the public's fury, informer Robert Bond received guests. He was the only outlet for the sensational story that the key players relied on. By the winter of 1987, steel bars contained the convicted killer at Somerville in Connecticut. The Constitution State was familiar turf to the Yale alum wanting to close the door on the death of his daughter. The Buick station wagon headed north, and according to Bond, the Websters signed in to pay him a visit the winter of 1987.

Trooper Andrew Palombo forged strange alliances in the cases surrounding his nemesis. A Doyle family member affirmed that David and the undercover cop were actually friends; the pair formed an unusual relationship before the Iannuzzi trial. The odd couple rendezvoused twenty to thirty times for undocumented meetings. The camaraderie was a patently inappropriate association between a lead cop and one of the prime suspects in the case. After all their clandestine meetings, it is not surprising the trial outcome was to Doyle's advantage.

Bond disclosed yet another strange twist; he had a pen pal. According to the confined informant, Palombo corresponded with his rat up to the time authorities unearthed Joan's remains in the northern community of Hamilton, Massachusetts. The undercover cop supposedly instructed the con not to change his story. However, cooperation with the state had complicated the man's caged existence throughout the penal system. He made enemies wherever he went.

Fellow Somerville inmate Kenneth Crawford posted a letter to still another attorney that took up Paradiso's challenge. He wrote Marie Altieri that Bond blatantly boasted his favor with the state for jamming the patsy and setting him up. Bond allegedly threatened other prisoners not to tell, but Crawford confessed to an act of self-preservation. Fellow inmates made a preemptive strike against Bond—they stabbed him. Injuries landed Bond in the infirmary in June of 1988, and administrators moved recidivists to new locations. In an unusual move, Robert Bond shifted to the Federal prison system on September 29, 1988, accommodations that were more comfortable.

Authorities paid an unusual amount of attention to the unsavory sorts they had gotten in bed with. Taking Paradiso to trial for Joan's murder was a tough challenge, undoubtedly, but one the Websters apparently wanted to pursue. The resolute team had come this far. They had to have Bond, the "credible" witness they trusted, because there was one glaring obstacle to hurdle—proof that there was a crime.

"It is very difficult to prosecute a case where there is no body," Burke conceded in November 1987 with the 1850 Webster case in the back of his mind. "Joan Webster's body has never been found."

CHAPTER 21

Dib's Truth

My tear crusted eyes opened after a few hours of restless sleep. The scene replayed day after day, but the unfamiliar surroundings still startled me. I splashed cold water on my face, hoping it would wake me up from this nightmare, but it was not a dream.

"Why am I here?" I kept asking myself. "How did things get to this point?"

"You were forced out of this family for a reason," my daughter e-mailed her stinging rejection.

"We just want you to be gone." Steve's cruel words pounded in my memory.

Days, weeks, and months passed in isolated silence, but I persevered. The devaluation that left me in some dark, abandoned hole, where the family left me, made no sense at all. It felt like solitary confinement, a dark, dingy prison for some unspecified offense. I started to dig and dig deeper to instinctively find a way out of the hollow I had been dumped in.

"Eve doesn't know how to get along with people," George maliciously insinuated.

What was he talking about? This was not the feedback I'd received throughout the years. Eleanor always told me how much Grammy liked me, and George commended my kindness with his father, RN. The family repeatedly reinforced what a wonderful mother I was. I pulled out one of Eleanor's old letters and pinched myself as I read.

"We want to thank you so much for welcoming Marg, Fritz, and Cathy so warmly." My mother-in-law could not praise me enough after her sister and family paid a visit. "Fritz said Sunday, 'When Eve gave me a big hug, I knew I was going to like her!'"

"What in God's name was going on?" I racked my brain trying to understand their reversal.

The family had apparently moved on. How could they forget what hideous devaluation does to a human being? They saw what it did to their own daughter. Apparently, it was my turn; my family devalued and discarded me. I felt worthless. I was missing out on every part of my children's lives, but evidently, no one seemed to wonder why. The destructive false rumors that circulated back to me must have filled the gap in people's minds. Tears saturated my pillow as birthdays and graduations passed without my presence. Sleep was my only escape from deprived holiday cheer while the family "guarded" my angels from my loving arms. When troubles knocked at the door, the Websters sealed their lips, and they denied my children their mother's comfort. Friends were nowhere to be found—I ceased to be living in any meaningful sense of the word.

"You can be happy without us," my youngest encouraged me to move on. "Just tell people your children died."

What was hurting my children? I struggled to understand what my children believed. Why were they resigned for me to be gone? Digging out was slow, but I carefully sifted each handful of dirt to understand where I was. When papers quoted my former in-laws' support of Tim Burke's upcoming book, light broke through, and the daunting task of unraveling the family murder began. Finding the path to my children and me meant finding Dib's truth.

The sun trickled through the dense tangle of the spring's budding branches. Karen Wolfe Churgin walked her dogs on April 18, 1990, on her remote wooded property on Chebacco Road. The veterinarian spotted a white sphere obstructing a drainage ditch. Churgin's home sat on top of the bluff overlooking Chebacco Lake, and the lower-wooded basin was often flooded with water. The sparsely inhabited wilderness in Hamilton, Massachusetts attracted hikers and bikers, but was also a secluded setting known for criminal activity. From a distance, she saw an object, a white sphere. When she reached to dislodge it, she reeled back in horror. She immediately called the police.

"I saw something in the woods that looked like a punched-in volleyball," Karen told the *Beverly Times* on April 25, 1990. "I looked closer and it was a human skull. It had suture-like zigzagged lines. Those are unique to human skulls."

Officer Hatfield was the first to respond, and the initial conclusion determined the discovery was, indeed, a human skull. Hamilton Police Chief Walter Cullen arrived at the scene next and photographed the find. The Massachusetts State Police Crime Prevention and Control Unit, CPAC, dispatched Cpl. Dennis Marks to take charge of the crime scene. Local police sent the skull and a nearby black boot to Hunt Memorial Hospital to examine, but nothing else surfaced in the initial cursory search of the surrounding area. Notices went out to departments to assist the resident force, and names poured in to compare the cranium to known missing persons. Joan Webster's name appeared on the list, but the resting spot was more than thirty miles from the long-speculated crime scene at Pier 7 in Boston.

"My guess is it's not her," Det. Tom Spartachino diminished expectations to the *Boston Herald.*

Spokesmen quickly dismissed speculation that the remains might be those of the long-missing graduate student, and the parents agreed. Television cameras rolled as Spartachino discounted the notion that Joan was anywhere other than Boston Harbor. He maintained that Paradiso was the culprit who put her there. The detective was part of the Crime Prevention and Control unit in Middlesex County that originally handled Joan's case, and he was privy to the calculations Tony Pisa dropped into the plot when he dialed up the Middlesex County DA early in 1983.

Psychic Richard Phillips had led Beverly police inspector Richard Gordon incredibly close to the site in 1982, and the uncanny coincidence kept Joan's name in circulation as the possible victim. The new department in charge was the Hamilton Police Department in Essex County, and the local force organized a search for more evidence.

"Of course, it's being checked out, but the location doesn't seem to correlate," George pondered in front of the *Harvard Crimson* reporter. "Circumstances pointed to her being taken out in a boat and dumped at sea. This is something way up north and doesn't tie to anything."

Over the next week, volunteers teamed with authorities and police dogs for a grid search on both sides of the partially paved road. Searchers recovered a few bones and miscellaneous items, but nothing identified the young female victim dumped in the thick woods. A trio of cops stood in hushed dismay surveying the rugged terrain on April 25, 1990. By that time, the resigned officers felt nothing more would be found. Det. Scott Janes and Det. Paul Grant somberly watched Officer Paul Accomando bend down to reach into the decayed log at their feet. The lack of evidence depleted all hope, but there it was, in that log—the Almighty answered our prayers. The officer reached down and clutched a vertebra from beneath the rotted wood. They found the obscured grave of Jane Doe. Enforcers secured the site and planned the exhumation.

"We know the whole body's there," Hamilton Police Chief Walter Cullen confirmed to the *Beverly Times*. "That's the grave."

Video cameras documented the rebirth of Joan Webster. Nature's debris had fallen silently for more than eight years, adding layers to God's protective blanket. In His infinite wisdom, God willed to give Joan back to the living to help unravel the mystery.

Experts did not know the name of the victim when they unearthed the skeleton. A team, including the three heroes that found her, agonized over the horror that ended a young woman's life. The gruesome discovery left no doubt the victim had met an unconscionable fate. The fatal blow left a two-inch by four-inch hole that took out the entire right side of the skull.

Massachusetts State Police Lt. McDougal photographed the recovery, and Officer W. Wilson sketched what they found. Massachusetts State Police Cpl. Marks represented Essex County DA Kevin Burke, but the DA never soiled his own shoes at the scene. Teams recovered most of the skeletal structure, and Dr. Pierre Provost and Dr. Robert Belliveau, examiners called to the gravesite, transferred the remains to the pathology department. Det. Donald Dupray chronicled the events, while Chief Cullen huddled with Auxiliary Captain Ralph York.

Cars congested the rutted, winding way through the forest, and crime scene tape kept reporters at a distance. The police spotted someone watching from a nearby drive. The woodland was an out-of-the-way scene, but some man made his way north from Malden or Melrose to witness Dib's truth emerging from the cold ground. Who was the curious onlooker? My first thought was someone who had followed the case, or perhaps someone involved in the investigation. Carmen Tammaro lived in the Melrose area, and he was an interested party. Trooper Palombo was the lead officer on Joan's case, but he lived in Lynn. The recent discovery undoubtedly caught the attention of the Websters' primary law enforcement connections. Whoever it was, the recovery team noticed him, and the recording captured the observation—someone was watching.

"The cause of death was massive trauma to the head," was the conclusion after careful examination.

The fragile bones rested atop a black, plastic trash bag that had broken open beneath her. The power company had sawed logs to thin the densely wooded area in 1981. The piled wood was convenient for the stealth assailant to entomb her discarded, lifeless form. Years decayed the cut timber, but the power company's occasional thinning provided more logs that someone just happened to layer on top of the concealed grave later in time. Was it chance that someone buried Joan's body deeper, or had someone returned to the scene of the crime?

A gold serpentine chain once adorned the graceful hollow of her neck, but now lay entangled with all that was left of the victim. A gold and amethyst ring was still on the delicate finger, carefully lifted from the desolate site where she rested.

Somewhere between the reported bearded escort from the airport and the trash bag in the isolated woods, a cold-blooded killer stripped off the clothing of the devalued, young woman. Odds for identification diminished without clothing, and the monster that killed her probably knew it. The skeleton was bare, and searchers did not find a trace of decomposed remnants. DA Kevin Burke erroneously reported seekers found a button, but Det. Paul Grant debunked the suggestion. Nothing turned up in the investigation to reconstruct what the victim wore. Zippers, buttons, or synthetics that defy nature's course never materialized.

The Office of the Chief Medical Examiner was now in charge. The state formed the OCME in 1983 pursuant to Chapter 38 of the General Laws of Massachusetts. After medical examination, the attending physician ruled the cause of death was a homicide by blunt force. The substantial cranial fracture indicated an enormous force landed the blow to the right side of the head.

"It was probably caused by something like a bat or a board," Det. Paul Grant speculated what weapon the offender wielded to cause such massive trauma.

The defenseless quarry would have died in the instant and bled profusely from the gaping wound. As life drained from her being, the offender bagged her naked corpse like rubbish. The cold-blooded killer knew how to avoid detection, and hid his sin in the dark woodland many miles north of the city. Joan's body was not supposed to be found, and opened the door for other outlandish explanations.

"The area is known for violence. It's a secluded area. People go there to be alone," Chief Ronald Ramos, an officer from Manchester, New Hampshire, described the location to the *Beverly Times*.

"Whoever put her there knew the area real well," an unidentified investigator told the *Boston Globe*. "You'd have to know the area not to get lost."

The thought George and Eleanor held out hope Joan was still alive was an illusion maintained in front of the press. In the private moments with the family, the parents expressed their resignation that Joan was gone as early as Christmas 1981, less than a month into the search. Impassive mandates instructed the rest of us to move on.

Before pathologists identified the broken bones as his daughter, her father affirmed the conclusion Joan was dead.

"We believed all along she was murdered," George emotionlessly told the *Harvard Crimson* on April 28, 1990. No tears moistened his eyes over the possibility of Dib's resurrection.

Dr. Stanley Schwartz was the state's forensic dentist called in on April 30, 1990, to compare dental charts. He knew who it was the minute he laid eyes on the crumbled pieces on the examiner's table. He had seen Joan's charts before when he compared them to a jaw-bone that washed up on the shore back in November 1984.

"SKELETON ID'D AS LONG LOST STUDENT: FIND ENDS SEARCH FOR JOAN WEBSTER," topped the news in the *Boston Globe* on May 1, 1990.

Headlines heralded the discovery, but the family withheld comment. They were still leery that these remains were their daughter. Dentals matched; George had to adjust his earlier denial and confirm his baby girl had come back. This was Dib, the couple's youngest child, and after long agonizing years, God finally brought her home. Officials escorted George and Eleanor to the forsaken graveyard on May 2, 1990, before the couple stoically sat down in front of the cameras.

DA Kevin Burke hosted a news conference in Essex County that raised logical questions in the enduring mystery of Joan's death. A caring and outraged public never learned the specifics of the recovery, or what Joan's broken bones revealed. This press conference was a façade, once again. The parents kept some family members and close friends in the dark too, despite all the long years everyone suffered. George and Eleanor shielded themselves behind the screen of "privacy," and maintained the CIA oath into their daughter's murder. Public perceptions and pressure meant a new investigation; articles quoted the renewed determination to find the killer. The core delegated the responsibility for truth and justice gave their word, and everyone believed them.

Bulbs flashed, and Eleanor fixed her icy glare on her husband as he carefully picked his words. Dentals were irrefutable—it was Joan. It made no sense why she rested in the wooded fringe of a hamlet far removed from Tim Burke's construed crime. The fact did not jive with other parts of the story either. Regardless, the former intelligence couple pronounced they already knew the killer and believed Paradiso had confessed to the murder.

"Why do you still believe that Paradiso is the culprit?" the gaggle of reporters asked. The question has yet to be answered.

George refused to elaborate. He just did not answer in the same way extortionist Harvey Martel clammed up with the Boston FBI. Paradiso reasserted his innocence when rescuers found the skeleton, but George and Eleanor remained resolute.

"That's his opinion," Eleanor angrily quipped to the *Boston Herald*, with George following suit.

The fact was, Paradiso's guilt was the Websters' expressed opinion. Hidden facts supported Paradiso's declaration of innocence, and so did the recovery of Joan's remains. No matter how adamant George and Eleanor were about their view of Paradiso's guilt, their estimation never mustered the charges to try the merit of the circulated theory. The discovery of Joan's buried skeleton shattered the errant tales about her disappearance. Even so, when reporters pressed George Webster for his thoughts, his denial rejected the obvious fact that Robert Bond was a liar that the core group had relied on. Everyone cocooned the Websters and hid the facts from the public. Participants blocked the path to sort out the truth.

"It's my intention to release as little as possible about the condition of the remains," Essex County DA Kevin Burke announced to the hungry reporters clamoring for news.

The massive hole in Joan's head was inconsistent with Bond's tale of a whiskey bottle in a crammed floating cabin, or the fake .357 magnum a confidential source told ADA Burke he would find. However, the detail Bond gave, in the otherwise false statement constructed with the Massachusetts State Police, was eerily descriptive of what searchers found. The uncovered fact exposed a disturbing accuracy with the rat's information. Bond described a hole and pointed to the right side of the head. Excessive blood flowed from the victim, and Bond's statement actually linked different suspects to the crime. The state's star witness had deviated from the modus operandi crafted by authorities; a profile that projected Paradiso strangled his victims. The snitch gave that option when he talked to the Massachusetts State Police, but someone prodding the ignorant convict in the courthouse selected just how Joan died from Robert Bond's multiple choice. Sgt. Carmen Tammaro introduced Bond to the officers with him on January 14, 1983, when the clandestine group refined the tale of two murders. The interrogator introduced his cohorts: Trooper Andrew Palombo, Trooper Jack O'Rourke, Boston Police Sgt. Robert Hudson, and court officer John Gillen. By Monday, January 17, 1983, when authorities met with Bond again, the field narrowed to three: Sgt. Carmen Tammaro, Trooper Andrew Palombo, and Sgt. Robert

Hudson. One of them picked the right answer more than seven years before this beautiful, young woman resurfaced. That was too much of a coincidence for my shaking nerves.

Hidden facts failed to support the promoted theory, but the parents of this wonderful human being closed their eyes in denial as new details emerged. Of course, the Webster influence guided the public's opinion of the situation, but they clung to an increasingly irrational yarn. Reporters asked George about the jewelry found tangled in Joan's crumbled bones, but he answered evasively.

"Young people have a lot of jewelry," he said. "That's probably an area that needs more definitive investigation."

The intelligence-trained couple paid attention to the smallest details. No one outside the inner circle of participants knew about the photographed bracelet or the falsely projected modus operandi that Lenny stole jewelry from his victims. The confidential source dangled the concept to the Feds, and Tim Burke rallied to support it, but the tactic fell short. Contrary to what the source said, there was no jewelry missing from Marie Iannuzzi, nor did Charlene Bullerwell have any of Joan's gold charms.

Burke identified the bracelet to the Feds, but on whose verification that it looked just like Joan's? Burke and the boys may have gone out on a limb on their own, but not likely; only George, Eleanor, or Anne could positively identify the bracelet. Burke named the obvious source for the photograph lifted at the Weyants during a feigned Iannuzzi search, Trooper Andrew Palombo. The undercover cop attested that he knew how criminals avoided detection and handed SA Steve Broce the snapshot of Paradiso's infrequent date. The woman came forward with a whopper the public consumed, but the tale of Lenny the Quahog was no more convincing than Zanny the Nanny when the local police dug out the facts from the cold earth.

After Joan's discovery, Eleanor stopped sending the news clippings that tracked every twist, and other family made judgments without essential information. The evidence remained in tight-lipped circles while a convincing official version broadcast the renewed search for Joan's killer.

A new campaign started to control the damage. Tim Burke took a page from Iannuzzi suspect David Doyle, and the former prosecutor started coming up with new stories. He massaged the indisputable facts to suit the old thesis. The Websters' confidant backpedaled and adjusted his account.

"Even at the time Bond's information was brought to the attention of investigators," Tim Burke revealed to the *Boston Globe*, "there were questions as to whether Paradiso's boat was operable. The weather was very stormy that night, and one of the cables to the rudder—one of the cables was broken."

Burke knew the alleged crime scene had a broken rudder, and was not seaworthy. The revelation came in 1990 when Joan's broken bones appeared. However, players knew the inconvenient fact when divers recovered the boat in 1983. Regardless, authorities continued spewing that Paradiso dumped Joan in Boston Harbor. Palombo ordered the examination by marine expert Dave Williams. The boys also knew the weather was bad on November 28, 1981, because the Great Lynn Fire left the community in charred ruins. Why was Burke just admitting things now?

The morsel of truth that slipped out next should have raised a red flag, but DA Kevin Burke aided in the deflection and gave a sensible sounding excuse.

"A close reading of Bond's statements to police indicate that the inmate may not have specified whether Paradiso actually dumped the body overboard," the Essex County politician dodged.

The hell they didn't. Maybe the review of Bond's statements missed pages filed in the cardboard box in Tim Burke's office, who knows, but Bond's tale of two murders definitely alleged Joan was in the watery deep of Boston Harbor, and that is not where she was. The years of speculation tied Burke's credibility to Bond's. Miraculously, the statement took on a new meaning for the counselor defending his story. Now "way out" had to mean way out of town to Hamilton, Massachusetts. The Websters' chosen boy conveniently forgot the lobby conference with Judge Roger Donahue years before where he argued to get Charlene Bullerwell's testimony on record. The story then was that Paradiso did not bury his bodies, but disposed of the evidence in water.

The confidential source Burke identified as Trooper Andrew Palombo told the FBI that Charlene knew where the presumed killer dumped Joan's body. The FBI office in Boston protected their sources, even criminal ones, and the state still vehemently guards the records exposing the truth. The pressured witness refused to testify during the trial and promote the unverified assertion that Paradiso was a hit man for the mob that chopped up bodies before weighting the dismembered souls into the sea. George and Eleanor Webster had the lawyer's back and supported the twisted excuses tendered for Bond's false allegations.

"We still think Leonard Paradiso is the person who murdered Joan Webster," George insanely insisted. "The things that were said in the Charles Street Jail could not have been made up. There was no reason not to believe it."

True to form, but unfortunately, something I did not understand yet, my in-laws were keeping secrets. Common sense told me
Paradiso was not the culprit; after all, Bond said he dumped her in
the ocean, and that is not where she was. The informant's allegations
were false. I figured that out, and I did not even know the half of it.
Paradiso was not the right man, but I speciously presumed he had
been fairly tried for Marie Iannuzzi.

The next revelation that came out was unsettling, but authorities had an answer ready to explain it.

"A 'carry-on' suitcase belonging to Webster was found in a Greyhound Bus Lines warehouse," the *Boston Herald* reported on May 1,
1990. "The bag had been locked into a storage locker in Boston and
later shipped to New York, where it went unclaimed."

Had authorities recovered Joan's suitcase in New York contrary
to the official representations? For years, the papers reported the bag
turned up in the Greyhound station in Boston's Park Square. Burke
wiggled around the problem with the suggestion that the bus line
transferred the unclaimed suitcase. However, he never did explain
why there was such a lengthy delay in disclosing this fact. I am stymied
how anyone could determine the bag was in a Boston locker before
bag handlers found it in another city unless that person put it there,
or made it up.

Days turned in to weeks while we waited for the results of the
forensics tests. Det. Paul Grant of the Hamilton Police Department
was the new lead on the case in the small village where Joan surfaced.
New investigators scoured files, and officials huddled to renew
inquiries into the cold case. Eight and a half years had passed, and
storytellers had convinced the public of Paradiso's guilt already.
Grant was a dedicated officer and committed to finding justice for
Joan. Unfortunately, he faced obstacles that could not be hurdled.

"We would rather you not bother David Duncan," George dictated.

George Webster deterred the investigator from questioning the
close friend that first called when Joan failed to show up for class.
Others "lawyered up" and the landscape of witnesses fell silent.
Trooper Palombo flashed a broad smile, but offered nothing about
the case he had guided for years. Instead, the trooper pointed Grant
to Tim Burke to direct any questions. The former ADA pledged he
would never give up on this case, but he continued to peddle Paradiso's guilt without any real evidence to match up with the facts.

The foot-dragging was just his gut feeling, but Det. Paul Grant
sensed there was reluctance to pursue the investigation further. No
official statement declared the family's disposition, but they did not

seem engaged to go after their daughter's killer even in light of new facts. George and Eleanor remained fixed in a rut, presumably convinced Paradiso did it. Essex County DA Kevin Burke lent no real support to the Hamilton investigators asking renewed questions. Those in charge already had someone to blame—Paradiso—and the case slipped under the rug. The political force in the Essex County DA's office looked the other way.

Looking the other way seemed to be the standard practice in Boston. DA Kevin Burke had failed to indict the boyfriend for Marie Iannuzzi's death in 1979, despite overwhelming circumstantial evidence that made him the prime suspect. Now, the hushed inference was that someone would make a deathbed confession for Joan's murder. That is how they hoped to solve Joan's case?

Justice was bothersome when it raised questions about the inner workings of a broken system, and two cases handled by bearded Trooper Andrew Palombo and his moustached sidekick, ADA Tim Burke. Det. Grant, and his superior, Chief Cullen, voiced their educated concerns, but bureaucracy tied their hands. Both raised the red flag that facts did not match the promoted premise, and the accused was not likely the culprit. Statistics and circumstances suggested Joan might have known her assailant, as most murder victims do, and the seasoned Hamilton authorities agreed. My heart quickened as the numbing possibility settled into my bones.

"If Joan knew her killer," I thought, "I might have, too."

It felt like an eternity waiting for the forensic results. The good news was that the state now had a body and could move forward with their case if it had any merit. Not having a body was the only reason authorities gave for not prosecuting the case. The core group had accused Paradiso for years, and state, local, and Federal officials had submitted they developed enough evidence to conclude he was Joan's killer. Only in hindsight, and a lot of digging for answers, do I now understand what happened next, and it made me sick to my stomach.

Heat rose from the sizzling hot pavement during the dog days of July when word came that the family was finally able to make some arrangements. Medical examiners pronounced Jane Doe dead on April 18, 1990, at 12:10 p.m., not yet knowing who she was. Now, they knew it was Joan and the horrific fate that befell her. George Webster ratcheted up the heat at Harmony Grove on July 13, 1990, under the direction of the Murphy Funeral Home in Salem, Massachusetts. The parents cremated Joan's broken bones; they diminished her to ashes. The parents were the only ones who could make that disposition for their slain daughter, but the state had to release the bones for burning.

Rule 38 of the General Law of Massachusetts was clear, and DA Kevin Burke was responsible to spell it out in detail. The law allowed the target of any investigation into a suspicious death to attend any inquest with counsel. Death was determined a homicide, and Leonard Paradiso had been accused of her murder for years. However, Paradiso never participated in any such examination. He was entitled to autopsy findings and presenting witnesses if authorities followed due process. Instead, the press continued to plaster his presumed guilt all over their pages. The law required the court to report in writing any material facts regarding the death. They were to name anyone whose unlawful act contributed to the crime if known. The county's superior court was to impound any findings filed until the DA determined to take it before a grand jury, or if the DA had tried the supposition already. The state filed no charges; there were no visible indications DA Kevin Burke ever went beyond lip service in the papers.

Even more specifically, Section 14 of Rule 38 defined the status of Joan's case. The law states that a body released for cremation only occurred when no further examination or judicial inquiry was necessary concerning the death. The homicide was unsolved.

George and Eleanor Webster were hardly ignorant people who would not understand the finer points of the law. The ITT executive witnessed the progress of science and technology continuously, but deserted any chance of advancements to capture a killer. The finality of the flames closed that door to the truth, and helped perpetuate the Salem witch-hunt against Paradiso.

Det. Grant's instincts, the case was swept under a rug, had a concrete foundation when Joan's remains were incinerated. Ashes were easier to sweep than her mangled bones. Essex County and the State of Massachusetts turned their back on their responsibility to Joan Webster, and capitulated to George and Eleanor.

Eleanor's call was matter of fact, and there was no expectation for us to be present when Dib, as we affectionately called Joan, was interred. My sense of family ran much deeper, and I packed up my family to travel back East. Steve was indifferent, and the girls were young, but I resolved to be there to say my goodbyes.

"Why isn't Anne here?" I asked.

"Well, she couldn't make it," my in-laws' excused.

Joan's sister Anne had forgone the final prayer and peace with her sister. To me a sibling's absence was a wholly surreal disconnection, especially after what we had all been through, and I was certain Joan would have been there for her. The images of Joan's sister sorely contrasted; Anne uncharacteristically made the journey to wave goodbye at the airport after they had just spent several days together, but was absent graveside for a respectful prayer for her brutally slain sister.

George and Eleanor did not seem to need the support after years of the harrowing ordeal, and the service was closed to anyone else. Bucky, the old choir director at church, said a few words at the cemetery to the four adults that stood silently by the grave. The only tears were mine, and the brief farewell seemed remiss for a beloved, young woman. As we departed, George put his hand on the tombstone and dipped one knee to the ground. His homage failed to pay adequate tribute to the child whose justice he had just abandoned. After the internment, the family retired back home, and "fundador" resumed with the smiles and laughter of my beautiful children—George poured a stiff drink.

Even though questions lingered within the family, Joan was rarely a topic of conversation. Eleanor composed a dedication later posted on Panel One of the Murder Wall at the Parents of Murdered Children website. In closing, Joan's mother broadcast the unverified theory of Joan's ending. I thought perhaps reality just had not settled in yet, and it would take time.

"Her case has never been prosecuted because of scanty (and hostile) witness information," Eleanor wrote, "and a belief by her family and law-enforcement officials that her murderer is already serving a long sentence for other crimes."

Bond was not willing to cooperate a second time. The merits of their theory were not tested after they found what was left of Joan's body. The murder was savage and brutal. What loving parent would say, "Oh well, he's serving time for something else?" The state never prosecuted the suspect, but the core group stuck to the same old story. The parents were in league and lockstep with law-enforcement officials, and in their minds, case closed. Authorities officially declared their conclusions on July 24, 1985, to the Department of Justice and branded an untried suspect as the assailant. Those in charge locked their deceitful maneuvers away safely and sealed their lips.

The family gathered again in August for the annual ritual in Nantucket. Anne made the trip this time, and the "fundador" began as usual. We all unpacked our bags in the gray-shingled rental that was home base for the next week. Residents on the quaint island identified cottages by name, and the name of our rental was particularly ironic—"Whale of a Tale." Despite the idyllic setting, recent events were too fresh, and the subject of Joan came up. There did not seem to be any word about the renewed investigation, and the stall was minimized.

"It's just been too long," my in-laws evasively answered. "The trail has simply gone cold."

Was the passage of time the obstacle to the truth of what happened? It seemed obvious that the boat theory was all wet, even assuming time was the impediment. Doubt crept in for other family as well, and my brother-in-law gently challenged George and Eleanor's judgment.

"Why are you convinced Paradiso murdered Joan?" Anne's husband cautiously asked.

"Paradiso's girlfriend had a ring of Joan's," Eleanor answered matter-of-factly.

Anne's husband heard a different story than anything I had been told. Eleanor took advantage of his trust and spun the story that Paradiso's girlfriend had a piece of Joan's jewelry. Good heavens, that would have been a slam-dunk prosecution if the accused had anything of Joan's, regardless how much time had gone by. The populace in Massachusetts was ready to burn the man at the stake, they now had the body, and the intelligence-trained mother of the victim said the culprit's girlfriend had Joan's ring. However, Anne's husband did not know a ring was found on the skeleton. Neither did I. Nor did we know something else. The 1983 confidential report, alleging Paradiso took jewelry from his victims, and Burke's pronouncement that a girlfriend had Joan's bracelet, remained in FBI files. The attempted modus operandi failed to pan out.

After years of rumors, Tim Burke connected the dots in his book between Trooper Palombo and Paradiso's occasional date, Charlene Bullerwell, but she had nothing of Joan's as Burke claimed. The fact is, no real evidence connected Eleanor's daughter to the man she accused. The real clues remained hidden: the composite of the bearded man locked away in the files, and the undisclosed, private number in Glen Ridge, New Jersey.

CHAPTER 22

Dear God

A fter the family buried Joan, I settled into my life as a wife and mother. My daughters are the loves and joy of my life. Just as I cherish my memories of their childhood years, I have also steeled my resolve to find answers. The Midwest was far from the turmoil that continued in Boston's controlling circles, and I focused on being a hands-on parent in the schools and their activities. Problems erupted from time to time, giving the family the opportunity to witness the strong backbone at my core. My role as a devoted wife, mother, and in-law remained unchallenged on the surface, but our temporary harmony was headed for destruction in this secretive family. My in-laws muted conversations about Joan's devastating loss, the aunt my children never knew. My life was moving on, but the tides were about to turn. I was headed for a dark hole hidden deep in Hamilton County.

Almost one year to the day after the parents cremated Joan, a scandalous story exploded in Massachusetts. The Boston papers exposed corruption in the Suffolk County DA's office.

"PROSECUTORS CONFLICT OVER 'SECRET' SLAY CASE FILES," was the headline splashed in the *Boston Herald.*

John Kiernan headed the homicide division exposed for keeping secret and duplicate files. The case raised questions about all of the prosecutions conducted between 1980 and 1988. The misconduct flagged Suffolk County cases. The DA had a 1984 case based entirely on gossip. ADA Tim Burke aggressively condemned a man based on "evidence" collected by the core group and disseminated through the tabloid press. Unfortunately, colleagues were in charge of the files in the DA's office and kept a tight lid on their secrets. The news failed to travel out to the Midwest, and Eleanor's frequent news clippings missed this entire story. Key players dodged another

304

bullet to examine what happened to Joan, or the related cases hung on Leonard Paradiso.

Elle Gates walked into the state troopers' office at the courthouse. She pensively stared at the yellowing poster still tacked on their wall. Joan smiled back, but her words could no longer be heard to help solve the mystery of what really happened or why. Elle saw a familiar face; a trooper from the Crime Prevention and Control unit in Middlesex County, that first handled Joan's case, was in the office.

"She's so pretty. It's a shame they never found her killer," Elle sighed.

"There were many men in her life. She was a whore," Trooper Billy Lisano coldly dismissed.

Elle described Lisano as a close friend of Bruce Latham, the former trooper the Websters hired as a private investigator in 1985. The callous comment was a disgusting confirmation of an age-old quandary—blaming the victim. However, the incident hit some nerves that unsettled me. Who was spreading destructive and degrading images about Joan in law-enforcement circles? The characterization was not the beautiful, young woman I knew at all. Zealots prolonged an unrelenting conquest to hang her loss on Leonard Paradiso with other women branded as having similar characters.

"Why would the Websters go along with this?" I asked Elle.

"Officials convinced them," Elle concluded. "They wanted to spare Joan's reputation."

The thought was repulsive that parents would succumb to such gossip and abandon justice with a scapegoat. George and Eleanor knew their daughter. However, appearances overrode everything in the family. Personal experiences provided the lens to understand the family's position. I was an embattled veteran of the Websters' image control. It was not funny; Trooper Lisano's hurtful blather hit so close to home.

"Is this what you called your daughter?" Sarah O'Brien pointedly accused.

"No," I replied to the girls' counselor. "I talked to her about behavior and how people can get the wrong impressions."

My child had angrily charged me with labeling her a bad name. It had to hurt right to the core to believe it; she understandably felt devalued. I had not said that, so why did she believe it? Clues trickled out just bits at a time. Her father had seeded false insinuations about a family dog. The most logical explanation was Steve's distorted view and his habit to speak for others. Rather than communicate and heal the wrongful impressions my children suffered, the family rallied behind other false sensations. The family dishonestly circulated that I was off my rocker and abusive. Examining the destructive portrayal of Joan further nauseated me when I thought about my daughters. I repeatedly protested Steve's neglect of the girls, and the enabling that could sully their names. His "grooming" paralleled the way Lisano maligned his sister.

George and Eleanor were not protecting Joan's good name by supporting the state's ludicrous theory, even if they believed hurtful gossip. Joan was dead. They guarded themselves and kept people out of their closet—it was about their "honor." The family placed my children at the same risk, and I could see behind the family's screen. My children felt devalued, and I experienced the Websters' cruel and unjustified rejection firsthand. Abuse and gossip came from within the secretive family and punctuated with the dictate, "Don't tell." The John Mulholland underhand slapped me right across the face.

"Just tell people we died," my baby resigned. "It's never OK to cry. Mom couldn't and I can't either."

Poor Lenny continued to rot in prison, making the futile, wildly unsuccessful attempts to fight back. Meanwhile, Burke absolutely thrived. When the infamous Marshfield mansion went on the market, Burke jumped right in to snatch it up. Built by drug trafficker Frank LePere and financed by his ill-gotten gains, the mansion was, apparently, what Burke envied.

Over a decade had passed since troopers photographed the drug king in the Lancaster Street Garage where Burke attempted to plant bugs to wiretap Whitey Bulger. LePere was an associate who paid Bulger off to keep his illicit business running smoothly. The warrant to break into the garage and eavesdrop on criminal activities was an effort to ensnare Bulger, but internal leaks always tipped the mobster off. Now, this self-declared crime-fighting counselor signed his name with LePere's family trust for his new summer home. The Early Bird Trust became a co-plaintiff with Burke in 1998, when greedy Rexhame Beach landowners wanted to take over the seaside. Land court is still sifting the sand, weighing the decision whether Burke and his cohorts can have their way.

According to Burke, two paths crossed during the unsuccessful 1980 wiretap operation. Burke asserts he met Trooper Andrew Palombo for the first time during the operation to bug Whitey Bulger. The State Police Major Crime Unit conducted the investigation targeting the mobster when the novice prosecutor wrote warrants and connected with the bearded, and pony-tailed, undercover enforcer. The scheme was a Trojan Horse style plan. A van parked inside the Lancaster Street Garage for the night concealed a trooper carefully hidden under a pile of furniture.

"Whitey Bulger had remarkable success avoiding detection. He was a protected player," Burke told *Greater Boston's* Emily Rooney. "An administrative assistant, who was very attractive, and also another trooper with very long hair, we used them to con the garage owner."

The pair were part of the plot driving the van into Bulger's garage so the concealed trooper could plant listening devices during the night. Coincidentally, or maybe not, Palombo's superior, Carmen Tammaro, had leaked his involvement with the FBI's agenda to go after the mafia. Paradiso documented his meeting with "Buster," and added specifics where the FBI hid cameras for their surveillance of the Angiulos. Bulger was the bureau's protected informant handled by SA John Connolly, and the mobster was more than willing to undermine the competition to keep his nefarious mayhem unchecked. Connolly supervised another young agent, Paul Cavanagh, Trooper Palombo's good friend. Cavanagh played a part infiltrating the mafia. Authorities handed down indictments on January 5, 1995, for the protected players: James Whitey Bulger, Steve Flemmi, and Frank Salemme. However, it was foiled once again. Bulger slipped through the fingers of a dedicated pursuit. Excrement hit the fan in 1997 when headlines exposed Boston's FBI office for corrupt practices shielding criminal informants.

Joan's saga had faded from the headlines in 1997, when Andrew Palombo nervously approached young Angela Paradiso again. "Things are falling apart," he told her.

This time, Angela knew exactly who he was, and their unsettling encounter at the airport on December 12, 1982, rushed back into her awareness. She avoided further contact with him and never did find out what he meant. When justice finally caught on to the Feds' part in handling Bulger, the district court found, "There had long been allegations of leaks by [John] Connolly from the Massachusetts State Police."

The papers quoted Joan's parents on December 29, 1997, but George and Eleanor neglected sharing another piece of news with the family, or at least within my earshot. Reports circulated that Leonard Paradiso was near death.

"We still believe he killed our daughter, and it would be nice if he said, 'Yes, I did this,'" George said about his slain daughter to the *Boston Herald*. "It would be the final cap on things. But knowing the type of individual he is, and how he has lied all the way through, I cannot believe he would turn around."

The notion of Paradiso confessing to an impossible crime just because the Websters believed it was crazy. The power of their persuasion and the unwavering delusion of his guilt never reached my holiday table.

George and Eleanor's focus was to manipulate my guest list, adding Anne's married boyfriend for Christmas against my objections. Anne was married too, but to someone else, and it was not a very positive model in front of my impressionable girls. Anne had it all figured out just who would sleep where.

"It's your decision, Eve," Steve slyly set me up.

"He can come the day after Christmas for a family brunch," I compromised. "He will have to stay at a hotel."

By time George and Eleanor arrived, the plans had changed, and George announced Dave was now coming Christmas day. I was not happy being manipulated, even when my in-laws buffered their control with a velvet glove. I left the house and spent the night at a friend's to calm down from the blatant disrespect for my healthy boundaries. My children were hurt and confused, and of course, I was the bad guy. Supposedly, Anne chauffeured Dave to a nearby hotel, but her paramour was suspiciously in my basement shower very early the next morning.

Another incident was simmering that Christmas too, that apparently exposed a part of my character the family did not like. An egregious hazing incident at my girls' swim club brought my backbone into full view of the in-laws.

"Oh, you're a whistle-blower, like Cherry Provost," my mother-in-law said with utter disdain.

My mother-in-law constantly reinforced a reward for someone to blow the whistle for Joan. How could these conflicting sentiments be from the same woman? Her good friend, Cherry Provost, stood up when a hideous rape incident tarnished five popular athletes close to home in Glen Ridge, New Jersey. In hindsight, the dagger sliced open the problem. Family dictated secrecy under the nom de privacy, and maintained their image at all costs. However, I put forth clear evidence that I had a much different character. In their minds, I was a mole that had burrowed deeply into the family's secretive world and had not signed Form 368.

While I struggled in vain to establish and maintain boundaries in my own home, papers rebroadcast their opinion that Paradiso was guilty. They did not say one word about that. Nothing new buttressed their judgment that Paradiso was the one who crossed Joan's name off the list for the family gathering. No new proof surfaced to connect the condemned man to their daughter, and in fact, exculpatory evidence remained locked in the files.

The family must have sensed I did not buy the theory that circulated for years, because they never discussed it in my presence. Nevertheless, four, well-educated blood-relatives of Joan's immediate family refused to consider the possibility that this man simply had not done it. Every breaking method the team tried utterly failed to prompt a deathbed confession for an impossible crime. Either the report of impending death exaggerated his condition, or Paradiso somehow improved. For more than a decade longer, he lingered behind bars. The condemned man professed his innocence continuously, but he could not reach the secreted facts that supported his claim. The Websters had rendered their sanctimonious verdict.

After the holidays, depression gripped my oldest daughter. Normal childhood maladies clouded my ability to understand what was wrong. Tears saturated her pillow, and the stellar, fifth-grade student struggled to feel good about herself.

"It doesn't matter if I'm good or bad," she sobbed, "I always end up in trouble."

"Come on, honey—you are wonderful, you are smart, and you are loved," I told her repeatedly, but my encouragement fell on deaf ears.

Buried pain sprouted suicidal thoughts in my child's heart and mind. She felt devalued; the same abuse Joan had undeniably suffered. Every effort to bolster her confidence came up short, and I could not get to the root of her suffering.

"I can't make Daddy unhappy," she announced to me, and the silence that followed undermined any help. The mantle of "don't tell" burdened another generation as if my child had signed Form 368.

Andrew Palombo revved his Harley. Crowds dispersed about eleven p.m. on Friday night after the fireworks were over. Traffic clogged the roads around his familiar hometown of Lynn, Massachusetts, as vehicles streamed out of the Independence Day celebration. The experienced biker passed a car turning right at the intersection of Rock and Grant Streets, and followed the curve at the top of the hill. Wind swept through his long hair as he traveled through the intersection not far from his destination. Speed was not a factor, but an oil spill spun the motorcycle out of control and into the guardrail. His riding partner saw the flashing brake lights and rounded the bend in time to witness the scene. The hulking undercover trooper lay sprawled on the pavement beside the mangled metal. Palombo was pronounced dead just after midnight on July 4, 1998—his lips silenced forever. Only the trail he left behind could reveal the truth about Joan's case.

Bagpipes played at the funeral, and fellow officers joined the procession. Trooper Bill Johnson was spiraling down when Palombo met his Maker. The department shunned Palombo's former "by the book" colleague after Johnson tangled with Whitey Bulger at Logan. Doing the right thing was not always met with favor, and fellow law enforcement distanced themselves from a man who honored the commitment of his badge. Johnson walked to the door with his partner on July 6, 1982, to arrest Leonard Paradiso for the murder of Marie Iannuzzi. Attorneys never called him to corroborate or refute Paradiso's alleged confession to the bearded, undercover cop that relentlessly pursued him. Now, isolation depressed Johnson to a critical point. The defeated defender told family he did not want the force that abandoned him saluting when he was gone. The devalued trooper's death on September 25, 1998, was determined to be suicide. A gunshot wound inflicted by his service revolver ended his life.

Federal prosecutors handed SA John Connolly an indictment on December 22, 1999, and dampened his holiday spirit. Reported scandal bared the inner workings of Boston's FBI office to a horrified public. The office deeply involved in Joan's investigation was corrupt and had shielded informants. Connolly's misconduct centered on organized crime, but the problem ran much deeper. Confidential records stuffed in Joan's files detailed the false information that a protected source had provided to the Feds. Reports connected former prosecutor Tim Burke to the misprision by name, and the solicitor connected more dots in his book of "true crime." Trooper Andrew Palombo coaxed SA Broce to find the witness Charlene Bullerwell detailed in the account. Connolly went to prison for his misconduct, but Bulger got away. Secrecy still guarded names and controlled damage in the shamed office. Protected players were still able to avoid detection.

My youngest was thriving when her temperament turned. Nothing explained the hostility that seethed into our lives, and her daily provocation challenged my patience. The list of family counselors increased, but nothing restored harmony in our home.

"I know that things happened before we were born." Her words dripped with venom, and anger charged every word. "We never killed anyone."

Worry and depression settled into my bones as I watched my extraordinary children fight for survival. What hidden secret threatened their existence? The question was always on my mind, and I simply could not grasp the answer.

Discord never fazed Steve—he did not miss a beat of "fundador" while more Webster women sank into devalued depression. His sister had come face to face with the ultimate devaluation, but he childishly blocked the turmoil.

Then I found the letter to God.

I pulled her desk drawer open looking for keys. Instead, I discovered three painful pages written to the Almighty for help. The letter folded in the back of the drawer for probably more than a year was now tucked in my pocket to try to get help. Hurt and confusion poured from every penned word. What my child could not tell me was lifted to God. She recognized all three Webster females under the roof were sinking into suicidal despair. Dad was a fun guy, but she went on to make allegations of a felony against him.

"He hurt me," she wrote, but resolved not to cry. She headed down the path of the same emotional disconnection that poisoned the CIA family.

Carol Metzger confronted Steve first, but his denial raised the question whether he had hit her. The girls were a unified force and refused to talk. The home front turned into a battleground of three on one, and efforts to eliminate a threat to the family image escalated. Preserving theirs meant destructively framing mine, and the relentless witch-hunt left me helpless to get to the truth. Two family counselors were now in possession of the incriminating letter, but failed to report it. The explanations kept coming, and I grappled trying to trust family while sorting the confusion.

Stirring misperception and diverting the issues were the hallmarks of Joan's case, but the parallel was still beyond my view. Devalued victims in the Webster family continued to accumulate. Suicidal thoughts came dangerously close to ending the pain for each feminine Webster, and my children felt as hopeless as Joan must have on that painful night in November 1981.

Any path toward discussion was blocked; they couldn't make Daddy unhappy. I had to rely on the things they had written to understand what was wrong. He definitely was not happy about the letter, or that I had found it. The fun and charming side of my spouse everyone knew quickly evaporated in lockstep with his parents. The family image was at risk even further, because I acted like a responsible parent and sought help. However, one written admission defined the problem.

"It was the biggest family screaming fight of all time," my oldest remembered. "My dad wanted to talk to her and see what made her write down something that suggested he may have raped her."

Eleanor had tutored my children discreetly that it was wrong to read what others had written. These were not her children, and this was not the CIA. Communication is essential in healthy relationships, and the family was blocking my dialogue with my children. Every time I caught wind of her meddling, it made me cringe. I wanted to look her in the face and ask her a pointed question, but regretfully held my tongue.

"How would you feel about someone's right to 'privacy' if it blocked help for Joan?" I muttered under my breath.

This mom did not keep secrets within our four walls, but that was apparently a problem for the Websters. Seeking proper help with counselors to sort out the troubles was hardly the approach the family had taken to plaster accusations against Paradiso all over the news. Something her father had done was causing my child distress, and the Websters, of all people, should have known that abuse is not a private family matter. If there was some misunderstanding in what I had read, open dialogue was the only way to decipher it. Fear, shame, and confusion were the controlling forces undermining my efforts in a war to keep Daddy happy.

The isolation compounded daily, and I started hearing the same rumblings thrown at Leonard Paradiso, but this time it wasn't Tim Burke running from one courtroom to the next.

"I mean, it's confusing to me that you say you love me, then threaten me. I would much rather deal with the issues that we have in a private setting," my oldest child e-mailed. "Are you implying here that you are going to deal with this publicly? How is that not a threat? You have to wait until I'm ready."

"As I indicated to you in the past, any threats or pressure to meet are not effective," Steve warned.

"What threats?" I repeatedly challenged.

"The girls consider this a violation of their privacy," Steve coldly calculated to protect his nice-guy façade.

Sarah O'Brien aped Steve's accusations; confronting what the family considered privacy issues was emotionally abusive to my girls. Like Leonard Paradiso, I had people running around maliciously suggesting I had threatened my children. What became clearer to me was that my children's sense of security, in their minds, depended on keeping secrets, and they did not trust me to keep them. The reality was that Steve did not trust me, and it infected my children.

"Privacy is an important thing that I'm not sure you ever fully grasped," my daughter misguidedly suggested.

My child had made allegations of heinous abuse, and domestic abuse is not a private family matter. I had done a lot of soul searching during my forced retreat. Although I had my share of flaws, like every human being on the planet, I knew I was a decent, honest, and caring human being who loved my children. Yet, I was treated like a villain at every turn. George, Eleanor, and Steve kept up the pretense of a supportive family, but my children saw through it. The paternal forerunners mistrusted the mother of their grandchildren, and my children adopted their mindset.

There was no way to know exactly what had happened to my children, but I could certainly see what was happening to me. I needed to understand the attitude of victims who had suffered the abuse my daughter suggested in her letter to God. Determined to educate myself, I read *Victimized Daughters* by Janet Liebman Jacobs and learned that the mother was often blamed for such horrors. In fact, victims will often identify with their attackers lulled by a false sense of security and a desire to avoid further harm. Victims feel betrayed and devalued by a mother they believe must have known and could have protected them from all harm. My girls' paternal grandmother influenced an example of secreted shame. Eleanor's illegitimate beginning was not her fault, but a burden nonetheless, that she carried throughout her life. Now, horrifying allegations surfaced in a family with a bizarre, unresolved murder. Shame controlled the codependent, Webster family in an unhealthy pact to keep each other's secrets.

Over spring break in 2003, my spouse struck the final blow. While in Hilton Head with their negligent father, my children walked in on him with Kim, a woman half his age. Kim nearly ran them both down making her escape, but Steve cowardly lied to the girls in the next breath.

"It's just your overactive imagination. There isn't anyone else in the condo. You know, I think you created this in your own minds, just like that crazy harassment, in order to get me in trouble." He was eerily convincing.

When they returned and counseling resumed, Steve shut the door in his mind and refused to talk. "It's Eve's problem to get over," he fumed in a complete state of denial.

Anticipating my departure, the girls gleefully chatted online with friends, but instead, Steve was asked to move out. Three days later, a hysterical drama played out, reminiscent of Charlene Bullerwell's sensational headlines. Like most households, we still had some prescription painkillers in the house left over from a recent wisdom tooth extraction. In the middle of the night, my daughter raided the medicine cabinet, and she found and ingested the Vicoden. The painkiller numbed her senses and set the stage to report to the school she was terrified of her mother. This horrible day concluded with Sarah O'Brien's suggestion that I take a hiatus. I was in shock. Steve was back in the house, and I was in the hospital in complete despair.

The net nanny captured my daughter's jubilation. "Dad's the happiest I've ever seen him!" she celebrated online.

Steve's exuberance at my despair reminded me of the same childish glee he expressed when his nemesis at work had fallen to his malicious gossip. An invisible foe had maligned Mike Orscheln at Baxter in an anonymous letter years before. Image management took a malignant tact to take care of a source of Steve's embarrassment at work, and now the embarrassment he faced with me, or worse.

In December of 2003, the Christmas spirit failed to warm the family's hearts. The Websters were fighting a cold war without a truce to set aside turmoil for a moment of peace. I sat alone in Brown County, still trying to find some way to connect, still struggling with just what was the truth. Why was I in the hospital, and Steve in the house? The only definitive answer I could uncover was that I had invaded their privacy. My feedback was frustrating, because there were genuinely distressing reasons for the heightened vigilance over my daughters. However, too many people make up hideous accusations that when someone actually does find such horrors, they are defenseless.

No one seemed willing to hear my point of view, nor was I able to even see the whole picture. Over the holidays, the potent combination of familial betrayal and extreme devaluation was more than I could endure. I poured a glass of wine, lined up every pill that I had, and stood in front of the mirror. I sang "I'll Be Home for Christmas" at the top of my lungs, and washed another numbing pill down my throat.

I did not want to wake up anymore, but when my eyes finally opened, I was glancing around the emergency room in Johnson County. The ambulance ride was a blur, but counselor Carol Metzger was there as I checked back in to the hospital's stress center. Christmas day dawned, but not a soul came to see me. Steve picked up the phone for a five-minute call and described the somber scene at the house. They were all reenacting the Christmas of 1981. George Webster's resigned words, lamenting his daughter, pounded in my head, "She's gone, but we have to move on." History repeated, and another family member was eliminated from the gathering.

Eleanor's birthday gift came a day late when Steve traveled down to Brown County on January 30, 2004. His visit was the beginning of the dissolution of our marriage, and a premeditated end to their privacy leaks. Sarah O'Brien had colluded with Steve and given his lawyer a letter that I had not seen. This letter unmasked the Websters' dysfunction and refusal to sit down and talk. The manipulated counselor's solicited comments gave my children control whether they ever spoke to me again. The girls were trapped; they could not make Daddy unhappy, so I was "dead" to my children. Threats that I would never see them again echoed from Webster camps. I would never see Joan again in this lifetime, but the barrier to my children defied all reason. At the time, I knew nothing about the similar threats levied against Christine DeLisi and Jean Day during the obsessed pursuit of Leonard Paradiso. My only real "offense" was not going along with the secrecy to safeguard the family picture.

By December 21, 2004, my quarter-century marriage had come to an abrupt end without a comprehensible explanation. Gathering my belongings was a challenge at best. On the handful of occasions I dared to return to my old home to begin sorting out my life, Steve shadowed every step. Later attempts to recover my things were met with paranoia; Steve barred me at the door and made me sort possessions in the garage. Steve cruelly answered my simple request to have copies of photographs with the flippant response he would think about it. Apparently, he's still thinking whether to share treasured moments of my life—no pictures. As I hurriedly scooped what I could recover, Steve snatched copies of the girls' birth certificates as if I was not their mother. In his nervous surveillance, however, he did miss something else—secrets walked out the door with me. The girls' journals were outside the family's control.

Reading their words was one of the most painful experiences of my life. With each page I turned, tears streamed down my face. Their words painted me as a monster comparable to the portrayals of Leonard Paradiso, but snippets trickled through their destructive image of me to expose the root of their pain. Carol Metzger got a crack at them first, but apparently never bothered to read them. Evidently, everyone was satisfied they had their scapegoat—now the Websters wanted to move on.

I carefully copied pages in the journals that reinforced the concerns in the letter to God and gave them to Sarah O'Brien. When Sarah confronted my child, the Websters knew things had leaked, and Steve demanded the incriminating pages be returned.

"There's more about me no one knows," my child wrote in desperation. "I know no one can help."

Steve sat on the counselor's sofa demanding the journals my girls had written. "Those are private!" he insisted.

Undoubtedly, I had hit the Websters' exposed nerve. The girls made serious allegations in those journals, and my job was to try to protect them, but I was up against a family with a particular set of skills.

"She will have to ask me herself," I firmly refused. Privacy or not, the issues had to be dealt with.

The pages corroborated concerns of a felony, and I would not comply with Steve's desperation. Sometime between April 29, and May 1, 2005, Sarah had a break-in at her office, as stealth as the intrusion of Chilean diplomats. The girls' advocate contacted Steve that an intruder disturbed the Webster file, but I had to hear about it through the inadequate grapevine. The perpetrator riffled only selective papers.

An unidentified agent found Sarah's secluded setting and avoided detection when no one was there. Their interest was what was contained in our files. The girls' crafty behavior to pick locks at home was suspicious conduct considered when I spoke with Carol Metzger, but professionals shied away from confronting them. Sarah obstructed my request to talk to police, and her agitation seemed to stem from the fact that I'd learned about the incident. Steve maneuvered a change in counselors to a new front where there was greater control of the input. The shift to a different couch was equivalent to the strategy to slip Joan's case out of Middlesex into another office in Suffolk County, and redirect earnest efforts. Again, professionals never verified what they heard, and another witch-hunt continued.

My focus remained on the problem of what was hurting my girls. When counseling failed to follow the law with the new pages that bolstered concerns about the behavior of Joan's brother, I went to police to report it. I held nothing back, and handed a binder of painful pages to Det. Nancy Zellers of the Carmel Police in Hamilton County. The curved walk to the door, on the warm June day in 2005, was not the typical path to find an offender. The serene upscale neighborhood was not riddled with crime. Instead, it was an ideal setting for dogs and joggers in an affluent suburb. Rather than struggle with violent crime, children achieved and went on to college. The girls answered the door, and unified denials convinced a source of help that nothing was wrong, again. The imprinted image branded Mom with the problem, and cunningly diverted attention from the desperate words my children had written.

Distress signals continued to seep into my awareness. My exile had not dulled my instincts that the right stones still had not been turned. Even though people knew my devotion to my children, no one was looking for a mom missing out of their lives. Worse yet were authorities and professionals who missed the signals. Uncovering secrets others want hidden is undoubtedly a catalyst that leads to terrifying stories in the news of missing women, some who end up murdered. There already was one unresolved murder in the Webster family.

I continued to reach out. Instructors read the loving letter I wrote to my oldest while she was on a school retreat, but strangely, she had a complete meltdown. Around the same time, drugs surfaced as a coping device to numb the pain, and their reckless father enabled the underage drinking parties that put every guest at risk. To make matters worse, the girls brazenly posted photos online for all to see. My attempt to convince professionals and authorities to intervene proved futile.

"Whatever you are thinking is not true and has no factual basis," my youngest fired back. "It is not in anyone's best interest for you to be spreading lies, rumors, or delusions."

"I would strongly advise you to cease this nonsense (libel/slander)," Steve warned in complete denial. In another e-mail he threatened, "You continue to libel/slander all of us. My parents, the girls, and myself stand ready to legally deal with you."

Nevertheless, the pictures told the real story that he labeled slanderous. Who was threatening whom? The net nanny software had captured both girls' discussions, and they had boldly posted their activities online. Another parent confirmed my concerns, but Daddy was in denial. When the waters calmed, Steve and I met face to face, and he privately admitted what was already abundantly clear.

"The girls are my biggest concern, you know that." No, I did not know that at this point, and Steve's actions were not matching up with his words. "It's recreational; it's not major at all. She's definitely experimented recreationally, but if you ever quote me on this, I'll never speak to you again!"

The truth was what threatened the family. A paranoid father and ill-informed counselors denied the girls loving guidance and help once again.

When my mother became sick, Steve ratcheted his rhetoric. She was critically ill, and doctors scheduled lifesaving surgery. The Websters shunned the whole Carson side of my children's gene pool as if we did not exist, and the severity and depth of the alienation was clear. My family is filled with good, decent people who love the girls unconditionally, but the controlling, paternal family devalued all of us. The control conflicted with the image of the parents that looked for their daughter in front of the cameras.

Calls, cards, and e-mails all failed to reach the caring, young ladies I knew, so I called officials at their schools to notify them of Grandma's surgery. The hostility spewed back at me left me stunned, and intensified my anxiety coping with my gravely ill mother.

"They feel terrible about Sue's condition," Steve disingenuously spoke for the girls. "However, they don't trust your motives. They are asking me to protect them from you."

This was complete insanity. When my father died, the girls tucked notes in with Grandpa's ashes and silently whispered to his spirit, "If he only knew the truth." Compassion did not appear to be part of the Websters' true colors; it took more than five months to pay meager tribute to my dad after his death in 2003. Why was Steve insinuating my motives were suspect? Now that the family had flipped the switch on my existence, Steve twisted the knife. He felt my children needed him to protect them from me and letting them know, in any way I could, that Grandma was seriously sick.

My knowledge of the girls dwindled. I lived in daily fear wondering whether they were all right. No news, good or bad, came from the Websters' secret fortress. The family that suffered the horror of a missing loved one inflicted the same terror for me to relive. The Websters' sentence was the hideous nightmare of not knowing about my children. Not knowing was torture I suffered with them when Joan disappeared. The fractured grapevine and occasional piece in the newspaper were my only fleeting glimpses of the girls' lives to reassure me that they were, in fact, still alive. My name was noticeably omitted from an article boasting one daughter's achievements; Steve was her father, but apparently, she had no mother. I was not even told of the honors, and the family smothered my pride for their achievements.

Doctors admitted one of the girls into the hospital, evidently under a suicide watch. There was not a word from the family. I had to hear it from the counselor, who still filled me in on what morsels she learned. The Webster family banded together to deny my children their mother's comfort. The years of holding out hope about Joan for the papers did not prevent the elders from wreaking the same hell for me and my children, but I had discovered a damaging letter. Their "privacy" had ended up in the hands of a family member who would not remain silent.

Counselor Ari Gleckman added a missing component. He observed that the depersonalization and disconnection in my daughter had reached a dangerous level. My child did not know what was real, but counselors did not verify what they were told. My oldest fired back tersely that I had been forced out for what I did to the family. I was at a loss. My knowledge had not yet been assembled into a logical place to explain it. With measured intent, the family had successfully constructed an image and eliminated an important influence to discern reality for my children. The Webster elders eliminated a voice of reason and a beacon of truth—they dangerously controlled the persuasion.

On the twenty-fifth anniversary of Joan's disappearance, former prosecutor Tim Burke announced the tome he billed as "true crime." Words jumped off the page that concerned me.

"Terry [Eleanor] Webster said they are cooperating with Burke's book because 'It keeps Joan alive,'" the *Boston Herald* reported.

George and Eleanor supported the book, and planned to contribute to the reworked tale. I expressed my concern for the irresponsible position to publicly condemn a man who had not been tried. Authorities had no real evidence that I knew of, and the grand jury rejected the theory. Joan was found buried, ending years of speculation that she had been dumped at sea, and informant Robert Bond was exposed as a liar.

My e-mails to Steve and his parents expressed my concern that the girls would end up like Aunt Joan. The e-mail bounced back once because George blocked anything I had to say, just as he had tuned out any rational thinking about the boat theory, but the second bounce told the story. Steve forwarded the e-mail from his office, but his father's mailbox rejected my protestation again. I'd hit a nerve. The root of the problem was now understood with Steve's knee-jerk reaction. The Websters influenced the girls to believe impossible things, or coerced them to keep the secrets. However, everyone shied from confronting the family's entrenched and inexplicable belief about Joan.

"You wait until you've been exiled out of the Webster family to start opening up these old wounds for the poor Webster family." The poster's comment underscored the problem.

The Joan Webster murder was an open and unresolved crime, but apparently, people had forgotten. The notion to let the "poor Websters" believe it if that gave them some peace was grossly misguided. It also meant that the family controlling my children's thoughts encouraged things that were not real; an ailment Gleckman described of my daughter. Like everyone, I had trusted the authorities and the Websters' judgment until it no longer made sense. As far as I am concerned, it is abusive not to tell the family the truth, though it is painful, but doing the right thing is not always met with favor. The truth is the only thing that allows genuine healing. At the core of the problem was the fact that everyone involved was sticking to the Websters' modified story that ignored the facts.

CHAPTER 23

Copies of Crazy

"Dear God," I prayed, "where do I start?"

My journey to unravel the truth began half the country and a quarter of a century away from the crime. For years, the offenders avoided detection and confabulated stories; wild speculation diverted attention. Genuine healing comes with the truth, but obstacles to healing surfaced from those in positions of trust. There was no recipe to follow to know just where to start. George and Eleanor visited Tim Burke in 2005, and settled into the same seats where Frank LePere's illicit drug deals went down when Joan disappeared.

"I started writing this book after Terry [Eleanor] and George visited my home in 2005," Tim Burke published. "They talked about the need for the victim's family to know as much as possible about the death of their family member."

They were the encouragement that inspired Burke to write his book, but the book depicts impossible gut-wrenching graphics to memorialize their daughter. The secretive family fell silent over conflicting details I knew, and influenced my children into thinking that I was not in my right mind. As far as they were concerned, I was crazy and delusional, but they conveniently concealed their underhand in manufacturing that illusion.

The Commonwealth and the next of kin were a formidable alliance promoting the theory Leonard Paradiso murdered Joan on his boat. The case of Joan Webster had filled the papers for years, and the first task was digging out as many articles as I could on her case. The clippings Eleanor regularly sent, that filled my scrapbook at the time, were inadequate to give a complete picture. Seeing some of the stories in print after so many years sent chills up my spine, and I began reliving the nightmare all over again. The tabloid accounts Eleanor selectively sent slanted perceptions and heavily promoted

Paradiso as the culprit. The regular news deliveries dwindled after the Iannuzzi trial, and apparently, our subscription had expired completely by the time searchers discovered Joan's bones. What I had at the time left the image of the shell fisherman's presumed guilt, and none of the quotes from the doubtful authorities sifted through.

"Was there a composite?" I asked after reading the *Boston Globe* article from January 19, 1982. "Why was it never broadcast?"

They were straightforward questions that only needed a simple answer, but there was no response. I asked about the extortion incident, too. I could not find it in any of the papers, but remembered Steve's excitement in telling the story. It's not the kind of life experience someone forgets, but I couldn't find anything about it anywhere.

"Why do you believe Robert Bond's statement?" I inquired. "What is it that I might not know?"

Dead silence.

The Essex County DA's office was now the custodian of Joan's files. I addressed my letter to them hoping for more information about my murdered sister-in-law. I asked them about the extortion incident, too. It gnawed at me; authorities never charged the man, and it bothered me more that the incident completely missed anyone's awareness. About this point in time, I thought Steve had made up the whole thing just to make me sound nuts if I dared to repeat it. The DA's office had nothing to say, and I got a canned answer.

"The case file materials remain confidential," first ADA John Dawley wrote.

I had learned from the prison that Paradiso was no longer confined at the Old Colony Correctional Center, his latest housing on record.

"Has Paradiso been released?" I asked Steve.

"That's an unpleasant thought for all of us," he scolded as if I were spreading rumors.

The comment was a question, not a statement, but Steve bristled. As it turned out, administrators had moved Paradiso to the Lemuel Shattuck Hospital; he suffered from cancer. Steve's mood was swinging when I got him to sit down and talk face to face. Every other word was how much he wanted the girls to have a healthy relationship with their mother, but agitated when I insisted we needed to sit down and talk. He ended the meeting with an unsettling look, and made an unexplained arrogant exclamation.

"You haven't figured this out yet," he smugly toyed.

I was not getting anywhere. My recollections included the bizarre tangent in Joan's case that tried to link her to the Zodiac murders. Therefore, I started searching online to see what I could dig up. A discussion board dissected Gareth Penn as a suspect for the Zodiac crimes. He had calculated an incredible theory that a Harvard professor was the notorious serial killer, and according to Penn, ended his spree with Joan Webster. If I were to unravel this mystery, no stone could be left unturned, and certain theories, however far-fetched they seemed, had to be checked out. The discussion board's concentration had focused on Penn as the diabolical killer and suggested he had murdered Joan.

Participants on the site had already made up their minds, so having someone contributing, connected to a case they discussed, didn't really matter that much to their theories. However, there were other areas on the site that piqued my curiosity and opened new doors of investigation. They had a thread about Boston's corrupt history during the time Joan disappeared, and a member directed me to look into the nefarious dealings of the CIA and ITT, George's former employers. I had my homework cut out for me. Someone else quietly followed the discussions, someone with a unique insight into Joan's case. I made my first significant contact, a member of the Paradiso family.

Theories fell one by one without concrete evidence, and common sense drove my instincts to turn the focus toward the Websters' incredulous story. The questions I really had were why does this family believe Paradiso murdered Joan, and why am I such a monster for asking?

I learned that the boat did not even exist at the time, and I already knew the offender buried Joan miles from the alleged crime scene. It made no sense. Why did the Websters cling to this explanation? I asked, but they weren't answering any questions. No one wants to believe people they have loved and cared about, family they trusted, are capable of terrible things. Nevertheless, I would not close my eyes in denial to any possibility. Did officials lie to the family, or threaten them to go along with the story? As each new morsel dropped in, it became obvious this case was a hoax. The boat theory was one whale of a tale, and I pressed harder to find something to justify the family's support.

The computer became my portal to learn whatever I could. I started my own discussion group to start pulling things together. One problem with Joan's case was how dissected the whole investigation was. George and Eleanor were the only ones that knew all the various aspects of the case, or so it seemed. One thing I knew about my intelligence-trained in-laws was that they paid close attention to every finite detail. That is what I had to do; if I were going to understand why they believed this, I had to try to think as they did. Members signed on to the group, each adding a bit to the discussion, and I got the magnifying glass out so I would not miss anything that might help.

Boston's system shielded Burke from having the case files opened for two reasons. First, the case was never officially resolved, so it is protected against Freedom of Information requests. Second, the remains were located in Essex County, giving them jurisdiction and reasonable deniability for Burke that he could not do anything about it. It also helped having friends and colleagues in the right places. Burke was a protected player, at least as far as the authorities go. Did authorities protect the Websters because they believed Burke's story, or to hide the state's wrongdoing from them?

"I'm glad there are some people aware that this is an open case, and that Leonard Paradiso may have been the victim of a frame-up." Dave made astute observations and had contacts in the law-enforcement community to discuss the case knowledgeably. "There is a natural tendency to 'circle the wagons.'"

He was right about that. The Essex County DA's office summarily dismissed requests as if authorities still used their valuable resources scouring the files to find the true killer. What had surprised most observers discussing the case was the intense effort officials made to pile charges on Paradiso and severely tack sentences on one after the other. Dave's comments hit a familiar chord; not only had George and Eleanor described the strategy to find things to use against Paradiso, it was also the schema my girls outlined in writing for their war against me. So whose strategy was it?

"I had also heard that Webster's father had many prominent contacts in the Mass law community." The contributor's observation was unquestionable from my vantage point. The Websters kept their hand in the investigation, albeit discreet, but it was there.

I relentlessly reached out to my children, and forwarded them a loving tribute to Aunt Joan on the anniversary of her birthday in 2007. One of the girls had an irrational response to my remembrance of Joan; she responded with the uncharacteristic venom I could never get used to. I was hitting nerves.

"You are completely crazy! You were forced out of this family for a reason!" My oldest revealed the premeditated malice of the family. "The real tragedy of the Webster family is you!"

What had I done to warrant being forced out of the Webster family? I had not killed Joan and lovingly embraced her memory. My mind drifted back to the useless counseling sessions where I was left dangling, and in CIA fashion, they could not tell me what I had done. I flashed back to the dictate outlined in the girl's war room to find things to use against Mom. Once again, the confusing accusation came without explanation, but invasion of privacy resounded among the ranks. The family that had bemoaned Joan's loss for the tabloids now placed me in the same category of the devalued and discarded. Legitimate investigation looks for behavioral patterns; there were three more devalued victims in Joan's immediate family.

Burke haughtily sat in front of his audience reading a passage from his new book, *The Paradiso Files: Boston's Unknown Serial Killer*, on March 8, 2008. He heralded his fiction as "true crime" at the book signing and graphically described his fabricated accounts about the murder of a member of my family. Did he think everyone would forget? It's unlikely Burke, in his narcissistic moment in the spotlight, noticed the tears welling up in my eyes. Burke's decision to commit these delusions to print underscored his confidence that he was a protected player, but his publication was now evidence in an open capital case.

"I tried to contact you," I quietly charged the author poised at the table to sign copies of his book.

"I know," he sheepishly dodged as he turned his gaze away from meeting my eyes. "I hope you enjoy the book."

The canned words he penned on the page were completely disingenuous. They hurt to the core. He could clearly see how flagged my copy was, but completely ignored it. Carmen Tammaro was there taking his bows. Burke portrayed "Carmenooch" as one of the heroes in the fictitious drama. When the former enforcer saw that Burke's prose dismayed some members of the audience, he rushed to cover the attorney's back.

"Don't worry," Tammaro whispered within the earshot of the next woman in line.

Broadcasters screened calls to weed out unfavorable questions as Burke made the rounds promoting his book. Reporters lauded the tome, but in truth, Burke's rendition buried Joan's case deeper into a cavern of deceit. The Essex County DA's office announced they were looking at other cold cases based on the fictitious book, but the office did not include Joan's case in their statement. It seemed everyone dreaded telling George Webster that Paradiso was not the right guy. In other words, "the emperor had no clothes," not to mention not having the boat, but George would not listen. The shame of Joan's case stained an already darkened system. Reputations were on the line.

The next step was obvious; I needed help, so I retained a private detective in Boston to help dig out the facts. The investigator submitted Freedom of Information, FOIA, requests to the Essex County and the FBI. Someone did not like me stirring up the unresolved case. A published version was circulating, and I, apparently, asked too many questions.

"Who is your client?" ADA John Dawley was agitated and called the private investigator asking for confidential information. "The Websters haven't hired you."

The discussion group was making progress, and I posted a sampling of recovered documents online. Then another interesting observer joined the mix. John James, if that was his real name, was intrigued by the LePere connection to Tim Burke. The man claimed to have some association with Frank LePere, a criminal who operated during the corrupting influence of organized crime in Boston. He e-mailed remarkable details of murder and mayhem during Whitey Bulger's reign of terror that I forwarded on to the FBI. The communications grabbed SA Bob Patenaude's interest, an agent assigned to the Whitey Bulger task force hunting the evasive mobster. The contributor on the other side of the keyboard obviously knew what he was talking about when it came to Bulger's former associate. James wanted to squelch any notion that the amiable drug pusher had anything to do with Joan's murder. Frankly, I did not think that LePere did, but was more interested in the company Burke was keeping.

The progress was measured by taking two steps forward and ten steps back. The collective truth-seekers online reviewed old trial transcripts. The recovered records bolstered retired private investigator Ray Morgan's memory of events. Morgan told me about the Bond interview with the Massachusetts State Police from the recording he heard during his involvement with the case. The transcript confirmed his recollection, and the honest and dedicated professional adamantly maintained Paradiso's innocence. Recovered documents debunked the state's story in numerous cases surrounding Leonard Paradiso, and Burke had colleagues in the right places. Burke, who had privileged access to files inappropriately stashed in his office, published a mangled and false explanation that he hoped would close the door on Joan Webster. However, he distorted accounts, omissions skewed the picture, and fabrications altered the facts.

The private investigator and my lawyer visited Robert Bond at Shirley MCI. The attorney thought Bond might have been the least intelligent person he had ever encountered—a profound statement from a defense attorney. Bond was skeptical and shared very little, but said the "Man from New Jersey" had sent people to see him.

The Webster household broke every rule in the care of my children as the family guarded their secrets. The time had come to face off with Steve in court. I filed a contempt suit and wrestled the demon pro se on May 23, and July 9, 2008. By representing myself, I could ask questions that broached on family history and enter my daughter's letter to God into the record. The author raised her right hand in front of Judge David Naffir. Steve's lawyer objected and urgently rushed through questions to whisk the witness away on a conveniently prearranged trip. She did not deny writing the letter, but the story had changed much like David Doyle's efforts to distort incriminating evidence. My daughter hoped to change her written doctrine of fresh complaint.

"There are parts of this that were forged," she defensively accused.

She caught me off guard. The letter was sitting in two counselors' folders and police files. Steve and the girls had denied this letter meant what I increasingly feared. Counselors asked her to sign a statement getting her dad out of the hot seat. The original in Metzger's office was out of my reach, and the patterned stationery could not be reproduced. Witnesses had affirmed she wrote the letter, including her sister.

The parts she alleged were forged were certainly the parts that would get Daddy in trouble. The Webster image was on the line again, so the story changed just like the pressured testimony of Jean Day and ITT lobbyist Dita Beard. The truth placed my daughter in a vise trying to make Daddy happy; I feared others in control coerced or enticed the perjured testimony to spare the family embarrassment.

My firstborn took the stand, too, and she turned down her eyes when she read the online chats she had with her sister. Apparently, the bullying tactics to force me out—that left her father the happiest she had seen him—pricked at her conscience. Nevertheless, Steve's attorney was quick to the rescue and objected.

"We had to worry constantly about some outburst and rampaging out to school which she did," my daughter swore to the court. "The reason I'm saying it's a rampage is because you didn't call me and tell me you were coming out."

Selective words promoted a false image, and my very intelligent children certainly knew that. The dictionary defines rampage as violent or excited behavior that is reckless, uncontrolled, or destructive. It is a state of violent anger or agitation. In fact, I had not called her in advance. If my children answered their phones at all when I called, they screamed in my ear before hanging up. Phoning ahead was pointless. The visit was a pleasant meeting with the dogs, and her boyfriend, Blake, walked alongside us. My companion was a tape recorder just in case things were distorted, and indeed, they were. The button I apparently hit was to ask about the welfare of her sister. I had learned about drug use and wanted to get help, exactly what a loving and concerned parent should do. Again, I had stepped into the secretive world they wanted to keep hidden.

When it was Steve's turn to take the stand, I laughed to myself when he raised his right hand. By this time, I knew my ex-husband made up his own truth and was very convincing.

"I don't remember," he sprinkled throughout his testimony. He had the same problem with recollection that David Doyle did.

"What did your parents do?" I pointedly asked him. "What was their job when you were born in Washington, DC?"

"They worked for the Federal government," he evasively answered.

His attorney's objection was timely to avoid further questions that might get specific. In his mind, he could not see what possible difference it would make what the girls' grandparents did. The average person was not accustomed to the secretive world of intelligence operatives; I had not been either. Clandestine collaboration with the CIA in international affairs was not the first thing to come to people's minds thinking of an executive with ITT either. The disadvantage was that no one understood the particular set of skills I was up against; the judge sustained the objection. The Websters had an image people saw, but the image was not what I dealt with in my personal life.

I cautiously broached the subject of Joan's unresolved murder, too, but the court deemed the topic too far afield. The small Midwestern family court, hearing contempt charges, had no concept of the bizarre mystery that plagued the family. Steve leaned over to his attorney with a smirk on his face to suggest I was crazy.

"The guilty man died in February," Steve audibly whispered, perpetuating the family's groundless contention.

Alienation had deepened and entrapped my children. One side of the girls' family controlled the input, but I continued to hammer at Webster barriers that blocked a loving mother from her children. Intentional malice planted the notion I was evil in the terrorized minds of my children, and the elders cajoled them to force me out of their lives. Now, the girls were the front line to shield the family image while the older Websters cowered behind them. In their terms, I was a mole that threatened the family picture they wanted people to see.

Another interested viewer with relevant insight contacted the discussion board. Elle Gates knew the players in Boston and enlightened me to what went on in the broken system in Massachusetts. She had worked for ADA Carol Ball on Joan's case, beginning in December 1981. She had a new employer by the fall of 1985. Tim Burke hired Elle when he opened his new practice with the signed contract for the Massachusetts State Police.

"I know what happened to the boat that you may not know," Elle disclosed. "Burke had another friend who was an investigator in the Suffolk County DA's office. I found out that Tim and Tony were in BIG trouble with the Suffolk County DA, because he found out that Tim told Tony that he could HAVE the boat for his own personal use."

It took some reflection, but she remembered the name Anthony Pascucci. Apparently, Tim handed the keys to his declared crime scene to the gopher that worked on the taxpayer dime. The case was still open. Elle vaguely recalled that Pascucci might have painted the hull of Burke's so-called evidence white. First Assistant Paul Leary called repeatedly to chew out the incompetent litigator's generosity.

"He gave the (expletive deleted) crime scene away?" I was stunned by the assistant's revelation knowing that authorities would not let that little tidbit out of their bag.

Elle answered the heated calls and filed documents in Joan's box, the carton Burke inappropriately shifted to his new office. She knew who came in and out, and conducted "business" with Burke. The attorney's clique of friends stumbled over the labeled cardboard file every time they reached for the white powder to sweeten their coffee. The presumption that Burke's legal coworkers in the office knew it was wrong for the files to be out of the DA's office was a given. Mark Newman, Joe Kittredge, and Brian Rogal were all attorneys who shared the office space on occasion. The close quarters made it inevitable Elle would overhear Burke's latest problems with Suffolk County regarding the Chris Craft, and the beneficiary of Burke's lavish giveaway kept coming back through the door. There was no reason to doubt her astute observations, because she was there.

The Internet was a powerful tool; it was a resource for research and an avenue to expand awareness of Joan's unresolved murder. Those who followed the thread expressed views on both sides of the case. Everyone's input was welcome as long as it was respectful. Documents were posted so everyone could see the concerns, but some readers did not like it.

"Pictures of state troopers, DA, and state officials alluding to corruption without solid proof is not acceptable!!!" the defensive poster protested.

If the reader cared to check, I posted documents online. The actual records raised legitimate concerns about what was going on during Joan's investigation. The notion no one could challenge what authorities did was rather frightening to consider, and even the poster's comments revealed her internal conflict.

"If Burke wasn't such a chicken shit he wouldn't have screened his phone calls on the radio station the night he was on," the "Great One" added. "He knew he was wrong."

The questions narrowed the search to persons involved in the investigation itself, but apparently, some people thought that was out of bounds. A thorough review meant no stone left unturned, and unfortunately, the investigation itself was where the stink came from. Why wouldn't there be an effort to divulge answers in the secreted files if they supported the Paradiso theory? Authorities vilified Paradiso so badly during the witch hunt that the image lingered after his death. The defensive posture was in sheer denial of what the actual records revealed.

"Your energy would be better focused on helping find missing children or abused children and break the cycle," the person on the other side of the keyboard instructed.

Breaking a cycle of abuse was exactly what I was trying to do, even if the poster could not figure that out. I tried the DA's office again without much success. I discussed the nature of abuse allegations with Trooper Brian O'Neil in the Essex County DA's office without giving my name. He said that information was extremely important in a family with an unresolved murder, and encouraged me to come forward. O'Neil took a shot thinking it was an open case in New Hampshire. When copies of my girls' distressing documents reached their office, officials sang another tune—this was the Joan Webster case. Massachusetts' dictionary had a word for their brand of blindfolded justice for the privileged and well connected—Chappaquiddick. They stopped answering the phones.

The Essex County DA's office rejected another request for information.

"The investigation into Ms. Webster's murder had been renewed prior to his [private investigator's] request," the assigned underling represented to my attorney. "We are in contact with Mr. and Mrs. George Webster, and they relate they have not hired your client and do not waive their privacy interest in the materials."

There it was again, "privacy," and I was violating the Websters' carefully guarded secrets. Murder is the state's responsibility and not a matter of privacy dictated by the family. Joan's parents came out with some sort of executive privilege to guard their secrets instead of looking for answers about who brutally murdered their daughter. George and Eleanor made no privacy claims when Burke published his book; on the contrary, the family supported it. *The Paradiso Files* was the tale they endorsed, and they did not want anyone to see it any differently. They had the answer they wanted, though the state never tried and decided the case.

A stealth correspondent underhandedly placed an anonymous letter in my mailbox without being posted. I filed a police report naming my ex-husband, Joan's brother, as the possible source. He had used that tactic before; he was a logical suspect for the harassment. The letter suggested that I had a mental disorder and hinted that I should admit it. These methods had not pressured a confession from Paradiso for a crime he could not have committed. Now, someone wanted a false submission from me, despite the fact the evaluation done by Dr. Larry Davis in 2006 contradicted the anonymous mailer's diagnosis.

A thick packet landed on my private investigator's desk. The voluminous FBI records took time to digest, and I scoured them incessantly looking for clues between the redactions. I could envision Burke's disappointment with each lab report filed. Examiners found nothing on the *Malafemmena* that supported the theory Joan had ever been there, or any evidence of any crime other than sinking the boat. Lab reports stamped "no match" for Joan's fingerprints on Lenny's *Maya* volume no matter how many times the obsessed litigator sent it in. The simple fact was, there was no real evidence to connect Leonard Paradiso to Joan's disappearance—period.

However, there were disturbing reports of a confidential source that tipped the Feds with false information. The nature of the disclosures narrowed the field to just a handful of players. Robert Bond's whale of a tale, the killer dumped Joan in Boston Harbor, was the first clue the informant revealed. Boston's G-men protected their snitches, but only insiders knew the Boston bureau made up their own rules. Collaborators hid the damning disclosure in files stamped with the case number for the bankruptcy case, 49B-1306, in the personal crimes division. Leonard Paradiso was the named subject and Joan Webster listed as his victim.

"Tim Burke advised that the MSP had been attempting to identify and locate Charlene for some time," the agent typed. "The bracelets Charlene was wearing in the photo may be identical to ones belonging to Joan L. Webster."

The confidential source told the Boston office that Paradiso stole jewelry from his victims, and falsely indicated there was missing jewelry in the Iannuzzi case. The tattler went on and deceptively suggested Charlene knew where the offender disposed of Joan's body. Burke's book revealed Trooper Andrew Palombo handed SA Steve Broce the picture to find the compelled witness that got on the stand and said Paradiso chopped up bodies before weighing them down in the ocean. That is not where Joan was, nor did Charlene have Joan's jewelry. It's a crime to lie to Federal authorities, but in Boston's corrupt system that seemed to be routine.

The thick file contained something else, reports of the extortion incident I remembered, but could not find until then. My brother dialed the phone while I listened. The implication was clear that I was delusional and needed help. My brother asked Steve about the extortion incident that was never publicly reported after reading the reports for himself. There was not a damn thing wrong with my memory. Denial slipped off Steve's tongue with ease.

"Honest to God, I don't recall anything like that," Steve pretended.

Honest to God nothing, I thought. Steve probably ducked to avoid lightning bolts bursting from the heavens. How could anyone forget such a traumatic event in the search for his sister? The FBI wired his dad in a car that crossed state lines with known felon Harvey Martel—but Steve "forgot" it. Repeating the incident sounded crazy without records to back it up. The family circulated the image I was out of my mind, but of course, I had found a letter that shattered the family image.

"You can't make copies of crazy and put it in a safe," I protested in an unopened e-mail to Steve. "You can't corroborate delusions in FBI files."

The postman knocked on my door, and dropped the thick envelope on my doorstep. The Glen Ridge, New Jersey police, in the Websters' hometown, finally answered my FOIA request. The department carefully documented everything learned through their office, a lot of detail to sift through, so I settled in for another sleepless night of reading. If I did not know the files were about Joan, I would have thought I was examining a whole other case. Only an occasional reference to the authorities in Boston brought me back to the concoction circulated in the tabloids speculating Joan's fate. There it was again, another copy of crazy. The New Jersey detectives corroborated my so-called delusions, too. This time there were no redactions to obscure names of the participants in the extortion drama that Steve couldn't seem to remember.

My phone rang. Retired Det. Paul Grant from the Hamilton Police Department, a dedicated enforcer, was on the other end of the line. He told me the shocking condition of Joan's remains on July 16,

2009. My limbs went numb; I had the same gut-wrenching sensation when I found the incriminating letter my daughter had written. Again, reality brought on dry heaves, and I collapsed into bed for two days. I realized that George and Eleanor had to know the condition of Dib's remains, but had turned their back on the truth for their daughter.

"Do you remember a composite?" I asked Grant.

"I remember something about long hair," he recalled.

Grant and I exchanged a few e-mails before reticent players discovered a hole in their dyke. My source went silent without explanation, and presumably, someone with influence abruptly plugged up the leak. Who was running the operation to shut me up, and what were they saying?

Intimidation, rumors, and smears were not going to silence my questions. The postings online had stirred unrest in the ranks. The Websters safeguarded the story and supported Burke's unworkable theory. New scrutiny had put different players under the microscope, and the inspection hit nerves. A new participant to the online group defensively added to the discussion. The observer had followed considerations for more than a year, and concurred that some things brought out actually made sense. Names on sworn documents raised concerns about misconduct during the investigation, but people held certain images of the individuals involved.

"I've reached out to Dave Moran. I'll let you know what he says," the woman wrote.

Soon after, however, her attacks became personal. Moran was an attorney in Salem well connected to the Massachusetts State Police, and in the same town with the tightly knit circle of the DA's office that maintained Joan's files. Shortly after the branch to help was extended, I was threatened with lawsuits for examining the unresolved murder of my sister-in-law, a scrutiny that cast authorities in a questionable light. Again, unsubstantiated gossip swirled from the town of the seventeenth-century witch hunts.

"You have no idea what I actually know about this case, as well as events surrounding abuse allegations," the official's daughter implied.

The question was, who was telling this woman stories. The root of the defensive individual's charges about me grew from the Webster family's destructive portrayals of me after I lawfully reported my daughter's allegations. The comments did not address the documents relevant in Joan's case; the motive for personal attacks stemmed from something else. It was not that hard to follow the most logical trail. The DA's office affirmed they had spoken to George and

Eleanor Webster, and the DA and Massachusetts State Police were the probable sources for Dave Moran to inquire about Joan's case.

"You really shouldn't believe everything you read," the angered poster deflected.

The answer was really quite simple to anyone with a lick of common sense. If you cannot discuss the issues raised by the documents, then discredit the person bringing it out. Shoot the messenger. Controlling forces swept legitimate questions about the professional conduct of authorities involved in Joan's search under the rug again.

Heavy steel bars closed behind me. The private investigator and I went through the maze of security at Shirley MCI on October 9, 2010, and came face to face with the known killer. The man, the metal, and the armed guards watching the room heightened my senses, and my nerves tensed; it was a daunting encounter. Robert Bond strolled through the crowded visiting room and sat down in the private cubicle where we waited. His shaved head glistened under the light, and his glass eye drifted as we sat in the small room. His one good eye remained fixed on his unexpected guests; it was obvious he did not trust us.

Bond stuck with the same basic story that Paradiso had confessed that he murdered Joan Webster. "The cops knew nothing about Paradiso before I told them," he mistakenly boasted.

The authorities sent Paradiso's prints in to compare with Joan's case a month before guards situated Bond close to the target. Despite the man's ill-informed claim that he was the source guiding police, the informant unwittingly made disclosures that raised the red flag higher. He had told the private detective that the "Man from New Jersey" had sent people to see him. George's liaisons were Sgt. Carmen Tammaro, Trooper Andrew Palombo, and ADA Tim Burke. Bond told us Tony Pisa saw his notes, and Palombo swore in warrants to the court that Bond's notes were in his possession. Bond also alleged Palombo corresponded with him until the time Mother Nature helped unearth Joan's remains. According to the state's star witness, the bearded, undercover cop told him not to change his story. The pretense of surgery was the height of the officials' misconduct. An attempt to plant the rat next to Paradiso's deathbed just before Burke's book rolled off the presses made me sick to my stomach.

The next day I drove down to New Haven hoping to connect with my daughter. The school directory listed an address, but when I got there another name was on the placard. She would not answer her phone, and no one answered the door. Like Jean Day, my youngest child had gone into hiding.

I addressed my e-mail to Steve and copied it to George and Eleanor.

"The investigator has learned a great deal more concerning the informant, Robert Bond. Bond's recent input has been almost shocking," I sincerely extended. "A sad piece of news, the garden dedicated to Joan outside Gund Hall is no longer there."

Every correspondence extended an opportunity to speak with the family about what I had uncovered, but the family never responded. The hardened criminal I had just met with was more credible in their eyes than the mother of their grandchildren who had lived through this tragedy with them. Instead, George forwarded the e-mail to Cyveillance, an Internet surveillance company in Washington DC. The company's Chief Executive Officer, Stephen Cambone, is a former Under-Secretary of Defense for Intelligence under President George W. Bush and a kindred professional to the Websters' own CIA background. The company, however, touts government and corporate clients in their surveillance activities, not individuals, so George had to have used his influence and connections. Researching the company uncovered reports about the firm's dodgy methods of Internet spying. My God, was the family spying on me? Was I some threat to national security? All they had to do was accept the invitation to sit down and talk in a proper setting. If the family had some intelligent reason to believe the con, I was eager to hear it. However, I was coping with a different mindset—once a spy always a spy.

Instead of looking for truthful answers, someone submitted a new tribute to Joan. In 2009, a stone engraved with Joan's name was added to the Garden of Peace in Boston, a serene park-like setting in memory of the city's murder victims. The organization posted a dedication online that hit a familiar chord.

"While her case has never been prosecuted because of scanty witness information, her family believes the murderer was convicted in another murder case."

The family, or someone on their behalf, reinforced their conviction that Paradiso was guilty of murdering Joan. The closing remarks were almost word for word the same piece Eleanor had written years before and submitted to the Parents of Murdered Children. The boat theory was the family's explanation, and they were sticking to it. Something interesting posted in the memorial caught my notice, too—I had the family's attention. The photograph of Joan used in the homage was one of mine from my wedding. The picture taken by a member of my family was not something they had access to until the picture appeared on discussion boards discussing Joan's case. Eleanor was not very technically savvy, but Anne was, and so were my children. The family clearly followed things online that refuted their theory of Joan's death.

The December night was cold and quiet as I walked to the door. The calendar page had turned to Christmas Eve. Only a couple of months had passed since my Bond update had unsettled George. I banged the doorknocker three times and listened to the panicked inhabitants behind the portal. I carried two small books for my girls filled with family quotes. George sipped his Scotch in the green leather chair by the bookcase when they heard me at the door, and they hurriedly stumbled to get out of sight. The girls followed the example of their elder and frantically rushed for refuge in the basement before Steve opened the door. The family trembled as if the ghost of Christmas past had come to visit. Any spirit of the season quickly drained from Steve's face as he warily challenged my presence.

"What are you doing here?" he skeptically asked.

Any seasonal gesture had to filter through him to reach my adult children. He stood paranoid and defiant behind the cracked door, and protected the girls from a mother bearing holiday gifts. When I lived there, the door was always opened warmly to share the joy of the season. Now, Steve turned out the lights and left me standing on the stoop in the dark—holding presents.

"This office, in cooperation with other law-enforcement agencies, has renewed the investigation into Ms. Webster's murder." The Essex County DA's office denied access to Joan's files again. "Such materials implicate the core policies behind the shielding of investigatory materials, namely, 'the encouragement of individual citizens to come forward and speak freely with police concerning matters under investigation.'"

"I would like to schedule a meeting to discuss the Joan Webster murder case handled by your office." My e-mail was directed to First Assistant John Dawley.

"Thanks for the offer," he condescendingly replied. "I have several thousand pages of documents."

Dawley wanted copies of the documents before he would schedule a date, but I insisted on a meeting face to face. After several exchanges, he finally agreed to a discussion on May 20, 2010. Wheels touched down in Boston again to discuss the unresolved murder of my sister-in-law. Officials listened to one discarded Webster asking questions about the tragic case of another. My private investigator sat by my side with three Massachusetts State Troopers across the large conference room table. I unzipped the portfolio with a large selection of records the detective had helped me recover; documents refuted assertions in Tim Burke's published book. It took only a few minutes to list some of Burke's erroneous statements in an open case out of their office, but the demeanor that came across was, "So what?"

"Is there a pair of shoes listed among Joan's recovered belongings?" I asked the question knowing Burke had placed the item in the possession of the Massachusetts State Police. The item was not in her suitcase as their colleague claimed, but an item that could only have been in the tote bag, the item never recovered.

"I don't recall," the custodian of Joan's records avoided. "I would have to look."

"Trooper Palombo was apparently acting as a source to the FBI," I remarked with the confidential source's false representations in my packet.

"It's not unusual for a trooper to work with the agency," Det. Lt. Norman Zuk dismissed.

"Giving false information?" I redirected. "There was no missing jewelry in the Iannuzzi case."

The private detective reinforced that the recovered documents raised serious questions about Trooper Palombo's involvement in the Joan Webster investigation. Under the circumstances, it was a fair concern to inquire about the officer's death. He was in his hometown when an unusual accident occurred in 1998.

"That is irresponsible coming from you, sir," Zuk admonished the sleuth. "You have a license."

These authorities evidently did not want this case stirred up, but they went on to affirm their inadequacy to resolve the twenty-nine-year-old case. Dawley acknowledged they did not know Joan's parents, but had only spoken to them over the phone. The custodians also admitted they knew nothing about the extortion call that played out in real life, not some melodrama acted on a big screen. They passed one of the reports around the room for each of the experienced public servants to study.

"My daughter made allegations of serious abuse against Joan's brother," I continued while pulling her gut-wrenching letter from my folder for them to read.

The conference room was dead silent for a few moments; the state's reinforcements had no comment regarding the assorted pages they had just skimmed. The representation the case was being reviewed was completely disingenuous; they failed to ask for copies of records to include in their obviously deficient files. You do not need to be Sherlock Holmes to figure out if you are trying to solve a case you need as much information as possible, and they weren't interested.

"Have your children been threatened?" Det. Lt. Zuk asked.

"I don't know, detective," I did not hesitate to answer. "The family has a reason to malign me."

I did not know precisely what the family told my children. The girls felt threatened if I spoke out about events in the family, or invaded privacy as the Websters defined it. The family aggressively and severely alienated my children from me. The bottom line was this group of experienced detectives had just seen my daughter's letter to God, and in my mind that constituted a real threat to my children's well-being.

"Have you examined the Marie Iannuzzi case?" I asked about the case inextricably entangled with Joan's. The 1979 murder involved the same suspect, and the same core group handled both probes.

"That was in Suffolk County," Dawley deflected. "You'll have to speak with them."

ADA John Dawley adjusted his glasses, then proceeded to administer the state's brand of justice to discredit a witness. "When were you divorced, Ms. Carson?"

Presumption and dismissal were the same tactics used to demean Candy Weyant when Burke had to eliminate obstacles to his theory. Apparently, in Dawley's mind, the fact Steve Webster's ex-wife brought things forward nullified what was in the actual records. In truth, a member of Joan's immediate family raised an alert about a family that irrationally went along with a bogus story, and a mother who had evidence of possible abuse.

"My marital status doesn't change what's in these records," I replied.

"Are you going to suggest George Webster was responsible for the crime?" the delegated defender flippantly asked.

The notion of accusing my former father-in-law in a subtlety hostile room that was not interested in gathering the facts was not a trap I wanted to step into. Maybe there was something in their records that implicated him in the crime, or maybe there wasn't. However, they were not about ready to let me look. The indisputable trail in recovered documents exposed the misconduct of authorities that threw the case off the track.

"It could have been vindictive. George's division at ITT was in serious trouble in the years leading up to Joan's disappearance," I responded. "What I will suggest is the motive has something to do with George and Eleanor's secrets, and had nothing to do with Joan."

The two leading forces that should have wanted the answers were the Commonwealth and the parents. Instead, they both were the obstacles I encountered. Dave, the online poster, was right. The wagons had circled to protect their own and completely ignore the state's obligation to the victim, or public safety. Shame handed the mantle to the next generation of colleagues covering up the misdeeds of the people before them. It is a reasonable conclusion the state's disgrace saddled the next generation professionally, just as Webster secrets burdened my children.

An update was on its way to George Webster's inbox. The informant he relied on was coming up for parole. Eleanor was on her deathbed, but George opened the correspondence several times during his vigilance. Eleanor died on June 15, 2010, and faced her Maker. Her obituary described George and Eleanor's roots in the CIA where they met. Thinking back, they were proud of their allegiance, so it was confusing why Steve dodged the question during the contempt hearing a couple of years before. The e-mail unsettled George during his moment of grief; he forwarded the news to Joan's sister, Anne, in Phoenix. She had assumed Eleanor's job to block any discomfort and keep her daddy happy.

I opened another private e-mail address when George blocked previous communications. Two e-mail addresses, created exclusively to inform the Websters, openly announced updates about their daughter's unresolved case. In my way of thinking, it would have been terribly abusive and vindictive not to share things I had learned, though it was painful. The requests were simple; I wanted to discuss the discrepancies in recovered documents regarding Joan's case and give my children information about Robert Bond. What happened next exposed the family's John Mulholland secretive hand in obstructing the truth in Joan's case. It is hard to describe to a regular person what it has been like dealing with spies.

On July 12, and July 16, 2010, 13 subscriptions glutted my two private inboxes. The insinuations were similar to the anonymous letter hand delivered a year before. The harassment was a caution to mind my own business. It eliminated any question about who was behind the mysterious letter dropped in my mailbox. Steve was the only one in town to initiate that little message, and it was consistent with the latest warning. A government maintained list included the originating IP address of the covert offender playing head games. Every digit and dot matched with the Bond update that George had forwarded. Further digging traced the IP address to a company computer at Syntellect in Phoenix, AZ—Anne's employer.

"Eve 'Paranoid' Carson," the secretive bully filled in the blanks.

I did not know anyone else who worked there, and no one knew me except Anne. My middle name is Elizabeth; it is a middle name Anne and I shared in common. New technology replaced Eleanor's clipped articles in the mail, but the methods were the same. This time I caught them red-handed.

Word was spreading about Joan's case. I would not stop talking and raising the questions that needed to be asked. It hit more nerves.

"Did you think we would not look into this?" Dawn fumed. "Wow, the sick things we found out about you. You were exposed as a thrown away member of the Webster family."

The eerie comparison escaped the angered woman's mental capacity to see the similarity. The Websters didn't discuss their problems, they got rid of them. Another member of the Webster family was discarded in a black plastic trash bag miles from the suggested crime scene. Bond's statement was undeniably false in Joan's case, but his statements also included Marie Iannuzzi's murder.

It was not clear who David Doyle's defensive wife had talked to, but he had a special inside track with the cops during the Iannuzzi trial. She went on to charge that I had made false allegations against my ex-husband. Her information was wrong; my child wrote the letter to God handed to ADA John Dawley and the three Massachusetts State Police officers seated at the table in Salem. Was there a witch hunt spreading from Salem? Undeniably, false rumors were swirling to discredit my input. Someone twisted confidential information disclosed to authorities in an open murder case. Then someone spewed destructive gossip to a family facing consequences if the truth in the documents reopened the Iannuzzi case. The real records revealed the Iannuzzi case was a sham, and the same players pressed on to go after the state's predetermined suspect for Joan. Exposing a wrongful conviction might put Doyle back in the hot seat for the death of his girlfriend. The man had a lengthy police rap sheet and known violent behavior. Authorities reasonably suspected Doyle in a murder case. Who put a target on my back in unsavory circles? Officials delegated with the responsibility of public safety were the ones with the information.

It was a chilly and damp spring day in New England as I pulled my rental car to a stop along Chebacco Road. The calendar had turned winter away and thawed the cold ground in the desolate graveyard. Birds chirped gleefully among the branches collecting their twigs for the season's nest. Mud squished beneath my feet as I traipsed through the wooded retreat following the very path of Joan's killer. Twenty-one years to the day that Joan surfaced, I stood in silence on her hidden grave. Wind rustled through the dense branches, a spirit's whispered warning about what happened here. I shivered and wiped away a few tears. The Almighty had given Joan back to tell us what happened. My prayers were lifted to God, once again, in that solemn place, but there were still too many guarding the secrets.

The next day, I walked into the Massachusetts Parole Board Office in Nattick with a prepared statement to oppose Robert Bond's release. The board knew I was coming and had advance copies of documents exposing the deceit of the man sitting before them. Board Chairman Josh Wall walked into the lobby and announced his decision to suppress a properly certified witness at an open hearing.

"Are you Ms. Carson?" he asked with his cell phone still plugged in his ear. "Oh, I see the book, so of course you are."

Following the obvious trail was elementary, but not reassuring to the cause of justice. When my packet arrived for the board, the logical place to inquire about Joan Webster's case was the Essex County DA's office of Jonathan Blodgett. Prior to his appointment to the parole board, Wall was the first ADA in Suffolk County where his predecessors had praised the inmate under review as a credible witness. His former counterpart in Essex County was ADA John Dawley, custodian of Joan's case, and Dawley had affirmed talking to George Webster.

The photographer moved around the room to shoot every angle as the con made his plea for release. Laura Crimaldi from the *Boston Herald* scribbled her notes to report to the city how the newly appointed board defended the city from the monster that wanted out. Coincidentally, Crimaldi wrote a piece when Tim Burke released his book. His published account trumpeted Bond's moral code to come forward for the Commonwealth. The latest edition of the paper accurately reported the board's scathing review, but neglected the felon's involvement in Joan's case completely. Some puppeteer pulled strings, telling the press to forget it and disconnect Bond from his complicity with the state. The board's scalding opinion was in stark contrast to the authorities that held up the con as a man to believe. The wagons circled—Joan's justice denied.

"It costs so much to be a full human being." Those were the words posted on Joan's dorm wall before she died. She lived up to them, but it was crystal clear there were too many others in Massachusetts who did not.

An extraordinary confluence of events brought together skilled storytellers that influenced perceptions. The resources merged to "resolve" Joan's case were astounding, and each group had a particular set of skills. The passage of time uncovered problems; the bared corruption was a missing ingredient necessary to unravel the lingering mystery. The Suffolk County office of DA Newman Flanagan, exposed for secret and duplicate files, influenced Burke during the years he pursued Leonard Paradiso. Relentless pursuit of a ruthless mobster unveiled corruption in the Boston office of the FBI, a department that shielded criminal informants when Joan disappeared. ITT knew the power of the press to spread propaganda. George's division got in bed with the CIA to undermine a foreign government with disastrous results, and fell under the Senate's scrutiny. The intelligence mentality of Joan's parents influenced the direction the investigation took, but no one understood their thinking. The best the collective team could concoct was an impossible crime on a boat that did not exist. It is their story, and they are sticking to it.

"There is no crueler tyranny than that which is exercised under cover of law, and with the colors of justice." - *U.S. v. Jannotti*, 673 F.2d 578, 614 (3d Cir. 1982).

Society is vulnerable to the powerful few who can pick someone out for unjust persecution. Tyranny in the system effectively covered the tracks for numerous crimes and denied a voice for victims left in the wake. The controlling factions supplanted a scapegoat in our minds to divert a legitimate search for Joan Webster and the monster that killed her. Misprision deceived decent people to look the other way, and fall prey to the malice of disconnected and amoral pretenders left in our midst.

CHAPTER 24

Persons of Interest

The bass of the girls' stereo vibrated through the walls of the house. I had retreated to my bedroom to put a few things away and get ready for bed. Compared to most days, this one had been relatively free of strife, except for the conflicts in the nightly news on the television. The girls stealthily slipped into my space to unsettle the calm, which for once, I thought, was ending my day. In moments, they surrounded me and angrily spewed verbal assaults. Irrational hatred infected their reasoning, and they tormented me relentlessly.

When I was a kid, I was taught not to speak to my parents that way and strictly corrected when I lost my tongue. Anger distorted the girls' thinking, not a good time to talk, and it was better to move away from the badgering until cooler heads prevailed. My first exit strategy was to leave the room through the door, but the girls quickly rushed to block my path. I turned around and moved toward the bathroom door to retreat. However, the girls moved faster and barred an escape from the hostility they brought into the room. I reached for the handle to the closet, but my daughters slipped between their quarry and any portal to freedom again. The only option I had left was to see whether there was a path through the window to a quieter location away from the unrelenting harassment. My youngest looked scared as she pulled me away from the window, but I was not irrational or about to hurt myself. The girls were respectfully asked to retreat and leave me in peace repeatedly.

Steve locked the door to the guest bedroom and cranked the volume on his sound machine to drown out the commotion. Steve had taken up sleeping across the hall in his haste to escape our marital bed, even though I had not banished him to another room. I leaned against the bureau in defeat, the girls staring me down, and cried for some help.

"STEVE! STEVE!" I pleaded.

The girls had committed to do whatever their dad asked and ignore me. They marched to his orders to leave the room. Steve's part was to play the hero protecting me and shield the John Mulholland dirty tricks going on under the radar. I collapsed into bed alone, crying silently into my pillow.

The girls' laced their counseling sessions with accusations of the mental trauma I supposedly inflicted and outrageous behavior that scared them. The dictate laid down was that they would not speak to the counselor if the counselor spoke to me. It was not even my word against theirs for the image they created; it was their portrayal and nothing else, like the presumptions ordained by elder members of the Webster family.

"You were in the master bedroom of our house, and something, I don't remember what, upset you," my youngest child represented to the court. "It's a second-story window, and right below it is concrete. I went over there and grabbed your shirt and pulled you back."

"We talked about this, how you tried to escape from a window," the girls' counselor, Sarah O'Brien, presumptively pronounced. "That was very traumatic for her. She felt like it was her responsibility to keep you alive sometimes."

Thank God, the net nanny caught the reality of the "trauma" they described.

"Y me? Y me?" the girls ridiculed my anguish. "STEVE! STEVE!"

"Hahahaa! Oh, that was a good time—she was so humiliated."

"As she should be, because she sounded like cattle—dying."

"Haha!"

"That was actually one of the best moments I've ever had with her! I was crack! -ing up!"

"She's such a bitch."

"What started the STEVE! thing?"

"All those times she would scream in the middle of the night we were 'badgering' her."

"Yeah, but there was one time when it was really bad, and I can't remember what we did."

"It was the time she climbed out the window," my youngest daughter mocked. "All we did was we wouldn't let her leave the room."

My own family framed me.

"You were forced out of this family for a reason," my oldest daughter e-mailed without explanation. "You are the real tragedy of the Webster family."

The influence over my children was well hidden from people's view. Occasional pangs of conscience troubled my children over what had happened, but they could not face me to say why. I had been vilified in the minds of my terrified children, who then acted out like the Websters' own little Manchurian candidates. They were not capable of the psychological warfare on their own any more than they could bend the steel shaft of the car key.

"I'm such a bitch to Eve sometimes. I wonder if it's been me all along," my loving baby somberly confided to her friend Ben.

"We probably won't ever be able to sit down and talk this through." My firstborn's inner beauty was shining through all the chaotic pain in her heartfelt apology. "I cannot justify the hurtful things I said and did, the lies, the sneakiness, and any other wrong I may have forgotten about. But I can try to improve myself now so I never hurt someone again the way I hurt you."

It took years to get the input the family desperately had needed to set our course on a healing path. It was not until Ari Gleckman took an oath to tell the truth and explained my youngest child's seemingly irrational trepidation.

"When she normally would bring that up [Aunt Joan's murder]," Gleckman said identifying a source of her fear, "it was out of concern that there might one day be a publication or legal matter that she could be drawn into, or forced if you will, to interact with her mom."

Why was my child afraid of talking about Joan's case?

The dog days were brutally hot, and bottle rockets flared into the night sky. My room was dark except for the dim light from my computer, the lifeline that had opened doors into Joan's investigation. The only sounds that broke into my solace were the loud bangs of the firecrackers revelers set off to celebrate the upcoming Independence Day and the occasional siren that rushed down the street. As I stared at the haunting image on my monitor, the noises outside transported my thoughts back to the bloody battles on Boston's streets when Joan disappeared. I flinched with every crack of the explosive powders.

Police logged the template numbers in the New Jersey reports that I had obtained, and I had waited anxiously to see whether I knew who it was. Two professionals independently reconstructed the image, and the bearded man now stared back at me from the screen. A cabbie believed he saw this man leaving the airport with my sister-in-law on November 28, 1981. The numbing thought, I was looking at the face of someone who knew what happened to Joan, paralyzed the limbs dangling uselessly at my side. The penetrating eyes frightened me to the core and left my hair standing on end, but I could not turn away. I shook uncontrollably and felt a cramping nausea settle into my stomach. The morning light broke through the window to snap me out of the trance, and I laid down in a futile effort to get some sleep.

Who was this man? The image was definitely not Leonard Paradiso in any stretch of the imagination. The New Jersey report contained one clue to the identity; the man's hair was less frizzy than depicted. I did not have the report that interrogators took from the eyewitness with added details, modifications, or any other hint to the monster's identity. The second clue came from retired Det. Paul Grant who remembered long hair. The final piece I had was the fact this bearded man was at the airport.

Authorities had suppressed the composite, and Sgt. Tammaro had coordinated the efforts among the various departments and agencies, according to some early accounts. The picture was never published in the paper or broadcast on television, as someone would reasonably expect when you're searching for a missing person. The individual in the drawing possibly gained Joan's confidence and discreetly whisked her away from Logan Airport. The authorities' negligence to follow up the lead was upsetting and baffling enough, but something else troubled me even more. Det. Richard Corcoran on the New Jersey force had reconstructed the likeness from template numbers provided by Lt. Larry Murphy of the Harvard Police. He hand delivered it to Eleanor Webster. The parents who broadcast desperate entreaties to find their daughter kept this clue secreted in their files.

An uncanny exchange took place the day New Jersey enforcers received the call from Massachusetts about the composite. Bizarre coincidences surfaced throughout the records. The obsessed prosecutor conveniently produced a replica .357 magnum that meticulous diving teams missed. The Suffolk County DA's office miraculously supplied the Feds with a fake boat license, instrumental for the bankruptcy case that addressed Burke's alleged crime scene. The lead cop befriended the most logical suspect in the Iannuzzi case—the boyfriend. Police arrested Doyle in Newark with a pair of panties in a brown paper bag and car keys. ITT security in New Jersey scheduled a strategy meeting with the local police on the same day guards transferred Bond to the Charles Street Jail. Finding another strange coincidence in the reports was more than too many flukes to happen by chance. George's corporate connection clouded the issues each time there was information witnesses saw Joan; McEwen diluted the importance of the composite—the bearded man avoided detection.

Lt. Murphy from the Harvard Campus Police left a message for Sgt. Tom Dugan at 10:10 a.m. on December 21, 1981, but the sergeant was not in when the call came. Within the hour, Sgt. Dugan took a call from Jack McEwen, the head of ITT security. Departments kept George and Eleanor abreast of every development, so it made sense that authorities would notify the parents when officers forwarded a composite for them to see. The call came in at eleven a.m. on Monday morning.

"Detective, this is Jack McEwen," George's close confidant began.

"Yes, Jack. What are the latest developments in the case?" Dugan replied as he poised his pen to jot down the notes.

"ITT may be offering a very substantial reward this week up in Boston," Jack announced. "We hope it will bring in some concrete leads."

Then the head of ITT security, a resource at George's beck and call, just happened to bring up the same subject as the previous caller.

"Oh, and I may try to put together a drawing," he continued. "We've been working with some psychics. One of them has given us a description of a suspect."

Twenty minutes later, Dugan received the composite template numbers from Lt. Murphy in Cambridge for the man they believed left the airport with Joan. In the first few days of Joan's disappearance, McEwen raised a red flag that squelched reports in the Newark paper. The story said observers saw Joan talking to a man behind a counter at Logan. What a coincidence for McEwen to suggest another composite to muddy the waters, produced from a psychic's image, at the same time law-enforcement officials constructed a composite from a witness description.

The lead reported in the *Boston Globe* on January 19, 1981, affirmed that a cabbie at Logan provided police with details to construct the composite. Lt. Larry Murphy was one of the officers quoted in the article that day, but the lead quickly disappeared from any further articles. Those in control silenced crucial information that witnesses noticed Joan with someone at Logan. Instead, George's inner circle stirred confusion that undermined a legitimate clue.

Every night I stared at the cold eyes in the picture, though I knew it would give me nightmares. I dug and dug through the records and scoured the photographs I had collected. There it was.

"Oh, dear God," I cried into my trembling hands. My fingers reflexively covered my mouth like Rosemarie Doyle—horrified when reality set in. "Now it all makes sense."

I put the two images side by side and forwarded them to my boss for his opinion. Formerly, he was a recognized private investigator. The two added details, long and less frizzy hair, fit the description of the man captured in the snapshot. My boss had no idea who was pictured. I wanted his frank and unbiased impression of the comparison to the composite of the bearded man a cabbie believed left the airport with Joan.

"Same guy. Too close," my experienced boss thought. "Based on that, he should have been picked up and questioned."

The chance of that was slim to none, especially if the drawing was of the man I suspected. The recovered picture bore an uncanny resemblance to the face put together from the taxi driver's description. The same pattern of a receding hairline, the nose, the mouth, and the full beard were too close; the man in the photograph could not be crossed off the list of suspects. All the confusion and tangents that diverted Joan's investigation now fell logically into place if the composite depicted Trooper Andrew Palombo.

The missing student rested in a remote forest not far from the bearded trooper's address while he aggressively promoted the tale that Paradiso dumped her in the harbor. Palombo lived at 247 Lynn St. in Peabody, Massachusetts at the time Joan disappeared. His house was just enough west of the blaze, that scorched the neighboring town of Lynn that night, to avoid the roadblocks and travel north. The address was two blocks from the onramp to Route 129 and just minutes from exit 16 that led to Chebacco Road in Hamilton. The secluded gravesite was in an area known for criminal activity, information law enforcement would know. After searchers recovered the skeleton, the hulking undercover cop simply smiled and passed questions to somebody else.

The undercover cop worked at Logan, the last place anyone saw Joan alive. Palombo's skills to gain a confidence and give young women a ride became evident when he followed his targeted suspect's daughter and her friend at the airport in 1982. The calculated maneuver coincided with Bond's shift to the Charles Street Jail to stand trial for his second murder.

Joan's purse and wallet were the first clues discovered in the fractured pursuit to find her. Someone avoiding detection tossed the belongings in the Saugus marshes along Route 107, the Lynn Marsh Road. The boggy area was familiar turf for the lead investigator on the Marie Iannuzzi case, but passing the known dumping ground was also a logical direction for the cop's daily commute to work at Logan Airport.

News articles reported the Massachusetts State Police found Joan's suitcase at the Greyhound station in Boston's Park Square for years. Articles quoted Palombo's destructive and unsubstantiated gossip suggesting Lenny hung out at the terminal. That is what I believed, but then Burke published the suitcase was recovered in New York; he detailed the discovery down to the hour in his confounding explanation.

"Police were able to determine that Joan's suitcase had been placed in a thirty-day storage container at the Boston bus terminal," Burke published in *The Paradiso Files*, "sometime between Joan's arrival at 10:35 p.m. on November 28 and 9:00 a.m. the following morning."

As far as I could determine, the only way someone would know that was if they put it there themselves or saw someone do it. There were other possible explanations for the suitcase showing up in New York City, but they did not follow the core team's premise that Paradiso was the culprit that murdered Joan Webster. A stealth assailant could have quietly departed the city that night on a bus, or someone could have put the bag in the luggage hold to make the trip unattended. Did authorities stage the discovery in Boston to throw off the investigation? They misrepresented other evidence, and it makes sense the boys fabricated the Boston locker, too—they controlled the media. The fact was, there was undercover activity at the Park Square station that connected the Massachusetts State Police to the terminal, not Paradiso. Lynda Walsh got a ride from a helpful, incognito, public servant.

Palombo represented an out-of-print coffee table book as one of Joan's textbooks. The seasoned officer distorted Candy's common, red silk jewelry pouch as the bag where Joan kept her pearls. Tim Burke misled Federal officials that the camera captured Charlene Bullerwell wearing Joan's jewelry, and the "confidential source" said the pressured witness knew where the presumed assailant discarded Joan's body. A battalion of enforcers confiscated the wrong brand of marine equipment, but the concealed fact perverted impressions and manufactured an assumption of guilt. The core group secreted the negative results on the recovered boat, and sworn warrants and statements to the court misrepresented their findings. The Suffolk County DA's office produced a fake identification for the Federal charges Burke instigated to address a nonexistent crime scene. Guards roughed up Paradiso to go after a splinter and warp an injury that did not match the mangled elucidation of Joan's slaughter. Disinformation is rule number one in any covert intelligence operation.

The whole time authorities tainted the evidence, Tim Burke claimed the Massachusetts State Police had a gray pair of shoes in their possession. The counselor fallaciously boasted that Joan packed her shoes in the suitcase, but that was not the case. The ill-fated student probably carried them in her tote bag as reported—the Massachusetts State Police never recovered that piece of luggage. According to the puppet prosecutor with privileged access to files, the Massachusetts State Police possessed an item that connected them to Joan Webster after she landed at Logan. Piece by piece the puzzle was finally coming together.

Burke manipulated another case in his obsession to pin the crime on Paradiso, and Trooper Palombo just happened to be in charge of that investigation, too. He knew Paradiso and could exploit the man's vulnerabilities; the parolee was susceptible to accusations. Sgt. Tammaro, Palombo's superior, knew him as well; they grew up together in the North End with Patty Bono. Bono makes an anonymous call and drops the dime on Paradiso to the Websters in January 1982, just a few weeks into the search for their missing daughter. After that call, the central figures decided that Paradiso was guilty of an impossible crime. Two cases, insurance fraud and bankruptcy fraud, both tried in Rhode Island, revealed that the *Malafemmena* did not exist when Joan Webster disappeared from Logan Airport. The authorities promoted the boat as the gruesome crime scene where she lost her life. The core group concealed the facts based solely on the false statement of convicted murderer Robert Bond. You simply cannot murder someone on a boat that did not exist at the time, but I am the person labeled crazy.

The way the operation played out was incredible. Middlesex County kept dredging ponds in search of the Zodiac killer, and New Jersey officials trailed extortion callers claiming Joan was alive. Under the radar, Newman Flanagan's Suffolk County office set their course to go after the Websters' suspect in one of Essex County's cold cases. They paired Tim Burke and Trooper Palombo to nail Paradiso for Marie Iannuzzi's murder, ignoring every fact in the files. Feigning objectivity, Burke stated that a John Doe grand jury convened on March 5, 1982, to distinguish which of two suspects killed Marie Iannuzzi, but the counselor lied. The first session for cause number 038655 began as the *Commonwealth v. Leonard J. Paradiso* and deceptively changed the next time jurors heard one-sided testimony. Days after the March grand jury, a trooper cast dispersions to Paradiso's parole officer, implicating him in another crime—the disappearance of Joan Webster.

Trooper Palombo had a questionable relationship with Marie Iannuzzi's boyfriend and met with him twenty to thirty times for undocumented meetings. Some higher authority usurped the officers in charge and curiously assigned the covert enforcer to the case. Doyle told the officer what he heard on the streets. Shifted responsibility in a murder case to an undercover cop that worked with informants was troubling in an environment where players protected unsavory sorts, and David Doyle was a prime suspect for the crime. The circumstantial evidence was overwhelming, but Essex County inexplicably failed to indict him.

The Logan detectives usefully introduced a snitch just when they needed someone to solidify the story. The rat corroborated a documented meeting between Paradiso and Sgt. Carmen Tammaro on August 1, 1982, in his statement. The written account of that meeting identified "Buster" as the source of the boat story when he prodded Paradiso for a confession in Joan's case. The sensational story surfaced four months later when Tammaro led a caged criminal through the maze of two murders. Trooper Palombo, the lead investigator on both cases, sat in the room when his superior arranged to get a letter from Bond. Then the Websters' designated hitters lied. Burke proclaimed to the public and the court that he received an unsolicited letter on January 5, 1982, and set up the meetings that followed. Burke deceitfully had the cart before the horse. The false statement wasn't mailed until the tenth, the day Bond was sentenced for his second murder, and he relied on promises dangled by the authorities. The core team withheld facts that contradicted Bond's tale of two murders at the time, but the court sealed the document, preventing an objective review.

However, the contrived correspondence did contain a morsel of truth. Badges manipulated their conduit to spread the state's story; Bond offered a choice for the manner of Joan's death. The Massachusetts State Police produced the letter, after they reviewed it with Bond, which picked the correct manner of Joan's death from Bond's multiple choice. My jaw clenched reading the exacting details, in an otherwise false statement, and developed seven years before Joan's soul whispered from Chebacco Road. The reasonable conclusion is someone in the chilled room at the courthouse knew how Joan died. The list was short and included the obsessed, bearded investigator from Logan leading the charge against a marked man.

Palombo turned up everywhere to influence Paradiso's guilt for numerous crimes, though the facts in the files pointed elsewhere. Witnesses all took their turns talking to the undercover cop. Interviews miraculously restored vivid memory after the experienced enforcer took each one into his confidence, and testimony changed. Recovered documents unmasked the heavy hand of officials to get the stories they wanted; law enforcement threatened prosecutions and pressured witnesses to give false testimony during the Iannuzzi trial against Paradiso. The pattern was obvious in the state's persecution of the targeted scapegoat and his girlfriend, Candy Weyant. In addition, participants threatened terrified mothers that they would never see their children again—a fate the Websters cruelly executed against me.

Burke identified his paired partner as the confidential source to the corrupt FBI office in Boston that protected criminal informants. Burke's published admission revealed that Trooper Palombo was the source that leaked disinformation to the Feds. Dave Moran uncovered the informant too, recording Palombo as the source to find the sunken boat. SA Broce pledged that an undisclosed tipster told him where to look for the craft, but Moran published his name; Palombo dug up the lead. The zealous ADA represented a pictured bracelet as Joan's distinctive jewelry, but only the family could identify it to be certain. The FBI's protected player inflated the story; the woman allegedly wearing Joan's missing gold links knew where the culprit purportedly dumped Joan's body. Two interrogators pressured Bullerwell for her sensational testimony, and tabloids plastered the headlines that made sensitive stomachs heave.

Palombo said it himself in sworn warrants to the court, "I am familiar with many procedures criminals use in attempts to avoid detection." He sure did.

Flanagan's office cut Burke loose, and the solicitor suspiciously carried a box of Joan's files with him. He set up in private practice with a signed contract to defend the Massachusetts State Police. It was a natural fit; the force defended his ludicrous theory. The next prosecutor on the DA's list never picked up the unresolved case to pursue, and the Websters maintained their confidence with Paradiso's primary, legal predator. Current custodians of Joan's case claimed they did not know about certain events that took place, but did not ask for the records.

The evidence was clear; Palombo sat in the room when Robert Bond stuttered through the tale of two murders. The letter the boys got from Bond was correct about the hole in Joan's head, and as long as there was no body, the story satisfied the public outcry for justice. Enforcers went over Bond's statement and whittled the con's multiple choice down to exacting detail, but the contrived blow with a bottle was inconsistent with the wound. Palombo gained the confidence of at least two, young women and gave them a ride from Logan Airport—he was an undercover cop assigned to F Barracks. Two insiders

pegged him as the FBI's confidential source feeding false information to a corrupted agency that protected informants. The cop's boss
had a friend that anonymously dropped a name to the Websters just
a few weeks into the case. The inner circle kept the name quiet for
months while they created an image. Scattered items threw off the
hunt while Joan's discarded life decayed silently in the woods not far
from Palombo's home.

It is a reasonable conclusion that the State of Massachusetts has
circled the wagons to protect the Commonwealth's purveyors.
Unfortunately, that is nothing new in Massachusetts' shameful history. The recovered documents bared an aggressive and purposeful
investigation that diverted attention down a dead-end path. Here was
a high-profile case involving prominent people. Was the DA's office
simply setting up a fall guy to bloat Flanagan's self-image and pander
for votes? Wasn't their obligation to Joan and everyone else these
public servants victimized? The concept authorities pressed forward
in a noble pursuit of a legitimate suspect because the Websters were
convinced, simply abdicated the state's responsibility to the "Man
from New Jersey." The idea the state cooked up the fish tale just to
hand gullible kindred some explanation for the loss of their daughter had some troubling flaws. Both the authorities and Joan's parents
withheld the first clue—the composite. The quest against Paradiso
started early in the case with an anonymous call to New Jersey from
an involved officer's friend. The core team worked closely with the
trained intelligence couple from the Garden State, and George and
Eleanor kept close tabs on the case. The operation was a well-orches-
trated effort to implicate Paradiso for the crime that kept legitimate
investigation off the scent. When you lose someone violently, a decoy
does not ease the pain for loving family left behind. Was the dysfunctional Boston system protecting a violent offender? Were they protecting Palombo?

Joan was an intelligent, young woman with a bright future in
store. To my knowledge, there was no hint of drug use, or seamy and
illicit friends entangled in the affairs of Boston's organized crime.
The boyfriends I knew were upstanding, young men, and tarnishing
her reputation in police circles was a destructive cop-out to blame
the victim. To speculate that the Harvard graduate student had
lethal knowledge, that she interfered with the nefarious dealings of
the city's opposing factions, bordered on the absurd. Sinister activity
conducted under the cover of a badge, or by criminal elements at
large, were not likely the secrets Joan knew. However, the possibility
that a cop had knowledge or even involvement in the crime was a

frightening risk that needed exposure. Protected players inside the investigation itself assured a culprit could avoid detection.

Recovered documents support Boston's broken system framed Leonard Paradiso.

If the authorities' interests were not their own, whose were they? The exposed tactics in recovered documents did not look like a legitimate investigation. The evidence looked like a deliberate cover-up, an excuse for Joan's murder the blood family defends. The unthinkable reality was obvious to me; I had to look in places everyone else had avoided. A diabolical killer remained hidden behind the curtain. The starting point was simple; if someone was not part of the solution, they were part of the problem, and the Websters were impeding the truth. The family's fixation on Paradiso, despite the conflicting facts and no real evidence, denied their daughter justice. What was missing to explain their unwavering conviction? Thinking George and Eleanor had been deceived defied reason; they were intelligent, educated people with a unique background, and they were very involved. It crossed my mind that someone threatened them to go along with the story. There was evidence in the records that authorities threatened family members and friends in the Iannuzzi case. If so, any hazards affected everyone in my family, but no one warned me of any risks. I could not identify anyone with the muscle to hold a club over George and Eleanor's heads. Simply stated, the Websters were the influential players with high-powered connections. Nevertheless, the family was clearly in denial of the obvious facts.

Did the authorities lie *to* the Websters, or did the authorities lie *for* the Websters? One possibility I could not shake was the heartbreaking chance that the family was complicit. I had to look there; I had no choice. Something was hurting my children, and I needed to decipher the truthful answers. My determination is to protect them— period. Even taking the most favorable view of the family, the fact was they were misleading my children. The lack of reality was the obstacle keeping us torn apart.

Flanagan's protégé had concocted a story that thrust him into the 1979 Essex County cold case that targeted the Websters' suspect. The victim's sister, Kathy, supposedly read the *Boston Globe* article, "AN OBSESSION TO FIND KILLER," then called an undistinguished novice in another county to draw him into the case. Burke proffered that justification to hunt his prey, but the paper published the article on February 27, 1982; the piece was too late for Burke's timeline. The story covered up for the Websters and their interest to go after Paradiso. Burke named his target in the grand jury he convened on March 5, 1982, shortly after the Websters' February 1982 meeting. Collaborators dispatched an officer in the next few days who planted unsubstantiated rumors in other departments. George and Eleanor returned the favor in kind and secretly locked away the composite that bore a haunting resemblance to the lead officer they frequently met with. The bearded, undercover cop operated out of F Barracks at the airport—where Joan disappeared.

Authorities ignored seemingly insignificant facts, details not in plain view. Uncharacteristically, George Webster traveled that weekend, and he probably passed the New York City Greyhound station as he turned into the Lincoln Tunnel for home. The parents were heavily involved in the campaign. On the surface, appearances looked sincere, the John Mulholland upper hand. However, George and Eleanor seemed to overstep appropriate boundaries to guide the case. They enlisted unprecedented groups to pursue the investigation out of several offices; the strategy dissected the search. George presumptively directed the Middlesex office to dredge Walden Pond in a wild goose chase for the Zodiac killer. Meanwhile, Eleanor prodded Gareth Penn's obsession and sent him a credit card slip she mysteriously removed from the Crimson Travel office.

The parents of a missing daughter withheld evidence. They never disclosed the composite, nor did they provide George's private number for scrutiny. Moreover, my in-laws supported an irrational explanation without concrete evidence. These were people trained to examine the smallest detail, and they did in our personal lives.

The family only shared selective information, or at least topics discussed within my earshot. I did not learn about Leonard Paradiso until the Bond allegations leaked in the papers, but George and Eleanor had him in their sights for a year before the state produced their star witness. I had very little knowledge of the Iannuzzi case, or that there was another strong suspect considered for the crime. The two most important influences for Joan's justice inexplicably pledged their allegiance to the implausible story the authorities pitched. Federal, state, and local representatives reached unsupported conclusions that Paradiso slew Joan Webster; the collective group removed resources from the case. Authorities had no real evidence against Paradiso, and the state never tried their calculated premise. In truth, facilitators secreted the exculpatory facts in files out of reach to the man the Websters accused of murder.

Eleanor's endless stream of news clippings strangely stopped when searchers unearthed Joan's bones; seasoned investigators doubted the Paradiso theory. True to Form 368, my in-laws never divulged the condition of Dib's remains. God had not forsaken the search for Joan's killer. The cold hard earth in Hamilton, Massachusetts yielded the first clue in many years. Nevertheless, Eleanor fixed the same icy glare on her husband that stifled his CIA secrets at the family table, and George buttoned his lip. It defied common sense; the parents resolutely maintained Paradiso's guilt despite the new facts. George refused to elaborate why they believed an obviously fallacious story promoted by the state. The core group stuck to the story. Two months after Joan's investigation regained new life, the state released the body for cremation at the parents' request—they slammed the door on Dib's truth.

After years of uncertainty, there now was an undeniable fact— Joan was not missing anymore. The recovery uncovered reality the family ignored. The stealth offender buried Joan in a remote copse more than thirty miles from the alleged crime scene. The undetected assailant inflicted a fatal blow to her skull that left a 2" x 4" hole on the right side of her head. The emotionless executioner stripped Joan's lifeless body naked and discarded her in a black plastic trash bag like rubbish. The predator undermined an earnest search from the start by widely dispersing her belongings. Robert Bond's fabricated statement was irrefutably false. The boat did not exist, and divers pulled it from the waters right where Paradiso stripped it months before Joan disappeared. Examiners found nothing to connect the team's sensational speculations to Joan or any wrongdoing, but the lack of evidence was a secret locked in the files.

George and Eleanor had Dib's body. If they thought they had their man too, a prompt inquest was the next logical step. Instead, the next of kin incinerated their daughter's battered remains and effectively shut down the investigation. The family remained in league and lockstep with the core group's premise and repeated their condemnation. The family had all the pieces to move forward, but the case was a hoax. The state never charged the man the parents inexplicably accused, or tried the merits of the theory they endorsed.

Anne could not be bothered to attend her sister's interment, and Steve would not have been there either if I had not insisted. Joan's disappearance violently altered the course of my life, but the Websters never seemed to miss a beat.

The family stamped their approval on Paradiso's guilt again with each public acknowledgement that defended Tim Burke's senseless explanation. A significant difference distinguishes Joan's case from other cases currently in the news. Police exposed Casey Anthony's lies; she also withheld evidence to help find her daughter, and the public reviled her. Josh Powell blurted an absurd explanation; he took his boys camping in the middle of the same frigid night their mother disappeared, but the public saw through it.

In Joan's case, similar behaviors slid under the radar, but the Websters kept their hands clean. According to Bond, the "Man from New Jersey" sent people to see him, and the people who saw him were the Websters' core team. The boys with the badges spread the stories, and the Websters simply concurred. The strategy of delegating an operation to subordinates allowed reasonable deniability. A protected covert source inside the investigation distracted legitimate rescuers, and a ruthless accoster escaped detection. Players got in bed with unsavory sorts to get a dirty job done—finding someone to blame for wasting Joan. The unfolding reality in recovered documents smacked of the methods and mentality of skilled CIA personnel.

File custodians and Joan's blood kin rebuffed every question— dead silence. The current DA spoke with George and Eleanor, and stamped information requests with "privacy." Murder is not a private family matter; murder is the state's responsibility to resolve. The unified front obstructed an independent examination of Joan's unresolved case.

Leonard Paradiso was nothing more than an Ephraim Littlefied; the janitor was John Webster's scapegoat in 1850 to conceal his guilt for George Parkman's murder. The authorities manufactured a crime scene; like Zanny the Nanny, Casey Anthony's fictitious babysitter, the boat did not exist. The envisioned crime scene for Joan's slaughter was worthless chicken feed that Burke allegedly gave away.

The public had the vision of an aggrieved family; everyone projected his or her own human emotions, feelings that normal people suffer losing a child. Photographers snapped George and Eleanor's stoic faces during the Iannuzzi trial and plastered them all over the papers. Their presence influenced people to believe them; if they went along with the state's story, so would the rest of us. George and Eleanor knew all about using the media and did so to their advantage—it entangled the cases. As long as George and Eleanor "believed" Paradiso was guilty of murdering Joan, law-enforcement and legal delegates cemented an impenetrable wall to promote a false story. The time, the place, and the players created a perfect storm for a criminal to avoid detection.

Joan Webster's murder is not resolved.

Fast-forward to the chaos that descended into my life; the family's true colors bled through the façade inside their inner sanctum. Red flags flapped distress signals, and something terrorized my children. The more I sought help and support, the more isolated I became. Then I discovered the letter my child had written to God. Instead of sorting out the concerns, the elders forced me out of the family using my children as the front line of their defense. Malicious rumors and gossip swirled; the Websters branded me evil. The destruction paralleled the witch hunt of Leonard Paradiso, the man they accused of murdering Joan.

"You're sick!"

"You're completely crazy!"

"You're delusional!"

"Quit threatening us."

The fact was I found a letter that alleged violent abuse inflicted against my daughter, an act of control. She lifted a desperate cry to the Heavenly Father; it is hard to believe my twelve-year-old child lied to Him. I sought help. The family silenced my input with professionals involved with the girls, and stifled the feedback I needed to uncover what was wrong. The Websters choreographed the damaging persona portrayed. Counselors did not know the family was repeating a performance; they churned malignant perceptions about Leonard Paradiso. Accusations about the behavior of Joan's brother shattered the well-honed image of the family, a family with a sensational unresolved family murder. Abuse is not a private family matter, and I took concerns outside the family barriers. I was a liability with a damaging letter, a problem to get rid of. Specialized training paid off, and the family subjected me to the equivalent of a CIA break down—devalued like Joan—and isolated like a threat to national security. The only things I threatened were the family secrets. I never knew what hit me—I pray Joan did not either.

The family alienated me from my children. They took down Christmas greetings and hid like roaches when I knocked on the door. Joan and I shared a similar fate; we were both forced out of the family. Webster enigmas shut down any chance of being part of my children's lives, but troubling behavior trickled through my window online. The enabling neglect of the Webster elders put my children at risk. I raised concerns, as any loving parent should, but responsible parenting triggered hostile reactions. The family faced the truth with denials and claimed I was spreading slanderous gossip. The threats came out of all the ranks; you will never see or hear from your children again. A frightening reality set in when I found similar warnings against Christine DeLisi and Jean Day that pressured them to go along with a story. The elders that lamented the pain of losing a loved one blocked the path of reconciliation with my children. Was it because I did not go along with their stories? Investigation looks for patterns; the Webster family behaved in the same horrible ways they accused others of acting.

The conflicting images of the family do not reconcile.

My uneasy questions did not stop, and the family did not like it.

"Your so-called quest to find Joan's real murderer is extremely abusive," my youngest hurled her trepidation.

No, the person who murdered Joan was abusive. The authorities that concocted a sensational and impossible story that covered up the crime were abusive. Current gatekeepers obstructing an honest review are abusive. Telling the truth is not abusive—but it hurts. Shooting the messenger that dug out the facts only raised the level of suspicion. Because the family refused to look at the verities, they have no standing to object. It is a reflection of them that they do not seem to care. I have made some enemies digging into Joan's case, but it was frightening where the protesters surfaced. Making enemies only meant I hit some nerves; it meant I stood for something—the truth.

The topic of Joan had gone quiet for years, but the family broke the silence by supporting Burke's tome, a book billed as "true crime." Ari Gleckman diagnosed my daughter; she did not know what was real. Apparently, she was not the only one; the Webster family aggravated the problem. Their parenting approach protected family members from the painful truth; they were the ones in denial.

The family's particular set of skills and the expertise to execute them with precision, made it easy to "take care" of me. I loved and trusted them—an easy target—and they knew my every move to deflect it. An operative's objective is to find the weakness; my children were my natural vulnerability. The calculated measures to force me from my children took time, and they had a head start. My attention focused on the girls, not on the issues surrounding Joan, and I was not cognizant that my knowledge threatened their imposed point of view. I was an unwitting mole for years and the only "outsider" in the immediate family when Joan disappeared. Demonizing me to my children nullified a defender my girls needed. My daughter made allegations of criminal deeds that experts recognize as controlling behavior. If that is what happened, then shame unfairly forced them to guard secrets. The girls' poor coping mechanisms reflected patterns of similar victims, and I shuddered seeing the broader picture.

If the allegations were true, the secretive family compelled a form of compliance with Form 368. The same Webster influence raised Joan. George and Eleanor dictated what the truth was to be, regardless of what facts revealed.

Steve showed his intentional malice, the John Mulholland underhand. He told my brother he knew nothing about the dramatic extortion incident his father played out with a known felon. That is absurd. Steve tried to persuade my family of birth I suffered from delusions. The documented events I recovered told the factual story; traumatic events seared into my memory were the reality.

Paranoia set in when my detections got too close. First, an incognito courier dropped an anonymous letter in my mailbox suggesting some mental disorder. After Eleanor's burial in Glen Ridge, Anne made an additional trip to White Horse Village to comfort her father. An invisible bully flooded the private e-mail addresses, the conduit to give the family updates, with anonymous subscriptions soon after Anne's trip. The secret correspondent dished out more of the same destructive malaise painting me as a disturbed lunatic. Yes, I was disturbed all right, but not in any way that diminished my mental capacity, or negated the facts found in the records. I was scared to death what this family was hiding, and what that meant to my girls.

The news is full of tragic stories of the missing and murdered who discovered things people want hidden. My daughter felt pressure to keep me alive. There was already one unresolved murder in the family, and they did not want to talk about it. Instead, someone posted a new tribute reaffirming the family's irrational belief that Paradiso did it. A new wave of false and malicious gossip started to swirl attacking my character. It looked to originate out of offices in Salem, the infamous town of the seventeenth-century witch hunts, and the tight-lipped group that had contacted the Websters. Apparently, current custodians relied on demeaning representations from a family that "believed" Joan was murdered on a boat that did not exist when she disappeared.

The family has secrets.

Counselors deposed under oath finally revealed my offense— violating privacy, in accordance with how the Webster family defined it. My daughter suffered not knowing what was real, but none of the so-called professionals verified what the reality was. The girls wrote it down in their journals in between their assaults on me. Daddy told them real events were their imagination. Two counselors and her sister affirmed who authored the letter and what it implied, but terrified children waged war against Mom to make Daddy the happiest they had ever seen him. Ari Gleckman disclosed my child's fear that Joan's case would gain attention one day and force her to interact with me. I was a person with unique insight of the case and knowledge that conflicted with the family's endorsed version of Joan's murder. According to Burke, George and Eleanor were the encouragement that spurred his bogus book. The fallacious representation of my sister-in-law's death stirred my concern to dig deeply into the case.

Joan's mystery unfairly hangs over my children.

Their words pounded in my mind.

"Oh, you're a whistleblower," Eleanor sniped with disdain.

"No one will ever believe you," Steve warned. "They'll think you're crazy."

Character assassination was the premeditated plan to neutralize me. The sentence imposed was cruel torment, a slow and agonizing dismemberment from my children, but I still had a voice. Real terror settled into my bones with the same intense fear Joan must have faced, and evil flashed a foreboding into my conscious awareness. Devaluation had taken a toll on the feminine gender in the Webster family. History repeated patterns found in Joan's case, and victims continued to suffer silently. The burden of secrets, and the pressure to keep them, hangs over the next generation.

"It cost so much to be a full human being," Joan posted in her dorm room at Perkins Hall.

"Dear God, what secrets cost Dib her life?" I choked on the tears streaming down the confused furrows of my face.

"And Ye shall know the truth, and the truth shall make you free," was the inscribed motto on Langley's wall touting the CIA's credo.

George and Eleanor walked past the carved Bible passage of John 8: 32 after they took their oath of secrecy on Form 368. Honesty was all I was asking for. However, the sad reality is facts are scary to people who lie. For my children and me, only knowing the truth will allow genuine healing.

Examining a cold case is a daunting task. It has taken sheer determination, but my children are worth the courage I could muster. Legitimate investigation starts at square one, and examines each piece until facts cross a name off from a list of suspects. Current authorities in charge, colleagues of the predecessors involved in Joan's case, vehemently guard the files that hold the last clues. The Websters claim privacy and go along with the story. A whistleblower daughter-in-law glimpsed family secrets, and the family devalued and discarded one of their own. Apparently, no one noticed another Webster had suffered the same fate—purged. It meant probing deeply into the family who once sat at my table and embraced lovingly.

My search for a killer pulled together the confused and fragmented pieces of the diversionary tactics deployed to throw obstacles along the trail. Stripping the confabulated excuses away from the facts opened the path to Joan's justice. Insincerity reared up from those delegated with the responsibility for the truth and those who should have most cherished her vibrant life.

The case really broke down to three probable groups. The culprits involved in the physical crime and accomplices that covered it up after-the-fact were the obvious players. However, the real evidence supported premeditated evil that lifted the mask of the third group—those who possibly knew what was coming. It undoubtedly took a lot of influence and cunning to pull off the deception that cluttered the course to find a killer. Only two names remain on my list as persons of interest for the heinous murder; I cannot cross off their names. They were involved together, concealed evidence, lied, and stuck to the story.

The circle of participants expanded to cover their trail. Misprision and gossip had poisoned common sense during the Iannuzzi case and infected Joan's. The same team steered both cases with an obsession to "prove" guilt where it did not belong. One bore a frightening resemblance to the bearded man in the composite—the man who knew what happened to Joan—and the other was a gullible puppet easily controlled. It's taken stubborn perseverance in the face of an unfathomable challenge to close in on Joan's killer. Essex County stated that the case is still open, but the Websters declare privacy at every turn. In effect, these are the forces collaborating in a way that buries the truth.

A monster eliminated Joan from the Webster family. It happened again under the guidance of the Webster elders using innocent children to force out their own mother and guarding secrets. In my case, there was deliberate malice aforethought. The family does not work through their problems; they get rid of them, as they did with me. Did the same thing happen to Joan? George, Steve, Anne, and Eleanor all marched in lockstep to the tune the state was playing—Paradiso is guilty. They are intelligent and well educated, but very secretive. In addition, the parents had specialized training, a fact negating an excuse of ignorance. Eleanor and Anne accompanied Joan to the airport on the night she died while I lay in the hospital losing a life I had hoped to bring into this enigmatic family.

The persons of interest were right in front of us the entire time. The people who made up a whale of a tale and went along with an impossible crime are the people to scrutinize. The closely-knit inner circle, that contrived and supported the unworkable story, are the very same people that everyone logically trusted. George and Eleanor Webster, Tim Burke, Andrew Palombo, Carmen Tammaro, and Steve Broce were the core team that supported this plot.

Society shies away from the topics I have had to face. When the abhorrent comes into view in the news, human nature reviles the offenders. When it remains hidden, poison infects thinking. Pretenders vilify victims who force others to see what is there. Too often, society turns a blind eye until further tragedy shocks us into reality. I live with the very real fear that Joan may have lost her life because she challenged the control of dangerous secrets. She conquered the demons in the shadows; she was a full human being. A brutal death cemented my relationship to Joan, and my progeny, Joan's nieces, have kept me connected. Joan's soul still transcends this world reaching out to protect. Sadly, Joan was not the only abuse victim with the last name of Webster. My children are undeniable victims who felt debased. Moreover, like Joan, I was devalued and thrown away; labeled crazy and abusive for violating Webster privacy. The glaring reality that I was the only non-blood relative in Joan's immediate family with a glimpse inside the fortress escalates the concern for my children. Over time, I could see the John Mulholland underhand of the family.

My moral authority is certain.

Protected players inside the investigations created confusion and diversions that avoided detection. Files controlled by the Essex County DA's office hold the final pieces in the thirty-year-old mystery of Joan's death. Copies of some recovered documents should be contained in the Commonwealth's records, files concealing the state's disgrace and hiding Joan's killer. Files may be incomplete; collaborators hid things under other headings and within out-of-reach folders. In addition, Tim Burke waltzed out of DA Newman Flanagan's devious office carrying Joan's carton across town. Among the real evidence that exists, there are allegations of violent abuse within Joan's family—allegations of incest. However, authorities took the tact to discredit a witness, a person who lived through Joan's tragedy in the midst of the family. They have repeated the strategy of name-calling, because they cannot discuss the facts. They have lost the debate and copped out—blaming a victim.

The Webster family lied to my children and lied to me. The secrecy and deceit made us terribly vulnerable. Ridicule and rumor were dangerous weapons in the rhetoric warfare that prosecuted

Joan's case in the tabloids and then eliminated me as a threat to a family image. The widening circle trampled on anyone who dared to tell the truth in Massachusetts' infamous fashion. Authorities easily control others not in the know. An unholy alliance existed to cover up Joan's murder, but they underestimated one thing. Another Webster mother was a mole in their midst, and my children were hurt. I will not be intimidated or settle for scapegoats. My children are still vulnerable. Joan gave me an incalculable gift, the avenue to find the answers, but my cost has been steep. My children do not need to pay a further price for the secrets of the elder Websters. An independent investigation is warranted, and the right eyes are needed to expose the real killer to everyone.

My children's terror was as real as Aunt Joan's when she took the last breath of her life. I left no stone unturned in my efforts to assure their safety. Sadly, the Websters are insecure people unable to examine the facts, unhappy to have their image disturbed. I will not be silenced like so many victims that have been in my position, discovering lethal secrets. I will not be silenced like Joan.

"The rules mean more than if we die," my oldest child nervously said. "I can't make Daddy unhappy."

"I know no one can help me," my youngest desperately wrote.

These could have been the words of Joan Webster, but instead, they were now coming from the mouths of my innocent children.

"You haven't figured this out yet," Steve smugly taunted.

"Dear God," I cried.

No more secrets. Mommy's a mole.

Index of Characters

Middlesex County DA Scott Harshbarger
ADA Laurence Hardoon
ADA Tom Reilly
ADA James Sahakian
Suffolk County DA Garret Byrne
Suffolk County DA Newman Flanagan
ADA Tim Burke
Anthony Pascucci, Suffolk County investigator
Ruth Scully, exhibit illustrator
ADA Paul Connolly
ADA Ellen Donahue
John Kiernan, head of homicide division
ADA James Larkin
ADA Margaret Steen Melville

Massachusetts State Police
Trooper Barrett
Trooper Charles Eastman
Trooper Joseph Flaherty
Trooper Rick Fraelick
Cpl. Marty Headd
Trooper Bill Johnson
Trooper John Kelley
Trooper Bruce Latham
Trooper Billy Lisano
Trooper MacDonald
Cpl. Dennis Marks
Trooper Dave Moran
Lt. Col. John O'Donovan
Trooper Brian O'Neal
Trooper Jack O'Rourke
Trooper Andrew Palombo
Trooper Carl Sjoberg
Det. Tom Spartachino
Sgt. Carmen Tammaro
Det. Lt. Norman Zuk

FBI & Department of Justice
SA Frank Barletto, Newark office
SA George Bertram, Boston office
SA Steve Broce, Boston office
AUSA Marie Buckley, prosecutor
SA Paul Cavanagh, friend of Andrew Palombo

SA Dennis Condon
SA John Connolly, Bulger and Flemmi handler
SA Roger DePue, Quantico psychological profiler
AUSA Maurice Flynn
SAC James Greenleaf, special agent in charge, Boston office
Patricia May, Quantico fingerprint lab
Oliver Revell, assistant to FBI Director William Webster
SA Paul Rico
SAC Lawrence Sarhatt, special agent in charge, Boston office
Chief Richard Steiner, Interpol
USA W. Stephen Thayer
AUSA David P. Twomey,
Director William Webster, director of the FBI
USA William Weld

Judges
Judge Paul Connolly
Judge Roger Donahue
Judge Harry Elam
Judge Robert Keeton, federal district court MA
Judge Paul Liacos
Judge James McDaniel
Judge James McGuire
Judge Bruce Selya, federal district court RI

Medical Examiners
Dr. Robert Belliveau
Dr. Donald Dixon
Mark Grant, chemist
Kathleen Higgins, senior chemist
Dr. George Katsas, pathologist
Dr. Pierre Provost
Dr. Stanley Schwartz, forensic dentist

Defense Personnel
Marie Altieri
Frank Bruno
Judd Carhart
John Cavicchi
James Cipoletta
William J. LaParl, polygraph examiner
Ray Morgan, private investigator
John Palmer

Walter Prince
Stephen Rappaport
John Roscoe Schifone, process server
Dennis Slawsby, private investigator
Walter Underhill
Owen Walker

Massachusetts Local Law Enforcement
Officer Paul Accomando, Hamilton Police
Victor Anchukaitis, parole officer
Det. Arthur Cook, Saugus Police
Chief Walter Cullen, Hamilton Police
Lt. Harold Fulton, Revere Police
Det. William Gannon, Revere Police
John Gillen, Suffolk County court officer
Det. Charlie Gleason, Saugus Police
Det. Sgt. Paul Grant, Hamilton Police
Officer Arthur Hatfield, Hamilton Police
Sgt. Robert Hudson, Boston Police
Det. Scott Janes, Hamilton Police
Inspector Howard Long, Saugus Police
Sgt. Neil Meehan, Saugus Police
Supervisor Murphy, parole supervisor
Sgt. Jack Murphy, Boston Police
Lt. Larry Murphy, Harvard Police
Jim O'Neil, parole officer
Det. Gordon Richards, Beverly Police
Lt. James Russo, Revere Police
Officer Nick Saggese, Boston Police
Inspector James Stoddard, Saugus Police

NJ Law Enforcement and Resources
Det. Richard Corcoran, Glen Ridge Police
Det. Tom Dugan, Glen Ridge Police
Patrolman Thomas Guthrie, Glen Ridge Police
Det. David Martinez, Newark Police
Jack McEwen, head of ITT security
Det. T. McLaughlin, Glen Ridge Police
Det. Ken Swain, Glen Ridge Police

Iannuzzi Case
Dennis Albano, friend of Christine DeLisi
Patty Bono, anonymous caller from North End

Peter Brandon, friend of Leonard Paradiso
Charlene Bullerwell, occasional date of Leonard Paradiso
Patty Cappozi, waitress at Cardinale's Nest Bar
Jimmy Cardinale, bartender at Cardinale's Nest Bar
Patty Cardinale, owner Cardinale's Nest Bar
Elaine Covino, friend of Leonard Paradiso
Edward Day, false name given to NJ police
Jean Day, Marie Iannuzzi's stepsister
Christine DeLisi, friend of Marie Iannuzzi
Michael DeLisi, friend of David Doyle
David Dellaria, friend of David Doyle
David Doyle, boyfriend of Marie Iannuzzi
Rosemarie Doyle, David Doyle's mother
Eddy Fisher, friend of Marie Iannuzzi
Marie Iannuzzi, 1979 murder victim
Mary Iannuzzi, Marie Iannuzzi's mother
Michael Kamer, friend of Marie Iannuzzi
Anna Marie Kenney, friend of Marie Iannuzzi
Kathy Leonti, Marie Iannuzzi's sister
Tony Leonti, Marie Iannuzzi's brother-in-law
Janet McCarthy, assault victim
Alfred Milano, David Doyle's uncle
Freddie Milano, David Doyle's cousin
Jimmy Milano, David Doyle's cousin
Michael Milano, David Doyle's cousin
Leonard Paradiso
Constance Porter, assault victim
Benjamin Puzzo, Marie Iannuzzi's uncle
Carol Seracuse, Cardinale's Nest Bar patron
Rosemary Sullivan, David Doyle's cousin
Louis Tontodonato, friend of Jean Day
Candy Weyant, Paradiso's girlfriend

Felons
Robert Bond, two-time convicted murderer
Kenny Crawford, inmate
Harvey Martel, known kidnapping felon
Anthony Manni, convicted drug dealer
Ralph Anthony Pisa, convicted murderer

Bankruptcy Case Experts
Arthur Capozzo, bankruptcy court clerk
Philomena Cipione, Haymarket Cooperative Bank executive

Dante Mayano, MA Marine & Recreational Vehicles record keeper
Carl Raichle, crime lab postal inspector
Rodney Swanson, Liberty Mutual Insurance claims manager
Dave Williams, marine examiner

Webster Family Counselors
Dr. Larry Davis, psychiatrist
Ari Gleckman
Carol Metzger
Sarah O'Brien

Massachusetts Parole Board
Josh Wall, chairman
Roger Michel, board member

Others
Joseph Alvoarra, Good Samaritan
The Angiulos, Boston mafia crime family
Anthony Anko Angiulo, son of mafia boss
Joe Barboza, protected FBI informant
Anthony Belmonte, clam digger
Ken Bramber, Glen Ridge, NJ resident
Billy Bulger, brother of James Bulger
James "Whitey" Bulger, protected FBI informant
Albert De Salvo, alleged Boston Strangler
Francis Dion, witness during Pisa trial
David Duncan, Joan Webster's classmate
Gov. Michael Dukakis
Harold "Doc" Edgerton, MIT professor
Robert Fitzpatrick, former FBI ASAC and author of *Betrayal* with Jon Land
Stephen Flemmi, protected FBI informant
Willie Fopiano, Boston NE wise guy and author of *The Godson*
Louis Greco, wrongfully convicted
Beau Herr, Joan Webster's classmate
Pierre Ivanoff, author of *Maya: Monuments of Civilization*
Walter Johnsen, friend of Joan Webster
The Joys, Webster family friends
Bill Kampiles, friend of Steve Webster
Gov. Ed King, MA governor
Joe Kittredge, colleague of Tim Burke
Keith Krach, friend of Joan Webster
Jon Land, author of *Betrayal* with Robert Fitzpatrick

Epilogue

Three things kept me going to get to the answers: faith in God, that admittedly faltered at times; my unconditional and unyielding love for my children; and the truth.

Former prosecutor Tim Burke's announcement to publish his theory of Joan's death in *The Paradiso Files: Boston's Unknown Serial Killer* was the catalyst that propelled me into this lingering mystery. Representations from his book are quoted. There was no expectation of what I would find, but I had the knowledge that the pieces of his implausible theory did not fit. His incompetence to investigate became immediately obvious in his book. In his first edition, he erroneously wrote Leonard Paradiso was born in Italy. The fact his prime suspect was born in Boston on December 8, 1942, was an elementary finding.

My children struggled to know what was real; what the Webster family influenced was not. The malfeasance I found in recovered documents was appalling, and further devalued a wonderful life that ended violently. Joan's murder is a real case and still open in Essex County, Massachusetts.

When I stepped into the Websters' circle in 1977, I unwittingly crossed into a secretive world. The family told me Reginald Webster had sold his company, Standard Thomson, to the Japanese, and there was no reason not to trust their representation. Research into Joan's case meant probing into the family I thought I knew. RN Webster sold Standard Thomson to the Allegheny Corporation in Pennsylvania in 1974. The Otto Corporation was the enterprise sold to the Japanese, but the family never uttered that company's name in my presence. The distortion may not be significant, but that realization opened the floodgates to verify what they said. My knowledge of the family is greater today than when they sat at my table.

The Church Senate Hearings submitted a lengthy report of their findings. In addition, the subcommittee reports on ITT's complicity with the CIA, their activities in Chile, are available to the public. Methods implemented in the CIA during George and Eleanor's employment were also under the scope of the Senate's inquiry into the agency's illegal and immoral activity. Jack Anderson and Brit Hume both published accounts of the scandals that erupted from both of George Webster's employers. Personal knowledge helped pull pieces together, out from under a veil of privacy.

Numerous books and court proceedings documented Boston's history when Joan disappeared. Multiple sources gave a broad review of the corruption of the various agencies involved in Joan's search. SAC James Greenleaf, who approved FBI methods used in Joan's investigation, was suspected of covering leaks that benefited Whitey Bulger. The internal fighting that went on in the bureau put good agents and earnest law enforcement at risk; leaks resulted in the murders of whistleblowers that would have exposed the corruption.

A private investigator helped in the recovery of documents surrounding Joan's case and the suspect the state incriminated. He conducted interviews with persons who held pieces of the puzzle. Robert Bond shed insight previously unknown, though he maintained his story was true. The Massachusetts Parole Board deflated his credibility completely. Retired police officers from Hamilton, Massachusetts sincerely sought justice and shared the horror of Joan's recovery. Det. Paul Grant, Det. Scott Janes, and Chief Walter Cullen all share the common goal—finding the truth. Elle Gates worked in the Middlesex County DA's office assisting ADA Carol Ball on Joan's case and affirmed that their office never received the composite of a bearded man. In October 1985, she went to work for Tim Burke, and observed events for the next two years. It took enormous courage for Elle to speak out.

FOIA requests produced hundreds of pages from FBI files. Requests made using two different search parameters uncovered the facts. Lab results on the recovered vessel, the suggested crime scene, yielded no evidence of Joan or any criminal activity. Use of a confidential informant in the case provided false information to the Feds in an office that inappropriately protected their sources. Records recovered from the Glen Ridge (New Jersey) Police Department included composite templates to reconstruct the suppressed image of the man believed seen leaving the airport with Joan. Detailed extortion attempts in both sets of documents corroborated other aspects of the case never publicly reported. Joan's brother Steve now denies any knowledge of the real event. The Interpol Blue Notice took more than a year for the family to file and amplified concerns why the family delayed in reporting Joan was missing in the first crucial days. Significant gaps in time hindered a legitimate search.

I read hundreds of news articles recurrently to see how the story shifted when facts interfered with the fable being presented. My scrapbook was insufficient to see the whole picture, but my information was controlled. The family's frequently quoted desire was to find Joan's killer, but they avoid reviewing the recovered documents now that tell a much different story. Articles named the sources who fed unsubstantiated images to the press—disinformation. Earnest enforcement analyzed facts when Joan resurfaced, but George and Eleanor's denial of reality dictated the course of the case.

Enormous thanks go to the Paradiso family, who provided hundreds of pages of critical documents surrounding Paradiso's cases. The Marie Iannuzzi case, the Federal bankruptcy case, Janet McCarthy's case, and others tried in the courts are part of the public record. The Paradiso family also provided affidavits and personal documents that showed how the case was constructed. Documents revealed the tactics used to entwine unrelated cases and kept exculpatory evidence hidden.

Mary Foreman's family was an inspiration. More than twenty-nine years after her senseless loss at the hands of Robert Bond, Mary's love was present in force at the parole hearing. The family lovingly embraced my presence and courage to be there. Each of them embodied the human connection that makes us full human beings. Joan strove to be complete before an unknown assailant viciously cut her life short, and her family, disconnected from emotions, failed to find truthful answers. Memory flashed back to my family of birth with the Foreman family's warm enfolds. Mary lives on, and people hear her through them. My experience and my voice will speak out for Joan. I was another Webster woman unjustly devalued and discarded.

It is also important to thank the sincere law enforcement community that genuinely pursued truthful answers for Joan. A broken system hindered their genuine efforts to find justice. Unscrupulous manipulators driven by other agendas diverted their attention and blocked the answers.

Recovered records uncovered serious discrepancies with published accounts. The Essex County DA in Massachusetts denied requests to release the files; they asserted the case remains open and privacy is requested by the family. The Secretary of State in Massachusetts denied a further request for documents in Joan's case, and relied on the representation from the DA's office that the thirty-year-old case is still under review. The Massachusetts Attorney General refused to examine the unresolved case despite her oversight responsibility. The top law enforcer in the state is responsible for the conduct of the public defenders. I provided documents to the Massachusetts Parole Board, the Suffolk County DA's office, and the Massachusetts State Police. I reviewed discrepancies with the Essex County DA's office and Massachusetts State Police investigators. The victim impact statement prepared for Robert Bond's parole hearing included supporting documents pertaining to Robert Bond, but the chairman silenced my voice in an open hearing. I have submitted further requests for an internal investigation, and pursued other legal remedies.

Former prosecutor Tim Burke had privileged access to files and published representations about several cases. Recovered documents dispelled his assertions. Essex County publicly stated they have opened cold cases based on Burke's published contentions. Decent citizens in the Commonwealth subsidize the continued witch hunt against Leonard Paradiso posthumously. The DA's spokesman confirmed that the unresolved murders of Melodie Stankiewicz, Holly Davidson, and Kathy Williams were under review based on Burke's book. The unresolved murder of my sister-in-law was not included in the announcement. However, the publication Burke upheld as a "true crime" account, became evidence in the open case of Joan Webster.

The dialogue in these pages came from primary sources. I have quoted directly from court transcripts, police records, sworn affidavits, correspondence, the media, and personal memory and recollections. In a few exceptions, dialogue was developed to illustrate actual events. The evidence is in black and white.

I have known the Websters for more than three decades and experienced a much different side of the family than their public image. Personal insight of their dysfunction behind closed doors and the John Mulholland invisible hand were missing pieces necessary to unravel Dib's truth. The grief has been enormous. I have made a necessary distinction between infringing on privacy and exposing behaviors that leave people at risk. My children's safety trumps the Webster "privacy" that effectively concealed crimes. Despite the family's devaluing treatment, I have given them a gift, truthful answers in Joan's loss.

Support systems are essential for any victim, but I struggled finding validation for some time because of the destructive images painted by the Webster family. Extraordinary events are difficult for even the most empathetic listener to absorb. Faith faltered at times, but God picked me up when I was ready to give up. My children are the gift that He gave me, and helping them see what is real is necessary for healing. I want to give special thanks to Deb Williams, an abuse advocate who often did not know what to say, but believed my painful entreaties to listen. Thanks also go to the online resources I found to analyze findings. It is impossible to name all the loving people I met who work selflessly to support people suffering through enormous tragedy.

My family of birth has remained solid during severe alienation from my children that cruelly was extended to them by the Webster family. They knew the core of my being, and never wavered in their love for me and for my children. At times, even they could not understand the tangled web I was unweaving, but they saw things in black and white that supported my instincts and recollections. Recovered documents exposed the reality of the unthinkable nightmares I was living. I uncovered the root of the evil that unfairly descended into Joan's life, the lives of my children, and my life. God has blessed me in many ways, and my blood family has been there every step of the way.

Three Websters must be thanked, too. My love for my children is unshakable despite the visible hostility they displayed. I know their beautiful inner core. The Websters influenced their actions. Premeditated disaffection was not of their own making, and emphasized the destructive forces of insecure people who alienated a loving parent. I do not know what threats may have been whispered to my children with the warning not to tell, but one child felt pressure to keep me alive. In their efforts to keep Daddy happy, they may have saved my life. Joan's case revealed that the Webster family was not telling my children the truth for whatever reason. My memory of Joan was a beacon of light guiding me through the deceitful maze that covered up unspeakable evil. I hold these three extraordinary Webster women, my children, and their aunt, Joan Webster, safely and securely in my heart.

Any suggestion the investigation is ongoing is disingenuous. Authorities failed to copy documents provided for their review relevant in Joan's case. Personal documents were also provided that these public servants ignored. Confidential information disclosed to authorities leaked. Frightening allegations made by my child were distorted and misrepresented to the public, putting people in jeopardy. The state has been derelict of their responsibility. Public servants violated the public's trust; citizens have to hold officials accountable. Steve smugly once told me I had not figured it out yet. Now, sadly, maybe I have. Control in the hands of a few with motivation that is not compatible with justice is redoubtable. The actual records revealed those in control were presumptive and destructive—they played God in people's lives. The Almighty is the final judge what is in a person's heart, and no one can hide his or her secrets from Him.

After this book was completed, the mask of a pretender slipped. On December 23, 2012, I extended Christmas greetings to George

Webster in an e-mail, and repeated my frequent request to discuss discrepancies with the family in a proper setting. Specific topics, all supportable with recovered documents, were extended: the December 1981 composite, the boat suggested as the crime scene, the January 1982 anonymous call identifying Leonard Paradiso, the Harvey Martel extortion incident, Robert Bond's false statement, exculpatory evidence in the Iannuzzi trial, the condition of Joan's remains, and her cremation.

Uncharacteristically, I received a direct response, out from under the shadows, on December 25, 2012, at 10:13 p.m. Unable to discuss our shared experience, and what is in the actual records, George Webster resorted to name calling and devaluation. He referenced civil litigation I filed in court, an ongoing matter, which was not disclosed to Webster family members through my sources. George's more familiar controlled façade fell to the darker personality and harrassment I experienced in the later years. The John Mulholland underhand was in full view.

"You have no f—idea," he typed, ignoring the invitation to examine what he and Eleanor left out.

George Webster, father of a murder victim, closed his comments in an explosive fashion. It immediately triggered the recollection of my child's concern to keep me alive. With his daughter's case still unresolved, George Webster's Christmas wish for the mother of his grandchildren was chilling.

"Die."

Timeline

1975	Irish mob boss, James Whitey Bulger, turns informant for FBI handler SA John Connolly in Boston
January 27, 1975	Senate hearings on 1950's CIA mind control project MKULTRA
August 3, 1975	Senate Church Commission hearings on ITT CIA activity from 1963-1974 in Chile
May or June 1979	Marie Iannuzzi stayed with Christine DeLisi following a physical argument with David Doyle
August 10, 1979	Marie Iannuzzi date with Eddie Fisher
August 11, 1979	Milano family wedding
August 12, 1979	Marie Iannuzzi murdered
August 14-16, 1979	Wake for Marie Iannuzzi
August 16-17, 1979	David Doyle arrested at Newark Airport
August 17, 1979	Marie Iannuzzi funeral
August 20, 1979	Rosemarie Doyle claims June motor vehicle accident cause of her son's scratches to Inspector Arthur Cook
August 28, 1979	Paradiso passes polygraph given by examiner LaParl at the direction of Attorney John Cavicchi

July 10, 1980	Det. Sgt. James Russo and Det. William Gannon of the Revere PD take assault report from Janet McCarthy
July 23, 1980	ADA Tim Burke obtains warrant to bug Whitey Bulger's Lancaster Street Garage
1980	FBI begin bugging Angiulo family in Operation BOSTAR against the mafia
October 29, 1980	Judge Paquet denies Anthony Pisa's seventh motion for a new trial
February 1981	Tr. Andrew Palombo assigned as chief investigating officer on the Iannuzzi case, replacing Tr. Carl Sjoberg
May 1981	Gareth Penn contacts the FBI with theory Harvard professor Michael Henry O'Hare is the Zodiac murderer
June 15, 1981	Robert Bond paroled from murder conviction of Barbara Mitchell
July 16, 1981	Inspector Howard Long interviews David Dellaria about the Iannuzzi murder
July 26, 1981	The *Malafemmena* reported missing and claim filed with Liberty Mutual Insurance
August 26, 1981	Paradiso files for bankruptcy
September 29, 1981	Liberty Mutual Insurance pays the claim for the *Malafemmena*
October 23, 1981	Community activist Mary Foreman murdered
November 11, 1981	Robert Bond lied to police, claiming he had not seen Mary Foreman on the night she was murdered

November 20, 1981	Robert Bond arrested for the murder of Mary Foreman
November 23, 1981	Joan Webster presents eleven-week project in class
November 26, 1981	Thanksgiving
November 28, 1981	The Great Lynn Fire in Lynn, Massachusetts
November 28, 1981	George, Eleanor, and Anne Webster drive Joan to Newark Airport for Eastern flight 960 to Logan
November 28, 1981	Joan Webster disappears from Logan Airport
Nov ?-Dec 1, 1981	George Webster travels to California
November 30, 1981	Classes resume at Harvard
November 30, 1981	Paradiso bankruptcy discharged
November 30, 1981	Paradiso has left index finger x-rayed at Lynn Hospital
December 1, 1981	Classmate David Duncan calls Websters to report Joan has not returned for classes
December 1, 1981	George Webster return flight from CA
December 1, 1982	Missing person report filed with Ptrl. Thomas Guthrie of the Glen Ridge, NJ Police Department at 11:12 p.m.
December 2, 1981	Missing person report filed with Sgt. Peter O'Hare with the Harvard Police at 12:34 a.m. and report copied to Lt. L. Murphy
December 1981	ADA Carol Ball in Middlesex County assigned Joan Webster case

December 2, 1981   Joan Webster's purse and wallet found in Saugus by Anthony Belmonte

December 3, 1981   SA George Bertram of the Boston FBI contacted by the Glen Ridge, NJ police

December 4-7, 1981   Interviews of airport personnel, cabbies, passengers

December 18, 1981   Extortion call placed to the Websters claiming Joan is alive

December 21, 1981   Composite of bearded man delivered to Websters by Det. R. Corcoran

December 25, 1981   George and Eleanor Webster make a pre-taped public appeal

January 9, 1982   Lynda Walsh given ride from Park Square Greyhound bus station from a man identified as an undercover cop

Jan 18, 1982   Websters hold press conference and ITT offers $10,000 reward

Jan 19, 1982   Anonymous call to Chief Donald Peters Saugus PD connecting Webster and Iannuzzi cases

Jan 19, 1982   Websters learn name of Paradiso from anonymous female caller

January 25, 1982   Boston Police Department receive anonymous letter suggesting Joan Webster murdered at fraternity party

January 29, 1982   Joan's bag found in New York or Boston

Jan or Feb 1982   Three males arrested by MSP for fraudulent information to claim reward money

February 1982   George Webster holds meeting with multiple agencies at Harvard

February 1982	Suffolk County ADA Tim Burke under Newman Flanagan takes over Essex County unresolved Iannuzzi murder case
February 27, 1982	Jeremiah Murphy published *Boston Globe* article about Tim Burke and a triple homicide on page one of the Metro section
March 2, 1982	Subpoenas issued for Iannuzzi grand jury
March 5, 1982	The *Commonwealth v. Leonard J. Paradiso* grand jury, cause number 038655 for Marie Iannuzzi murder, convened in Suffolk County
March 11, 1982	MSP Tr. Carl Sjoberg informs Paradiso's parole officer, Jim O'Neil, that Paradiso was subpoenaed in a John Doe grand jury and is a suspect in new Boston case
Spring 1982	Michael Delisi conversation with David Doyle at the Cardinale's Nest Bar regarding the Iannuzzi murder
April 1982	George and Eleanor Webster in contact with Gareth Penn regarding Zodiac theory
April 3, 1982	George Webster mails letter postmarked from Cambridge, MA
April 4, 1982	Report of anonymous letter mailed from Cambridge, MA to the Middlesex County DA
April 5, 1982	Renamed John Doe grand jury cause number 038655 reconvened
April 5, 1982	Walden Pond searched
April 8, 1982	Wenham Lake in Hamilton, MA searched on tip from psychic Richard Phillips
April 12, 1982	George Webster letter to the FBI

April 14, 1982	Multiple agencies meet with FBI psychological unit SA Roger DePue to develop profile
April 16, 1982	George Webster meets with FBI
April 20, 1982	Brian Bowen from the Central Parole Office requests Paradiso's records for Suffolk County DA's investigation
April 23, 1982	John Doe grand jury for cause number 038655 reconvened
April 29, 1982	George Webster letter to the FBI
April 30, 1982	George Webster conference in Boston
May 2, 1982	George and Eleanor Webster remove Joan's belongings from Perkins Hall
May 2, 1982	Anonymous call claiming Joan is alive
June 22, 1982	John Doe grand jury cause number 038655 reconvenes
June 28, 1982	First-degree murder indictment number 0438655 handed down against Paradiso for the Iannuzzi murder
July 6, 1982	Paradiso arrested for Iannuzzi murder by Tr. Andrew Palombo, Det. Lt. O'Connor and Tr. Bill Johnson
July 1982	Tr. Palombo searches records at the Registry of Motor Boats and Registry of Motor Vehicles
July 21, 1982	Joan Webster dental records provided by Dr. Joseph Pallis
August 1, 1982	Sgt. Carmen Tammaro meets with Paradiso at the Charles Street Jail
October 12, 1982	George and Eleanor Webster increase reward to $25,000 for information and

	$50,000 for information leading to the capture of offender
October 14, 1982	Extortion call placed to the Websters that Joan is still alive
October 15, 1982	George Webster meets with extortion caller Harvey Martel in Concord, NH, with FBI, ITT security, and Glen Ridge police
October 20, 1982	Tr. Andrew Palombo submitted report alleging Paradiso's statement at the time of arrest on July 6, 1982
October 25, 1982	Call placed to the Websters claiming Joan is alive in Maine
November 5, 1982	Leonard Paradiso fingerprint comparison in Joan Webster case submitted to FBI lab
November 24, 1982	Fingerprint analysis of Paradiso in Webster case is negative
December 8, 1982	Robert Bond and Paradiso both moved to Charles Street Jail
Dec 8 or 9, 1982	Meeting scheduled with private investigator, Glen Ridge, NJ police, and ITT security
December 12, 1982	Bearded man identified as Tr. Palombo followed two women at Logan Airport and gave them a ride
December 13, 1982	Robert Bond found guilty for the murder of Mary Foremen
December 29, 1982	Robert Bond moved to Concord facility
January 5, 1983	Date Tim Burke alleges receipt of unsolicited letter from Bond
January 10, 1983	Robert Bond sentenced to life at Walpole

January 10, 1983	Robert Bond meets with authorities at Suffolk County Courthouse
January 10, 1983	Robert Bond mails letter to ADA Burke from Concord prison
January 13, 1983	Robert Bond speaks with Deputy Carter at Concord prison regarding letter mailed on the tenth
January 14, 1983	MSP interview with Robert Bond at Suffolk County Courthouse
January 15-17, 1983	Sgt. Carmen Tammaro arranges to obtain letter from Bond's family
January 17, 1983	Sgt. Carmen Tammaro, Sgt. Robert Hudson and Tr. Andrew Palombo meet with Bond to go over statement
January 17, 1983	Tim Burke allegedly receives letter in mail from Robert Bond
January 18, 1983	Robert Bond polygraph with MSP Jack Nasuti at direction of Sgt. Carmen Tammaro
January 27, 1983	First Robert Bond reports in the news indicate a "break" in Joan Webster case
January 28, 1983	Boston FBI informed that a Massachusetts State Prison inmate named Paradiso for Joan Webster murder and claims Webster dumped in Boston Harbor
Late January 1983	Janet McCarthy sees Paradiso's picture on television with reward and comes forward
Late January 1983	Middlesex ADA Carol Ball informs ADA Burke about Anthony Pisa allegations
Jan or Feb 1983	Marie Iannuzzi stepsister, Jean Day, assaulted

February 1, 1983	Sgt. Carmen Tammaro's North End acquaintance, Patty Bono, comes forward to ADA Tim Burke
February 17, 1983	Grand jury regarding Iannuzzi case convened for rape charges
March 3, 1983	Interpol Blue Notice issued for missing person Joan Webster
March 4, 1983	Attorney Norman Zalkind appointed to represent Robert Bond
March 28, 1983	ADA Tim Burke travels to Quantico for FBI meeting regarding Joan Webster case
April 5, 1983	Tr. Andrew Palombo travels to Maine
April 25, 1983	Search warrant executed at Weyant home
April 28, 1983	Ralph Anthony Pisa takes new polygraph changing his involvement in the 1969 George Deane murder
May 3, 1983	ADA Tim Burke contacts Boston FBI over alleged bankruptcy fraud by Paradiso and Candy Weyant
May 10, 1983	FBI SA Steve Broce meets with ADA Tim Burke
June 1, 1983	Paradiso declines Commonwealth offer for a lesser plea in Iannuzzi case
June 2, 1983	ADA Tim Burke for the Commonwealth rescinds plea bargain offer to Paradiso
June 6, 1983	Grand jury hands down a true bill 043033 in the *Commonwealth v. Leonard J. Paradiso* for rape of Marie Iannuzzi
June 13, 1983	Anthony Pisa motion for new trial

June 17, 1983   FBI SA Steve Broce meets with Tr. Andrew Palombo

July 11, 1983   FBI SA Steve Broce interviews witness Elaine Covino

July 12, 1983   John Doe grand jury convened investigating disappearance of Joan Webster cause number 044570A

July 17, 1983   Judge Liacos grants immunity to Candy Weyant for Joan Webster case

July 18, 1983   US Attorney Marie Buckley meets with ADA Tim Burke

July 27, 1983   Weyant recalled to John Doe grand jury for Joan Webster case

July 28, 1983   Federal search warrant executed on Weyant and Paradiso's joint safety deposit box at Haymarket Cooperative Bank

August 11, 1983   Weyant pleads innocent to murder accessory charges brought by ADA Tim Burke in Marie Iannuzzi case

August 12, 1983   FBI confidential source provides SA Steve Broce with information to locate the *Malafemmena*

August 15, 1983   ADA Tim Burke meets with US Attorney Marie Buckley regarding Federal charges against Paradiso and Weyant

August 15, 1983   SA Steve Broce meets with ADA Tim Burke regarding location of Paradiso's boat, *Malafemmena*

August 20, 1983   Tr. Andrew Palombo requests Det. Tom Dugan of the Glen Ridge, NJ police secure Joan Webster's personal property

August 25, 1983	US Attorney Marie Buckley begins Federal grand jury against Paradiso and Weyant on bankruptcy and mail fraud charges
September 8, 1983	Judge Connolly finds Candy Weyant in contempt of court for taking the fifth during grand jury and sentences her to three months in Framingham
September 19, 1983	Grand jury indictments handed down against the Angiulo family
September 26, 1983	*Malafemmena* found submerged under its mooring at Pier 7
September 27, 1983	*Malafemmena* raised
September 27, 1983	FBI begins testing boat for evidence
September 29, 1983	Confidential source contacts FBI with name Charlene
September 30, 1983	Confidential source contacts Boston FBI again with additional information Charlene allegedly knows the location of Joan Webster's body
Oct - Nov 1983	Authorized divers continue search of Pier 7
October 3, 1983	Marine surveyor David Williams inspects *Malafemmena*
October 3, 1983	FBI SA Steve Broce locates Charlene Bullerwell from photograph
October 4, 1983	FBI SA Steve Broce and second unidentified individual interview Charlene Bullerwell
October 7, 1983	ADA Tim Burke claims jewelry bag in safety deposit box identified as Joan Webster's

October 12, 1983	David Williams conducts second inspection of *Malafemmena*
October 15, 1983	ADA Tim Burke meets with Websters
October 20, 1983	ADA Tim Burke instructs Officer Nick Saggese where to dive for gun at Pier 7 based on a tip from confidential source
October 24, 1983	Middlesex County ADA James Sahakian files Commonwealth's objection to grant Anthony Pisa's motion for new trial
January 19, 1984	Tr. Andrew Palombo and Det. Murphy of the Boston Police Department request, through Sgt. Easyrock at Walpole, to speak with Paradiso
January 22, 1984	Tr. Palombo and Det. Murphy attempt unsuccessfully to speak with Paradiso at Walpole
January 23, 1984	Attorney Stephen Rappaport appointed by court to represent Paradiso
February 9, 1984	John Doe Federal grand jury testimony
February 16, 1984	John Doe Federal grand jury testimony
February 17, 1984	Tr. Andrew Palombo interviews Janet McCarthy
Late February 1984	Ralph Anthony Pisa moved to Park Drive facility
March 2, 1984	Tr. Andrew Palombo John Doe Federal grand jury testimony
March 5-12 1984	Judge Roger Donahue presides over Iannuzzi pretrial hearing

March 6, 1984	Three additional indictments handed down from the Suffolk County grand jury—Paradiso pleads not guilty to all three
March 6, 1984	Candace Weyant declared hostile witness
March 7, 1984	Weyant immunized in Iannuzzi case, and testifies in pretrial hearing in front of media
March 8, 1984	ADA Tim Burke requests protective order of discovery for Robert Bond affidavit
March 9, 1984	Federal Grand Jury indictments against Paradiso and Weyant
March 12, 1984	Anthony Pisa Iannuzzi pretrial testimony alleging Paradiso involvement in Iannuzzi and Webster cases
March 13, 1984	Emergency bail reduction hearing for Anthony Pisa before Judge Elam in Middlesex County, and Pisa released
March 13, 1984	Court orders Robert Bond statement exhibit #15 be sealed and impounded
March 21, 1984	David Doyle has three counts dismissed on the motion of a prosecutor
March 28, 1984	Paradiso and Weyant arraigned in Federal court for bankruptcy and mail fraud charges
April 26, 1984	Weyant attorney Walter Underhill files motion to dismiss Federal charges against Weyant
June 16, 1984	Defense investigator Ray Morgan contacts George and Eleanor Webster
July 9, 1984	Iannuzzi murder trial begins, Judge Roger Donahue presiding

July 12, 1984	Charlene Bullerwell refuses to testify at Iannuzzi trial
July 22, 1984	Guilty verdict against Paradiso for second-degree murder in Iannuzzi case and assault with intent to rape
July 25, 1984	Paradiso sentenced
November 26, 1984	Joan Webster dental records hand delivered from NJ by Det. Tom Dugan at ADA Tim Burke's request
November 26, 1984	ADA Tim Burke meets with Det. Tom Dugan, and requests personal items secured in NJ, FBI SA Steve Broce is contact for transfer
November 28, 1984	Insurance fraud charges filed regarding *Malafemmena*
December 18, 1984	ADA Tim Burke petitions Judge James McGuire to x-ray Paradiso's finger and surgically remove a presumed splinter
December 21, 1984	SA Steve Broce arranges for transfer of Joan Webster's personal items unrelated to the bankruptcy and mail fraud case
January 3, 1985	Middlesex County ADA Laurence Hardoon files memorandum withdrawing Commonwealth's objection to Anthony Pisa's motion for a new trial
January 3, 1985	Ralph Anthony Pisa changes plea for 1969 murder of George Deane and sentenced to time served
January 4, 1985	SA Frank Barletto assists packing of personal items in NJ for transfer to FBI lab in Quantico

January 8, 1985	Glen Ridge police submit Joan Webster's personal items to Quantico
January 16, 1985	ADA Tim Burke argues before Judge James McGuire regarding splinter allegedly linking Paradiso to Joan Webster
January 21, 1985	Judge Robert Keeton changes venue of bankruptcy case to Rhode Island
January 29, 1985	Court hearing for insurance fraud regarding the *Malafemmena* begins in RI
February 13, 1985	X-ray ordered on Paradiso left index finger for clues in Webster case
February 15, 1985	Police allegedly used force to x-ray Paradiso's left index finger
February 16, 1985	Massachusetts Supreme Court injunction to prevent further x-rays of Paradiso's finger
February 18, 1985	Paradiso acquitted of insurance fraud involving *Malafemmena*
March 28, 1985	Sgt. Carmen Tammaro allegedly offers a deal to Walpole inmate Anthony Manni in return for a "confession" solicited from Paradiso
April 4, 1985	Federal bankruptcy fraud case begins against Paradiso
April 5, 1985	Paradiso receives treatment in RI for six-week-old broken finger injury
April 9, 1985	Paradiso found guilty on three counts in Federal charges
May 10, 1985	Paradiso sentenced for three counts of bankruptcy fraud by Judge Bruce Selya

May 28, 1985	Garden dedication for Joan Webster at Gund Hall at Harvard
July 24, 1985	State, local, and Federal investigators report they have developed sufficient strong evidence to determine Paradiso abducted and murdered Joan Webster
Sept 16-20, 1985	Tim Burke resigns from the Suffolk County DA's office during this week
Sept-Nov 1985	Former MSP Tr. Bruce Latham hired as private investigator in Joan Webster case
November 5, 1985	Paradiso files motion for a new trial in Iannuzzi case
November 15, 1985	Robert Bond filed motion that the state failed to fulfill promises naming Tim Burke, Andrew Palombo, Carmen Tammaro, and "Bill"
November 23, 1985	Informant Robert Bond convicted of murdering Mary Foreman in retrial
February 13, 1986	Trial Judge Donahue, acting as motion judge, rules to deny Paradiso's motion for a new trial without hearing
June 11, 1986	Paradiso files motion to reconsider his motion for a new trial
July 1, 1986	Trial Judge Donahue, acting as motion judge, denies Paradiso's motion to reconsider without hearing
July 3, 1986	Paradiso files notice of appeal
August 1986	*Trooper* by Dave Moran with Richard Radford published
August 13, 1986	Janet McCarthy assault case against Paradiso begins

August 15, 1986	Paradiso convicted in Janet McCarthy case
1987	Gareth Penn publishes *Times 17* implicating Harvard professor Michael Henry O'Hare as the Zodiac murderer, and alleging O'Hare murdered Joan Webster
September 25, 1987	Tr. Bill Johnson involved in incident at Logan Airport with James Whitey Bulger
Winter 1987	George and Eleanor Webster meet with Robert Bond at Somerville
June 1988	Robert Bond stabbed by fellow inmates at Somerville
September 29, 1988	Robert Bond moved into Federal prison system
April 18, 1990	Skull found in Hamilton, MA on Chebacco Road
April 18, 1990	Unidentified victim pronounced dead at 12:10 p.m.
April 25, 1990	Gravesite discovered by Det. Scott Janes, Officer Paul Accomando, and Det. Paul Grant of the Hamilton, MA Police Department
April 26, 1990	Excavation begins of shallow grave in Hamilton, MA
April 30, 1990	Remains identified as Joan Webster through dental records
May 2, 1990	George and Eleanor Webster visit Hamilton, MA gravesite
July 13, 1990	Joan Webster's remains cremated in Salem, MA

July 1990   Joan Webster's cremated remains buried in Glen Ridge, NJ

July 15, 1991   Suffolk County DA's office exposed for duplicate and secret files in homicide cases from 1980–1988 under the head of homicide, John Kiernan

September 25, 1992   Tim Burke buys property of former drug trafficker and Bulger associate Frank LePere in Marshfield, MA

November 1993   *The Godson* by Willie Fopiano with John Harney published

September 2, 1994   Tim Burke buys additional property in Marshfield, MA in another transaction involving the LePere family

January 5, 1995   Indictments for FBI informants Bulger, Flemmi, and Salemme compromised

October 3, 1995   President Bill Clinton acknowledges and apologizes to the victims and families of CIA MKULTRA mind control experiments illegally conducted on US citizens

1997   FBI corruption exposed in handling James Bulger as a protected informant

December 29, 1997   Paradiso reported near death

July 4, 1998   Tr. Andrew Palombo killed in motorcycle accident in Lynn, Massachusetts

September 25, 1998   Tr. Bill Johnson's death reported as suicide

December 22, 1999   FBI SA John Connolly indicted on charges for falsifying FBI reports, accepting bribes, and protecting informants Bulger and Flemmi

2000	*Black Mass: the True Story of an Unholy Alliance Between the Irish Mob and the FBI* by Dick Lehr and Gerald O'Neill is published recounting corruption in Boston's law enforcement and investigative agencies
December 2000	US Justice Department investigates FBI corruption in Boston and uncovers secret FBI informant files
June 2001	Letter discovered with criminal allegations in Webster family
May 29, 2002	FBI John Connolly convicted for his handling of FBI informants Bulger and Flemmi
Early 2005	Journal entries discovered corroborating concerns of criminal allegations in Webster family
Apr 29-May 1, 2005	Break-in reported at office of Webster family counselor Sarah O'Brien
May 2005	Police report filed for break-in at Sarah O'Brien's office
June 2005	Police report filed stemming from discovered letter and journal entries
Summer 2005	George and Eleanor Webster meet with Tim Burke in Marshfield, MA and Burke decides to write book
September 13, 2005	Parole hearing for Robert Bond
November 1, 2005	Parole denied for Robert Bond
November 28, 2006	Tim Burke announces upcoming book about Paradiso supported by George and Eleanor Webster
February 7, 2008	Robert Bond taken to Lemuel Shattuck Hospital where Paradiso is a patient

February 18, 2008	*The Paradiso Files: Boston's Unknown Serial Killer* by Tim Burke published
February 27, 2008	Leonard Paradiso passed away at Lemuel Shattuck Hospital
May 6, 2008	Private investigator and MA attorney meet with Robert Bond at Shirley MCI
May 13, 2008	Sworn depositions of Webster counselors Sarah O'Brien and Ari Gleckman
May 23, 2008	Webster contempt hearing
May 23, 2008	Perjured testimony regarding letter with criminal allegations
July 9, 2008	Webster contempt hearing
Late August, 2008	Former Paradiso witness harassed in MA with anonymous letter
December 8, 2008	George and Eleanor claim privacy for independent review of unresolved case
January 22, 2009	Hand-delivered anonymous letter placed in mailbox
July 2, 2009	Composite of bearded man reconstructed
October 9, 2009	Meeting with Robert Bond at Shirley MCI
October 15, 2009	George Webster forwards e-mail regarding Robert Bond to Cyveillance
May 20, 2010	Meeting with ADA John Dawley in Essex County, Det. Lt. Norman Zuk, and two MSP officers
May 28, 2010	George Webster notified of Robert Bond's upcoming parole opportunity

June 15, 2010	Eleanor Webster passed away
July 12-17, 2010	Multiple harassing e-mails received from company computer of Anne Webster's employer, Syntellect
April 19, 2011	Parole Board Chairman Josh Wall denies DOC certified victim from giving victim impact statement at open parole hearing for Robert Bond
January 2012	*Betrayal* by Robert Fitzpatrick and Jon Land published
January 18, 2012	Massachusetts Parole Board unanimously denies Robert Bond's petition for parole
December 23, 2012	Christmas greetings sent to George Webster and request to discuss discrepencies regarding unresolved Joan Webster murder
December 25, 2012	George Webster e-mail response to Eve Carson stating "Die"

SUPPLEMENTARY REPORT

<u>MISSING PERSON</u>
Classification

NO. 28900

NO _____

Name of Complainant	Address	Phone No.
Joan L. Webster	528 Ridgewood Ave., Glen Ridge, NJ	744-0322

Offense

Missing Person

DETAILS OF OFFENSE, PROGRESS OF INVESTIGATION, ETC.:
(Investigating Officer must sign)

Page No. ___R-10___   Date ___Dec. 1___ 19 81

Monday 12/21/81

1400 Hrs. Sgt. Dugan gave this officer the IdentiKitnumber used to make a
composit of the individual that may have left Logan Airport with
Joan Webster. The numbers were from the Identi-Kit II, NN09, AA09,
BB15, GG03, LL04, EE86, HH145, CC10. Sgt. Dugan also said the
person was around 42 years old, full beard, hair was less kinky than
the overlay.
This officer went to Bloomfield Detective Bureau to use their
Identi-Kit Composites made at Bloomfield Police Dept.
This officer then went to the Webster House and left a copy of the
composite with Mrs. Webster. I also picked up the tape of the
last extortion call made on 12/18/81 around 1840 hrs. This tape was
then turned over to Sgt. Dugan at Police Headquarters.

ES INVESTIGATING OFFICER(S) __Det. R. Corcoran__   26 REPORT MADE BY __Det. R. Corcoran__   DATE 1/14/82

27 CASE FILED   28 THIS CASE IS   Active ☐ 29 APPROVED BY
Yes ☐ No ☐ | Cleared by arrest ☐ Unfounded ☐ Inactive ☐ Other ☐ |

FORM 166-3R

Glen Ridge, New Jersey police report listed composite template numbers,
and the image was delivered to Eleanor Webster on December 21, 1981.

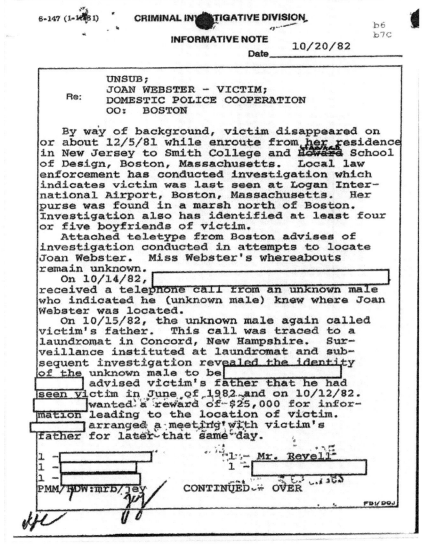

6-147 (1-14-81)   **CRIMINAL INVESTIGATIVE DIVISION**

INFORMATIVE NOTE

Date_____ 10/20/82

Re:
UNSUB;
JOAN WEBSTER - VICTIM;
DOMESTIC POLICE COOPERATION
OO: BOSTON

By way of background, victim disappeared on
or about 12/5/81 while enroute from her residence
in New Jersey to Smith College and ~~Howard~~ School
of Design, Boston, Massachusetts. Local law
enforcement has conducted investigation which
indicates victim was last seen at Logan International Airport, Boston, Massachusetts. Her
purse was found in a marsh north of Boston.
Investigation also has identified at least four
or five boyfriends of victim.
    Attached teletype from Boston advises of
investigation conducted in attempts to locate
Joan Webster. Miss Webster's whereabouts
remain unknown.
    On 10/14/82, [   ]
received a telephone call from an unknown male
who indicated he (unknown male) knew where Joan
Webster was located.
    On 10/15/82, the unknown male again called
victim's father. This call was traced to a
laundromat in Concord, New Hampshire. Surveillance instituted at laundromat and subsequent investigation revealed the identity
of the unknown male to be [   ]
[   ] advised victim's father that he had
seen victim in June of 1982 and on 10/12/82.
[   ] wanted a reward of $25,000 for infor-
mation leading to the location of victim.
[   ] arranged a meeting with victim's
father for later that same day.

1 -
1 -
1 -
PMM/RDW:mrb/jey

1 - Mr. Revell
1 -

CONTINUED - OVER

FBI/DOJ

A report (page 1) about the October 15, 1982, extortion incident was sent to
FBI headquarters and routed to Oliver Revell, assistant to FBI Director Webster.

b6
b7C

On 10/15/82, the meeting between victim's
father accompanied by a Special Agent of the
FBI, posing as Mr. Webster's cousin, took place.
[   ] provided an address in Boston where
victim could be found; however, this address
proved to be erroneous.
[   ] was subsequently interviewed by the
FBI. [   ] refused to answer any questions
or make any statements about this matter
during the interview.
U.S. Attorney, Boston declined prosecution
on [   ] due to the fact no demand made and
no other Federal laws were violated.
[   ] is a known felon. [   ]
was arrested in 1969 for kidnapping and
subsequently on numerous other charges.

APPROVED:
Director _____
Exec. AD-Adm _____
Exec. AD-Inv. _____
Exec. AD-LES _____

Adm. Servs. _____
Crim. Inv. _____
Ident. _____
Inspection _____
Intell. _____

Laboratory _____
Legal Coun. _____
Off. of Cong.
& Public Affs. _____
Fisc. Mgnt. _____
Tech. Servs. _____
Training _____

-2-

The FBI report (page 2) was initiated by Director William H. Webster.

038655   Grand Jury, March 5, 1982   ADA TIMOTHY BURKE

COMM. VS. LEONARD J. PARADISO

Murder - 1st

WITNESS SWORN
q identify yourself.
a Katherine Leonti.
q where do you live?
a 365 Meridian St. East Boston.
q are you married?
a yes.
q what is your husband's name?
a Anthony Leonti.
q did you know Marie Iannuzzi?
a my sister.
q how old was Marie at the time of her death?
a 20.
q she died on August 12, 1979.
a yes.
q did you know who she was living with at the time of her death?
a David Doyle.

The grand jury transcript (page 1), the *Commonwealth v. Leonard Paradiso* for cause # 038655 for the murder of Marie Iannuzzi, was convened by ADA Tim Burke in Suffolk County, Massachusetts on March 5, 1982.

-1-

038655   Grand Jury   April 5, 1982   ADA TIMOTHY BURKE
                                                      STENO. ROBERT BARRY

JOHN DOE INVESTIGATION

Re: Death of Marie Iannuzzi

WITNESS, SWORN

Q   Sir, tell us your name?

A   Charles George.

Q   Would you spell your last name for the court reporter, here.

A   G-E-O-R-G-E.

Q   Mr. George, are you employed?

A   Yes, I am.

Q   Where are you employed?

A   Atlantic Lobster Company.

Q   Where is the Atlantic Lobster Company located?

A   Saugus, Mass.

The grand jury transcript (page 1), the John Doe investigation for cause #
038655 for the murder of Marie Iannuzzi, was convened by ADA Tim Burke in
Suffolk County, Massachusetts on April 5, 1982.

D-36 (Rev. 5-22-78)

FBI

TRANSMIT VIA: PRECEDENCE: CLASSIFICATION:
☐ Teletype   ☐ Immediate   ☐ TOP SECRET
☐ Facsimile   ☐ Priority   ☐ SECRET
☐ Airtel   ☐ Routine   ☐ CONFIDENTIAL
                                          ☐ UNCLAS E F T O
                                          ☐ UNCLAS
                                          Date ___11/5/82___

TO   : DIRECTOR, FBI (62-119655)
           (ATTN: IDENTIFICATION DIVISION
           LATENT FINGERPRINT SECTION)

FROM   : SAC, BOSTON (62D-5738)(P)

SUBJECT: UNSUB;
          JOAN WEBSTER--VICTIM
          DPC
          OO: BS

      Re Latent Fingerprint Case C-13738.

          Identification Division, Latent Fingerprint Section is
requested to compare latent fingerprint in this case with any known
fingerprints for Leonard J. Paradiso, white male, date of birth
December 8, 1942.

                    62-119655 - 12

                                          16 NOV 1982

②-Bureau
2-Boston

GHB/aw
(4)

                  62 - 119655

Approved: _____   Transmitted _____ _____   Per _____
                                    (Number) (Time)
                    U.S. GOVERNMENT PRINTING OFFICE : 1982 O - 395

The submission of Leonard Paradiso fingerprints, on November 5, 1982, was
prior to the Robert Bond "break" in the Joan Webster case in January 1983.

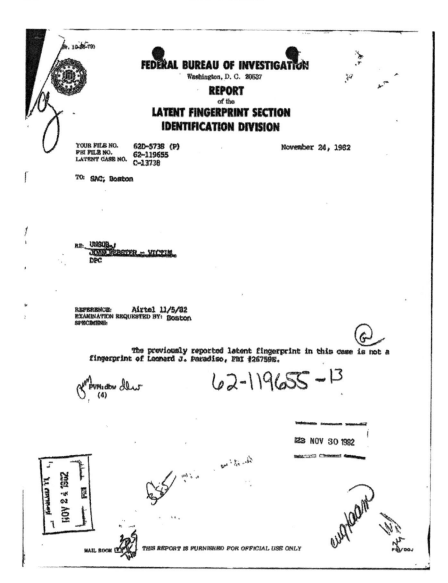

The lab reported negative fingerprint comparison on November 24, 1982.

The Boston office of the FBI withdrew domestic police cooperation on the Joan Webster case after the conclusion of authorities determined Leonard Paradiso was guilty of her murder.

U.S. Department of Justice

Federal Bureau of Investigation

In Reply, Please Refer to
File No.

Boston, Massachusetts

July 24, 1985

LEONARD J. PARADISO - SUBJECT;
JOAN L. WEBSTER - VICTIM;
DOMESTIC POLICE COOPERATION - INTERPOL

On November 28, 1981, JOAN L. WEBSTER, a HARVARD UNIVERSITY graduate student, departed Newark, New Jersey, on an EASTERN AIRLINES flight to Boston, Massachusetts. WEBSTER was last seen in the baggage claim area at Boston Logan Airport. WEBSTER's purse was later found in a marsh in Saugus, Massachusetts, and one of her two suitcases was discovered in a locker at the Greyhound Bus Depot in Boston, Massachusetts.

Since November, 1981, investigation conducted by state, local and federal authorities has developed strong evidence that WEBSTER was abducted and murdered by LEONARD J. PARADISO, a convicted murderer. This evidence is not currently considered strong enough to convict PARADISO mainly because WEBSTER's body has never been recovered. Although PARADISO has not been prosecuted for WEBSTER's murder, the consensus of the state, local and federal investigators of this case is that sufficient facts have been established to cancel the Interpol "Blue" notice.

This document contains neither
recommendations nor conclusions of
the FBI. It is the property of
the FBI and is loaned to your agency;
it and its contents are not to be
distributed outside your agency nor
duplicated within your agency.

1*

62-119655 — 49

Confirmation distributed on July 24, 1985, concluded Paradiso's guilt
for the Joan Webster murder. Guilt was determined prior to the
discovery of Joan Webster's remains in 1990.

COMMONWEALTH OF MASSACHUSETTS

SUFFOLK, ss.

SUPERIOR COURT
CRIMINAL NO.
037586

COMMONWEALTH OF MASSACHUSETTS   )
)
VS.   )
)
ROBERT BOND   )

MOTION TO ENFORCE PLEA BARGAIN AGREEMENT

Now comes defendant in the above matter and moves this
court to enforce the plea bargain agreement entered into
between defendant and the government's representatives in the
above matter.

In support of this motion, defendant relies on the attached
affidavit.

By his attorney:

Martin D. Boudreau
BOUDREAU & BURKE
One Milk Street
Boston, MA 02109
338-6721

Robert Bond's motion to uphold plea bargain agreement.

AFFIDAVIT

1. My name is Robert Bond and I am defendant in the instant matter;

2. I have been told on numerous occasions by the following representatives of the District Attorney's Office that in return for a change of plea to guilty in the instant matter I would receive a recommendation from the government of a sentence of 15 to 20 years:

    1) Tim Burke, Assistant District Attorney
    2) Andrew Palumbo, Massachusetts State Police Officer
    3) Carmine Tammara, Massachusetts State Police Officer
    4) Bill (last name unknown), Massachusetts State Police

3) My attorney has informed me that he has, through his discussions with the various representatives of the District Attorney's Office, been told that there is no such deal for a plea bargain agreement and that such plea bargain agreement is not possible;

4) I have specifically relied on the representations of above-mentioned representatives of the District Attorney's Office, to my detriment and the government has failed to fulfill its obligation as it has, through its authorized representatives, agreed.

Sworn under the pains and penalties of perjury.

Robert Bond   11/15/85

Bond named authorities.

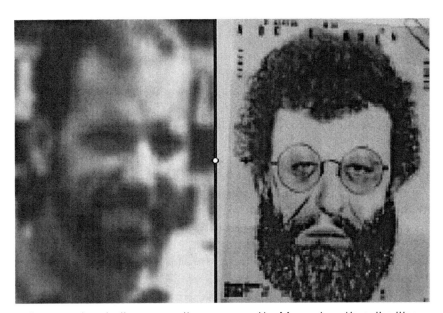

A comparison to the composite suppressed by Massachusetts authorities shows similarities to known individual.

E ve Carson was born in Danville, Illinois in 1953, and has lived in
the Midwest most of her life. She is a graduate of Purdue University with a degree in economics and industrial management. She
was a supervisor for General Motors and a marketing representative
for IBM before taking time to be a stay-at-home mom with her daughters. Presently, she works in the security industry.

Eve married Joan Webster's brother, Steve, on January 5, 1980,
and she was part of the immediate family when Joan disappeared. As
a mother, Eve was active in the schools and her girl's activities. She
volunteered time and skills to numerous organizations, fundraising,
and promoting a positive environment for her children. Ms. Carson
earned the reputation for speaking out when serious circumstances
warranted a voice and a backbone to stand up against abuse. Unfortunately, in our society, Eve learned blowing a whistle often has a personal cost.

She brings a unique insight into the enigmatic Webster family
and the devastating events that have spanned more than a quarter
century. Trauma continued to plague members of the Webster family.
Without justification, Eve found herself in Joan's shoes, alienated
from her children, and missing from their lives. Joan's blood relatives
devalued and discarded a member of their family. Repeated history
and a horrifying allegation were the catalysts for Ms. Carson to
unravel the lingering mystery of Joan's loss.

When Tim Burke published events surrounding Joan's unresolved case in 2008, Eve pressed to recover documents, interview witnesses, and research the case. Insight, instinct, and memory,
corroborated in files, unveiled a complex and secretive manipulation
of Joan's murder investigation. The search for truthful answers followed a path filled with obstructions and exposed evidence of public
corruption.

Examining a cold murder case opened new avenues Eve would
like to share with others who have suffered devastating tragedy. Writing, interviews, and presenting facts are tools to shatter the silence
and dispel myths. Too often, society blames the victims. There is a
serious need to educate professionals; imprudent and erroneous
judgments compound the abuse.

Ms. Carson undertook a daunting challenge, fighting a system that obscured justice in the brutal murder of a loved one. Supported with facts documented in files, she persevered through personal attacks. Faith was tested, but God showed the way. Eve hopes her experiences will lead to stronger sunshine laws that remove control from those who fail to protect the vulnerable. The public needs to see the personal faces, innocent people further victimized by injustice.

Eve is the loving mother of two daughters who never had the joy of knowing their Aunt Joan. Only the truth, even when it is painful, allows genuine healing.

CPSIA information can be obtained at www.ICGtesting.com
Printed in the USA
LVOW06s1518170415

435048LV00002B/303/P